If I'd Only Listened to My Mom, I'd Know How to Do This

Hundreds of Household Remedies

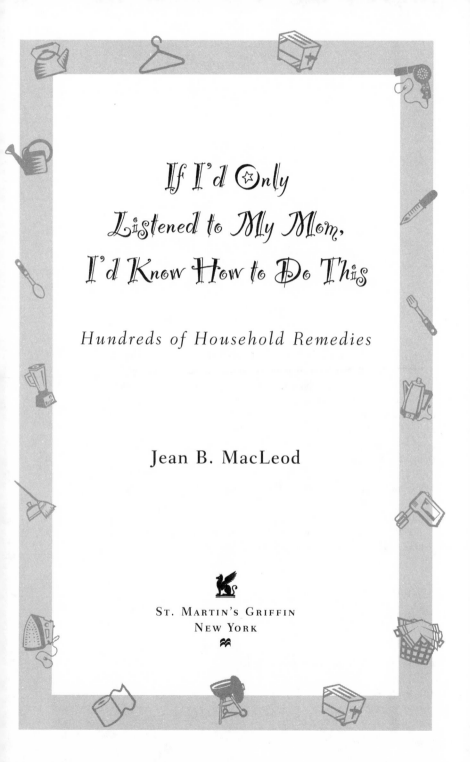

If I'd Only Listened to My Mom, I'd Know How to Do This

Hundreds of Household Remedies

Jean B. MacLeod

ST. MARTIN'S GRIFFIN
NEW YORK

IF I'D ONLY LISTENED TO MY MOM, I'D KNOW HOW TO DO THIS. Copyright
© 1997 by Jean B. MacLeod. All rights reserved. Printed in the United States
of America. No part of this book may be used or reproduced in any manner
whatsoever without written permission except in the case of brief quotations
embodied in critical articles or reviews. For information, address St. Martin's
Press, 175 Fifth Avenue, New York, N.Y. 10010.

Design by Maureen Troy

Library of Congress Cataloging-in-Publication Data

MacLeod, Jean B.
    If I'd only listened to my mom, I'd know how to do this : hundreds of
household remedies / Jean B. MacLeod.—1st ed.
        p.   cm.
    ISBN 0-312-15589-1
    1. Home economics.   I. Title.
TX158.M23   1997
640—dc21   97-7595
                                                                 CIP

First St. Martin's Griffin Edition: August 1997

10   9   8   7   6   5   4   3   2   1

*Dedicated to
Ian Alan, Ian Murray,
Elizabeth, Pamela,
and Colin Breac*

Acknowledgments

To my mother, Helen Blake, for providing the impetus for the book, and my family for their help and support—my appreciation and gratitude.

To my agent, Jeremy Solomon, and the people at St. Martin's Press—my editor Jennifer Weis; Madeleine Findley, editorial assistant; Mara Lurie, production editor; Maureen Troy, designer; and Debby Manette, copyeditor—my heartfelt thanks.

To the individuals who have contributed their knowledge, and to you, the reader, for granting me the opportunity to share it…thank you sincerely.

Contents

Introduction

. . . .

While mothers don't have all the answers, we do have more than a few household tricks up our sleeves, under our belts, and at the back of our minds. And, like most mothers, what I had acquired I wanted to pass on to my children. Why learn everything the hard way. Consequently, I set out to compile solutions to everyday household concerns, plus all the time and money-saving nuggets I had accumulated along the way. And, most important, to arrange them in a concise, quickly accessible, A-to-Z format.

A goodly portion of my informational tidbits was scattered around—in my personal notes, in the back of recipe files, in the front of gardening books, and in a bulging file of newspaper and magazine clippings. I'm a compulsive collector of practical information, and what I had collected and recorded was useful—really useful—that is, if I could find what I wanted when I needed it. There had to be a better way to quickly locate known information, filed, and subsequently forgotten.

What started out as a desire to correlate information for the family blossomed into *If I'd Only Listened to My Mom*.

When I started writing the book, research confirmed that there are many ways to solve most household challenges. And in questioning friends, relatives, co-workers, even strangers (I solicited information from everyone), it was obvious that each family has its own tried-and-true, dear-to-the-heart methods. We come from different backgrounds and all have our favorite time-tested procedures. As a result, I have included all available options beginning with the simplest and most environmentally friendly, to the more complex. Playing it safe, I have also included some basics. We can't assume that what we think of as common knowledge is known by all.

Most of the ingredients included in the book are to be found in most households. Toxic products have been omitted as much as possible and included only as a last resort. (Let's not forget that most commercial household cleaning products contain toxic ingredients and carry warnings.)

Unlike other books on the topic, *If I'd Only Listened to My Mom . . .* is arranged in an easy-to-use, recipe-style format. Devoid of preamble, each entry starts with a verb and gets right to the point.

Packed with A to Z tips, *If I'd Only Listened to My Mom* is for the domestically savvy, the newlywed or unwed, cooks/foodies, gardeners, pet owners, do-it-your-selfers, senior citizens, consumers, tightwads, mail-order shoppers, travelers, recyclers, the chemically sensitive, and the ecologically conscious.

This comprehensive reference of thousands of time and money-saving hints, efficient low-cost solutions to everyday household dilemmas, alternatives to toxic or costly commercial products, plus a vast, second-to-none resource guide of useful addresses and 800 numbers can save you time, effort, and money from the very first page.

Helpful Hints, A to Z

ADDRESS, To give in a hurry:
- Tear off the address portion of your deposit slip.

ADDRESS BOOK, Hint on:
- Identify it with your name and address in case of loss; also keep a photocopy of the book.

ADDRESS LABELS, RETURN, Uses for:
- Stick on redemption coupons that require a name and address.
- Label items that you've lent out, such as books, tools, etc.
- Tape on the bottom of a serving dish or utensil taken to a potluck or food sale.
- Identify an item for repair.
- Put one on the tongue of your running shoe as identification.
- Put one on your gas cap.
- Put one inside your eyeglass case.
- Put one on the metal shaft of your umbrella next to the handle. Cover it with cellophane tape.
- Keep one in each piece of luggage and in your gym bag.

ADHESIVE RESIDUE FROM LABELS AND DECALS, To remove:
- Saturate the area with prewash spray, WD-40, or cooking or baby oil and leave for a couple of hours, then scrub away the adhesive with a cloth or nylon scrubber.
- Rub with a cotton ball saturated with rubbing alcohol.
- Apply mineral spirits with a piece of terry cloth.
- Use nail polish remover on a cotton ball.

AIR PURIFIERS, Natural sources to use:
- Use plants. According to research by NASA (National Aeronautics and Space Administration), a spider plant removed 96 percent of the carbon monoxide and 86 percent of the formaldehyde from a sealed test chamber in 24 hours. English ivy removed 90 percent of the benzene. Other plants that removed pollutants were golden pothos, peace lily, and several species of Dracaena.
- Keep some charcoal briquettes in a basket in the room that needs the

benefit of its air purifying properties. Later they can be used for the
barbecue.

- Put out zeolite (see USEFUL ADDRESSES AND PHONE NUM-
  BERS, "Toxin-Free/Low Toxin Products").
- Boil 1 or 2 cut-up lemons in 2 or 3 cups of water and pour the liquid
  into bowls, then place the bowls throughout the house.
- Cut up leftover orange and lemon peels and place them strategically
  about the room.
- Put some baking soda into jar lids and place out of sight.
- Place a saucer or small bowl of white vinegar in the room.
- Put 1 teaspoon vanilla in an uncovered container and place it where
  needed.

ALARM CLOCK, To make ring louder:
- Set on a tin plate, metal baking dish, or ceramic tile.
- Use a clock radio alarm with the volume turned up if you have a hard
  time being awakened by an alarm clock.

ALARM CLOCK, To muffle:
- Wrap in a face cloth or towel or turn it upside down.

ANIMAL HAIRS ON FABRIC, To remove:
- Rub a rubber glove over the upholstery.
- Scrape off with a dampened squeegee or lightly dampened sponge or
  chamois.
- Wrap a length of duct tape, adhesive tape, or masking tape around
  your hand, sticky side out, and brush over the area. The animal hairs
  will stick to the tape.
- Place the dry garment in the clothes dryer with a damp towel and tumble dry for about 15 minutes.

ANTS, To get rid of:
- Place whole cloves, sage, or tansy around windows or wherever they
  are entering the house. Or keep tansy growing in the kitchen.
- Plant mint, pennyroyal, southernwood, and tansy by doorways to drive
  ants away. Crush some leaves periodically to release the oils.
- Put out mint leaves or sticks of mint chewing gum. There is no need
  to unwrap the gum.
- Disrupt their invasion paths by drawing a chalk mark where they are
  appearing; or sprinkle baking soda, talcum powder, borax, dried mint,
  chili powder, cayenne pepper, kitchen scouring powder, or lemon juice
  in the area. The ants will not cross the barrier.

- Kill the ants by spraying them with 1 tablespoon liquid dishwashing detergent mixed with water in a sixteen-ounce spray bottle.
- Track them down where they are entering the house. Wash all areas where they appear with full-strength white vinegar. Let the area air-dry.
- Find the nest and stir several tablespoons of Epsom salts into the top inch of soil within a 6-inch circumference of the nest entrance.

ASHTRAY, OUTDOOR, SUBSTITUTE:
- Invert a small clay flowerpot over a saucer. Cigarettes can be put into the small hole, and the lack of oxygen will put them out. Or fill a small container with sand or gravel.

ASHTRAYS, To clean:
- Apply a thin layer of floor wax to brass or copper ashtrays after washing. Allow to dry, then polish well. When wiped clean, no ashes or moisture will cling. Or wipe the clean ashtrays with your furniture waxing cloth, then polish well.

BALLPOINT INK ON PLASTIC, WOOD, CLOTH, To remove:
- Coat with mineral oil or petroleum jelly. Allow to set, then use cleaning fluid to remove the lubricant and the mark. See also STAINS chapter, "Ballpoint Pen Ink."

BALLPOINT INK ON WALLS, To remove:
- Dab white vinegar on painted walls and keep dabbing until the ink is removed. Or rub gently with silver-polishing cream, then rinse.
- Spray hair spray on wallpaper, allow it to dry, then brush it off.

BALLPOINT PEN DRIED UP, To rejuvenate:
- If the point is plastic, boil a small amount of water and place the filler in the water. Turn the heat off. When the water is cool, remove the filler, wipe dry, and replace in the penholder.
- If the point is metal, hold a lighted match or cigarette lighter to the tip of the pen until the metal is heated slightly.

BARBECUE, Hints on:
- Trim excess fat from meat to avoid excessive smoke and flare-ups.
- Handle meat with tongs, not forks, to avoid losing natural juices.
- Get maximum heat from the coals by knocking the white ashes off with tongs. Doing so will nearly double their heat for the next 5 minutes.

- Get low heat by spacing out the coals after they have a white coating. Use tongs to position them so they don't touch.
- Add more coals by placing them at the edge of the fire. Don't put fresh coals on top of those already burning.
- Revive coals by sprinkling a few teaspoons of cooking oil on top.
- Extinguish coals when finished by closing all the barbecue vents.

BARBECUE COALS, To check the temperature of:

- Hold the palm of your hand at cooking level (about 4 inches above the coals), and count the number of seconds you can hold it there: 3 seconds for hot coals; 4 seconds for medium coals; 4 to 5 seconds for medium-low coals.

BARBECUE COALS, To extinguish flare-ups:

- Sprinkle on baking soda or salt.
- Throw a lettuce leaf on the flame.

BARBECUE COALS, To save after use:

- Use tongs to put the coals in a bucket filled with water. Or put the coals in a large can with holes and run water through them. Let the coals dry out thoroughly before using again. Or spray the coals with water and leave them in the grill to dry out.

BARBECUE COALS, To start:

- Make sure your charcoal is dry. Charcoal absorbs moisture and will not burn well if damp. Store in a dry place. If stored outdoors, keep it in a weatherproof container with a tight lid.
- Fill an empty waxed cardboard milk carton with crumpled newspaper. Put the coals on top and light the carton. The carton should burn long enough to ignite the coals.
- Use a cardboard egg carton. Put one briquette in each section, then light the carton.
- Twist sheets of folded newspaper or paper towels into cylinders. Dip one end of each in cooking oil or cooking grease. Place the oil end under the coals and ignite the dry end.
- Presoak briquettes ahead of time. Put the briquettes in a coffee can and add enough charcoal starter to cover them. Keep the sealed can in a cool spot. When you start the barbecue, put in 4 or 5 presoaked briquettes, then cover with dry ones from the bag.
- Buy a tin chimney made for the barbecue. Set it on the firebed, put in 4 or 5 presoaked briquettes (see above) or a crushed milk carton and fill the chimney with briquettes. Light the carton or presoaked bri-

quettes and wait about 15 minutes or until the coals are glowing, then remove the chimney with tongs.

- Soak a brick ahead of time with starter fluid. Put the brick in the firebed, stack briquettes around it, and light it. Remove the brick after the fire is established.

BARBECUE DRIP PANS, To make:

- Fashion drip pans from two layers of heavy-duty aluminum foil. Or mold the double layers of foil over an inverted baking pan. Pinch the corners together and remove from the pan. A drip pan should be larger than the meat so that all the drippings go into the pan, not on the coals.

BARBECUE, GAS, BRIQUETTES, To clean:

- Turn the briquettes upside down, light the grill, and set to high. Close the cover and let the fire burn for 15 to 20 minutes.

BARBECUE GRILL, To clean:

- Clean the grill after using and while it's still hot with a long-handled wire brush dipped in water, a brass grill brush, or crumpled aluminum foil, then wipe with paper towels. Wear oven mitts to protect your hands. Or try any of the following.
- Spray the grill with window cleaner while it's still warm, then scrub or wipe clean.
- Cover the grill with heavy-duty aluminum foil, shiny side in, after you have finished cooking. Close all the vents and the cover and let it sit until the grill is cool enough to handle. (Leave a gas grill on for 20 minutes.) Then scrub with a wire brush or crumpled foil and wipe with damp paper towels.
- Steam clean by wrapping the grill in wet newspaper while it is still hot, then wipe clean when it's cool.
- Soak the grill overnight in a strong solution of dishwasher detergent.
- Allow the grill to cool down, then put it between layers of paper towels or newspaper and place it inside a large plastic garbage bag. Pour 1 to 2 cups ammonia into the bag to saturate the paper towels or newspaper. Tie the bag shut and let the grill soak outdoors overnight. The next day, wash in hot, soapy water. Use a plastic scrubber or steel wool pad to remove any stubborn deposits. Rinse with clear water.
- Wait for a sunny, hot day, then put the grill in a black plastic trash bag. Pour 1 cup ammonia into the bag, seal with a twist tie, and leave out in the sun. Remove the grill at the end of the day and rinse it off with the hose.

BARBECUE GRILL, To prevent food from sticking:
- Oil the grill before using with a paper towel moistened with vegetable oil, or spray it with a nonstick cooking oil spray.

BASEMENT, DAMP, To dry and remove odor:
- Mix together 1 10-pound bag cat litter and 5 pounds baking soda. Place an inch or two of the mixture in shallow pans and set out around the room. Replace the mixture once a week. Or sprinkle the mixture liberally over the floor. Let it sit for a week, then sweep or vacuum up.
- Place coffee cans filled with salt in the basement. The salt will absorb the moisture from the air. When the salt becomes damp, stand the cans on a warm stove or put the salt in the sun. The heat will cause the moisture to evaporate so you can reuse the salt again in the basement.
- Fill sturdy cloth bags with calcium chloride, and hang them from the ceiling. Calcium chloride will absorb moisture, the cause of mildew and mustiness. (Obtain calcium chloride from a builder's supply warehouse.)
- Put bags of zeolite in the damp basement to absorb the odors. Cleanse the zeolite by putting the bags in the sun, then put them back in the basement. (See USEFUL ADDRESSES AND PHONE NUMBERS, "Toxin-Free/Low Toxin Products.")

BASKETS, To clean:
- Brush out dust and grime with a stiff brush or clean paintbrush.
- Clean with warm soapy water and rinse in clear water.
- Wet periodically to prevent basketware from becoming brittle.

BASKETS, VARIOUS SHAPES AND SIZES, Uses for:
- Making a bed for a small pet.
- Holding potted plants from the nursery.
- Filling with food for an attractive and welcome gift food basket.
- Lining with plastic and filling with potpourri.
- Serving as a plant pot, if plastic-lined.
- Filling with charcoal briquettes and using as a room deodorizer.
- Storing newspapers or magazines.
- Serving as a cutlery and napkin holder at buffets and picnics. (Wrap each cutlery serving in a napkin.)
- Holding bathroom accessories such as guest soaps, rolled-up guest towels, or face cloths.

- Keeping pens and pads together by the phone.
- Holding edibles: fruit basket, bread basket, chip and cracker basket, and lined with greens for a fresh veggie basket.
- Serving as an incoming or outgoing mail receptacle.
- Holding pet's or children's toys.
- Holding gadgets and items in kitchen drawers and cabinets.

BATTERIES, To prolong the life of:
- Scrape both ends with sandpaper, a nail file, or an emery board to give them more mileage.

BEADS OR PEARLS, To thread:
- Let the melted wax from a burning candle drop on the end of the thread, or dip the end in the wax. Twist between the fingers, then let it harden.
- Use waxed dental floss.

BED SLATS SLIDING OUT OF PLACE, To prevent:
- Slip wide rubber bands over the ends to keep them from moving.

BELT, To make extra notches: See "Leather Belt, To make extra notches."

BERRY BASKETS, Uses for:
- Hold condiments in the kitchen cupboard, such as sauce packages, soup mixes, etc.
- Put them in the bottom shelf of the refrigerator and in the vegetable crisper for small items such as garlic, ginger root, lemons, etc.
- Nestle two together for support and keep frequently used spices in the cupboard or refrigerator.
- String together with twist ties and use to separate different cleaning rags.
- Separate various items in drawers.
- Store your vitamin bottles in them.
- Utilize as mini colanders.
- Keep one on the kitchen counter to hold paper towels you've dried your hands on. You can reuse the towels to mop up spills or wipe up stains on the kitchen floor.
- Line with plastic, fill with potting soil, and use as planters inside ceramic containers.
- Turn upside down in a large vase and use as a frog for flowers.

BICARBONATE OF SODA (BAKING SODA) FOR CLEANING, To save money on:

- Buy large bags in a Chinese supermarket, or buy a box from the drugstore instead of the small ones you buy for baking.

BLIND CORDS, VENETIAN, To clean:

- Soak them in a solution of ½ cup water and ¼ cup chlorine bleach in a jar or bowl for about 1 minute. Check after a minute to see if they are white; if not, keep in a little longer. Rinse in a clean container of water, then dry with a towel.

BLIND CORDS, VENETIAN, To replace:

- Tape or sew the end of the new one to the old one. Slowly pull out the cord and you'll pull the new one into place.

BLINDS, FABRIC, To clean:

- Cover the blind with a paste made of fuller's earth, a little detergent and water. Leave on for 2 hours, then wash off. (Obtain fuller's earth from drugstores.)
- Rub with a rough flannel cloth dipped in cornmeal or flour.
- Water and mildew stains: Dampen the blind and rub salt well into the fabric. Leave the blind in the sun and keep it damp until the stains disappear.

BLINDS, FABRIC, To repair:

- Use clear nail polish to repair small tears.

BLINDS, MINI/VENETIAN, Care of:

- Dust with a feather duster, lamb's wool duster, clean 2-inch paintbrush, or the dusting attachment of the vacuum. Close the slats flat, dust the front, then close them in the opposite direction and dust the other side. Follow with a soft cloth.
- Put an old sock on your hand and spray it with window cleaner. Close the blinds and, starting at the top, go over them side to side, then do the reverse side.
- Take them down and wash them outside. First hose them off, then lay them on an old blanket and scrub the slats with an all-purpose cleaner or a solution of ¹/₂ cup ammonia to 1 quart warm water. Scrub the slats using a soft-bristle brush or terry-cloth rag. Turn the blind over and do the other side. Hang the blind on a ladder or clothesline and rinse with a hose. Shake, then dry with a towel or let air-dry.

- Put an old blanket or quilt on the verandah or porch, then lay the blinds on top and wash them with a solution of $1/2$ cup nonsudsy ammonia to 1 gallon warm water. No rinsing is necessary.
- Use a commercial product made for chandeliers.

BOOK LICE, To get rid of:
- Put books in plastic freezer bags or wrap them in newspaper and store them in the freezer for 3 to 4 days.

BOOK PRICE STICKERS, To remove:
- Put a cloth over the book and press the sticker for a couple of seconds with a medium-hot iron, then gently pull the sticker off.

BOOKENDS SUBSTITUTE:
- Fill hollow decorative pieces or fancy tin cans with sand.

BOOKS, To clean:
- Use a wide paintbrush or a feather duster to make the job go faster.
- Clean the book covers by rubbing them briskly with a clean cloth wrung out in a solution of 1 part white vinegar and 2 parts water.
- Rub book covers with waxed paper and they will stay cleaner.

BOOKS, BEST-SELLING, To save money on:
- Request your local library to reserve them for you if you can't find them on the shelves. The fee, if any, is about 50 cents.

BOOKS, CRUMPLED OR FOLDED PAGES, To straighten:
- Set a steam iron at the low setting, then cover the page with a pressing cloth and press firmly to steam the page flat.

BOOKS, LEATHER- AND VINYL-BOUND, To care for:
- Treat leather-bound books occasionally with a lightweight oil so that the leather won't dry and crack. (See also "Leather, To condition," "Leather, To preserve," "Leather, Dirty, To clean," "Leather, Faded, To renovate," "Leather, Greasy, To clean," "Leather, Mildew On, To remove," "Leather, Stains On, To remove.")
- Wash vinyl books with a mild detergent solution, then rub in well a light coating of petroleum jelly and buff it off.

BOOKS, MUSTY ODOR OR MILDEW ON, To remove:
- Place the books outdoors in the sun and fan the pages frequently so the air can get to them.
- Sprinkle baking soda, baby powder, talcum powder, or cornstarch

through the pages. Use a shaker or sieve to distribute the powder evenly. (Make sure the pages are dry first.) Leave for several days, then gently brush out the powder.
- Put sheets of newspaper between some pages and place the book along with crumbled newspaper in a suitcase, closed box, or paper bag. Repeat until the odor is completely gone.

BOOKS, STAINS ON, To remove:
- Place a piece of blotting paper, tissue, or paper towel over the spot and press for a few seconds with a warm (not hot) iron.
- Rub with soft white bread crumbs.
- Clean soiled edges with a gum eraser, holding the pages tightly together.

BOOKS, TORN, to repair:
- Paint the tear with the white of an egg using a small brush.
- Put wax paper under the torn page, then brush white glue along the torn edges with a small brush. Carefully join the torn sections together and press the edges. Remove excess glue and set another piece of wax paper over the glued section. Weigh down the page with another book for several hours.
- Use book tape or strips of rice paper or thin onionskin with non-acid-forming adhesive. (Ask at your local library for a source.) After repairs, put wax paper on both sides of the mend to prevent the pages from sticking together.
- Think twice about getting old books rebound if they are valuable. It will lower their resale value.

BOOKS, WET, To dry:
- Put them in a frost-free freezer for several hours or overnight to dry out.
- Put them in a microwave for 1 minute. Repeat, if necessary.

BOTTLE CAP, To open without an opener:
- Pry cap up in a couple of areas with a key or needle-nose pliers.

BOTTLES/JARS, To deodorize:
- Put 1 tablespoon dry mustard in the jars, then half fill with cold water. Shake to mix and let stand overnight. Rinse thoroughly.
- Fill the jars with warm water, 1 tablespoon tea leaves, and 1 tablespoon white vinegar. Let stand 3 to 4 hours, then shake out and rinse.

BOTTLES, ORNAMENTAL, STAINED: See "Vases, Stained, To clean."

BRASS ANDIRONS AND FIRE TOOLS, To clean:

- Rub the metal in one direction with extra-fine steel wool (grade 000) or fine emery cloth to remove burned-in resins. When clean, polish with brass polish.

BRASS, LACQUERED, To clean:

- Dust and occasionally wash with mild dishwashing detergent and lukewarm water. Rinse and dry. Do not polish. Do not use hot water or allow it to soak, as this might crack the lacquer. Damaged lacquer can be removed with acetone. Cover small articles with boiling water to soak off the lacquer. To re-lacquer, polish the piece with brass polish, wipe it with acetone to remove all traces of polish, then brush or spray on water-white transparent metal lacquer. (Obtain acetone from a drugstore.)
- Take the item to a professional to have it re-lacquered.

BRASS, UNLACQUERED, To clean:

- Wash brass in hot soapsuds and rinse and dry before polishing. This makes polishing easier. After polishing, wash the piece thoroughly with soapsuds to remove any remaining polish, then rinse and dry. Rub lightly with a cloth moistened with olive oil or apply a coat of protective wax to prevent rapid tarnishing. Remove tarnish and corrosion by any of the following methods.
- **Antique brass:** Rub with lemon mineral oil and polish it softly.
- **For a bright finish:** Mix 1 teaspoon salt, 1 tablespoon flour, and enough white vinegar to make a paste. Rub the paste on with a clean sponge and let it dry completely. Rinse in hot water and polish dry.
- Rub with a cloth dampened with Worcestershire sauce.
- Make a paste of lemon juice and either baking soda or cream of tartar. Apply to the surface and leave on for 5 minutes, then rub with a soft cloth. Rinse and dry.
- **For a soft finish:** Rub with a thin paste made of rottenstone and linseed oil. Wipe off the excess oil and polish with a clean cloth. (Obtain rottenstone and linseed oil from a hardware or paint store.)
- **Badly corroded:** Dip a piece of lemon in salt or in hot white vinegar and salt, and rub it on the corroded spots, then rinse and dry. Or sprinkle salt on a sponge or cloth saturated with vinegar or lemon juice and rub lightly, then rinse and dry.

BRASS/COPPER CLEANER, To Make:

- Stir together ¼ cup water, ¼ cup ammonia, ½ cup rubbing alcohol, and 1 cup diatomaceous earth to form a very thin paste. Store in a clean glass jar with a piece of wet sponge. Rub the damp sponge on the brass. Dry completely, then polish with a soft cloth. (Obtain diatomaceous earth from a garden or pool supply store.)

BRICK OR STONE FLOOR, To clean:

- Put ½ cup washing soda in a bucket and pour in 1 gallon warm water to dissolve the soda. Wearing rubber gloves, mop, rinse, and dry.

BRONZE, To maintain:

- Dust, then wipe over with a little vegetable or mineral oil and polish with a soft cloth.

BROOM, Hints on:

- Avoid standing a broom on its bristles.
- Drill a hole through the top of the handle and hang it on the wall.
- Put two nails a couple of inches apart and store it upside down.
- Put a screw eye in the end and thread a piece of string through it. Then hang it by the string.
- Prevent the broom from making marks on the wall when resting against it by buying a rubber tip (the kind that fits on kitchen stool legs and crutches) and putting it over the top of the broom handle. Or cut a finger off an old rubber glove and slip it over the handle, or put rubber bands around the top.
- Slip a pair of old pantyhose or an old T-shirt over the bristles when sweeping wood floors. The dust will cling better.
- Spray bristles with water, furniture polish, or a commercial product such as Endust to make the broom more effective in collecting dust.
- Prevent corn brooms from becoming brittle by wetting them occasionally.

BRUSHES AND COMBS, To clean: See "Hairbrushes and Combs, To clean."

BUBBLE WRAP, Uses for:

- Line a toolbox to cushion the tools.
- Line a manila envelope to make a padded mailing bag.
- Wrap around a soft drink can to keep it colder longer.

BULB, BROKEN, To remove from socket:

- Turn off the electricity at the circuit box or unplug the cord. Use an oven mitt, a child's rubber ball, half a raw potato, a wad of newspaper taped together, or a bar of soap. Insert in the socket, press down and twist counterclockwise to remove the broken bulb from the base. Or unscrew the broken bulb base, using needle-nose pliers.

BULLETIN BOARD, CORK, Hint on:
- Use sandpaper to make a discolored board look like new.

CAMPING FIRST-AID SUPPLIES, Items to include:
- Include antiseptic, bandages, gauze, Band-Aids, aspirin, a pair of blunt scissors, white vinegar for insect bites and sunburn and to act as smelling salts.

CAMPING STOVE, To make:
- Suspend a square of thin sheet iron across large stones on either side of the firepit.

CAMPING TENT, To keep clean:
- Buy a painters' drop cloth the same size as the tent. Place the drop cloth on the ground before setting up the tent. It keeps the bottom of the tent dry and clean.

CANDLE HOLDERS, To clean:
- Place candle holders in the freezer until the wax is chilled, then peel off wax. Remove used votive candles the same way.
- Soften the wax with a hair dryer set on high heat, then remove.
- Spray the inside of the holders lightly with nonstick cooking spray before putting in the candles. The candles will slip right out.

CANDLES, To prolong their life:
- Store in the refrigerator to make them burn slowly and evenly with no dripping.
- Soak them for 2 hours in a solution of 2 tablespoons salt with enough water to cover, then rinse well and dry. Wait at least a day before using so the wicks can dry. This procedure will make them burn without dripping.
- Keep them clean and unbroken by storing them in empty cardboard tubes from paper towels or gift wrap.

CANDLES, Too large for the holders:
- Dip the candle ends in hot water, or melt them slightly with a match or cigarette lighter, then press them down firmly into the candle holder.
- Trim off the excess with a sharp knife that has been heated in hot water.

CANDLES, Too small for the holders:
- Use florist's or modeling clay to hold them in place.
- Twist a rubber band around the base of the candles.

CANDLES, DECORATIVE, To reuse:
- Put a small candle into the hollow that has burned down and is hard to light. The decorative candle will serve as a candle holder.

CARPET SWEEPER, To clean:
- Keep it empty and clip the threads in the brushes with scissors before pulling them out. Wash the brushes in warm water and mild dish-washing detergent, then rinse in cold water and let air-dry.
- Rub a damp paper towel over the brushes before using; they will pick up the dirt better.

CDs: See "Compact Disc, To clean," "Compact Disc Player, To clean," and "Compact Disks, To categorize."

CEDAR-LINED CHEST, To renew:
- Sand the interior lightly to restore the cedar odor.

CEILING, HIGH, WITH COBWEBS, To dust:
- Brush with a broom that has an old T-shirt wrapped over the bristles held in place with a rubber band.
- Use a dust wand with a telescoping handle.
- Throw a tennis ball wrapped in a cloth or pillowcase at the cobwebs.
- Let a helium balloon on a string drift up to the cobwebs. Keep a tight hold on the string so you can get it down.

CEMENT STAINS: See "Cement, Unpainted, Stained, To clean," and "Concrete/Cement, Grease/Oil/Transmission Fluid Stains, To remove."

CEMENT, UNPAINTED, To clean:
- Sweep with a soft broom or vacuum cleaner floor attachment. Wash with a wet mop or scrub with a brush, then rinse. For a thorough cleaning, add a couple tablespoons washing soda to a pail of water and wash with a mop or scrub brush. Or scrub with a stiff broom dipped in thick detergent suds, then rinse.

CEMENT, UNPAINTED, STAINED, To clean:
- Scrub with a solution of 1 cup chlorine bleach to 2 gallons warm water, then rinse thoroughly. Scrub any remaining stains with a solution of ½ cup washing soda to 2 gallons water.

- Scrub with a solution of 1 cup ammonia to 1 gallon water, then hose off.

CERAMICS, MEMORABILIA, To put to use:
- Put vinegar in bowls and place strategically to remove odors.
- Store toothbrushes (bristles up) in mugs in the bathroom.
- Use as flower or potpourri containers.
- Use to hold pens and pencils.
- Keep on your desk for such items as rubber bands, paper clips, etc.
- Use your imagination.

CHAIR AND TABLE LEGS MARKING THE FLOOR, To avoid:
- Wax the bottoms of the chair and table legs when waxing the floor.
- Glue small circles of carpet remnants, felt, or moleskin to the bottoms of chair or table legs. Or use bunion pads or adhesive-backed felt.
- Put plastic or metal glides on the table and chair legs.
- Press thumbtacks into the bottom ends of wooden chair legs to enable them to slide more easily across a wood or tile floor.

CHALK, To make easier to use:
- Wrap the end you hold with masking tape.

CHANDELIER, To clean:
- Make sure the chandelier lights are off, the bulbs are tightened and cool, and the table or floor beneath the chandelier is covered with plastic or towels covered by several thicknesses of newspaper before starting to clean.
- Wear cotton gloves and dip your hands in a solution of 1 quart warm water to 2 tablespoons ammonia. Squeeze out excess and wipe each pendant by hand.
- Mix a solution of ¼ cup rubbing alcohol and ¾ cup water in a narrow container. Dip each pendant in the solution for a few moments and swish it back and forth. Let the pendants air dry.
- Cover each bulb with a small plastic bag and secure it with a twist tie. Then spray enough window cleaner on each pendant so that the dirt runs off and the pendants can drip dry.
- Combine 2 teaspoons rubbing alcohol, 2 cups warm water, and 1 tablespoon dishwasher antispot product in a spray bottle. Cover the bulbs as above, then spray the chandelier and let drip dry.

CHECKING ACCOUNTS, To save money on:
- Look into credit union share draft accounts. They pay interest on your balance and can be used like checking accounts. To locate a credit union you might be eligible to join, call 800-358-5710 to find the phone number of your state's credit union league.
- Shop around for a bank that offers free checking accounts with no strings attached.

CHECKS, BANK, To save money on:
- Order preprinted checks from a major discount printer that sells checks for almost half of what most banks charge. Current (800-426-0822) and Checks in the Mail (800-733-4443) both sell a wide variety of plain and decorated checks at $4.95 for a box of 200. Checks in the Mail has been printing checks since 1916.

CHEESECLOTH SUBSTITUTE:
- Use a piece of nylon stocking.

CHEWING GUM IN HAIR, To remove:
- Work peanut butter, mayonnaise, or cooking oil around the wad to break up the gum, then shampoo as usual.

CHINA/POTTERY, BROKEN, To mend:
- Clean, then roughen the broken edges slightly with sandpaper. Carefully glue the pieces together with slow-drying epoxy glue. Remove any excess glue with rubbing alcohol. If the item is broken in more than two pieces, glue them one at a time, allowing the adhesive to set between each repair. While the glue is drying, support the pieces in position. If it's a plate, fill a pan with sand and place the plate in the sand with the broken edge straight up. Gravity will hold the pieces in place. If necessary, use clothespins to clamp the pieces together, or wrap strips of masking tape around the item, or stretch rubber bands around a small item such as a cup or vase.

CHINA/POTTERY, CRACKED, To mend:
- Immerse the cracked article in a pan of milk, simmer for 45 minutes, and then wash and dry.
- Soak in a solution of ½ cup chlorine bleach and 2 quarts water. Then wash the piece and let it dry. Use slow-drying epoxy to fill the crack, filling slightly higher than the surface. Smooth the area with a superfine abrasive (such as grade 0000 sandpaper) after the glue hardens.

CHOPSTICKS, Uses for:
- Use to extract bread stuck in the toaster.
- Use to turn over crêpes, tortillas, meat, fish, and poultry, and to remove deep-fat fried food from the oil.
- Measure and mark on a chopstick ⅛, ¼, ½, ¾, and 1 inch, and use as a seed-sowing guide.
- Use as stakes for small plants.

CHRISTMAS CARDS, To recycle:
- Cut off the fronts and send them to a charity, such as St. Jude's Ranch for Children, P.O. Box 1426 NE, Boulder City, NV 89005.
- Use as Christmas postcards by removing the front and cutting them down to postcard size. Put the address on one half and the message on the other.

CROCHETING, See SEWING, KNITTING, CROCHETING chapter.

CHROME, To clean:
- Rub with the inner white part of a lemon, then rinse.
- Rub with baking soda that has been sprinkled on a damp sponge or cloth. Or make a paste of baking soda and water. Rinse well with warm water, then polish dry.
- Wipe with a cloth or sponge saturated with white vinegar, rinse, then polish dry.
- Dampen a cloth with rubbing alcohol, apply, then polish dry.

CHROME RUST SPOTS, To remove:
- Rub the spots with crumpled aluminum foil dipped in cola. Be careful to rub only the rust spots so as not to scratch the chrome. When the rust is removed, apply a sealer.
- Scrub the spots with superfine steel wool (0000) dipped in turpentine. When the rust is removed, apply a sealer.

CLEANERS, ALL-PURPOSE, To make:
- Put 1 tablespoon ammonia (sudsy or clear), 1 tablespoon liquid dishwashing detergent, and 2 cups water in a spray bottle. Spray on surface and wipe, then rinse with clear water.
- **For appliances and tile:** Combine 2 tablespoons ammonia, 4 tablespoons washing soda, and 2 cups warm water in a spray bottle and shake vigorously. Apply and rinse.
- **For appliances, countertops, mirrors, metals, tiles, windows, hard plastics, and fingermarks on painted walls and wood:** Put

½ cup to ⅔-cup nonsudsy ammonia and 2 cups water in a spray bottle. No rinsing is necessary after applying.

- **For bathroom fixtures, kitchen fixtures, appliances, chrome, countertops, and painted surfaces:** Mix ½ cup rubbing alcohol, 1 teaspoon dishwashing detergent, 1 teaspoon ammonia, and 2 cups water in a spray bottle. Rinse with clean water after using.
- **For countertops, appliances, sinks, bathroom fixtures, and tile:** Pour 1 cup white vinegar into a spray bottle. Spray on and wipe off. No rinsing is necessary.
- **For kitchen appliances, chrome faucets, and greasy surfaces:** Mix ¼ cup ammonia and 1 cup rubbing alcohol in a spray bottle. Rinse with clear water after using.
- **For spot-cleaning woodwork and walls:** Mix 2 to 3 tablespoons liquid laundry detergent and 1 cup water in a spray bottle. Rinse with clear water after using.
- **For windows and mirrors:** Use either 2 tablespoons clear ammonia or 2 tablespoons white vinegar to 2 cups warm water. Mix ingredients and put in a spray bottle. Spray on surface and polish clean. See also "Windows, To wash."

CLEANING, Hints on:
- Stop dirt from being tracked in by having mats at all entrances to the house, including verandahs and balconies.
- Dust before you vacuum. Work from high to low. (Dust falls down.) Remove dust from a feather or lamb's wool duster frequently while dusting by twirling it around by the handle inside a brown paper bag, or take it outside and twirl it around.

CLEANING CLOTHS AND RAGS, Hints on:
- Use old washcloths and cut-up terry towels (hemmed to avoid loose strands) for jobs that require a little abrasion, such as tiles, porcelain, and hard kitchen and bathroom surfaces.
- Use soft, lint-free, nonsynthetic cloth, such as old flannel and cotton, diapers, old T-shirts, linen tea towels, napkins, and cotton socks, for furniture and surfaces that are easily scratched. Call a local diaper service if you have no rags. It may sell old diapers by the pound.

CLEANING POWDER/LIQUID, SCOURING, To make:
- Fill a clean, used shaker-top container with 1 cup baking soda and 1 cup table salt. Shake well.
- Combine 1 cup baking soda and 1 cup washing soda in a shaker container.

- Combine 1 cup baking soda, ¼ cup borax, and 2 tablespoons sodium perborate or oxygen bleach in a shaker container.
- Make a liquid scouring cleanser by mixing ¼ cup baking soda with enough dishwashing liquid to make a creamy lotion. Pour into a plastic squeeze bottle.

CLEANING PRODUCTS, Hints on:
- Buy only one or two products that will clean a variety of surfaces.
- Buy the least harmful and hazardous product. Read labels. Look for the key words "Danger/Poison," "Warning," and "Caution." "Caution" indicates the lowest level of toxicity; "danger," the highest. If ingredients are not listed, choose another product.
- Do not drink, eat, or smoke while using hazardous products. Traces of chemicals can be carried from hand to mouth.
- Do not wear soft contact lenses when working with solvents and pesticides. They can absorb and hold chemicals next to the eyes.
- Do not be fooled by the word "nontoxic." The word is an advertising term not defined by the federal government, so it can be used as manufacturers choose. Also know that much of the lemon in household products isn't lemon at all but a combination of chemicals that smell like lemon.
- Make your own cleaning products. Work in a well-ventilated area, label containers carefully, and do not mix more than a month's supply at a time; the chemicals may lose their effectiveness.

CLEANING SOLUTIONS, Important warning:
- Never mix bleach and vinegar or bleach and ammonia. The fumes they produce can be deadly.

CLEANING SUPPLIES, To store:
- Keep them together in clearly marked containers in a permanent location.
- Carry them around easily in a cleaning caddie; make one by cutting the top off a large plastic milk or bleach bottle and leaving the handle on.
- Keep baking soda handy in an empty plastic container with a plastic top. Add a few marbles to keep the soda from caking.
- Keep white vinegar on tap in a plastic spray or squirt bottle.

CLOCK, ELECTRIC, NOT RUNNING, To fix:
- Turn it upside down for 3 days to redistribute the oil. Or put it in a slightly warm oven (under 150°F) for 1 hour.

CLOSETS, DARK, To remedy:
- Buy a battery-operated light fixture that mounts on the wall or ceiling if the closet has no electrical outlet.

CLOSETS, MILDEW IN, To remove:
- Tie several pieces of blackboard chalk together and hang them up to reduce dampness.
- Line shelves with a double layer of blotting paper and renew it from time to time.
- Dissolve ¼ cup borax in 2 cups hot water and mix thoroughly. Saturate a sponge with the mixture and wash the mildewed areas. Leave the solution on for a couple of hours or overnight, then rinse well. If the mildew has penetrated deeply into the walls, leave the solution on for a number of days until it is completely dry. Then sweep or vacuum up the powder.
- Use a commercial dehumidifier such as silica gel or activated alumina, both of which work well in closets. (Obtain silica gel or alumina from a hardware or craft store.)

CLOTHING, To make last longer:
- Brush with a good natural-bristle clothes brush and air overnight to get another day's wear. Machine washing and drying make clothes wear out more quickly.

COCONUT FIBER MATS, To clean:
- Wash them first with a strong, stiff brush dipped in ½ cup washing soda to 1 gallon water. (Wear rubber gloves.) Then dip the brush in a solution of ½ cup table salt and 1 quart cold water, and brush it over the mats. The salt helps to keep the fibers stiff.

COMBS, To clean: See "Hairbrushes and Combs, To clean."

COMFORTER, DOWN, To clean:
- Sprinkle fuller's earth over the whole comforter. Roll up tightly and leave rolled up for 2 or 3 days. Then shake it well and leave it to air. (Obtain fuller's earth from drugstores.)
- Have it professionally dry-cleaned.

COMFORTER/QUILT, SLIPPING OR TOO SHORT, To remedy:
- Sew a piece of material on the end and tuck that into the end of the bed.

COMPACT DISC, To clean:
- Handle by the edges. Wipe off dust with an antistatic cloth and remove fingerprints with a soft lint-free cloth dipped in rubbing alcohol. Wipe in a radial direection across the grooves.

COMPACT DISC PLAYER, To clean:

- Use canned compressed air to remove dust. (Obtain canned, compressed air from a photographic or electronics store.)

COMPACT DISCS, To categorize:

- Stick small colored dots on the spine of the jackets according to classification—classical, jazz, rock, vocal, etc.—and keep the colors together.

COMPUTERS, Hints on:

- Keep the computer on for the first 30 days after purchase. If anything is going to go wrong, it will show up earlier rather than when the warranty expires.
- Purchase an extended warranty. This is one appliance where the warranty will pay for itself if anything goes amiss.
- Dust the keyboard with a paintbrush. Remove keyboard grime by unplugging the keyboard and cleaning it with a cotton swab dipped in rubbing alcohol. For a quick once-over, use a moist towelette.

CONCRETE/CEMENT, GREASE/OIL/TRANSMISSION FLUID STAINS, To remove: See also "Garage floor, stained with oil and grease, To clean."

- Wet the cement and sprinkle dishwasher detergent on the stain. Let the detergent remain for a few minutes, then rinse with a kettle of boiling water. Hose off any residue.
- Spread TSP (sodium carbonate and sodium sesquicarbonate) over the stain and sprinkle with enough water to dampen the powder thoroughly. Let sit for 30 minutes, then scrub and rinse well.
- Smear with a paste of washing soda and water and allow to sit for about 1 hour, then rinse. Repeat if necessary.
- Cover the stain with an absorbent such as fuller's earth, baking powder, baking soda, cornstarch, or cat litter (ground fine with a brick). Let it sit for a day or so, then sweep it up.
- Saturate the spot with cola and immediately cover with an absorbent as above. Let it sit for a couple of hours, then sweep up. The cola will bring the grease to the surface.
- Paint or pour paint thinner onto the spot. Saturate the spot as well as an area 6 to 8 inches beyond it. Cover with a thick layer of absorbent, let it sit for about 1 hour, then sweep it up. Two applications may be required.
- Use oven cleaner. Let it sit for a few minutes, then rinse. Repeat if necessary.

- Spray on engine degreaser and let it sit for about 10 minutes, then hose off.

CONCRETE, RUST STAINS, To remove:
- Sprinkle on Portland cement powder, then sprinkle on water and work the cement into the stain with a stiff brush. Rinse.
- Hire a professional with a pressure cleaner.

CONCRETE, STUBBORN STAINS ON, To remove:
- Scrub with a solution of 1 cup chlorine bleach to 2 gallons warm water, then rinse thoroughly. Scrub any remaining stains with a solution of ½ cup washing soda to 1 gallon water.
- Scrub with a solution of 1 cup ammonia to 1 gallon of water, then hose off.

CONTACT LENSES, To clean:
- Avoid losing lenses in the sink by washing and rinsing them in a small spice or herb jar with a perforated plastic lid (thoroughly cleaned and sterilized).

CON-TACT (OR SELF-ADHESIVE) PAPER, To apply:
- Rub the sticky side very lightly with a damp sponge containing a little soap. This will prevent the paper from sticking while positioning. The paper will slide until you get it in position and then will stick without any problem.
- Remove a wide border of the backing on all four sides of the paper, leaving the center with its backing intact.
- Smooth out bubbles and creases in the paper with a chalk eraser.
- Remove a bubble in the paper by cutting a small X into the bubble with a single-edge razor blade and smoothing the four parts back in place.

CON-TACT (OR SELF-ADHESIVE) PAPER, To remove:
- Facilitate future removal by leaving the backing on in the center when you install it. Remove only the edges before putting the paper in place.
- Use a hair dryer set on warm. Work on one section at a time and gently pull at the edges.
- Place a rag over the paper and iron it. The warmth will loosen the adhesive.
- Lift up a corner and spray on hot water. Pull and continue to spray a little at a time.
- Remove adhesive left behind by saturating the area with prewash spray, WD-40, or cooking or baby oil. Leave it on for a couple of hours,

then scrub with a cloth or nylon scrubber. Or rub with rubbing alcohol, or use a commercial adhesive remover.

COOKBOOKS, To keep clean:
- Cover with self-adhesive paper, plastic wrap, or plastic book covers.

COPPER, LACQUERED, To clean:
- Dust and occasionally wash with mild dishwashing detergent and warm water. Rinse with warm water and wipe dry. Do not polish. Do not use hot water or allow it to soak, as this might crack the lacquer.

COPPER, UNLACQUERED, To clean:
- Wash utensils and ornamental pieces with soap and water, rinse, and dry. Spots caused by corrosion can be removed if rubbed with any of the following:
- Lemon juice and salt: the juice of 1 lemon and 1 teaspoon table salt. Leave on the copper piece for 30 minutes. Wash thoroughly with detergent and water to remove all traces of the salt and lemon juice, then rinse well. Or rub with a cut lemon or lime dipped in salt. Let the juice sit for a while, then rub it off with a soft cloth.
- Hot vinegar and salt: Use as instructed for lemon juice and salt.
- Toothpaste and baking soda in equal portions. Rub in, then wash and dry thoroughly.
- Cornmeal, table salt, and white vinegar in equal portions stirred to a paste. Use a dampened sponge to apply the mixture, then rinse with warm soapy water and dry with a soft cloth.
- Flour, table salt, and white vinegar, in equal portions, mixed to a smooth paste. Rub on with a soft cloth. Wash in hot soapy water, then rinse and polish with a clean cloth.
- Ketchup applied with a sponge and rubbed in thoroughly. Leave it on for 1 hour or so if badly tarnished, then rinse with hot soapy water and polish dry.
- Whiting or rottenstone mixed to a paste with olive oil. Rub it on, then wash, rinse, and dry. (Purchase whiting and rottenstone from a hardware store.)
- Commercial polish made especially for copper.
- Wash copper thoroughly with soapsuds after using acid or commercial polish, or it will retarnish rapidly.

CORD, ELECTRIC, To shorten:
- Buy a cord shortener or make one by using a small piece of cardboard or plastic. Make a notch in the cardboard or plastic to guide the cord

through, then wind the excess cord around it. Finally, make a notch to guide the cord back out. Don't wrap the cord too tightly.
- Wrap a too-long cord tightly around a broom handle for a day. This will spiral and shorten it.

CORKS, Hints on:
- Sterilize by boiling or clean with an emery board or emery cloth. Use as a missing knob for a pot lid. Attach with screw.

CORK SUBSTITUTE:
- Soften a candle stub in the microwave for 1 or 2 seconds, wrap in a piece of wax paper, and insert into the neck of the bottle.

COSTUME JEWELRY, To clean:
- Pour rubbing alcohol on the item and let it sit for a few minutes on paper towels, then wipe off the tarnish.
- See "Silver, Sterling Jewelry, To clean."

CRAYON MARKS ON VINYL OR LINOLEUM, To remove:
- Rub the marks gently with silver polish.

CRAYON MARKS ON WALLS, To remove:
- Use baking soda on a damp cloth to wipe the marks off the wall safely.
- Use turpentine or lighter fluid to dissolve the wax in the crayon.

CREDIT CARDS, For best interest rates on:
- Check money magazines such as *Barron's Weekly* at the library, the financial section of the newspaper, or the Internet for cards that offer the best interest rates.
- Charge a large-ticket item right after the bank's closing statement date.
- See also USEFUL ADDRESSES AND PHONE NUMBERS, "Credit Cards."

CREDIT CARDS, To keep track of:
- Make a photocopy of all your credit cards on one sheet of paper. Write the toll-free number under each card. Take a copy with you when traveling and leave a copy at home.

CRYSTAL WITH CHIPS OR ROUGH EDGES, To smooth out:
- Rub the edge gently with an emery cloth until the rim is smooth and the chip smoothed out.

CURTAIN HOOK SUBSTITUTE:
- Use a bent paper clip if you are missing a hook.

CURTAINS, To freshen:
- Put them in the dryer for a few minutes on the air cycle.

CURTAINS, SHEER, To hang:
- Avoid snags by cutting a finger from an old glove and slipping it over the rod end before feeding the rod into the curtain. Or cover the ends of the rods with cellophane tape.

DECALS, To remove: See BATHROOMS chapter, "Bathtub Appliqués, Adhesives, Decals, To remove."

DECANTER, STAINED, To clean: See "Vases, Stained, To clean."

DECANTER STOPPER STUCK IN BOTTLE, To loosen:
- Pour a few drops of glycerin around the neck of the bottle. Leave until the glycerin has worked down and the stopper can be removed.

DENTAL WORK, Hints on:
- Get routine dental care at a dental school. Services at the dental school training clinics are high quality and 60 percent less expensive than normal dentist's fees. Check your phone book or your local dental society.
- Ask your dentist if he or she gives a discount for cash. Most dentists will give a 10 percent discount if you pay at the time of your visit instead of waiting to be billed.

DEODORANT, NATURAL:
- Use baking soda applied dry on a cotton ball.

DETERGENT SCOOPS, Uses for:
- Give them a thorough cleaning and use for flour, sugar, cereal, and coffee scoops.
- Check to determine how much they measure and use as measuring cups.
- Use them to start seeds or propagate cuttings.

DISHWARE BROKEN, To mend: See "China/Pottery, Broken, To mend."

DISHWARE, CRACKED, To mend: See "China/Pottery, Cracked, To mend."

DISINFECTANTS TO WASH SURFACES:
- Use a solution of half vinegar and half water, or straight white vinegar, to wash surfaces. Let air-dry.

- Dissolve ¼ cup borax and ⅛ cup white vinegar in 1 gallon very hot water. Wash the surfaces with a sponge or mop and let dry.
- Use rubbing alcohol and allow to air-dry.
- Add 1 cup borax to 1 gallon hot water to disinfect any household surface. Rinse and let dry.
- Use a solution of pine-oil cleaner or chlorine bleach mixed with water. Follow directions on the labels.

DOOR, CREAKING, To silence:
- Rub the hinges well with the lead of a pencil, or give them a shot of WD-40 or graphite.

DOOR LOCK, STICKING, To loosen:
- Rub the key across soft pencil lead (graphite) several times, then slide the key in and out of the lock a few times.

DOWN PRODUCTS, OLD, To recycle:
- Make a down pillow, a pair of bootees for cold weather, a throw rug to snuggle up in while reading or watching television, a baby quilt, a car seat.
- Use the down to stuff homemade throw pillows.

DRAINS, To keep clean, free-flowing, and fresh:
- Keep them odor-free by running very hot tap water through them. Periodically use one of the following:
- Put in ½ cup baking soda followed by 3 cups boiling water. Let soda and water bubble for a while before rinsing with hot tap water.
- Pour in 1 cup white vinegar. Let it stand for 30 minutes, then run very hot water through the drain.
- Put ½ cup table salt down the drain followed with very hot water.
- Put ½ cup baking soda down the drain followed with ½ cup white vinegar. Leave for 15 minutes, then rinse with hot water.
- Pour 1 cup chlorine bleach down the drains to disinfect them.
- Mix 1 cup baking soda, 1 cup table salt, and ¼ cup cream of tartar in a small bowl. Stir thoroughly and pour into a clean covered jar. Pour ¼ cup of mixture down the drain and immediately add 1 cup boiling water. Wait 10 seconds, then flush with cold water. Use weekly as maintenance.
- Dissolve any grease build-ups by once a month pouring ¼ cup washing soda down the kitchen drain and then slowly running down very hot water.

DRAINS, STOPPED UP, To open:

- Fill the sink with about 4 to 5 inches of water. Close the overflow vent and the other drain, if a double sink, with wet rags. Put a little petroleum jelly around the rim of the plunger for better suction. Put the cup of the plunger over the drain and press down hard, then pull the handle up, push down again, and repeat 10 to 12 times.
- Try very hot soapy water or dishwasher granules dissolved in boiling water to open a sluggish drain. Pour it down, then run in plenty of hot water.
- Pour ½ cup borax into the drain, then slowly pour in 2 cups boiling water. Let sit 15 minutes, then flush with water.
- Open a drain clogged with grease by pouring 1 cup salt and 1 cup baking soda down the drain. Follow with a kettle of boiling water. Cover drain and wait 1 hour. Repeat, if needed.
- Bail out the water, then pour 1 cup each baking soda and white vinegar down the drain and plug the drain. Let the mixture bubble for 20 minutes, unplug, then rinse with hot water.

DRAPERIES, To keep clean:

- Dust them when you clean the room. Use a hand vacuum, upholstery attachment of a regular vacuum, or a soft-bristled brush and work from top to bottom. Dusting prolongs the time between dry cleaning.

DRAPERIES GAPING IN THE MIDDLE WHEN YOU CLOSE THEM, To remedy:

- Sew a small magnet into both center seams where the draperies gape open.

DRAWER KNOB, LOOSE, To tighten:

- Remove the screw, wrap a piece of cotton ball around it, and dip it into glue. Place the screw back in the hole and wait until the glue is completely dry before using the knob.
- Insert wooden toothpicks or pieces of match stick in the hole to give the threads something to grip. Or wind a few strands of steel wool around the screw.
- Paint the tip of the screw with fingernail polish or glue before inserting the screw. When it dries it will hold more tightly.
- Put a plastic plug of the correct size into the screw hole.

DRAWERS, STICKING, To make glide smoothly:

- Apply candle wax, paraffin, or soap to the sticking areas.

- Lightly sand the bottom edges of the drawer sides and the tops of the runners with 100 grit sandpaper. Then wax them.

DRIVEWAY STAINS: See "Concrete/Cement, Grease/Oil/Transmission Fluid Stains, To remove."

DUSTERS, Hints on:
- Speed up dusting by using a feather or lamb's wool duster.
- Use old cotton sweat socks cut open, old T-shirts, diapers, or any soft cotton absorbent material for dusters.
- Fold a large dusting cloth in half and in half again, so there are several clean sides to use.

DUSTERS, To prevent scattering dust:
- Dip dusting cloths in a solution of 2 cups of water and ¼ cup lemon oil and allow to dry before using.
- Put the dusting cloth in a jar with a little turpentine. Roll the jar around to make sure the turpentine covers all the interior, then put the cloth in for a few days. Store the dusting cloth in the jar.
- Soak the duster in turpentine and allow it to dry. Store in a covered glass or metal container.
- Spray the duster with a commercial product, such as Endust, and keep in a covered jar for 24 hours before using for the first time.

DUSTING HIGH PLACES:
- Use a telescopic duster.
- Wrap a towel, T-shirt, or old pantyhose over a broom or dustmop and fasten in place with a rubber band.

DUSTING NARROW AND HARD-TO-REACH PLACES:
- Use a long-handled barbecue brush.
- Put a heavy sock over a straightened-out wire coat hanger, fly swatter, yardstick, or flattened-out gift-wrap cardboard cylinder.

DUSTING NOOKS AND CRANNIES:
- Use a natural-bristle paintbrush to remove dust from the inside corners of picture frames, chandelier chains, cloth lamp shades, ruffled or pleated lamp shades, pleated tops of draperies, carved furniture, the area where chair padding meets the wood, and other places where a duster is inadequate for the task.

DUSTPAN, Hint on:
- Spray with furniture polish and buff. The dust will slide right off.

HELPFUL HINTS, A TO Z / **29**

DUSTPAN SUBSTITUTE:
- Cut a paper plate in half and moisten the edge.
- Take a half sheet of newspaper and dampen 1 to 2 inches. Press the dampened edge to the floor and sweep up the dust.
- Dampen a paper towel or napkin and scoop up the dust.

ELECTRIC PLUG, HARD TO PULL OUT OF THE SOCKET:
- Rub the prongs with a lead pencil. The graphite acts as a lubricant.

ELECTRONIC EQUIPMENT BARGAINS:
- Call the Department of Defense at 800-468-8289 for information on military base auctions. Auctions are held regularly at hundred of bases around the country and are a good source for bargain-priced VCRs, electronic equipment, and other items.
- Inquire at local electronic repair shops for items that have been abandoned by their owners. Sometimes you can acquire an item for the price of the repair.

EMERGENCY PREPAREDNESS, Hints on:
- Contact your local emergency management or civil defense office and American Red Cross Chapter for information about how to prepare for a hazard in your community. (See also USEFUL ADDRESSES AND PHONE NUMBERS, "Emergency Preparedness.")
- Keep a battery-powered radio, flashlight and extra batteries, along with the emergency supplies, bottled water, and first-aid kit.
- Plan two escape routes out of each room and practice fire drills at least twice a year.
- Teach family members to stay low to the ground when escaping from a fire.
- Install smoke detectors on every level of your home. Clean and test them at least once a month. Change batteries once a year.
- Keep a whistle in each bedroom to awaken the household in case of fire.
- Hang pictures and mirrors away from beds.
- Strap the water heater to wall studs.
- Keep some money in the house. In case of a power failure, you won't be able to cash checks or use the ATM.
- Make sure family members know the location of emergency supplies, fire extinguishers, first-aid kits, and utility shut-off points and how to turn off the water, gas, and electricity.
- Pick one out-of-state and one local friend or relative for family mem-

bers to call if separated during a disaster. (Often it is easier to call out of state than within the affected area.)

- Find the safe spots in your home for each type of disaster.
- Post emergency telephone numbers near the telephone.
- Always keep your car half filled with gasoline. Fill it up when it gets half empty.
- Keep your family records in a water- and fireproof container.

EMERY BOARDS, To make last longer:
- Cut them in half lengthwise with scissors. This gives each board two more good sides.

ENVELOPE, SEALED, To open:
- Place a damp cloth over the seal and press quickly with a hot iron.
- Hold it over the spout of a steaming kettle to melt the glue.
- Put it in the freezer for a few hours, then slide a table knife under the flap. The glue will be good as new.
- Heat it in the microwave for 20 seconds.

EYEGLASSES, To clean:
- Avoid using tissue or paper towels on plastic lenses. They will scratch the surface.
- Put a drop of white vinegar, rubbing alcohol, or vodka on a piece of soft, clean cloth and polish clean.
- Wet under hot running water, then rub a drop of mild dishwashing or liquid soap on the lenses with your fingers. Rinse under hot running water, then dry with a soft, clean lint-free cloth.
- Clean eyeglasses with anti-reflective coating with a product made for the purpose.

EYEGLASSES, To make emergency repairs:
- Use a pencil eraser to tighten a screw if you don't have a tiny screwdriver. And keep the screw in place with a dab of colorless nail polish if it keeps working loose.
- Replace a missing screw with a stud-type earring or a bit of wire from a twist tie.

EYEGLASSES, OLD, Uses for:
- Take them to the optician and have the lenses darkened so you can wear them for sunglasses.
- Keep them for an emergency in case you lose your present pair.
- Pass them on to an organization such as the Lions or Vision Habitat

(Habitat and Church Streets, Americus, GA 31709), which give glasses to people in Third World countries.

FABRIC SOFTENER SHEETS, Uses for:
- Shining shoes.
- Dusting and shining furniture.
- Deodorizing shoes.
- Scenting closets or drawers.
- Preventing empty suitcases from acquiring a musty odor.
- Polishing silver.

FELT MARKER, To prolong the life of:
- Store markers capped with the tips down.
- Slice off a piece with a single-edge razor blade at the same angle as the tip to get it flowing again.

FELT MARKER STAINS ON HANDS, To remove:
- Spray with hair spray, then wipe off with a tissue.
- Rub off with rubbing alcohol.

FILM CANISTERS, Uses for:
- Holding jewelry when at the gym.
- Holding coins for the Laundromat or in the car glove compartment for tolls or emergency phone calls.
- Keeping sewing supplies for work or travel.
- Holding pills, aspirins, vitamins, sun screen, hand cream.
- Using as hair rollers.
- Using as a stamp dispenser. Cut a 1½ inch slit in the side of the can and slide a roll of stamps inside. Feed the stamps through the slit.
- Making a cat toy to hold a paper clip, pen top, or anything that will rattle.

FILM DEVELOPING, To prevent loss:
- Print your name and address on letter-size paper with the words "This film belongs to" and take a picture of it when you start a new roll.

FILM NEGATIVES, To find easily:
- Store those you want to keep behind corresponding prints in the photo album.

FINGERNAIL POLISH, To dry quickly:
- Put your hands with the fingers spread apart into the freezer compartment of the refrigerator.
- Hold your hands under a hair dryer or blow on them.

FIRE, GREASE OR ELECTRICAL, To extinguish:

- Use salt or baking soda for small grease fires, and baking soda for electrical fires. Don't use flour on grease or electrical fires; it can explode.

FIREPLACE, To extinguish the fire:

- Throw salt on the fire, and in a few seconds the flames will be extinguished.
- Let the flames burn down, then cover the embers with ashes before you retire.

FIREPLACE, BRICK/STONE, To remove soot stains:

- Wash with ½ cup TSP (sodium carbonate and sodium sesquicarbonate) mixed in 1 gallon hot water.
- Dissolve ¼ cup washing soda in 2 gallons hot water. Scrub the area with a brush or nylon pad.
- Mix 1 cup washing soda with enough hot water to make a paste. Rub on the area with a nylon pad, then rinse well.
- Use scouring powder and a stiff brush.
- Brush off as much smoky stain as possible with a stiff brush. Then mix ½ cup laundry detergent with 1 quart hot water. Add ½ pound powdered pumice stone and ½ cup ammonia and mix thoroughly. Apply the solution and let it sit for half an hour. Scrub off and rinse thoroughly with warm water. (Obtain powdered pumice at a hardware or paint supply store.)
- Sprinkle a few tablespoons of table salt into the fire while it is burning. The salt helps to remove the black off the chimney and disperse the soot.

FIREPLACE, BRICK, POROUS, To clean:

- Scrape soot off frequently with a stiff wire brush.
- Dab with white vinegar, which also brings out the natural color of the bricks.

FIREPLACE DOOR, STUBBORN SOOT ON, To clean:

- Mix ⅛ cup white vinegar, 1 tablespoon ammonia, and 1 quart warm water. Spray or wipe on with a cloth. Rinse and dry with a clean cloth.
- Cover each panel with a thick layer of newspapers saturated with ammonia, and put inside a heavy-duty garbage bag. Close the bag and let it sit for 10 minutes or longer. Scrub away the softened soot with a plastic mesh scrubber, then rinse with clear water.

FIREPLACE FIRE STARTERS AND KINDLING, To make:
- Ask the local lumberyard for leftover wood scraps to use as kindling.
- Roll old newspapers tightly and fit them into empty cardboard paper towel tubes.
- Light a "puff-out-proof" birthday candle and poke it into the kindling. The candle will burn long enough to ignite the kindling.
- Roll wet newspapers around a rod until about 5 inches in diameter. Tie the roll or use heavy rubber bands, then slip off the rod and stand up to dry, usually from 1 to 3 weeks. Don't use the colored ads or colored paper such as the comics.
- Save waxed cardboard milk cartons and candle stubs, which make good kindling.
- Toss dried orange peel into the fire for a pleasing fragrance.

FIREWOOD, To obtain free:
- Gather free firewood from any of our 155 national forests. Contact your regional office of the U.S. Forest Service for a permit, which allows you up to six cords of downed or dead wood. (See USEFUL ADDRESSES AND PHONE NUMBERS, "Firewood Permit.")

FLASHLIGHT, To find in the dark:
- Paint a strip of luminous paint around the handle or put on a strip of fluorescent tape.

FLEAS, To trap:
- Fill a flat dish with water and float a little dishwashing detergent on the top. Place on the floor next to a 25-watt lamp or night-light. Position the bulb about 1 to 2 feet above the dish so it shines directly onto the water's surface. (A goose neck lamp is ideal.) Make sure it is the only light on in the room. Do this every night until no more fleas are caught.
- Place a plate of milk in the infested room at night. The white of the milk attracts the fleas. No light is needed for this.

FLIES, To get rid of:
- Hang bunches of bay leaves, mint, pennyroyal, or eucalyptus by your door to repel them.
- Dampen crumpled newspaper with ammonia and rub on windows to keep flies away.
- Dip a sponge in boiling water and place it in a saucer or shallow container. Pour ½ teaspoon oil of lavender on the sponge. (Flies do not like the aroma.) Moisten the sponge twice a day with boiling water and once a week with the oil.

- Trap flies in an old clean jar containing 1 envelope of yeast and enough water to fill the jar a quarter full. Drill three ⅜-inch holes in the lid of the jar and leave it out.
- Hang clusters of cloves in each room to keep flies away.
- Spray a fly with water or hair spray to stun it, then swat it with a newspaper.

FLOORS, PAINTED, To clean:
- Mop porch, verandah, or other painted wood or concrete surfaces with clear lukewarm water or water to which a little ammonia or white vinegar has been added. Generously swab one portion at a time, then mop up the dirty water with the wrung-out mop.

FLOORS, TILE, LINOLEUM, OR CERAMIC, To clean:
- Add ½ to 1 cup ammonia to a gallon of warm water. No rinsing is necessary.
- Mix 1 cup white vinegar with 1 gallon water. No rinsing is necessary, and it won't leave a film.

FLOORS, WOOD, To clean:
- Dilute white vinegar in cold water and wipe with a well-wrung-out mop or soft cloth. Never use plain water on wood floors.
- Remove water spots on finished wood floors by rubbing gently with a cloth moistened with rubbing alcohol, then wiping with a cloth dampened with vegetable oil.

FLOWER STEMS, DAMAGED, To fix:
- Insert the stems into plastic straws.
- Tape a toothpick to the stem to act as a splint.

FLOWERS, DRIED OR SILK, To clean or freshen:
- Steam briefly over a pan of boiling water and reshape.
- Clean by putting them in a large bag with a handful of table salt or cornmeal and shaking gently.
- Air-dry silk flowers in a pillowcase for 15 minutes. Tie the pillowcase in a knot and put in the dryer with a damp cloth.
- Spray lightly with hair spray when arranging to make the flowers last longer.

FLOWERS, FRESH, CUT, To make last longer: See GARDENS chapter, "Flowers, Cut, To make last longer."

FLOWERS, MINIATURE, SHORT OR WEAK STEMMED, To arrange:
- Put the short, narrow flower stems through the sprinkle holes of an empty spice jar with a shaker top.

- Arrange them in a bowl or vase of well-watered sand.
- Put a cut-in-half potato in a bowl, cut side down, and punch holes in it with a nail or ice pick, then insert the flowers.
- Pour melted paraffin into a bowl. Punch holes in the paraffin after it hardens and insert the flowers.

FLOWERS, NOT ENOUGH TO FILL VASE, To improvise:
- Put them into a tall narrow jar, such an olive jar, then put the jar into the vase.
- Reduce the size of the vase opening by placing strips of cellophane tape across the top. Crisscross several strips so that the flowers can be arranged in the openings.
- Turn a berry basket upside down and use as a holder in a deep, wide vase. Anchor the basket with florist's clay.
- Put a piece of crumpled clear plastic wrap, crumpled chicken wire, florist's foam, marbles, pebbles, bubble wrap, or coarse sand in the vase.
- Join together plastic hair rollers with tape and place in the bottom of the vase to keep the flower stems in the same position.

FLOWERS, SUBSTITUTE FOR:
- Use a few branches from a shrub to add greenery to an arrangement. Use small branches alone if you have no flowers. They make a nice display. Or use fresh green weeds.

FLOWERS, WILTED, To restore:
- Cut off the ends at an angle and stand them in hot water. Allow the water to come to room temperature before arranging.

FLOWERS WITH DROOPING HEADS, To prop up:
- Inset toothpick halves into the heads and centers of the stems. Push the toothpicks deeply into the flowers so they will be covered by the petals.

FOOT ODOR, To treat:
- Air shoes thoroughly between wearings.
- Dust feet with baking soda, and sprinkle baking soda in shoes and leave overnight. When you dust your feet, put each foot in a shoe box first to avoid getting the baking soda on the floor.
- Sprinkle the insides of shoes with talcum powder, cornstarch, or crumbled sage leaves and leave overnight.
- Boil 2 tea bags in 2 cups water for 10 to 15 minutes, then add about 2 quarts water and soak feet for 20 to 30 minutes.

- Add ½ cup white vinegar, ½ cup kosher salt, or 1 tablespoon baking soda to each quart of water. Soak feet 15 minutes twice a week to 10 days.
- Rub feet with a natural deodorant crystal.

FRUIT FLIES, To avoid:
- Keep fresh basil in the fruit bowl or a pot of basil nearby.

FUNNEL SUBSTITUTE:
- Cut the bottom off a cone-shaped paper cup.
- Cut the corner off a heavy plastic bag.
- Use a clean empty plastic bleach or milk container. Remove the lid and cut down to any size you want the funnel to be.
- Cut a long-neck plastic shampoo, water bottle, or other type of plastic bottle to the size you want the funnel to be.
- Hold a pencil across the opening of the pouring container. The liquid will follow the pencil to its end.

FUSE BOX, Hint on:
- Identify all the fuses.

GARAGE FLOOR STAINED WITH OIL AND GREASE, To clean: See also "Concrete/Cement, Grease/Oil/Transmission Fluid Stains, To remove."
- Spread several thicknesses of newspaper over the area and saturate them with water. Press the newspapers firmly against the floor, then allow them to dry before removing.
- Apply paint thinner, mineral spirits, or cola to the oil or grease, then cover with a layer of fuller's earth, cat litter, sand, baking soda, washing soda, or cornmeal and leave overnight, then sweep it up. Scrub away any remaining stain with ½ cup TSP in 1 gallon hot water. If the stain remains, pour on full-strength chlorine bleach, then wipe up the excess.
- Soak with mineral spirits for 30 to 45 minutes, then scrub with a brush while adding more mineral spirits. Scoop up the grease and allow the stain to dry. Finally, wash with a solution of 1 cup laundry detergent, 1 cup chlorine bleach, and 1 gallon cold water. Repeat until stains are gone.
- Mix liquid all-purpose cleaner with talc or powdered chalk to make a thick paste. Spread ¼ inch thick over the stain and cover it with plastic wrap. Put masking tape around the edges to seal in the moisture and leave it until it dries. Scrape it off, then rinse the area thoroughly with plain water.

- Scrub the stain with TSP and hot water, then apply an oil-dissolving solvent (obtainable at an auto supply store) or MEK (mek methy ethyl) (obtainable at a paint store) mixed with fuller's earth to a thick paste. Proceed as above.

GARAGE SALE, Hint on:

- Forgo pricing items. Let customers make you an offer. Sometimes it may be more than you had anticipated.

GARBAGE CANS, To sanitize:

- Wash with hot suds, rinse, then wash with a solution of 3 tablespoons chlorine bleach to 1 quart water. Keep wet for 5 to 10 minutes, then rinse.

GARLIC ORDOR ON BREATH, To avoid:

- Eat a few parsley sprigs or dip a sprig of parsley in apple cider vinegar, then chew it thoroughly.
- Chew on a few anise or fennel seeds.
- Suck a clove or a piece of cinnamon bark.
- Crush 1 or 2 cloves into a hot lemon drink.

GIFT, Giving a hand-knitted or crocheted item:

- Give one of the skein packages if it contains information and instructions. Also include some extra yarn for future repairs.

GIFT, Giving one that carries a warranty:

- Open the package, if necessary, and fill out the form, or provide the information to the recipient. Most warranty cards ask for the place and date of purchase.

GIFT, Giving to an elderly relative or friend:

- Consider festive food items or homemade goodies or a gift certificate stating that you will give a soup, bread, or fruit of the month to the recipient.
- Give a book of stamps, stamped postcards, or a box of all-occasion greeting cards—or all three.
- Give a gift certificate for service (carpet/upholstery cleaning, window cleaning, yard or maid service); for a department store, catalog company, or grocery store; or ask the telephone company for a gift coupon. The recipient mails in the coupon in place of money with the monthly phone bill.

GIFT GIVING, Hints on:

- Ask for two receipts when purchasing a gift—a regular one for your records and one that has the description but no price. Enclose the description one with the gift in case it has to be returned.

- Include the care instructions when giving a plant, plus any information or hints you can offer about it.
- Give a bookmark when giving a book. Write the date on the bookmark plus a comment or two.

GIFT, LARGE, To wrap:
- Use a disposable party tablecloth for a very large package.

GIFT WRAPPING PAPER, Hint on:
- Buy a roll of white butcher paper and use it to wrap gift items for all occasions.

GIFTS, Received from out-of-town senders:
- Enclose a photo of yourself with the gift—holding the flowers or wearing the article—with your thank-you note.

GILT FRAMES, DISCOLORED, To renew:
- Pat the frame with a sponge dampened with a solution of half ammonia and half rubbing alcohol. Pat it dry, then apply a little lemon oil.
- Rub the frame with a clean cloth dipped in warm turpentine. Do not heat turpentine on the stove as it is highly flammable, just stand it in a bowl of hot water.
- Wipe the frame with equal parts of methylated spirits and water. Dry well.

GLASS, BROKEN, To pick up:
- Use a piece of bread to pick up shattered pieces of glass.

GLASS CLEANER, To make:
- Mix 2 ounces rubbing alcohol, 2 ounces nonsudsing ammonia, and 12 ounces water in a clean 16-ounce spray bottle.

GLASS ORNAMENTS, To clean:
- Soak for 1 hour in lukewarm water to which 1 teaspoon ammonia has been added, then leave to dry.

GLASS TABLETOPS AND SHELVES, To clean:
- Apply rubbing alcohol on a soft cloth and rub dry.
- Wash with a mixture of 2 cups warm water and ½ cup liquid fabric softener. This will clean the surface and retard dust.

GLASS VASES, CARAFES, CRUETS, STAINED OR CLOUDY, To clean:
- Fill them with water containing 2 teaspoons ammonia and let them

stand for several hours or overnight. Wash and rinse. This method also works for mineral deposits.
- Shake tea leaves and white vinegar around in the item.
- Rub with a paste made of table salt and water.
- See "Vases, Stained, To clean."

GLASSWARE WITH CHIPS OR ROUGH EDGES, To smooth:
- Rub the edge gently with an emery cloth until the chip is smoothed out.

GLASSWARE, TINY SCRATCHES ON, To remove:
- Polish the scratches with nongel toothpaste.
- Mix 1 ounce water, 1 ounce glycerin, and 1 ounce iron oxide (jeweler's rouge). Rub the paste gently on the scratch with a soft cloth, then rinse with clear water. (Obtain jeweler's rouge from a jeweler who makes settings.)

GLOVES, LEATHER, To clean: See "Leather Gloves, To clean."

GLUE, Dried in the bottle:
- Put a little white vinegar into the container to moisten the glue and make it liquid again.

GLUE, To avoid drying out:
- Keep tubes of partially used glue in a tightly closed glass jar.
- Coat the threads of the tube and the cap lightly with petroleum jelly.

GLUE, To make:
- Mix 3 teaspoons cornstarch with 4 teaspoons cold water to make a smooth paste. Boil ½ cup water and stir into the paste. The mixture should become clear. Use when cool.

GLUE, HARDENED, To remove:
- Remove old glue from items with hot white vinegar.

GOLF BALLS, To clean:
- Soak them in a solution of 1 cup water and ¼ cup ammonia until clean. Rinse and dry.
- Rub them with a damp sponge dipped in baking soda. Rinse and dry.

GOLF BALLS, To identify:
- Mark them with a dab of colored nail polish. Or use golf balls of a specific color.

GOLF BALLS, To store:
- Keep them in egg cartons.

GREETING CARDS, Hints on:
- Buy in bulk to save time and money.
- Put the patient's home address as the return address when sending a card to someone in the hospital. If the person has been discharged, it will be sent to that home.

GUITARS AND STRING INSTRUMENTS, To remove dust from interior:
- Put ½ cup uncooked rice in the opening, shake it around, then pour out the rice along with the dust.
- Blow the dust out with canned compressed air. (Obtain canned compressed air from a photographic or electronics store.)

HAIR RIBBONS, To keep from fraying:
- Paint a narrow strip of colorless nail polish across the ends.

HAIR WITH STATIC ELECTRICITY, To control:
- Rub a slightly dampened sheet of fabric softener over your hair and on your hairbrush.

HAIRBRUSHES AND COMBS, To clean:
- Soak for a couple of minutes in warm mild sudsy water, or suds to which 1 or 2 teaspoons ammonia has been added. Rub the brushes and combs against each other. Rinse thoroughly and dry them on a towel with the bristles down. When they are nearly dry, turn them so the bristles are up. Stiffen natural bristles by adding ½ teaspoon alum to the final rinse water. (Obtain alum from a drugstore or the spice section of a supermarket.)
- Dissolve 1 teaspoon liquid dishwashing detergent and 1 tablespoon borax in 2 quarts warm water. Soak for 30 minutes, then rinse in hot running water. Finish with cold water.
- Clean your brush or comb while shampooing your hair. Dab the brush or comb on your shampoo-covered hair a couple of times, run it through your fingers, then rinse by holding it under the running water.

HAMPERS, CLOTHES, To keep fresh:
- Sprinkle baking soda in hampers to eliminate odors. The baking soda can go in with the clothes to boost cleaning.

HANGER MARKS ON WOOLENS, To remove:
- Dampen each bump with a wet washcloth. The item will dry quickly and the bumps will disappear.

HANGERS, CLOTHES FALLING OF, To prevent:

- Put strips of masking tape, sticky side up, on both ends of the hangers.
- Slip rubber bands or strips of Velcro on the ends.
- Cut a piece of foam padding and slip it over the hanger.

HEARING AID, USED, Hint on:

- Donate it to a nonprofit organization that restores and recycles used hearing devices for those who need but can't afford them. Send your tax-deductible used hearing aid to Hear Now, 9745 East Hampden Avenue, Suite 300, Department MO, Denver, CO 80231. Or check whether your local library collects them.

HEATING PAD, MOIST, SUBSTITUTE:

- Moisten the pad of a disposable diaper, then heat the diaper in the microwave. You'll have a reusable heating pad that will seal in the moisture and is easy to wrap and secure around joints and aching muscles. Be careful not to overheat the diaper. If that happens, let it cool before applying.

HEATING PAD SUBSTITUTE:

- Fill an old sock with uncooked rice or gravel. Close or tie the end and place in the microwave for 3 minutes. It will stay hot/warm for 2 hours and can be reused many times. Because of its flexibility, it's ideal to wrap around aching joints. If you add a few cloves to the rice, it will be aromatic and soothing.

HEIRLOOM CLOTHING AND LINENS, To preserve:

- Remove from a garment any metal parts that might rust. Wash the item, rinse, then rinse again in a solution of 2 tablespoons white vinegar to 1 gallon cool water. Do not starch or iron. If possible, dry in the sun if the item is white. Wrap in acid-free tissue paper, muslin, cotton, or cotton/polyester sheets. Don't wrap in plastic, Styrofoam, cardboard, or regular tissue paper. If you are using new sheets, wash them before using. Place wrapped pieces in acid-free boxes in a cool, dry, dark, well-ventilated area, or put them in a drawer lined with acid-free tissue, or cotton or muslin sheets.

HIGHLIGHTER PEN, DRIED OUT, To renew:

- Remove the felt tip or the end plug and add water. Or add water mixed with food coloring.

HOT OIL TREATMENT FOR HAIR, To warm the towels:

- Put them in a little hot water in the washing machine, then turn the washer to the spin cycle. The towels will be hotter than if wrung by hand.

HOT WATER BOTTLE, OLD, Use for:

- Fill it with rags, old hose, or Styrofoam popcorn and use as a kneeling pad. Cut off the end and seal with sturdy tape.

HOT WATER BOTTLE SUBSTITUTE:

- Fill a 2-liter soda bottle with hot water.
- Warm a brick in the oven and cover it with aluminum foil, a cloth, or towel.
- See also "Heating Pad Substitute."

HOT WATER HEATER, To conserve energy:

- Insulate it and turn it down to 120°F.
- Turn it off if you plan to be away for a while.

HOUSEPLANTS, See "Plants, Indoor."

HUMIDIFIER, To remove odor from:

- Put 1 tablespoon strained lemon juice into the water to keep the humidifier odor-free.

ICE TRAY SUBSTITUTES:

- Use clean Styrofoam egg cartons if you don't have enough ice-cube trays.
- Freeze water in well-washed-out cardboard milk cartons, then take them outside and hit with a hammer to break up the ice. Hammer well for crushed ice.

INCOME TAX HELP, Hint on:

- Call your local university to see if it provides tax service. At least 16 law schools sponsor free clinics. Some help only the poor, but others accept people of any income who have tax bills that do not justify payment of an accountant's fee.

INSECT REPELLENT, To make:

- Rub vinegar on your skin with a cotton ball and allow it to dry. The smell disappears as it dries. Or dilute oil of citronella with a little vegetable oil and rub it on.

INSURANCE, AUTOMOBILE, Hint on:

- Shop around. Your State Insurance Department (listed in the white pages of the phone book under State Government Offices) will provide you with information on cost, service, and complaint statistics on insurance companies.

IRON, NONSTICK SURFACE, STARCH BUILDUP, To remove:
- Rub gently with a dampened plastic pad, or spray prewash spray into a washcloth and rub it gently over the soleplate.

IRON, STAINLESS STEEL, STARCH BUILDUP, To remove:
- Rub a small piece of superfine (No. 0000) steel wool gently over the bottom of the iron, then wipe off with a clean, wet cloth and dry well. (Purchase No. 0000 steel wool at a hardware store.)
- Wipe with a cloth dampened with rubbing alcohol, then buff with extra-fine steel wool (No. 000) and wipe off any residue.
- Turn the iron on a low setting and run it several times over a piece of wax paper. Then run the iron over an old towel or piece of cloth to remove any traces of wax.
- Run the iron several times over a washcloth saturated with white vinegar. Then run the iron over a damp cloth to wipe off any remaining starch.
- Sprinkle table salt on a sheet of wax paper and slide the iron across it several times. Afterward, rub the iron lightly with silver polish to remove the stain.
- Mix 2 tablespoons of table salt with water to form a paste. Rub on with crumpled newspaper, then wipe it clean with a damp paper towel.

IRON, STEAM, To fill:
- Use a clean ketchup or mustard dispenser or a turkey baster to fill the iron with water.

IRON REST SUBSTITUTE:
- Use a brick. It won't draw the heat from the iron as quickly as metal.
- Wrap a thick magazine in heavy-duty aluminum foil.

IRON SEDIMENT BUILDUP IN THE PORTS, To remove:
- Unplug the iron and clean out the ports with a straightened paper clip, cotton swab, or pipe cleaner. Then fill the iron with a mixture of equal parts white vinegar and water and turn it on to a low-steam setting. Allow to steam in a well-ventilated area until all the vinegar is gone. Or heat to the highest steam setting and steam for 5 minutes. Unplug and let cool. Empty the vinegar mixture and loosened mineral deposits. If the iron is still clogged, repeat the procedure with full-strength vinegar. After steaming, empty the vinegar and rinse the iron

well with water. Finally, heat the iron and run it a couple of times over a damp piece of terry-cloth to remove any mineral residue.
- Check for steam. If no steam is coming out of the iron after you have treated it with full-strength vinegar, it is too badly clogged to be fixable.

IRON SOLEPLATE, To clean:
- Rub the soleplate with a damp sponge sprinkled with baking soda.
- Wipe the soleplate with a cloth sprayed with laundry prewash solution.
- Use a plastic scrubber, which won't damage the finish.
- Run the iron over table salt sprinkled on a brown paper grocery bag.
- Spray on oven cleaner, then sponge off.

IRONING, Hints on:
- Iron when fabrics are still slightly damp, except for wool, which should be dry to avoid shrinkage. Sprinkle or dampen items with warm, not cold, water.
- Sprinkle linens lightly with water, place them in a plastic bag, and keep them in the refrigerator until the items are uniformly dampened. Or place the items in a 1-gallon plastic bag. Twist loosely to close and microwave on high for 1 minute or until the cloth is warm to the touch.
- Keep handy a plant sprayer or an ice cube wrapped in a thin cloth when ironing so you can dampen small areas as needed.
- Use a low-temperature setting for silk, high for linen, and iron clothes from the low setting to the high.
- Iron collars, cuffs, and hems on the wrong side first to prevent them from puckering.
- Press silk, corduroy, and dark-colored items on the wrong side.
- Press double-knits and "hand wash/dry clean only" fabrics.
- Press by using a nonterry cloth dishtowel, cotton diaper, man's handkerchief, or a piece of old cotton sheeting as a press cloth. Or use a dampened paper towel or a pressing sock. See "Ironing, Pressing Sock, Iron, To make."
- Put a big safety pin on the square end of the ironing board and run the iron's cord through the pin to avoid tangles.
- Hang the hangers you will need on the leg of the ironing board.
- Hold pleats in place with a paper clip slipped onto the ends or with straight pins stuck directly into the ironing board.
- Iron garments with grippe snaps, pearls, or rhinestones on the wrong

side on top of a bath towel. The decorations will sink into the towel, and you can iron over them.

IRONING PLASTIC, Hint on:

- Place a piece of cloth, such as an old sheet, over the plastic before ironing. The iron glides over the material and won't stick to the plastic.

IRONING, PRESSING SLEEVE SUBSTITUTE:

- Roll up a magazine and cover it with a cloth, then insert it in the sleeve. The magazine will fan open and fill the sleeve.

IRONING, PRESSING SOCK, IRON, To make:

- Make a pattern on paper first by tracing around the steam iron. Add 1 inch to the pattern, then cut the material out from a piece of cotton. Sew a piece of ⅛- or ¼-inch-wide elastic, ⅗ inch from the cut edge, stretching the elastic slightly as you sew. The elastic allows the sock to slip on and off the iron easily. A pressing sock is easier to use than a pressing cloth.

JEWELRY, GOLD AND SILVER, To clean:

- Soak in a solution of ½ cup clear ammonia and 1 cup warm water for 10 minutes. Rub gently with a cloth or soft brush and allow to dry. Do not use on pearls.

JIGSAW PUZZLE IN PROGRESS, To move around:

- Keep it on a large tray or a piece of thin wood. The puzzle can be moved as required without taking up needed space.

JUNK MAIL, To curtail:

- Put the material in the postage-paid, business-reply envelope that came with it, if there is one, plus the used envelope it came in, and send it back to the company.
- Request your name be removed from mailing lists. (See USEFUL ADDRESSES AND PHONE NUMBERS, "Direct Mail Relief.")

KEYS, To identify:

- Put a spot of colored nail polish or paint on the keys you use most frequently.
- Put a piece of tape at the end of a frequently used key.
- Drill an off-center hole in a key for instant identification in the dark. Or file a notch in the top.
- Use identification rings intended for the purpose. This is handy if you have many keys.

- Draw an outline of each key you have on a piece of paper and under it write what lock it fits.

KNEELING PAD SUBSTITUTE:
- Stuff Styrofoam packing pellets, old rags, or nylon hose into an old hot water bottle.
- Use an old piece of foam rubber or computer wrist rest.

KNITTING, See SEWING, KNITTING, CROCHETING Chapter.

LABELS, GLUE AND GUM RESIDUE FROM, To remove:
- Saturate the residue with vegetable oil and rub vigorously with a coarse cloth.
- Rub the glue with rubbing alcohol, being careful not to smear it onto the clean surface.

LACE, TO IRON, Hint on:
- Iron on wax paper.

LABELS ON BOTTLES AND JARS, To remove:
- Fill the container with hot water, put on the lid, and immerse it in hot water for 30 minutes.
- Cover the label with a wet paper, dish, or hand towel, and keep it wet until the label can be peeled off.

LADDER MARRING WALLS, To prevent:
- Put a sock over each ladder leg before propping it up in the house.

LAMB'S WOOL RUG, OLD, Uses for:
- Cut up and use as dusting mitts, polishing cloths, or car-washing mitts.
- Use as a cover for a car seat or tractor, or the office at work. It's a perfect insulating material—cool in hot weather and warm in cold.
- Make a pair of bootees or slippers.

LAMP SHADES, To clean:
- Dust regularly using the dusting attachment of the vacuum cleaner, a baby's hairbrush, or a feather duster.
- Clean periodically with a chemically treated dry sponge made for lamp shades and wallpaper.
- Have all hand-painted silk, linen, and chintz shades dry-cleaned professionally.
- Wash silk, rayon, and nylon shades if they are sewn, not glued, to the frames and the trimmings are colorfast. Dip shades in and out of a tub

of lukewarm suds, made with mild detergent. Rinse twice in clear, lukewarm water. Let drip for a few moments, then dry in front of an electric fan, turning the shades frequently to prevent the fabric from staining or the frame from rusting.

LAMPS, HURRICANE, To prevent smoking:
• Soak the wick in white vinegar and dry well before using.

LAVENDER, To dry:
• Pick heads in dry weather when about half the flowers on the spikes are open. Lay on trays and dry in the sun or in a light, airy room, turning occasionally. Or hang in bunches upside down with a paper bag tied around flower heads. The flowers will drop into the bag when they are dry.

LEATHER, To condition:
• Clean the leather first, then apply a small amount of castor oil or petroleum jelly with a soft cloth or the fingers. Rub in well, then remove excess with a soft cloth and buff.

LEATHER, To preserve:
• Avoid storing in plastic. Leather can't breathe through plastic.
• Rub with a mixture of 1 part neat's-foot oil (available at a hardware or shoe repair store) and 1 part castor oil. Heat the mixture over very low heat until it is just warm. Rub the warm oil into the leather with a soft cloth. Let it sit 15 minutes, then buff with a clean soft cloth.

LEATHER, BALLPOINT INK STAIN ON, To remove:
• Use cuticle remover. Test on a hidden area first.

LEATHER BELT, To make extra notches:
• Make the notches with a red-hot steel knitting needle.
• Use a one-hole punch, a nail, or the prong of a belt buckle.

LEATHER, DIRTY, To clean:
• Mix together 2 tablespoons white vinegar, 2 tablespoons rubbing alcohol, ½ teaspoon cooking oil, and ½ teaspoon liquid soap. Apply to the leather with a clean sponge.
• Apply saddle soap with a soft cloth and let it sit for about 30 minutes. Brush or rub vigorously with a cloth, then buff with a soft cloth. (Obtain saddle soap from the shoe polish section of a supermarket or a shoe repair store.)

LEATHER, FADED, To renovate:
- Treat with saddle soap to soften it up, then touch it up with leather stain.

LEATHER GLOVES, To clean:
- Wash them while wearing them in cold water with mild soap, saddle soap, or Murphy's Oil Soap. Rinse well and remove. If they are hard to remove, run water into them. Stuff clean tissue paper into them and air-dry flat.

LEATHER, GREASY, To clean:
- Mix 6 ounces water, 3 ounces rubbing alcohol, and 2 ounces white vinegar. Moisten a soft cloth or sponge with the solution and wipe the leather clean.

LEATHER, MILDEW ON, To remove:
- Rub the mildew stains gently with petroleum jelly. Wipe clean, then rub more petroleum jelly onto the stains. Let stand 24 hours, then polish with a clean soft cloth.

LEATHER SHOES, See "Leather, To preserve" and "Leather, Dirty, To clean."

LEATHER, STAINS ON, To remove:
- Mix 3 tablespoons castor oil and 2 tablespoons rubbing alcohol. Apply to the stains and leave on for 24 hours. Wipe off the mixture with a clean cloth.

LEATHER, TREATED, To clean:
- Wash with warm water and pure soap such as Ivory Snow or Fels Naphtha (not a detergent), taking care not to make the leather too wet. Rub stains gently with a soft nail brush or toothbrush. Rinse in slightly lighter lather, not in plain water. If a jacket, roll up in a heavy towel and dry away from the heat. If stiff, rewet in heavier soapsuds.

LEATHER, TREATED OR UNTREATED, To determine:
- Rub a small inconspicuous spot with soap on a damp cloth. If the color shows on the cloth, the leather is untreated. Most leathers are treated.

LEATHER UNTREATED, To clean:
- Polish with wax or cream polish.

LEGAL SERVICES, Hints on:
- Look into legal clinics and prepaid legal service plans.
- Belong to a credit union that offers a free legal service. Members can

call an assigned attorney and have their questions answered over the telephone. (To locate a credit union you might be eligible to join, call 800-358-5710 to find the phone number of your state's credit union league.)

- Check the yellow pages under "Attorneys" for the Lawyer Referral Service. The service can assign you to a lawyer who gives you half an hour of consultation for a small fee.

LEVEL SUBSTITUTE WHEN HANGING A SHELF:
- Fill a tall plastic bottle three-quarters full of water. Put the top on, then lay the bottle on its side. Adjust the shelf until the water is level. Or place a marble in the midpoint of the shelf.

LINENS, To store:
- Roll them around cardboard tubes from wrapping paper to avoid creases. Or roll and put them inside long mailing tubes to prevent soiling and creases.
- Fold the linens wrong side out. Any discoloration on the creases will be on the underside of the cloth.
- Keep infrequently used linens in a blue pillowcase or blue paper, or in pillowcases blued to a deep color with bluing.

LINT ON CLOTHING OR FURNITURE, To remove:
- Rub a slightly dampened sponge or coarse cloth over the fabric.
- Wrap masking tape or cellophane tape around your hand, sticky side out, and pat the fabric.
- Use a clothes brush or any clean soft brush.

LIPSTICK STUBS, To salvage:
- Remove lipstick from the dispenser with a toothpick and put in a small dish with an equal amount of petroleum jelly. Melt in the microwave on high for about 1 minute, stirring a few times with a toothpick. Put in a container and use as a lip gloss.

LOCK, STICKING, To loosen:
- Lubricate the lock by rubbing pencil lead (graphite) on the key and inserting it several times into the lock. Repeat if necessary.

LOUVERED DOORS OR SHUTTERS, To clean:
- Put plastic or newspapers under the door or shutters, then spray generously with an all-purpose cleaner. Include the tops of the slants and the corners. Leave for a minute or two, then wipe each slat with a

damp piece of terry cloth wrapped around a paint-stirring stick or a wooden spatula. Spray with clean water, then wipe dry with a clean dry cloth.

LOW-TOXIN PRODUCTS: See USEFUL ADDRESSES AND PHONE NUMBERS, "Toxin-Free/Low-Toxin Products."

LUBRICANTS, Uses for:
- Silicone spray such as WD-40 is an all-purpose lubricant.
- Powdered graphite is used to lubricate locks.
- Penetrating oil such as Liquid Wrench loosens rusted connections, screws, and nuts.

LUGGAGE, To remove musty odors:
- Stuff with crumpled newspaper. The newspaper will absorb odor.
- Put a shallow container filled with cat litter deodorizer in the suitcase or trunk. Close the lid and leave overnight. The next day put the open suitcase or trunk in the sun to air out.
- Put activated charcoal in the suitcase until the odor is gone, then air in the sun if possible. (Obtain activated charcoal from an aquarium supply store.)

LUGGAGE HANDLE, BROKEN, Hint on:
- Replace with a dog collar.

LUGGAGE, LIGHTWEIGHT, Hints on:
- Buy lightweight polypropylene or nylon, which is far lighter than leather and stronger and more practical than any other luggage fabric. Also look for nylon-coil zippers, which are continuous coil and self-repairing—no metal teeth to break.

LUGGAGE PACKED AWAY, To keep fresh:
- Put a cake of unwrapped soap inside or a couple of scented fabric softener sheets.
- Stuff with newspaper if storing for long periods.

LUGGAGE SIZES FOR AIRLINE CARRY-ONS:
Underseat bags: 9 × 14 × 22 inches, with a total dimension of 45 inches.
Garment bags: 4 × 23 × 45 inches, total of 72 inches.
Overhead bags: 10 × 14 × 36 inches, total of 60 inches.

MAGAZINES, FINISHED WITH, To indicate:

- Put your initial or name on the front of the magazine after you are finished with it. Have family members do the same. This eliminates guesswork and questions when it's time to discard the magazines or pass them on.

MAGAZINES, FREE, Where to obtain:

- Borrow them from the library.
- Ask your beauty shop, barber, doctor, or dentist if you can have them when they are ready to be discarded.
- Call the local library to inquire when it discards old ones and what publications would be available and where.
- Exchange them with friends.

MAILING REQUESTS FOR INFORMATION ABROAD, Hint on:

- Purchase International Reply Coupons from the post office when requesting information that requires a self-addressed stamped envelope. Sometimes you can buy stamps of other countries and receive a list of current mailing rates from the various consulates.

MAILING PHOTOGRAPHS AND BOOKS, Hints on:

- Cut Styrofoam meat cartons to use as protection.
- Line a manila envelope with bubble wrap you've saved from packaging instead of purchasing a padded envelope.
- Use a small paper bag for a mailer. The maximum size allowed is $6\frac{1}{8}$ × $11\frac{1}{2}$ inches. Fold it down to meet the requirements and tape it closed.
- Include your return address inside any package you mail.
- Mail books 4th class to save on postage.

MANICURE, Hints on:

- Apply glycerin, cuticle remover, or lotion to the cuticle. Massage it around the cuticle gently, gradually pushing the cuticle back. If cuticles don't respond readily, soak them in a solution of equal parts white vinegar and warm water for 5 minutes, then apply glycerin and rub with an orangewood stick. Dip a small piece of cotton in vinegar and wipe each fingernail to clean the nail and make the polish adhere longer. Let dry, then apply polish. Do not shake polish before using. Instead, turn the bottle upside down and gently roll it between your palms. Clean up any manicure splatters with an eyeliner brush, artist's brush, or cotton swab dipped in polish remover.

MARBLE, To clean:
- Wash with a mild detergent and water, then rinse off with clean water and buff dry.
- Scour with baking soda on a damp sponge. Let sit for a few minutes, then rinse with warm water and dry.

MARBLE ETCH MARKS, To remove:
- Sprinkle tin oxide (jeweler's rouge) on a surface that has been wet with clean water. Rub the powder into the marble with a damp cloth, and continue buffing until the marks disappear and the surface is shiny.

MARBLE GREASE STAINS, To remove:
- Place white paper towels saturated with mineral spirits on the stains until they are removed. Cover the towels with a sheet of plastic wrap, or place a Pyrex dish on them to hold the moisture in the towels. When the stains are removed, bleach the area with hydrogen peroxide, wash with mild detergent and water, rinse, dry, and polish with a nonyellowing wax.
- Place a white paper towel saturated with amyl acetate or acetone on the spots. Cover with a piece of plastic or plastic wrap and weigh down with something heavy.
- Mix whiting with acetone to form a paste. Apply to the stain area and cover with a piece of plastic wrap. Leave the paste on until the stain is removed. Then wash with a mild detergent and water, and rinse.

MARBLE RUST STAINS, To remove:
- Soak with paper towels saturated in commercial rust remover. Cover with a piece of plastic wrap and leave on for 4 hours, then remove the paper towels, and wash and rinse the area thoroughly.

MARBLE STAINS, To remove:
- Place white paper towels saturated with hydrogen peroxide and a few drops of ammonia on the stains. Cover the towels with a sheet of plastic wrap and seal with masking tape to hold in the moisture. Keep the moist towels on until the stains are removed. This may take several hours. After the marble is cleaned, rinse, dry and buff.
- Send for information from the International Marble Cleaning Company of Great Neck, Long Island, 39 Water Mill Lane, Great Neck, NY 11021. For $6.00 plus postage, it will send you a stain removal kit.

MARBLE, YELLOWED, To whiten:
- Rub with white vinegar, then rinse immediately.

MATCHES, LONG, SUBSTITUTE:
- Use a paper drinking straw or a piece of raw spaghetti.

MATTRESS, Care of:
- Vacuum with the upholstery attachment of the vacuum cleaner or brush with a whisk broom once a month.
- Turn the mattress over head to foot one month, and the next month turn it over side to side.
- Remove any stains with upholstery shampoo, then spray with a disinfectant air freshener.

MATTRESS METRIC MEASUREMENTS, To convert:
Twin	38 × 75 inches or .097 × 1.92 meters
Full	53 × 75 inches or 1.36 × 1.92 meters
Queen	60 × 80 inches or 1.54 × 2.05 meters
King	76 × 80 inches or 1.95 × 2.05 meters

MATTRESS ODORS, To eliminate:
- Neutralize urine odor by dampening the spot and sprinkling borax over it. Rub it into the area and let dry. Brush or vacuum to remove the dry borax.
- Sponge the area with white vinegar, then rinse with clear water.
- Freshen a mattress by sprinkling baking soda over it. Leave it on for a couple of hours or all day, then vacuum or sweep up the soda.

MEASURING WITHOUT A RULER, Hints on:
- Know the exact width of your hand with the thumb and little finger spread apart; then you'll be able to make a rough measurement if necessary.
- Remember that a dollar bill is about 6⅛-inch long if you need an approximation.

MEDICINE CABINET, Hints on:
- Keep a few supplies such as aspirin, Band-Aids, and over-the-counter remedies in the cabinet for easy access. Keep first-aid supplies all together in a container (a shoe box is fine), and keep medicines in a cool dry place. The bathroom is not the ideal place for prescription items.
- Put a piece of magnetic tape on the wall of the cabinet to keep metal nail files, tweezers, clippers, and manicure scissors within reach. Or keep them in a small plastic jar or container.

MEDICINES, To identify:

- Mark containers with the malady for which they were prescribed as soon as you bring them home; for example, for headache, for cough, for allergy. Call the pharmacist for information on how to take the medications (with meals, not with other medication, etc.) if the instructions are not printed on the container, or no instruction sheet was provided.
- Ask your physician for a free sample when he or she prescribes a medication to see if it agrees with you.

MEDICINES, To keep track of when taking:

- Ask your doctor or druggist for a free Counter Cap. It shows the day and dosage, and counts each time you open your pill bottle.
- Put a check on the calendar after you've taken your pill for the day. Make a check each time you take the medicine; for example, if you have to take it three times a day, you should put three checks on the calendar.
- Put what you need for the day in a small container and carry it with you.
- Put out the pills the night before in a small container or bottle cap. If you have to take many pills, label empty pill containers with the time of day the pills are to be taken, and put the pills in the containers the night before.
- Set the alarm for pills that must be taken at a certain time.

MEDICINES, HARD TO TAKE, To facilitate:

- Suck an ice cube for a moment before taking any unpleasant-tasting medicine. It will paralyze the taste buds.

METAL POLISHING, Hint on:

- Put an old pair of socks over your hands when rubbing off metal polish.

MICE, To repel:

- Saturate a piece of cardboard or a rag with peppermint oil or put out crushed fresh peppermint. Mice and rats hate the smell.
- Bait a trap with a cotton ball soaked in lard or bacon grease.
- Spread cloves or dried peppermint leaves around pipes and entrances and in the stove before leaving a summer cottage for the season.

MILDEW IN AREAS OF THE HOUSE, To curtail: See also BATHROOMS chapter, "Mildew, To inhibit."

- Leave a light on if the mildew is in the bathroom or closet. Or install a low-voltage light and keep it burning.

- Use a commercial product, such as silica gel or activated alumina, both of which work well in closets. Put a vent in the door or use louvered doors.
- Ventilate with fresh air as thoroughly as possible by opening all doors and windows and using an electric fan.
- Never dry a damp room or closet with an electric heater.

MILDEW ODOR ON AN ITEM, To remove:

- Put the item in a sealed bag or box with activated charcoal packed around it. Leave for a couple of weeks until the odor is gone.
- See also "Books, Musty Odor or Mildew, To remove."

MILDEW ON FABRICS, To remove:

- Wipe fabrics with cheesecloth dipped in equal parts of rubbing alcohol and water and then wrung out. Dry with a clean cloth. When dry, treat with fabric fungicide.
- Saturate the mildewed area with lemon juice and rub table salt on it, then put the item in the sun for several hours.
- Saturate a sponge with a solution of ¼ cup borax thoroughly dissolved in 2 cups hot tap water, and apply to the mildewed areas. Leave on for a couple of hours or overnight, until the stains are gone, then rinse well. Alternatively, soak the clothes in this borax and water solution.
- Mix a half-and-half solution of Lysol and water. Saturate the mildewed area with this solution and let sit for about 30 minutes, then brush the surface lightly. Put the unrinsed items in the washer and wash as usual. Test an inconspicuous spot first.
- Moisten with water, then rub in white powdered chalk. Leave for a while, then launder as usual.
- Remove mildew from white material by using a solution of 1 part chlorine bleach to 4 parts water. Soak for 15 minutes or until the mildew disappears.

MILDEW ON PAINTED AND HARD SURFACES, To remove:

- Paint the area with full-strength white vinegar.
- Apply a solution of one-quarter cup chorine bleach to 2 cups water. Leave on for 15 minutes. Repeat if necessary, then rinse.
- Make a paste of borax and water and leave on the area for a couple of days until completely dry, then vacuum up.
- See also BATHROOMS chapter, "Mildew, To inhibit."

MINIBLINDS: See "Blinds, Mini/Venetian, Care of."

MIRROR, SCRATCHED, To mend:
- Smooth a piece of aluminum foil a little larger than the scratch over the back of the mirror. Coat well with shellac or colorless nail polish and allow to dry.

MIRRORS, FOGGED, To prevent: See BATHROOMS, "Mirror Fogged, To dry in a hurry," and "Mirror Fogged, To prevent."

MITES, DUST, To curtail:
- Put carpets and rugs outside in the sun, upside down.
- Wash bedding in hot water.

MOSQUITOES, To repel:
- Put a few drops of camphor on a lump of sugar. Place the sugar lump on the bedside table.
- Place a pot of basil on the windowsill or outside on the patio to deter mosquitoes.
- Repel them at a picnic by putting 1 teaspoon oil of citronella in each of a few juice cans.

MOTHS, To repel:
- Wash clothes before storage and air regularly. Tumbling in a dryer will kill moth eggs.
- Keep moths away from drawers and cupboards by wiping with a solution of ½ cup ammonia and 1 quart water. Let the drawers and cupboards air-dry. (Use rubber gloves and work in a well-ventilated area.)
- Hang a small bunch of dried bay leaves (tied together with thread) in the wardrobe. Replace every 3 to 4 months. Also scatter bay leaves in the drawers and between layers of clothing you are putting away to store.
- Put a few cloves or cedar chips in the corners of wardrobes and cupboards or sprinkle the corners with Epsom salts.
- Make small cloth bags and fill with lavender, rosemary, or peppercorns, and put in the drawer with woolens.

MOUTHWASH, To make:
- Add ¼ cup apple cider vinegar to 2 cups boiling water, then let cool. Store in an old washed-out mouthwash bottle.

MOVING, Hints on:
- Leave clothing in drawers, but do not overload them.
- Designate one drawer for sheets and towels so that you won't have to rummage through boxes the first night in your new home.

- Pack a box of items that you will need immediately in your new home.
- Place pictures in boxes between sheets and blankets to give them added protection.
- Wrap dishes in facecloths, bath towels, tea towels, and other items from the linen closet.
- Put pillows, blankets, and other bedding requiring no wrapping in the bottom of wardrobe cartons provided by the moving company free of charge.
- Pack heavy items in small boxes, light items in large boxes.
- Wrap audio and video equipment inside a large plastic garbage bag to protect it from dust and dirt before packing.
- Pack plates and record albums on end vertically.
- Remove light bulbs before packing lamps.
- Put different colored pieces of tape or colored labels on boxes or items of furniture to indicate to which room they should go. Stick the colored tape or labels on the door of each room.
- Defrost your freezer and refrigerator 2 days before departure. Put a handful of fresh coffee, baking soda, or activated charcoal in a nylon stocking and place it inside the cleaned refrigerator to keep the interior smelling fresh. Or stuff the refrigerator with wadded-up newspaper.
- Carry valuables and financial and personal records with you.
- Take your current phone book with you. You may need it.
- Check with the Department of Agriculture in both origin and destination states before transporting plants. Some states specifically prohibit the entry and/or exit of certain plants. Water the plants upon arrival at your new home, but don't fertilize them until they've had a chance to adjust to the new environment.
- Record all utility meter readings (gas, electric, water) the day you leave.

MYLAR BALLOONS, To reuse:
- Have a local florist reinflate them for a small fee.
- Open them up and use them as gift wrap.
- Cut them into ribbons about 1 inch wide and attach them to branches of fruit trees to keep the birds away.

NAIL HOLES IN WALLS, To fill:
- Rub a cake of wet soap over the holes until filled. Let dry.
- Fill the holes with nongel toothpaste.
- Mix equal parts of table salt and dry laundry starch with enough

water to make a patching plaster. Fill the hole and smooth the surface.
- Combine equal parts of table salt and cornstarch, then add water until the mixture is the consistency of putty. Fill the holes and smooth the surface.

NAIL HOLES IN WOOD, To fill:
- Mix sawdust with glue until you get a stiff paste, then fill the holes with the paste.
- Use wood putty. Remove excess from the surface with a plastic playing card or credit card.
- Remove nails with a pair of long-nose pliers, rolling them as you extract them to prevent the hole from widening.

NAIL POLISH, CLEAR, Uses for:
- Paint over medicine bottle labels to preserve the information.
- Cover addresses on parcels to be mailed on wet days.
- Coat the back of metal necklaces or bracelets so the jewelry won't leave dark marks on skin.
- Coat the ends of ribbons to stop them from fraying.
- Harden the tips of shoelaces when the metal tips come off.

NAIL TOO SMALL TO HOLD, Hints on:
- Use a pair of snub-nosed pliers to hold it in place.
- Stick the nail through a piece of cardboard. Hold the cardboard in one hand and the hammer in the other. When the nail takes hold, tear away the cardboard.
- Hold the nail between the teeth of a comb or bobbypin.

NAILS, HAMMERING, Hints on:
- Use a nail punch for the final stroke when hammering nails into wood. This will prevent scars on the surface.
- Push nails through a cake of soap before using to prevent them from bending.
- Dip nails in hot water to heat them before driving them into plaster. There will be less chance of the plaster crumbling or chipping.

NEWSPAPERS/MAGAZINE ARTICLES AND SPECIAL PAPERS, To preserve:
- Combine 2 tablespoons milk of magnesia or 1 milk of magnesia tablet with 1 quart club soda. Refrigerate overnight. Pour the mixture into a shallow pan, then add the papers in a single layer. Soak for 1 hour. Remove and blot between paper towels, then spread on a flat surface

to dry. Do not disturb until completely dry. Place a weight on top of the clippings once they are semi-dry to prevent the ends from curling.

- Spread a thin layer of white craft glue over the papers. Let dry. You can coat just the side you want to preserve, or you can coat both sides. Let the first side dry before coating the reverse side. Be sure to choose white craft glue or paper glue that dries to a clear coat.
- See USEFUL ADDRESSES AND PHONE NUMBERS, "Mail-Order Companies, Acid-free tissue paper."

NYLONS AND PANTYHOSE, To extend the life of:
- Wrap freshly washed hose in foil or a plastic bag and freeze for 24 hours. After removing, let them thaw, then hang to dry. When dry, stretch them a little.

ODOR, To eliminate:
- Keep some charcoal briquettes in a basket in the room that needs the benefit of their air-purifying properties. They can be used later for the barbecue.
- Put out zeolite (see CLEANING PRODUCTS AND USES, "Zeolite," and USEFUL ADDRESSES AND PHONE NUMBERS, "Toxin-Free/Low-Toxin Products").
- Burn a scented candle or put some potpourri in a potpourri burner or in an old pot and simmer on the stove.
- Put a dab of perfume or aromatic oil on a cold lightbulb. When the light is turned on, the heat will release the aroma.
- Keep a vase of dried eucalyptus in the room.
- Boil some lemons and pour the liquid into bowls, then place them throughout the house.
- Cut up leftover orange and lemon peels and place them strategically about the room.
- Put some baking soda into jar lids and place out of sight.
- Place a saucer or small bowl of white vinegar in the room.
- Put 1 teaspoon vanilla in an uncovered container and place where needed.
- Keep a lemon geranium in the room. When the leaves are gently pressed they release their odor, filling the room with a pungent, lemony fragrance.
- Put 1 teaspoon nutmeg or cinnamon in an old metal pan or a frozen food container and burn it slowly on the stove burner until all the spice is dissipated.

ODOR, BOOKS, MUSTY: See "Books, Musty Odor or Mildew, To remove."

ODOR, BOTTLES AND JARS: See "Bottles/Jars, To deodorize."

ODOR, CARPET: See CARPETS chapter, "Carpet, Smelly, To freshen."

ODOR, COOKING: See KITCHENS chapter, "Odor of Fish or Vegetables Cooking, To minimize."

ODOR, DISHWASHER: See KITCHENS chapter, "Dishwasher, To remove odor."

ODOR, FOOT: See "Foot Odor, To treat."

ODOR, FURNITURE: See FURNITURE chapter, "Wood Furniture, Old, Musty Smell In, To eliminate."

ODOR, GARBAGE DISPOSAL: See KITCHENS chapter, "Garbage Disposal, To keep clean and sanitary."

ODOR, GARLIC AND ONION, ON COUNTERS: See KITCHENS chapter, "Garlic and Onion Odor on Counters, To remove."

ODOR, GARLIC AND ONION, ON HANDS: See KITCHENS chapter, "Garlic and Onion Odor on Hands, To remove."

ODOR, GARLIC ON BREATH: See "Garlic Odor on Breath, To avoid."

ODOR, HUMIDIFIER: See "Humidifier, To remove odor from."

ODOR, LUGGAGE: See "Luggage, To remove musty odors."

ODOR, MATTRESS: See "Mattress Odors, To eliminate."

ODOR, MILDEW, "Mildew Odor On an Item, To remove."

ODOR, PAINT: See PAINTING chapter, "Odor of Paint in Room, To remove."

ODOR, PERFUME IN BOTTLE: See "Perfume Odor in Bottle, To remove."

ODOR, PERFUME ON CLOTHING: See LAUNDRY chapter, "Perfume on Clothes, To remove."

ODOR, PERSPIRATION, ON WOOLENS: See LAUNDRY chapter, "Perspiration Odor in Woolens, To remove."

ODOR, PET ACCIDENT: See CARPETS chapter, "Carpet, Pet Accidents, To treat."

ODOR, REFRIGERATOR/FREEZER: See KITCHENS chapter, "Refrigerator Odors, To eliminate."

ODOR, SHOES: See "Shoes, Smelly, To remove odor."

ODOR, SUITCASE: See "Luggage Packed Away, To keep fresh."

ODOR, TOBACCO SMOKE, To get rid of:
- Soak a cotton ball with peppermint oil and put it in a small jar with a lid. When you need to scent a room or remove an odor, remove the lid.
- Keep small bowls of white vinegar in the room.
- Fill a bowl with 1 quart water and 1 tablespoon ammonia and leave it out overnight in the room.
- Dip a small towel in equal parts of vinegar and hot water. Wring it out and, holding the towel over your head as you walk around, wave it around the room.
- Place a little baking soda in a saucer or small dish and sprinkle with a few drops of ammonia and 3 drops oil of lavender. Add a few teaspoons boiling water and leave uncovered.
- Fill a plant-mister bottle with a solution of 3 tablespoons baking soda to 2 cups water and spray the area.

OIL STAINS ON DRIVEWAY, To remove: See "Concrete/Cement, Grease/Oil/Transmission Fluid Stains, To remove."

ORNAMENTS SCRATCHING THE SURFACE, To prevent:
- Put a corn or bunion pad on the bottom of the ornament.
- Paste a piece of foam rubber on the bottom.
- Purchase self-adhesive felt that is made for the purpose.

PACKAGES TO TRANSPORT, Hint on:
- Use a laundry basket to take packages to work, Christmas gifts to relatives, or to go shopping. It will keep all the packages together, and you have one container instead of many.
- Use a large trash bag.

PANTYHOSE, To make last longer: See "Nylons and Pantyhose, To extend the life of."

PAPER STUCK TO A POLISHED TABLE, To remove:
- Saturate the paper with cooking oil.

PARAFFIN, To melt:
- Place paraffin in a clean metal can, such as a coffee can. Bring 2 to 3 inches water to a boil in a large saucepan, then remove it from the heat and place it on a heatproof surface. Immediately set the can of paraffin in the very hot water and let it sit until it is completed melted.

PERFUME ODOR IN BOTTLE, To remove:

- Remove the scent from an empty perfume bottle by filling with it with rubbing alcohol. Let it stand overnight, then wash with warm water.

PERFUMED OIL, To make:

- Put eucalyptus leaves, rosemary, orange blossoms, rose petals, or other fragrant leaves or petals in a pottery jar or crock. Add some olive oil and seal tightly. Keep in a dark place for 10 days, then strain the oil into a bottle. Use the oil for freshening potpourri, adding to the bath water for a soothing aromatic bath, or putting on light bulbs to add fragrance to a room.

PEWTER, To clean:

- Wash with warm water and mild soap.
- Rub with cabbage leaves.
- **For a Bright Finish:** Mix whiting and rubbing alcohol to a thin paste. Let the paste dry, then polish, wash, rinse, and dry.
- **For a Dull Finish:** Rub with rottenstone and olive oil mixed to a thin paste, then wash, rinse, and dry. (Obtain rottenstone from a hardware or paint store.)

PHONOGRAPH RECORDS, To categorize:

- Stick small colored dots on the spine of the jackets according to classification—classical, jazz, rock, vocal, etc.—and keep the colors together.

PHONOGRAPH RECORDS, To clean:

- Wipe the records with a soft cloth wrung out in a solution of lukewarm water and a little mild dishwashing detergent, being careful not to get the labels wet. Then rinse with a cloth wrung out in clear water (preferably purified), and allow the records to air-dry.
- Use rubbing alcohol on a cotton swab to remove dust and dirt from the grooves.
- Wipe with a cotton ball moistened with methylated spirits.

PHONOGRAPH RECORDS, SCRATCHED, To fix:

- Dust and wash the records, then soak a clean cloth or handkerchief in 1 tablespoon olive oil and rub the record with it. Let the record dry for about a week without touching anything. When dry, the record should be fit to use.
- Rub scratches with a black felt marker and allow to dry. For bad scratches, play the records and rub again with the felt marker.

PHONOGRAPH RECORDS, WARPED, To straighten:

- Place between 2 sheets of glass on a flat surface in the sun and leave for 1 hour. Place a weight on the glass if it is badly warped. Take inside, still between the glass, and allow to cool to room temperature, then remove the glass.
- Place the record on a warm flat surface, such as on top of the television or refrigerator, then weigh it down with heavy books. Leave the record undisturbed for several days.

PHOTOGRAPHS, Hint on:

- Check finished snapshots before leaving the photoprint store. If you spot any processing mistakes, ask for reprints.

PIANO, Hints on:

- Get it tuned at least every 6 months and cleaned professionally every 3 years.
- Avoid tuning the piano for 3 months after you move. The wood needs a chance to settle.
- Avoid placing it near extremes of heat and cold, radiators, air conditioners or vents, or in direct sunlight.
- Put it at least 4 inches away from the wall.

PIANO KEYS, IVORY, To clean:

- Clean keys with a cloth dampened with milk or yogurt; follow with a cloth dampened with water. Wring these cloths very dry. Rub immediately afterward with a soft dry cloth.
- Use rubbing alcohol on a soft cloth to clean the keys.
- Clean really dirty piano keys with nongel toothpaste and an old soft toothbrush. Remove toothpaste with a cloth dampened with water and wrung dry. Rub immediately afterward with a soft dry cloth. Don't get the keys wet.

PIANO KEYS, YELLOW, To whiten:

- Rub with a soft cloth moistened with lemon juice, white vinegar, methylated spirits, or rubbing alcohol. Rinse with a clean cloth wrung out in clean water.
- Give the keyboard a chance to "breathe" by keeping the keyboard lid up. This helps prevent the keys from turning yellow.

PICNICS AND CAMPING, Hints on:

- Take salad greens in a self-sealing plastic bag. Add dressing at the last minute and shake.

- Fill a well-washed plastic milk bottle three-quarters full with water and freeze it. Then put it in your cooler for picnics or camping trips. After the ice melts, you have cold drinking water. Use juice instead of water if juice is your beverage of choice.
- Freeze water in margarine tubs and use one or two in a large beverage jug or pitcher instead of ice cubes.
- Line a plastic picnic bag with frozen bubble wrap or wrap it around the soft drink containers to keep them colder longer.
- Soak large sponges in water, then put them in self-closing plastic bags, seal, and freeze solid. Use in an insulated bag or cooler.
- Freeze wet washcloths in small plastic self-closing bags to take on picnics for wiping hands and cooling off.
- Put cutlery into an empty paper towel or gift wrap roll and fold in the ends to keep the utensils inside. Or wrap individual cutlery servings in napkins.
- Cut egg cartons into sections so they can fit in the cooler in the odd spaces. Use to hold eggs when camping, or hard-boiled eggs, tomatoes, or small fruits when picnicking.
- Keep pots and pans soot free by placing them on disposable aluminum pie pans when cooking.
- Put cans filled with water underneath table legs to stop ants from crawling up.
- Repel hornets by setting out saucers filled with apple cider vinegar.
- Prevent the tablecloth from blowing around by taping the corners to the underside of the table with masking tape, or put a stone in each corner and tie into a knot around the stone.
- Cover the food with a piece of nylon net weighed down around the edges. Or hem the edges and insert beads or a piece of wire in each hem.
- Invest in some cheap cotton napkins for picnics (or make your own). They don't fly around in the wind as do the paper ones.

PICTURES, FRAMED, To clean:
- Spray the cleaning fluid onto a cloth and apply it to the glass instead of spraying it directly on the glass.
- Use eyeglass cleaning tissues for small pictures.

PICTURE FRAMING, To save money on:
- Buy a matted/framed poster of the same size as the item you want matted and framed and exchange the poster for the picture. This will cost much less then getting it custom framed.

PICTURE HANGER, LIGHTWEIGHT, To make:
- Attach a soft-drink can tab to the back of the picture with a dab of epoxy glue.

PICTURES, To hang:
- Put 2 pieces of masking tape or cellophane tape on the wall in the shape of an X before putting in the nail. If you need to remove the nail, the tape will keep the paint from peeling off or the plaster from crumbling.
- Wet a fingertip and press it on the wall to mark the wire's inverted V point or make a mark with a pencil.

PICTURES, To keep straight:
- Affix corn pads or squares of double-faced tape to the frame's two lower back corners.
- Wrap masking tape around the wire on both sides of the hook so the wire won't slip.
- Position two parallel picture hangers on the wall a few inches apart to prevent the picture from moving.

PILLOWS, DOWN AND FEATHER, Care of:
- Fluff them daily and air them at least once a month outdoors or by an open window. Fresh air puffs them up and gives them a new lease on life. Pick a breezy day to hang them on the line, but keep them out of direct sunlight. Tumble them occasionally in the clothes dryer on an air setting for a minute or two.

PING-PONG BALLS, DENTED, To fix:
- Put them in boiling water until the dent pops out.

PLANT POTS, Materials to cover the drainage hole:
- Use cracked walnut shells, broken pieces of clay pottery, marbles, stones, pebbles, well-washed fruit pits, Styrofoam packing popcorn, activated charcoal, old sponges cut into squares, crushed eggshells, or several layers of nylon net or plastic mosquito netting.
- Line the bottoms of containers with no drainage holes with 1 inch or more of gravel or Styrofoam packing pellets. Use more for taller containers.

PLANT POTS, To disinfect:
- Immerse them in boiling water or heat them briefly in a 180° F oven, then let them cool.
- Wash them in hot soapy water and then soak overnight in a solution of

1 ounce chlorine bleach to 9 ounces water. Rinse off the pot the next day, and let air-dry.
- Soak clay pots in clean water for a few hours before using them for planting; otherwise they will draw water out of the soil.

PLANTS, INDOOR, Broken stem, To fix:
- Make a splint with a toothpick or matchstick and hold in place with tape.

PLANTS, INDOOR, Brown ends, To trim:
- Cut in the angle in which they grow, an inverted V, not straight across, and leave about one-half inch between brown and green, or else it will bruise and brown more.

PLANTS, INDOOR, Cactus, To repot:
- Use a pair of ice or bacon tongs or heavy oven mints to protect your hands.

PLANTS, INDOOR, Care of: (See also "Plants, Indoor, Feeding/fertilizing.")
- Dust them with a feather duster or blow the dust off with a hair dryer set on cool. Mist tropical plants afterward.
- Spray or mist nonhairy plants in the bathtub occasionally.
- Turn them from time to time so all parts will get their ration of light.
- Aerate the soil with a fork occasionally.
- Choose plants that are easy to care for if you have a brown thumb: cacti, dracaena, English and Swedish ivy, rubber plants, snake plants, spider plants, philodendrons, jade plants, or schefflera.

PLANTS, INDOOR, Cat repellent:
- Crush rue leaves and put them on the soil surface of the plants, or cover the top of the container with netting, screening, or strips of tape to prevent the cat using the plant container as a litter box.
- Grind up a few alfalfa tablets (not alfalfa sprouts) and mix with the cat's food or grow a box of grass for your cat to eat if the cat is chewing the leaves.

PLANTS, INDOOR, Deficiency of nutrients:
- Nitrogen (N): Lower leaves yellow; overall plant light green; growth stunted; burning tips and margins of leaves.
- Phosphorus (P): Small growth; delayed maturity.
- Potassium: Edges of leaves yellow, then brown; plants grow slowly; stalk is weak.

PLANTS, INDOOR, Feeding/fertilizing:

- Feed plants with a water-soluble fertilizer every 3 weeks or with a diluted amount every time you water.
- Give plants and bulbs 1 drop olive oil once a week as a tonic. They will grow faster and have glossier leaves.
- Give them a little praise or word of encouragement. Talking to your plants really does work, according to research.
- Treat an ailing houseplant with a few drops of castor oil dribbled on the soil followed by a thorough watering. It will also keep a healthy plant greener and improve blossoms.
- Save tea leaves and coffee grounds for the plants. They enrich the soil and give them a treat. Also occasionally give them plain leftover cold coffee with no milk or sugar. Don't do this too often because of the tannin.
- Water with leftover stale club soda because of the minerals.
- Use the water from boiling eggs. Let cool first. Or mix 3 or 4 crushed eggshells into 1 quart water and let sit overnight, then water.
- Use the water left over from cooking or steaming vegetables (without table salt). Cool before applying.
- Water ferns periodically with leftover tea. Or mix soggy tea leaves into the potting soil. Make sure ferns have a moist environment, otherwise they will be short-lived.
- Add 1 drop ammonia to 1 quart water to improve the color of the foliage and increase the growth. This is especially good for ivy.
- Try liquid seaweed extract for ailing plants. Liquid seaweed extract contains more than 60 minerals and can be applied to the soil to help remedy possible deficiencies.

PLANTS, INDOOR, Pests and disease, To get rid of:

- Wipe flat leaves with a wet cloth to remove most insects.
- Give the plants a shower to wash the pests off.
- Wash them with ½ teaspoon mild dishwashing detergent to 1 quart water.
- Put 1 whole clove garlic in each pot. If the clove sprouts, cut off the shoot so it does not take root and start to grow.
- **Aphids:** Squash aphids with your fingers or run under water to wash them off.
- **Aphids, whiteflies, red spider mites, mealybugs, soft scale, and thrips:** Mix 1 cup rubbing alcohol (70 percent isopropyl) and 1 cup water in a spray bottle. Do not use on plants with hairy leaves or on ferns.

- Spray plants with a solution of ½ teaspoon mild dishwashing detergent and 1 quart cool water.
- **Fungus:** Spray every few days with a mixture of ½ teaspoon baking soda combined with 1 quart water in a spray bottle.
- **Mealybugs or soft scale:** Dip a cotton swab or cotton ball in a mixture of 1 part water to 2 parts rubbing alcohol and touch it directly to the mealybugs or soft scale. Or dab on undiluted buttermilk.
- **Spider mites:** Mist plants frequently to control spider mites.

PLANTS, INDOOR, Putting outdoors:

- Give the plants a treat and put them outdoors when it rains. Avoid strong sunlight and don't leave them outdoors for an extended period or overnight; the change of climate may cause shock.
- Condition plants gradually if putting them outside permanently. Introduce them to outside conditions a few hours at a time, then gradually increase the time they are outside. The reverse holds true for bringing outdoor plants indoors.

PLANTS, INDOOR, Repotting:

- Put down lots of old newspapers or a trash bag to work on, then scoop up the old soil and dispose.

PLANTS, INDOOR, To clean the air:

- Use aloe vera, English ivy, fig trees, potted chrysanthemums, and spider plants, which absorb and neutralize air pollutants such as toxins, benzene, and formaldehyde.

PLANTS, INDOOR, To water:

- Water houseplants with room-temperature water. Cold water injures them.
- Water when the soil is dry below 1 inch from the top, and apply water until it runs out of the drain hole.
- Use a meat baster to siphon water out of the saucer if the plant is too heavy to move and the water has been sitting too long.

PLANTS, INDOOR, Vacation care:

- Set all your houseplants in the bathtub in a few inches of water. Put them on old towels folded once or twice or on thickly folded newspapers. The plants will absorb moisture as needed.
- Keep plants healthy for up to 1 month by watering them well, then enclosing them completely but loosely in clear plastic bags, such as those that come from the dry cleaners's. Tie the bags securely at the top and bottom. Place the plants in northern light. When you return,

untie the bags and let the plant adjust to room air for a day before completely removing the covering.

PLANTS, INDOOR HANGING, To water:
- Before planting, take a plastic bag and open it up. Poke holes in for drainage and line the pot with the plastic before putting the soil in. The lining helps the pots hold moisture longer.
- Slip an old shower cap over the bottom of the container before watering the plant, then later carefully remove the cap with the dirt and drips.
- Put a few ice cubes into the pots and let them melt.
- Use a large sports water bottle. The bent plastic straws make reaching the container easier.
- Buy a water wand from the hardware store. You squeeze the bulb and the water shoots into a high curved tube.
- Buy saucers that clip on the bottom of the container.

PLANTS, INDOOR, TROPICAL AND SUBTROPICAL, Care of:
- Boil and cool tap water before watering tropical and subtropical plants, to be on the safe side. A high chlorine content or too much lime in the water will poison a number of plants.

PLASTIC, To iron: See "Ironing Plastic, Hint on."

PLASTIC AND VINYL, To clean: See FURNITURE chapter, "Plastic and Vinyl Furniture, To maintain."

PLASTIC GLOVES SUBSTITUTE:
- Wear long plastic bread bags or plastic produce bags. Fasten or tape them to your wrists with a rubber band or a piece of tape.

PLUMBER, Hints on calling:
- Ask when calling if the plumber has the necessary equipment before coming to the house—extra-long snake, etc. This may prevent the plumber from having to leave and come back. Also have the plumber check on other minor plumbing problems you have if you will be charged by the hour.

POTPOURRI, Hints on:
- Stir occasionally and, if necessary, add a little rose, flower, or other essential oil to rejuvenate the potpourri.
- Put in the microwave for a few seconds, then stir to release the aroma.
- Simmer the potpourri in a mug or old cheese crock placed on a coffee-cup warmer. Or use an old fondue or chafing dish as a simmering pot.

POTTERY, CRACKED, To mend:
- Clean the area around the crack with a cotton swab dipped in soapy water. Then put the item in a 125° F oven for 30 minutes. Force a slow-drying epoxy glue into the crack with a toothpick. When the crack is full, remove any excess with a cotton ball dipped in rubbing alcohol or nail polish remover and leave to dry.

PREMOISTENED TOWELETTES, To make:
- Mix a few tablespoons of baby oil with 1 cup soapy water. Soak paper towels in this solution and tuck them into plastic bags to use in the nursery. Or carry them in a diaper bag or purse for quick cleanups.

PRESCRIPTIONS, To save money on:
- Ask your physician what milligram sizes the medication comes in when he or she prescribes it. If it comes in 10 mg size and you must take 5 mg and the per-pill cost is the same, ask if he or she can prescribe the larger size. Then cut them in half. Scored tablets are easy to break in half. Coated tablets should not be broken. Use a pill splitter from the drugstore to divide both scored and unscored pills.
- Shop and compare. Check out chain discount drugstores such as Cost Cutters, Drug Emporium, Drugs for Less, Drug Palace, Drug World, Phar-Mor, Freddy's, Rx Palace, and AARP (American Association for Retired Persons), which offers a slightly smaller discount to non-members. Also check warehouse clubs if they have a pharmacy department. Call for prices. In some states you can even get a printed price list to take home and some municipalities require price-posting. (See also USEFUL ADDRESSES AND PHONE NUMBERS, "Mail-Order Companies.")

PRICE STICKER LABEL RESIDUE, To remove: See "Adhesive Residue from Labels and Decals, To remove."

PRICE TAG ON A BOX, To remove:
- Cover the tag with cellophane tape. Rub over the tag with the back of a fingernail or the blunt end of a pen, and remove the tape. The price tag will come off with the tape.

PUMPKIN FROM HALLOWEEN, To save:
- Wash the seeds, salt them, and dry them in the oven.
- Keep the pumpkin firm indefinitely by spraying the inside and outside with an antiseptic, repeating periodically as necessary.

RAGS FOR CLEANING, What to use:

- Use terry cloth or cheesecloth for cleaning.
- Use 100 percent cotton underwear and socks, old diapers, cotton T-shirts, old cotton or linen tea towels or napkins, flannel, or any soft cotton material for dusting and polishing. Don't use material made from synthetic fibers. Synthetic material is not absorbent.

RATS AND MICE, To get rid of:

- Trap them, then seal off entrance holes by stuffing each entrance with steel wool. Cover floor vents and basement windows with hardware cloth. For bait, use peanut butter, fried bacon, bread spread with lard, bread soaked in sardine or fish oil, cheese, gumdrops, or hot-dog slices. Wash your hands before baiting the traps or wear gloves. Rodents detect human scent easily.
- Mix equal parts of baking soda and powdered sugar, or equal parts of cement powder and flour, and put in the infested area.
- Put cloves or dried peppermint leaves around kitchen pipes to deter mice when closing up a cottage for the season.

REAL ESTATE, BUYING, Hints on:

- Explore financing options and seek mortgage preapproval to make yourself a more attractive buyer. Look to banks and other mortgage holders as sources of bargains in the housing market and to corporate relocation specialists for hurried sellers seeking a quick sale and willing to bargain. (Ask your agent to phone other agents who are relocation specialists.)
- Ask your agent for a listing of what comparative properties in the neighboring area have sold for.
- Visit the property during the daytime, the evening, and the weekend to get an overall picture. Also talk to neighbors who live around the intended property to get their opinion of the neighborhood, the schools, snow service (if applicable), garbage pickup, mail delivery, and any concerns you may have.
- Obtain comparative information on school quality in the area from your real estate broker. Check on test results, comparing them to results from nearby schools, plus the percentage of high school graduates who go on to college.
- Find out what the previous owner paid for a house. If your agent can't supply the information, go to the County Assessor's office and ask for the green sheet. This is a copy of the tax information, including the sales history of the house.

- Have an independent professional inspection of the property made. Most sellers will pay for the inspection. If under pressure to sign a contract before the inspection, specify "Sale is subject to buyer's satisfaction based on the report of the inspection."
- See if the seller will cover all or part of the closing costs.
- Look into making your mortgage payments biweekly instead of monthly and discover how much interest you will save.

RING, STUCK, To remove:
- Rub hand lotion or baby oil over the finger and gently move the ring back and forth so some of the cream gets underneath, then gently slide the ring off.
- Rub the ring and finger with a bar of hand soap and work it under the ring, or put the ring hand in a bowl of ice-cold soapy water, then try pulling the ring off.
- Stick the end of a piece of thin string or dental floss under the ring toward the hand. Starting at the knuckle side of the ring, wrap the string snugly around the finger toward the end of the finger beyond the knuckle. Each wrap should be right next to the one before. Grasp the end of the string that is stretched under the ring and start unwrapping it. Push the ring along to take the place of the unwrapped string until the ring passes the knuckle.

ROACHES, To get rid of:
- Put borax or boric acid in dark kitchen cabinets, under the sink, and around baseboards and appliances. (Boric acid is poison. Keep out of reach of children and pets.)
- Mix 2 tablespoons borax or boric acid with 2 teaspoons sugar and place around the infested area on plastic lids, beverage bottle tops, or jar caps. The roaches will take the poison back to the nest. Leave it around for about 10 days. Repeat every 2 weeks until roaches are gone.
- Mix ½ cup borax and ¼ cup flour. Sprinkle behind cabinets and appliances, under the sink, and around baseboards, or put it in small shallow containers.
- Inject boric acid dust at 99 percent concentration into cracks and crevices with a dust bulb.
- Kill a crawling roach with a shot of rubbing alcohol from a spray bottle.

RUBBER BANDS, To keep organized:
- Keep them on a safety pin in the desk.

RUBBER BANDS, LARGE, SUBSTITUTE:

- Use the elastic bands from old pantyhose or men's briefs for large jobs, such as keeping boxes closed, etc. Use slices of an old inner tube from a 10-speed bike for jumbo jobs.

RUBBER FINGER SUBSTITUTE:

- Wrap a rubber band around your finger when sorting paperwork.

RUBBER GLOVES, Hints on:

- Apply a good dose of heavy-duty hand cream (not lotion or petroleum jelly) or sprinkle powder on your hands before you put on the gloves to make removal easier.
- Run cold water over your gloved hands if the gloves are hard to remove.
- Dry the gloves by turning them inside out, then dry with paper towels or a cloth, or with a hair dryer, or prop them over jars or soda cans to dry.
- Recycle an odd glove by turning it inside out and using it on the opposite hand. Usually the right glove is the first to go and you are left with a left-hand glove.

RUBBER GLOVES SUBSTITUTE:

- Wear long plastic bread bags or the bags provided for produce at the supermarket. Fasten or tape them to your wrists with a rubber band or a piece of tape.

RUST ON KNIVES AND TOOLS, To remove:

- Clean metal parts with a wire brush, emery cloth, or steel wool. Apply a protective coating of oil or petroleum jelly with a rag.
- Mix a little table salt and water to a paste. Rub on, leave for a little while, then rub it off.
- Rub a cut onion on the rust marks. Leave the juice on for 2 days, then wash off and clean.
- Rub with a soap-filled steel wool pad dipped in turpentine, then rub with a wadded piece of aluminum foil.

RUST ON METAL FURNITURE, To prevent:

- Melt ¼ cup lanolin and 1 cup of petroleum jelly in a double boiler over low heat, or in a microwave-safe bowl in a microwave set to defrost. Stir periodically until it melts, then remove from the heat or microwave and let it cool slightly. Apply while still warm and let dry on the article.
- See also GARDENS chapter, "Tools, To prevent rusting."

RUST-PENETRATING OILS, SUBSTITUTES:
- Use hydrogen peroxide. It works as a penetrating oil if allowed to sit on frozen bolts.
- Free crusted bolts by pouring a carbonated beverage on them. Let the carbonation work awhile before loosening.
- Pour on white vinegar or apply a rag saturated in vinegar to the rusted item.

SCENT SACHETS, To make:
- Cut up old nylons and fill with potpourri. Tie or sew to close, and hang up in the closet or put in lingerie drawers.
- Melt ½ cup paraffin in a double boiler over low heat or in a microwave-safe cup in a microwave set to defrost. (See also "Paraffin, To melt.") Remove from heat, let cool slightly, and then stir in 6 drops oil of rose, oil of lavender, or other perfumed oil. Coat the inside of caps from small jars with petroleum jelly. Pour the perfumed paraffin into the jar cap molds and let sit overnight to solidify. In the morning tap out the molds.
- Add a few drops of your favorite perfume to a few teaspoons of oatmeal or sawdust. Mix well and place in a small satin bag, and tie with matching ribbon.

SCENTING A ROOM, Hint on:
- Put a dab of perfume or aromatic oil on a cool light bulb. As the bulb heats it will release the scent.

SCISSORS, RUSTY, To clean:
- Mix a little table salt and water to a paste. Rub on, leave for a little while, then rub off.
- See "Rust on Knives and Tools, To remove."

SCREENS, ALUMINUM AND METAL, To clean:
- Rub a circular roller brush lightly over the screen to pick up the dust or use the dusting attachment of the vacuum cleaner.
- Roll a dry lamb's wool or synthetic duster over the screen, then wet the duster and rub it over the screen again. Be sure to wash the duster when finished.
- Remove the screens and place them up against a tree or fence or lay them on an old blanket. Scrub with a mixture of 1 cup ammonia to 1 gallon water or a solution of all-purpose cleaner and water. Scrub screens in two directions, up and down and side to side. Finish by

standing the screens up and rinsing them off with a hose. Put them in the sun to dry or dry with rags.

SCREW, HARD TO REMOVE, Hints on:

- Spray on WD-40 or saturate a cotton ball with vinegar, ammonia, lemon juice, or carbonated cola. Place the saturated cotton ball over the screw head, hold it in place with a little adhesive tape, and let it sit awhile.
- Heat the edge of the screwdriver before you insert it into the screw.

SCREW HOLE TOO LARGE, Hints on:

- Wrap a piece of cotton ball around the screw and dip it into glue, then place the screw back in the hole.
- Place a small piece of nylon fishing line in the hole, then insert the screw all the way to lock it in place.
- Wind a few strands of steel wool around the threads of the screw.
- Break a wooden toothpick in half and insert both pieces in the hole to give the threads something to grip.
- Squeeze wood filler into the hole and insert the screw while the filler is still wet.
- Insert a plastic plug of the correct size into the hole.

SCREWDRIVER HOLDER, Hint on:

- Nestle two plastic berry baskets together and put on the wall of your workshop or garage. The blades of the screwdrivers will slide through the holes in the baskets but the handles will not.

SCREWDRIVER, SUBSTITUTE FOR PHILLIPS:

- Try a metal potato peeler.

SCREWS, Hints on using:

- Make a small hole with a nail first before inserting a screw.
- Stick the screw into a bar of soap, or wax, or apply cooking oil or paraffin to the screw threads to make the screw go in easier.
- Rub chalk on the screwdriver blade to prevent it from slipping.

SHAVING CREAM SUBSTITUTE:

- Use hand cream or hair conditioner for soap or shaving cream. No lathering or rinsing is needed, and the skin stays softer.

SHEETS, To determine yardage:

1 twin-size flat sheet = 5¼ yards
1 full-size flat sheet = 6½ yards

1 queen-size flat sheet = $7\frac{1}{2}$ yards
1 king-size flat sheet = $9\frac{1}{8}$ yards
1 standard-size pillowcase = $1\frac{1}{8}$ yards
1 king-size pillowcase = $1\frac{3}{8}$ yards.

SHOE HEELS SCRAPED AND WRINKLED, To fix:

- Press a warm curling iron gently against the scraped area. The warmth of the iron will remove wrinkles so that you can smooth the leather and glue it back into place.

SHOELACES, WHEN THE METAL TIPS COME OFF, Hint on:

- Harden the tips of the laces with a little colorless nail polish.
- Dip the ends in glue, twist to a point, and allow to dry.
- Wind transparent tape around the ends a few times.

SHOE POLISH, HARDENED, To soften:

- Heat it in its metal container in a bowl of hot water.
- Moisten it with a little turpentine.

SHOE POLISH SUBSTITUTE:

- Apply olive oil to leather shoes of any color, then buff.

SHOE RACK SUBSTITUTE:

- Suspend a piece of board on two shoe boxes, books, or bricks. Put your shoes under and on the board to save space in the closet.

SHOES, ATHLETIC/FABRIC, Hints on:

- Spray with starch or fabric protector before wearing and after washing them, and wash them in a pillowcase in the machine. Stuff the toes with paper towels while drying.
- Bleach white ones ultra-white by adding lemon juice to the final rinse.
- Coat the eyelets with clear nail polish to prevent discoloration of the laces and tongues.
- Clean and deodorize by mixing $1\frac{1}{2}$ cups baking soda and 4 cups water in a container. Scrub the mixture onto the shoes thoroughly. Use an old toothbrush for crevices. Remove and scrub the insoles, if possible. Let stand for a few minutes, then rinse well. Repeat if necessary, then stuff paper towels into the toes and air-dry.
- Clean by spraying with carpet cleaner. Scrub with a toothbrush, let dry, then brush with a dry brush.
- Remove grease by sprinkling the spot with cornstarch or baking soda. Leave the absorbent on the grease for several minutes, then brush it off.

SHOES, BROWN LEATHER, Hint on:

- Rub them well with the inside skin of a banana. Let them dry, then buff with a piece of soft cloth. Polish afterward with brown shoe polish.

SHOES, LEATHER, To preserve:

- Polish before wearing to protect the leather. (See also "Leather, To preserve.")

SHOES, LEATHER, WET, To treat:

- Coat with saddle soap and stuff with paper to hold the shape. Avoid placing near a heat source while drying. When dry, rub the shoes with a little castor oil if you didn't initially coat them with saddle soap. This will soften and recondition the leather. Finish off by giving the shoes a good polish.
- Remove water stains by rubbing with a cloth wrung out in a solution of half water and half white vinegar.

SHOES, LIGHT-COLORED VINYL, SCUFF MARKS ON, To remove:

- Rub the spots with nail polish remover or lighter fluid.
- Scrub the scruff marks vigorously with a prewash spray.
- Use a matching color in acrylic paint, indelible felt marker, or crayon.

SHOES, PATENT LEATHER, To clean:

- Rub a dab of petroleum jelly or castor oil over the shoes and buff.
- Spray on glass cleaner and buff.

SHOES, SMELLY, To remove odor:

- Place crumpled newspaper in the shoes to absorb the moisture.
- Sprinkle with baking powder and remove the powder before wearing the shoes. (See also "Foot Odor, To treat.")

SHOES, TIGHT, To stretch:

- Saturate a cotton ball with rubbing alcohol and rub it inside the shoes at the tight spot. Then put the shoes on and walk around for a while. Or put them on shoe stretchers.
- Put plastic bags in the shoes, then fill the bags with water. Seal the bags, then put the shoes with the bags of water in a large plastic bag and freeze. When the water expands, it will stretch the leather.

SHOES, TOO LARGE, To shrink:

- Soak from inside with a wet sponge, then let the shoes sit outside in the bright sun to dry.

SHOES, WHITE, Hint on:

- Rub wax paper on the shoes after applying polish and letting it dry. This seals the polish and prevents it rubbing off.
- Spray with hair spray after polishing and drying.

SHOPPING, Hints on:

- Obtain at least three estimates on large purchases and services. Compare price, service, and guarantee.
- Keep estimates, receipts, warranties, canceled checks, and instruction booklets.
- Bargain on anything secondhand; on anything damaged; on rentals, services, antiques, art, cameras, cars, real estate; and with one-man operations and merchants catering to tourists.
- Ask in small shops for a discount for paying cash on large-ticket items since no credit-card service charge will be incurred.
- Shop for groceries from a list, have a plan, buy specials when they really are specials, remember the prices of items you purchase regularly or jot them down in a small notebook, read labels, check the price per unit (larger containers do not necessarily represent better buys), and avoid impulse buying.
- Buy generic and house brands if the ingredients listed are identical to name brands. Buy what's in season and, if possible, what's grown locally.
- Make the acquaintance of the butcher and the produce manager and don't hesitate to ask for advice.
- Limit your purchases at members-only warehouses to what you can use comfortably in a reasonable amount of time or share with others, except for paper products, detergent, soap, and nonperishable items you use continuously. Check the unit price or count to determine if bigger is better and if the warehouse prices are indeed lower than those in the supermarket.
- Put a cooler (or insulated food/beverage bag) containing an ice pack in the trunk when you go shopping on a hot day. You won't have to worry about frozen food defrosting if you make other stops.
- Save and use manufacturer's redemption coupons only on items you know you'll use and redeem them at stores that offer double the face value. And check comparable items and house brands to determine if the coupons truly represent a savings.
- Ask for a discount for produce past its prime and offer to buy in bulk at a roadside stand near closing time. The proprietor may be glad to get rid of the whole case or what's left.

- Frequent roadside stands and farmers' markets for fresh produce. If you live in a farming area, ask a farmer if you can pick the produce left behind by the pickers. Many farmers will allow you to do this.
- Stock up on seasonal items. Buy an extra turkey at Thanksgiving and other foodstuffs that traditionally go on sale at Thanksgiving and Christmas. Freeze for future use. Buy Christmas food items and chocolates after Christmas when they are reduced in price, and Easter, Valentine's, and other holidays after the occasion. Buy other holiday nonperishable items after the holidays when they're reduced and save for future holidays.
- Put a plastic laundry basket in the trunk before departing on a shopping spree such as Christmas shopping. It will keep all your small packages together and make them easier to carry to the house.
- Visit furniture showrooms for ideas on furniture and decorating. Buy classic, quality furniture and the best you can afford. Look for workmanship and construction. Hold out for wood rather than pressboard, which not only weighs a ton but contains formaldehyde. Watch the furniture store ads for loss leaders, end-of-season sales, clearance and close-out sales, and investigate the furniture section of department store basements. But avoid being swayed by a so-called bargain that doesn't fit your lifestyle or one you'll find hard to live with. Better to buy a quality piece of furniture at the Salvation Army store and have it refinished than a shoddy piece brand-new. You will spend the same amount of time caring for an inferior item of furniture as you would a quality item. Shop for specifics, hold out for your ideal, and always carry samples of your colors with you.
- Peruse the classified ads. Perhaps someone else is selling what you are seeking. Again, know prices and check for quality.
- Check the phone book for department store outlet warehouses and manufacturer's outlets.
- Be knowledgeable about prices. Do your homework and find the current prices on items you're interested in so you'll know what constitutes a bargain.
- Frequent cut-rate drugstores, discount houses, factory outlets, and grocer's warehouses to save money.
- Buy seconds and irregulars when it doesn't affect the appearance of the item.
- Look for good buys in secondhand stores, resale stores, pawnshops for unredeemed merchandise, flea markets, auctions, estate sales, farm auctions (which also feature furniture and household items), church sales, charity bazaars, and thrift stores, especially those supported by charities that have wealthy members.

- Explore mail-order catalogs for hard-to-find items. Be sure to factor in shipping and handling costs. Catalogs put out by museums and TV PBS stations feature some great gift ideas.
- Check before buying discontinued models to see if you'll be able to get replacement parts.
- Buy items when traveling that are native to the area, what you can't get at home, or what is far less expensive than at home. Shop where the natives shop, not in the tourist shops. Look around department store basements for unusual gadgets and in museum gift shops for prints, which also make good gifts.

SHOPPING FOR SERVICE, Hints on:

- Obtain three estimates; do business with local companies; inquire how long the company has been in business; avoid addresses with PO boxes; ask for references and call people in the middle or on the bottom of the list; find out whether you will get a written warranty of materials and workmanship; and, of course, bargain.

SHOULDER PADS, To recycle:

- Sew them together by hand to make a potholder.
- Use absorbent ones as polishing cloths or shoe shiners.

SILVER, Care of:

- Wash by hand. Dishwashing removes the patina.
- Keep rubber bands away from silverware. They can stain or corrode even when covered with several layers of tissue or cloth.
- Avoid prolonged contact with table salt, eggs, olives, salad dressing, fruit juices, vinegar, sulfur, and alcohol, including perfume and cologne. These items can leave marks on the silver that are hard or impossible to remove.
- Store in flannel bags specially treated to prevent tarnish or in pacific cloth. (Buy pacific cloth at fabric stores for about $15.99 a yard.)
- Keep a piece of chalk, alum, or camphor in the silver chest or where silver is stored. All three absorb moisture and slow down the tarnishing process.
- Put large pieces in plastic bags, and store in a cool dry place.

SILVER, To polish:

- Use long strokes rather than circular ones when polishing silver, and apply the polish with a small soft damp sponge.
- Use the gentlest silver polish and use it infrequently. All silver polishes are abrasive.

- Wash the silver after polishing with warm soapsuds, then rinse in clear warm water. Dry immediately.
- Avoid using rubber gloves when you polish; they create tarnish.
- Clean between the tines of forks by wrapping a cloth dipped in silver polish around a knife. Or stick the fork tines down in the paste for about 5 minutes.
- Use an old soft toothbrush to polish filigree.
- Rub ornamental pieces with a soft clean chamois after polishing. It will give them a truly deep shine. Use genuine animal skin, not a simulated chamois.
- Rub silver vases with olive oil or furniture polish after cleaning. Wipe off any excess oil or polish.

SILVER POLISH, To make:
- Add enough water to baking soda to make a soft paste. Rub it onto the silver with a damp sponge. Rinse with water and dry with a dry cloth.
- Add a little water to nongel toothpaste to make a paste.
- Mix white chalk or whiting with ammonia or rubbing alcohol to make a soft paste.
- Add water to diatomaceous earth to make a paste. Rub the mixture gently onto the silver. (Obtain diatomaceous earth at a garden or pool supply store.)

SILVER POLISH, HARD AND DRY, To renew:
- Add warm water and stir until it's creamy or of the right consistency. Keep a small piece of damp sponge in the container to avoid the polish drying out in the future.

SILVER, STERLING JEWELRY, To clean:
- Soak the jewelry for up to 1 hour in a solution of ½ cup clear ammonia, ½ cup warm water, and 1 tablespoon mild liquid dishwashing detergent. Rinse under warm tap water until clear, then put the jewelry on a clean towel and dry thoroughly.

SILVERFISH, To get rid of:
- Discard old papers and books.
- Scatter cloves around the area.
- Sprinkle the area with Epsom salts.
- Sprinkle boric acid in cracks and susceptible areas. Repeat weekly until the silverfish are gone. (Boric acid is poison. Keep away from children and pets.)

SLANT BOARD SUBSTITUTE:

- Use an ironing board propped up against a bed or couch to reverse the pull of gravity on internal organs and send blood to the upper extremities of the body.

SLEEPING BAG LINERS, To make:

- Sew single sheets up three sides with enough room at one end as an opening to get in and out of.

SLIDING DOOR TRACK, To clean:

- Spray generously with an all-purpose cleaner. Let soak for a few minutes, then wipe out loosened dirt with a paper towel. Or put a piece of terry cloth over a screwdriver blade or piece of wood and run it up and down the track a couple of times. Spray with cleaner again, wipe, and repeat until the track is clean. Run the door back and forth a few times to clean the wheels or glides, then wipe dry.

SMOKE ALARM TRIGGERED BY COOKING, To silence:

- Mist the air underneath the alarm with a spray water bottle.

SNOW AND ICE, To prevent slipping on:

- Put heavy socks over your boots or shoes.
- Wear golf shoes.
- Scatter cat litter or coarse sand on icy walkways. Table salt and deicing chemicals harm grass and plants. Cat litter and sand improve the condition of the soil.

SNOW SHOVEL, To prevent snow from sticking:

- Spray it with nonstick cooking spray or with lubricating oil before you use it.

SOAP, To make last longer:

- Take it out of the box or wrapping paper when you bring it home from the store to let it dry out. If you put a cake in a drawer or linen closet, it will provide fragrance and you'll always have a spare on hand.

SOAP, To use up bits and pieces:

- Stick the old, thin bar on a new bar by wetting them both.
- Put soap slivers in the blender, add some water, and set the blender for grate. Pour the liquid into plastic squeeze bottles or an old pump container.
- Melt the soap over low heat with water to cover, then add a few drops of glycerin and put in a pump bottle or a closed container.

- Shred the soap bits and put them in a microwave-safe bowl. Add water and microwave on high for 5 minutes, or until soap is dissolved. Stir every minute or so. Let cool and pour in a soap dispenser.
- Put the dry odds and ends in a mesh bag made from one that onions, oranges or lemons come in or in part of an old nylon stocking. Use as a scrubber for callused feet or elbows.
- Keep the scraps in a metal tea ball. Swish it around in the water when washing delicates.

SPONGES, SCRUBBERS, AND LOOFAHS, To clean and sterilize:
- Soak in a solution of half white vinegar and half water for 24 hours. Rinse thoroughly a number of times in cold water and dry in the sun if possible.
- Soak overnight in a solution of 4 tablespoons baking soda per 1 quart water, then rinse and dry in the sun if possible.

SPORTS BALLS, VINYL (Baseball, Bowling, Golf, Soccer, Volleyball), To clean:
- Soak them in a solution of 1 cup water and ¼ cup ammonia until clean. Rinse and dry.
- Rub on baking soda with a damp sponge. Rinse and dry.

SPRAY BOTTLE NOT SPRAYING, Hint on:
- Drop marbles or pebbles into the bottle until the level of the liquid rises enough to cover the tube and provide suction.
- Unscrew the sprayer from the bottle. Put it in warm water and pump a few times, then remove from the water and pump until dry.

STAMPS, POSTAGE, To buy without visiting the post office:
- Ask the cashier at your local grocery or convenience store if that store is an EASY STAMP outlet that sells postage stamps at post office prices.
- Order them from the Postal Service, which pays postage both ways. Request a "Stamps by Mail" envelope from your local post office or letter carrier. Return the envelope to the carrier or drop it in a collection box. There is no service charge.
- Call the toll-free number (800-782-6724) 24 hours a day, 7 days a week to place your order. Visa, MasterCard, or Discover credit cards are accepted. No minimum order is required, but there is a service charge based on the total price of the order. You can also fax your order.

STAMPS, POSTAGE, STUCK TOGETHER, To separate:
- Place them between two pieces of brown paper, iron them with a hot iron, and separate while hot.
- Place the stamps in the freezer for about 1 hour.
- Put in the microwave on high for 30 seconds.
- Return them to the post office for replacement.

STAMPS, TO REMOVE FROM ENVELOPE, Hint on:
- Dip the corner of the envelope in boiling water for a few minutes, then remove the stamps. To use the stamps, moisten the back and rub it over the glue side of an envelope.

STARCH SPRAY, To make:
- Add 1 tablespoon cornstarch to 2 cups warm water. Mix well, then store in a spray bottle. Rinse the nozzle after each use to prevent clogging.

STEEL WOOL, To prevent rusting between uses:
- Wrap in aluminum foil.
- Store it in 1 cup water with 3 tablespoons baking soda.

STEREO EQUIPMENT, To clean:
- Remove the dust around the stylus with a new, soft paintbrush and clean it with a small paintbrush dipped in rubbing alcohol.
- Give all the stereo control knobs a full twist and push in all buttons to help keep the contact points clean and avoid maintenance problems later.

STICKY RESIDUE ON APPLIANCE, To remove:
- Use rubbing alcohol or nail polish remover for glass and hard surfaces.

STORAGE SPACE, SHORTAGE OF, Hints on:
- Weed out your possessions on a regular basis. Decide if you're storing things you'll never use again, then throw them out, sell them, or give them away. Before making any purchase, consider if you have room for it and where you will put it.
- Investigate every available space in the house and put it to use—install a rack above the toilet, an overhead cupboard over the bathtub, a hanging shelf that slips over the shower head to hold shampoo and conditioner, open shelves on the wall, a spice rack on the bathroom or linen closet door to hold toiletries, a lightweight wire hanging shelf made to slip over the back of a door to turn it into an extra cupboard with narrow shelves.

- Utilize empty decorative pieces to hold small items. Just remember what holds what.
- Buy furniture that does double duty. A coffee table can be a wicker basket or refurbished trunk. Look for coffee tables that provide storage. Use small chests and cabinets as end tables and coffee tables. Use a storage hassock. Choose a dining room table that can be expanded with leaves rather than a massive one.
- Use a small drop-leaf table attached to wall or closet door for a desk or table.
- Put shoes in a shallow container under the bed, then pull the whole container out when you need a pair of shoes. Or put a board across two bricks or shoe boxes in the closet, and put your shoes under the board as well as on the top.
- Use multiple skirt and pant hangers that accommodate several items on one hanger. Hang a blouse on one hanger, and then hang the next hanger onto the first one, so that one overlaps the other.
- Attach a towel rack to the inside of a closet door to hold several pairs of slacks. Put up pegs and hooks to hold belts, housecoats, etc.
- Roll up bulky items such as sweat clothes and sweaters, and keep them on the closet shelf instead of in drawers.
- Install another shelf in the closet if there is room above the existing shelf. Add a shelf at the bottom or a half shelf. Or put drawer units at the bottom. Or stack see-through boxes.
- Color coordinate your wardrobe and stick to basics.
- Nestle suitcases together or keep purses, etc., in them. Or use the suitcases to store seldom-used items or out-of-season clothing.
- Buy boxes specifically designed to fit under the bed so that you can utilize wasted space. Or purchase a commercial under-bed dresser with drawers that takes the place of a bed frame.
- Put extra bedding, comforter, or quilt between the mattress and box spring. Cover extra pillows with shams and keep them on the bed. They look attractive and can be removed when retiring for the night.
- Investigate under the couch for storage space. Use covered shallow boxes or plastic garbage bags.
- Buy and use multipurpose cleaners or make your own.
- Confine your home library to books you treasure or need as reference. Give the rest away. Borrow books from the library rather than accumulating books that you will never read again.
- Have one staple all-purpose cookbook instead of many. Go through the cookbooks you now have and copy the recipes you indeed use. Put

them in a three-ring binder with page savers or in a photo album. Borrow cookbooks from the library for inspiration and to copy a recipe you'd like to try.

- Put books on the top of the bookcase as well as on the shelves. Use bookends. Stack paperbacks on top of each other, spine out, to save space on the bookcase. You can accommodate more this way.
- Install half shelves or stack rack half shelves in kitchen cabinets to utilize wasted space. Most containers fill only half the area allocated, leaving one-third free space.
- Install under-shelf baskets on any free shelves in the kitchen.
- Cut down on plastic food storage containers. You will rarely use all of them at one time. Buy square or oblong ones, which take up less space, and nestle them together, keeping the lids separate.
- Freeze food in casserole dishes or frozen food containers, then when frozen, lift out and wrap. This will free the containers. Or put foil in the casserole dish first or line a frozen food container with a plastic bag; then you can lift the food right out when it's frozen.
- Store bulky pans and large kitchen items in the dishwasher, microwave, or oven. Remove them when the appliance is in use, then put back afterward.
- Install sturdy plastic hold-alls on the walls or inside door of the utility closet to hold various items such as vacuum cleaner attachments, cleaning products, dusters, etc.
- Provide privacy for children sharing a room by dividing the room using open-shelf bookcases, partitions, suspended fabric, window shades, or beads.

STUFFED TOY ANIMALS, To clean: See "Toys, Stuffed, To clean."

SUEDE, To clean:
- Spray it with Suede Saver or Scotchgard to repel dirt.
- Use a suede brush, then go over it with a cloth that has been dipped in vinegar and wrung out well.

SUITCASES: See "Luggage," various headings.

SUN PROTECTION WHILE DRIVING, Hint on:
- Keep a sleeve cut from an old blouse or shirt in the car to slip over the arm that's exposed to the sun when you drive.

SUPER GLUE, To remove from hands:
- Soak a cotton ball or cloth with nail polish remover and hold it on the area until the glue disappears. Or soak the hand in nail polish remover.

TABLE TENNIS BALLS, DENTED: See "Ping-Pong Balls."

TABLECLOTHS, To store: See "Linens, To store."

TAPE, MASKING OR ELECTRIC, DRIED OUT, To revive:
- Put the tape in the microwave on high for 1 minute.

TAPES/CASSETTES, DAMAGED, To salvage:
- Put the tape or cassette in an airtight container with wet blotting paper for 4 hours. This will make the tape playable long enough to copy it.

TAPESTRY, To clean:
- Rub with warm bran.

TELEPHONE, To clean:
- Clean inside the dial and the crevices with a cotton swab dipped in rubbing alcohol. Then clean the rest of the telephone and the cord with a cloth or paper towel soaked in alcohol. The alcohol will clean the telephone and keep it germ-free.

TELEPHONE NUMBERS, FREQUENTLY USED, Hints on:
- Put them on a gummed label on the inside of the phone receiver or on plain paper covered with a strip of clear plastic tape. Also include emergency numbers and a return address sticker with your phone number. In a crisis it's handy to have on hand for a baby-sitter or visitor, even yourself.

TELEPHONE NUMBERS, OUT OF STATE, To find:
- Call 800-CALL-INFO to get up to two numbers, then have the operator connect you to the number requested at no extra charge. This costs 75 cents per call but does away with having to call your local operator for the area code, then call long-distance information to get the number.

TELEVISION SCREEN, To repel dust:
- Wipe the screen with rubbing alcohol or a fabric softener sheet.

TENNIS BALLS, To rejuvenate:
- Put them in the oven overnight with the door closed and the pilot light on. The slight heat will put the bounce back in the balls.

THERMOMETER, MERCURY DIVIDED, To remedy:
- Touch the glass with a magnet to pull the separated mercury back down into the bulk.

THERMOS BOTTLE, To store:
- Store with the lid off or make sure it's completely dry before putting it away for long-term storage. Put a couple of sugar cubes in to keep it fresh.

THERMOS BOTTLE, STAINED, To clean:
- Rinse the container first with cold water if the bottle has contained anything with milk. Then wash with hot water, dishwashing detergent, and a bottle brush.
- Fill the container partially with crushed eggshells, add hot water, and shake well.
- Fill the container with warm water and 1 tablespoon baking soda, let stand for 3 hours, then wash.
- Soak it with hot water and 2 tablespoons automatic dishwasher detergent for about 30 minutes, then rinse.
- Remove odors by filling the container with a mixture of half water and half baking soda. Cover and let soak overnight.
- Clean the interior of the Thermos occasionally by unscrewing the metal shelving of the case and carefully wiping the interior casing and the Thermos.

TOBACCO SMOKE ODOR: See "Odor, Tobacco Smoke, To get rid of."

TOOLS AND KNIVES, RUSTY: See "Rust on Knives and Tools."

TOXIN-FREE/LOW-TOXIN PRODUCTS: See USEFUL ADDRESSES AND PHONE NUMBERS, "Toxin-Free/Low-Toxin Products."

TOYS, STUFFED, To clean:
- Check the label. If washable, tie the toy in a mesh bag or pillowcase or tie a nylon stocking over the head to protect any parts that might come off. Wash with warm water on the gentle cycle, adding a couple of bath towels for balance. Push the toys down if they float. Dry in dryer except for toys stuffed with kapok or foam rubber.
- Put nonwashable toys in a large plastic bag and add ½ cup baking soda. Close the bag and shake vigorously. Remove the toys from the bag and shake off as much baking soda as possible before brushing with a hairbrush to remove the residue.

- Rub cornstarch into stuffed toys that are not washable. Let them sit for half an hour or more, then brush the cornstarch off.
- Kill dust mites by putting the stuffed toys in a plastic bag and leaving them in the freezer for 24 hours.

TRANSMISSION LEAKS ON GARAGE FLOOR, To remove: See also
"Concrete/Cement, Grease/Oil/Transmission Fluid Stains, To remove."
- Cover with an absorbent such as fuller's earth, cat litter, or cornstarch. Let it sit for a day or so. Sweep up, then scrub with a solution of ½ cup heavy-duty laundry detergent or TSP and one gallon hot water, then rinse.

TRANSPARENT TAPE, To find the end:
- Place the roll in a small container of hot water for a few seconds.
- Prevent the tape from sticking to itself in the future by folding a small portion of the cut end back under. Or put a paper clip, bread tab, soft drink tab, small button, or coin on the edge.

TRASH CAN LINERS, To keep in place:
- Cut off the elastic from men's shorts or old pantyhose to use to hold plastic garbage bags in place. For large garbage containers use slices of an old inner-tube from a ten-speed bike.

UMBRELLA, To carry in the car:
- Insert it into a tube from gift-wrap paper to store it without soiling. The cardboard tube makes it safe to carry in case of an accident.

UMBRELLA, To carry while shopping:
- Take a plastic grocery bag with you so you can put the wet umbrella into the bag and carry the bag over your arm.
- Slip it in a plastic sleeve that the newspaper is delivered in and you have brought along for the purpose.

UMBRELLA, Where to put it when wet:
- Keep it in the shower or bathtub until dry.

UMBRELLA, BLACK, To renovate:
- Dissolve 2 tablespoons sugar in ½ cup hot black tea, then cool. Sponge the open umbrella with the solution, then hang to dry. The sugar stiffens the fabric and the tea revives the color.

UMBRELLA, SILK, To renovate:
- Dissolve 1 tablespoon sugar in 1 cup boiling water. Sponge the open umbrella with the solution, then hang to dry.

UTILITY BILLS AND NATURAL RESOURCES, To save on:

- Call your local utility company to find out if it does energy audits and at what cost.
- Curb unnecessary waste of water and energy to heat water by installing a low-flow shower head, which can cut water flow by up to 50 percent without sacrificing its force. Check to see if you can get a free low-flow shower head from your utility company. Otherwise pick one up at your local home improvement store or mail-order one. (See USEFUL ADDRESSES AND PHONE NUMBERS, "Home Energy.")
- Reduce the amount of water used in the kitchen by installing an aerator in the kitchen faucet. The aerator reduces the flow but aerates the water to cause it to flow with greater force.
- Put an insulating jacket or blanket around the hot water heater. Ask if your utility company can provide one free of charge or sell you one.
- Set the temperature of the hot water heater to 120°F unless you have a dishwasher without a booster heater. The machine needs 140°F to do its job properly.
- Improve the water heater's efficiency by draining off a bucket or two of water twice a year.
- Install a timer on the electric water heater that switches the heater off during the night, then on again in the morning. For absences of longer than a day, switch off the hot water heater at the circuit-breaker box.
- Look into a tankless hot water heater if yours is electric and there are just two adults in the family. It can cut your operating costs by 50 percent over a traditional hot water heater. Call your hot water heater distributor for a Paloma and Aqua Star tankless heater or mail order one. (See USEFUL ADDRESSES AND PHONE NUMBERS, "Home Energy.")
- Control the flow of water needed to flush the toilet by putting a tightly closed plastic bottle filled with water in the toilet tank (clear of the operating mechanism). Or consider a low-flush toilet. Also check the toilet tank for leaks.
- Keep the freezer three-quarters to nearly full. Freeze and add well-washed-out plastic milk bottles three-quarters filled with water to help fill it.
- Rinse all clothes in cold water.
- Replace the most frequently used regular light bulbs with compact screw-in fluorescent bulbs.

- Unplug the television when not in use. A modern color television uses a certain amount of electrical energy even when it's turned off.
- Install a shelf above the radiator with a layer of aluminum foil on the underside. Or buy ready-made reflective shelves. This will direct warm air into the room rather than allowing it to rise to the ceiling.
- Take advantage of hot water in the bathtub and sink to add to the heat of the house. Let it get cold before you let it go down the drain. It also will add humidity.

VACATION, RETURNING FROM, Safety hint:
- Run the hot water faucets for a few minutes after arriving home after an extended absence. Doing so will release any hydrogen gas that may have built up in the water heater.

VACUUM CLEANER, Hints on:
- Attach a heavy-duty extension cord to your vacuum if the cord isn't long enough.
- Unclog the vacuum cleaner hose by pushing a garden hose through it, then drop a coin through to see if it's free.
- Empty the bag into a plastic garbage bag. Hold the mouth of the bag shut as you shake out the dust.
- Use a seam ripper, single-edge razor blade, or scissors to cut across the hairs and threads on the rotating brush.
- Place a scented fabric softener sheet between the inner and outer vacuum bag or into the bag of an upright vacuum clean. The scented sheet can be used for several weeks.
- Put in the vacuum bag some whole cloves, carpet freshener, baking soda, your favorite potpourri, or a cotton ball moistened with your favorite scent, liquid household soap, or lemon juice.

VAPORIZER SUBSTITUTE:
- Use an electric skillet. Fill the skillet with water, set the temperature at low, and place the skillet on the floor near the bed of the person who is ill. Refill the pan with water about every eight hours.

VASE SUBSTITUTES:
- Utilize old sugar bowls or milk jugs or pottery purchased at garage sales. Use a brandy sniffer, an old teapot, mug, glass, or whatever will hold flowers and look attractive.

VASE TOO WIDE FOR FLOWERS, Hints on:
- Put flowers into a narrow jar, such as an olive jar, then put the olive jar into the vase.
- Reduce the size of the opening by placing strips of transparent tape across the top in a crisscross arrangement. Then insert the stems in the openings.
- Put a piece of balled-up chicken wire in the bottom of the vase, and put the stems in the wire openings.
- Wrap the bunch of stems in a piece of bubble wrap.

VASES, STAINED, To clean:
- Use detergent and water and a bottle brush. If the bottle brush alone doesn't do the job, wrap a few folds of nylon net around the bristles and fasten with a rubber band. If the brush doesn't reach the bottom, put a wet tea towel or dishcloth into the vase and move it around with a wooden spoon.
- Pour in some automatic dishwasher detergent, fill the vase with water, and leave it to soak overnight.
- Fill the vase with water and some ammonia. Let it soak until clean.
- Fill it with water and drop in a few denture tablets. Let it soak several hours or overnight.
- Put crushed eggshells or small balls of steel wool, some detergent, and water in the vase. Shake until clean, then rinse.
- Remove a water line from a vase with a vinegar-soaked paper towel.
- Cut a potato into small pieces and place it in the vase along with warm water and a little white vinegar. Shake until clean. Then rinse with clean water.
- Fill a vase with white vinegar and let stand overnight, then add uncooked rice or beans and shake to remove the stains.
- Slice grapefruit rind into the vase and fill it with water. Let it sit for a day or two.

VCR, To clean:
- Use a wet-type cleaning cartridge (it's less abrasive than the dry type) to clean the VCR after 40 to 50 hours of use.

VELVET, To remove wrinkles:
- Hang the garment in the bathroom after closing the window and putting a folded towel at the bottom of the door. Turn the hot water on until the bathroom is thick with steam, and let the velvet steam for 30 minutes, then brush.

VENETIAN BLINDS, See "Blinds, Mini/Venetian, Care of."

VIDEOS, TAPES, CDS, To save money on:
- Borrow them from the library.

VINEGAR, To have handy:
- Keep in a squirt bottle for stain removal and general cleaning.

VINYL AND PLASTIC, To clean: See FURNITURE chapter, "Plastic and Vinyl Furniture, To maintain."

VINYL AND PLASTIC, NEW, To remove the new smell:
- Rub with a paste made of baking soda and water, then rinse well.

VINYL AND PLASTIC RAINCOATS, To remove wrinkles:
- Hang the coat in the sun or in the bathroom when you take a shower. (See "Velvet, To remove wrinkles.")

WADING POOL, SMALL, INFLATABLE, To clean:
- Squeeze all the air out, close up the valves, and wash it in the washing machine. Add 2 bath towels and a little bleach and pull it out before the spin cycle. Hang it on the line and rinse it off with the hose. Let dry.

WALLPAPER, NONWASHABLE, To clean and treat for spots:
- Rub with an art gum eraser, slices of stale bread rolled into balls, wheat bran sewn into cheesecloth or muslin bags, or a cloth dipped in borax.
- Put blotting paper over grease stains and press with a warm iron.
- Remove grease spots and crayon marks by applying a thick paste of cornstarch, baking soda, fuller's earth, or powdered chalk and water. Let the paste dry, then brush or vacuum off. Repeat the procedure a couple of times, if necessary.
- Smooth down a loose seam with the back of a spoon.
- Apply a coat or two of white shellac right around switch plates on the wall to make the area easier to clean.

WALLS/WASHABLE WALLPAPER, Crayon marks, To remove:
- Rub them lightly with baking soda sprinkled on a damp sponge.
- Use undiluted dishwashing detergent. Rinse well to remove.
- Use nongel toothpaste on a damp sponge. Rinse afterward.
- Rub them with silver polish on a damp sponge, then rinse.
- Sponge them lightly with a soft cloth moistened with cleaning or lighter fluid.

WALLS/WASHABLE WALLPAPER, Grease spots, To remove:

- Remove as soon as possible.
- Make a thick paste by mixing baking soda, cornstarch, fuller's earth, talcum powder, or other absorbent powder with water or cleaning fluid. Test an inconspicuous place to make sure the colors won't bleed, then smooth the mixture on the spot. Allow it to dry thoroughly, then brush it off. Two or three applications may be required for a bad spot.
- Mix 2 tablespoons borax and one-half teaspoon ammonia in 1 quart water and use to wash off areas discolored by smoke or grease. Rinse afterward.
- Buy a commercial stain remover (available at wallpaper stores) for old grease spots you can't remove by other methods.

WALLS/WASHABLE WALLPAPER, Mildew, To remove:

- Apply a cloth moistened in rubbing alcohol.

WALLS/WASHABLE WALLPAPER, Pen/pencil marks, To remove:

- Dampen the spot lightly with water, then wash with a mild soap in a circular motion.
- Use baking soda or nongel toothpaste on a damp sponge. Rinse afterward.

WALLS/WASHABLE WALLPAPER, To wash:

- Wash walls with circular overlapping strokes.
- Use a pine-based cleaning solution and water for latex paint.
- Dissolve 2 tablespoons mild dishwashing liquid and ½ cup borax in 1 gallon warm water. Wash with a sponge or cloth wrung out in the solution. Rinse with a solution of ½ cup borax dissolved in clean warm water and applied with a clean sponge or cloth.
- Combine 1 cup ammonia, ½ cup white vinegar, and ¼ cup baking soda or borax with 1 gallon of warm water. Rinse with clear water.
- Use a sponge mop to wash the places you can't reach, then throw a dry towel over the mop to dry the area.

WALLS/WASHABLE WALLPAPER, Transparent tape, To remove:

- Put a cloth over the tape and press a warm (not hot) iron against the cloth to loosen the tape's adhesive backing.

WASTEBASKETS, To keep fresh:

- Put a dry fabric softener sheet in the bottom.

WATER, To remove chlorine taste:

- Fill jugs or pitchers with tap water and leave uncovered or cover with a thin layer of cheesecloth if not refrigerated. Chlorine evaporates after 2 days.
- Stir water briskly or put it in an uncovered blender at a low speed. Aeration makes the chlorine in water evaporate.

WATER, EMERGENCY DRINKING, To purify:

- Add 10 drops chlorine bleach per 1 gallon water.
- Add 10 drops of 2 percent tincture iodine per 1 gallon water.

WATER SHUTOFF VALVE, Care of:

- Turn it off and on again once every 6 months to keep it in working order.

WICKER See FURNITURE chapter, "Wicker Furniture, Care of."

WINDOW FRAMES, To clean:

- Wash out the window grooves with a narrow brush or strip of cloth wrapped around a piece of wood. Or use the crevice tool attachment of the vacuum cleaner to remove dust. Be sure to wash window frames and sills before putting in a clean screen. Use a cotton swab dipped in the wash water to get in the corners.
- Brighten aluminum window frames with cream silver polish.

WINDOW PANE, CRACKED, To remove:

- Lay newspaper on the floor, then crisscross the pane on both sides with masking or duct tape. Wear heavy gloves or oven mitts, heavy shoes, and a pair of goggles, if you have them. Remove the putty and lift out the glass. Or put a cloth over the glass and hit it gently with the hammer. Take the larger pieces out first, then gently pull or knock out the smaller pieces.

WINDOW, PICTURE, SCRATCHES ON, To remove:

- Rub on some nongel toothpaste, then rinse off and polish.
- Apply automobile heavy-duty rubbing compound with a slightly dampened sponge. Work in the direction of the scratches, then wipe with a dry towel and use glass cleaner.

WINDOW SHADES, To renovate:

- Remove worn or stained shades from the rollers and turn them so the top is at the bottom. Hem the top and tack the bottom to the roller.

WINDOW SHADES, FABRIC, See "Blinds, Fabric, To clean:"

WINDOW WASHING CLEANING SOLUTIONS, To make:

- Use 1 or 2 tablespoons ammonia, white vinegar, or borax for each quart warm water.
- Use ¼ cup rubbing alcohol per quart water.
- Use 1 tablespoon borax and 1 tablespoon ammonia to 1 quart water.
- Mix 2 ounces rubbing alcohol, 2 ounces nonsudsing ammonia, and 12 ounces water. Store in a clean 16-ounce spray bottle.
- Use pure white vinegar to remove stubborn hard-water sprinkler spots and to clean really dirty windows.
- Use one-half cup nonsudsing ammonia per 1 quart water for really dirty windows.
- Use cola for grease marks and fingerprints. Saturate a sponge or rag with the soda and wipe clean.

WINDOWS, To wash:

- **Use a chamois:** Wipe the wet chamois over the window, then wring it out thoroughly to wipe the window almost dry.
- **Use crumpled-up newspaper:** Dip it into white vinegar or a cleaning solution and wipe the glass until almost dry, then finish off with a cloth or dry newspaper.
- **Use a pump spray bottle:** Spray cleaning solution on, then wipe dry with a lint-free cloth or paper towel.
- **Use a sponge or rag:** Apply the cleaning solution with the sponge or rag, then dry with a clean cloth or paper towels.
- **Use a squeegee:** Apply clear water or cleaning solution to the window with a squeegee. Or dip a sponge into the cleaning solution and wash windows, then use the squeegee. Wipe the blade of the squeegee with a damp cloth to help it slide easily, and wipe it with the cloth after each stroke. Work from top to bottom by pulling the squeegee across the window at an angle and down the side.
- Use a clean chalkboard eraser after washing to give extra shine.
- Use vertical strokes when washing outside and horizontal strokes when washing inside (or vice versa) so you'll know where the streaks are.

WINDOWSILLS, To keep clean:

- Apply a coat of hard wax. Rub in well, then polish. The dirt will wipe off easily. To remove for repainting, wipe the polish off with turpentine.

WOOD, BLACK MARKS ON, To remove:

- Apply undiluted white vinegar and let sit on the area for five minutes. Wipe dry with a clean cloth.

- Dissolve 1 tablespoon oxalic acid crystals in 1 cup water. Apply the solution to the area while wearing rubber gloves. Let it sit for 2 or 3 minutes, then wipe it up with a damp cloth. (Obtain oxalic acid from a paint store.)

WOOD FINISH, To identify:

- Rub on a drop of turpentine. If bare wood appears, the surface is coated with oil or wax. If the sheen persists, a stain, varnish, or polish has been applied.
- Rub an inconspicuous spot with a cotton-tipped swab dipped in denatured alcohol. If the finish softens and runs, it's shellac. If the alcohol has no effect, it's varnish.

WOOD FLOORS, Care of:

- Clean once a week with a dust mop, soft attachment of the vacuum, or a broom with the leg of old pantyhose over the bristles. Sweep with the grain of the wood.
- Buff once a month with an electric buffer.
- Wax once or twice a year, preferably with a paste wax.

WOOD, OUTDOOR, To protect:

- Paint it. Paint protects wood better than varnish, which allows ultraviolet light to penetrate and attack the wood. Outdoor varnishes need to be renewed every 2 years.

WOOD PANELING/CABINETS, DIRTY, GREASY, To clean:

- Mix together 4 tablespoons white vinegar, 2 tablespoons olive oil, and 1 quart warm water. Rub down the wood with a cloth well wrung out in the solution. Shake the mixture frequently to keep the oil emulsified. Wipe dry, then wax if desired.
- Pour ⅔ cup white vinegar into the blender and add ⅓ cup vegetable oil in a thin stream until emulsified. Apply with a soft cloth and buff to a shine.
- Mix 3 tablespoons linseed oil, 2 tablespoons turpentine, and 1 quart hot water in a container. Rub the solution over the wood surface with a clean cloth. Wipe dry. Repeat if necessary until the finish is clean. Apply polish, if desired.
- Mix ⅛ cup linseed oil, ⅛ cup white vinegar, and ¼ cup lemon juice in a glass jar. Rub into the wood with a soft cloth until clean.

WOOD, VARNISHED, To clean:

- Place used tea leaves in a basin full of water and soak for ½ hour. Stir and use instead of soap and water.

- Use Murphy's Oil Soap.

WOOD WHITISH AFTER CLEANING, To correct:
- Go over varnished wood with a cloth moistened with raw linseed oil. Use a cloth slightly moistened with alcohol for shellac, and go over it quickly and lightly to avoid damaging the finish.

WOODWORK, NATURAL, To clean:
- Moisten a cloth very lightly with a solution of water and a few drops of white vinegar.

WOOLEN BLANKETS, To fluff and freshen:
- Tumble them in a dryer on low- or air-setting for 3 to 4 minutes.

WRAPPING PAPER, Hints on:
- Save used wrapping paper and smooth out the creases and wrinkles with a warm iron. The heat also will remove any tape.
- Use full-page scenic photos from magazines as gift wrap on small parcels.
- Use plain white tissue paper or white wrapping paper for all occasions. A colorful bow or ribbon dresses it up.
- Use the comic section of the newspaper for children's gift wrap.

WRAPPING PAPER, To store:
- Roll it up and put it inside the cylinder it came in.
- Cut the legs off old pantyhose and store the rolls in them.

ZIPPER, STICKING, To remedy:
- Rub the teeth on both sides with soap, paraffin, candle wax, or a lead pencil point. The lead pencil point contains graphite.

AUTOMOBILE, To deodorize:
- Eliminate the odor of smoke, mildew, or pets by applying baking soda liberally on all dry carpets and cloth upholstery and leaving it on overnight. Vacuum it up the next day. Wash all other surfaces with a solution of 4 tablespoons baking soda per 1 quart water. Rinse thoroughly and dry.

AUTOMOBILE, To wash:
- Avoid washing in direct sunlight.
- Use a soft dusting mitt kept for the purpose, a dust mop head, a car washing mitt, a piece of deep-pile carpet, or a very soft, clean rag.
- Use cold or warm water (not hot) and a mild dishwashing detergent. Hose off the car first, then wash one section at a time and hose off. Loosen hardened spots by placing a wet rag on them for a few minutes instead of trying to scrape them off. Dry with a clean rag, paying special attention to where rust can collect.
- Remove tar and stubborn stains by spraying on prewash laundry spray. Or soak spots with linseed oil, then wipe clean with a soft cloth dampened in the oil.
- Wash bugs off the car with a pair of cut-up old pantyhose or spray with a mixture of one-half cup baking soda and 2 cups warm water. Wait 2 minutes, then respray and sponge off the bugs.

AUTOMOBILE AIR FRESHENER, Hints on:
- Keep a little baking soda in the ashtray if you are a smoker.
- Keep some potpourri or whole cloves in the ashtray if you are a non-smoker. (Buy cloves in bulk at the health-food store.)

AUTOMOBILE ANTENNA, Hint on:
- Apply a coat of wax and buff or rub with wax paper. It will slide out easier.

AUTOMOBILE BACKREST, To make:
- Fold up a towel and put it in the small of your back for better support.

AUTOMOBILE BATTERY CABLES, CORRODED, To clean:
- Scrape the corrosion off with a stiff brush.
- Make a thin paste of baking soda and water. Rub it on the cables with a soft toothbrush, then rinse it off. Or wet the cables and sprinkle on the baking soda, then brush and rinse it off.
- Pour a carbonated drink such as club soda over the cables.
- Prevent further corrosion by coating the cables with petroleum jelly after cleaning and after they have dried.

AUTOMOBILE BUMPER, To wash off bugs:
- Spray with a nonstick cooking spray, then wash off.
- Use a pair of cut-up old pantyhose and soapy water.

AUTOMOBILE BUMPER STICKERS, To remove:
- Scrape away very gently with a single-edge razor blade or putty knife.
- Put white vinegar on the sticker and allow to soak in, then scrape it off with a plastic scrubber.
- Spray on a lubricant such as WD-40, leave it for a while, then rub off with a nylon scrubber.
- Heat the sticker with a hair blow dryer, then lift the corner with a knife or old credit card and peel it off. Repeat if necessary. After you've peeled off as much as possible, let the surface cool. Saturate a soft cloth with mineral spirits, alcohol, or rubber cement thinner, then gently rub the glue until it comes off. Keep the rag saturated so it doesn't scratch the bumper. Rinse and polish.

AUTOMOBILE CARPET, To clean:
- Vacuum thoroughly, then use a spray foam carpet cleaner or any product you use to clean your carpets at home. Follow directions.
- Absorb grease stains with equal parts baking soda and salt. Sprinkle it on the stain, brush lightly, and let it sit for a few hours, then sweep or vacuum. Clean the stain with a solution of 3 parts baking soda to 1 part water. Rub the paste into the stain, let dry, then brush or vacuum. (See also CARPETS chapter, "Carpet, To clean" and "Carpet Stain.")

AUTOMOBILE CHROME, To clean:
- Rub with baking soda that has been sprinkled on a damp sponge or cloth, or with a paste made from baking soda and water. Rinse well with warm water and polish.
- Rub on leftover club soda.
- Use a soft cloth moistened with rubbing alcohol.
- Wipe with a cloth saturated with vinegar. Buff dry.

- Polish with automobile chrome cleaner, if necessary.

AUTOMOBILE CHROME, To remove rust:
- Rub with crumpled aluminum foil dipped in cola or water. Rub just the rust; otherwise the foil will scratch the chrome.

AUTOMOBILE DOOR OR TRUNK LOCK FROZEN, To defrost:
- Cup your hands around the lock and blow on the keyhole.
- Heat the key with a match or lighter, then quickly put the key into the lock and turn it gently. Repeat if necessary.
- Keep locks from freezing by squirting graphite lubricant in them. Close and lock several times.

AUTOMOBILE GLOVE COMPARTMENT, Items to keep in:
- Keep a little money (bills and change) for emergencies in a plastic bag or empty film canister, a list of emergency phone numbers, a few plastic sandwich bags to slip over your hands when pumping gas or checking the oil, a couple of individual packs of premoistened towelettes for fast cleanups, a small flashlight, pen and paper, spare pair of glasses, and a reliable tire gauge. (Studies show that gauges built into air pumps at service stations are generally wrong.) Keep maps, car instructional booklet, maintenance log, and receipts from repairs in a self-closing plastic bag(s) under the seat(s). Also keep a rolled-up plastic bag from the grocery store to carry library books and assorted items, and a large black plastic garbage bag to protect yourself in case of rain (make holes for your head and arms to slip through) or to kneel on when making repairs.

AUTOMOBILE OIL FUNNEL SUBSTITUTE:
- Use a clean empty plastic bleach or milk bottle. Cut the body down to make the funnel the size you want and remove the lid.
- Use a magazine, newspaper, or brown paper bag to guide the oil if no funnel is available.

AUTOMOBILE REPAIRS, Hint on:
- Check with local auto repair schools for estimates.

AUTOMOBILE STAINS ON DRIVEWAY, To remove: See HELPFUL HINTS, A TO Z, "Concrete/Cement Grease/Oil/Transmission Fluid Stains, To remove."

AUTOMOBILE STUCK IN SAND, MUD, OR SNOW, To remove:
- Use a hubcap as a shovel.
- Let a little air out of the tires. Place boards, pieces of cardboard, or

the mats from the car in front of the rear wheels to provide traction.
- Always carry sand or cat litter in the trunk in icy weather. Keep the sand in clean, washed-out plastic milk or bleach bottles or in a heavy black plastic garbage bag.

AUTOMOBILE TRUNK, Items to keep in it:
- Keep a flashlight with extra batteries, an extra umbrella, small blanket, small first-aid kit, and emergency/earthquake supplies. Keep these all together in a large clear plastic bag, such as the type blankets are sold in. Wrap a wide, heavy rubber band around the flashlight to use to strap it to your forearm and keep your hands free. Also carry a set of jumper cables, flares or reflective devices, duct tape for temporarily patching a belt or hose, and a flat-tire inflater. Wrap those in the small blanket.

AUTOMOBILE UPHOLSTERY, ANIMAL HAIRS ON, To remove:
- Rub a rubber glove over the upholstery.
- Scrape off with a dampened squeegee or lightly dampened sponge.
- Wrap a length of duct tape, adhesive tape, or masking tape around your hand, sticky side out, and brush over the area. The animal hairs will stick to the tape.

AUTOMOBILE UPHOLSTERY, FABRIC, To clean:
- Use 1 part ammonia to 3 parts water. Using a cloth, clean one area at a time, changing cloths frequently. If treating only a stain, work from the outside toward the center to keep a ring from forming. Blot dry with a cloth or towel or blow dry with a hair dryer.
- Use a spray-on dry-cleaning product made for cars, such as Coral Dri-Clean Upholstery, or a spray-on carpet cleaner.

AUTOMOBILE UPHOLSTERY, LEATHER, To clean:
- Wipe with a damp cloth, then dry the leather thoroughly.
- Wipe with a cloth dampened with stale beer, then dry.
- Treat difficult stains with saddle soap and water. After cleaning, rub the leather with a leather preservative.
- Clean dirty and greasy leather with a mixture of 1½ cups water, ¾ or 1 cup rubbing alcohol and ½ cup white vinegar. Dampen a soft cloth or sponge with the solution and wipe the leather clean.
- Remove stains with equal parts of warm water and white vinegar, then polish with a cloth dipped in linseed oil.
- Restore faded leather by applying 2 parts linseed oil to 1 part white vinegar. Shake the mixture in a jar and wipe on with a soft cloth.

AUTOMOBILE UPHOLSTERY, VELOUR, To restore:

- Moisten a section with the spray from a steam iron. Then, using a stiff hairbrush, brush the upholstery against the direction in which the pile has been crushed. Next move the brush in a circular motion to work the pile back and forth. As the first section dries, repeat the procedure in another section.

AUTOMOBILE UPHOLSTERY, VINYL, To clean:

- Wash with mild soapsuds and water or 1 ounce liquid dishwashing detergent in 2 quarts hot water. Rinse well and wipe dry.
- Wipe with a damp sponge that has been sprinkled with baking soda. Rinse and dry.
- Spray on foaming bathroom cleanser, wipe, then rinse and dry.
- Dissolve ¼ cup washing soda thoroughly in 1 cup boiling water. Let it cool, then saturate a sponge with the mixture and, while wearing rubber gloves, rub it over the upholstery. Rinse with clean water.

AUTOMOBILE WINDOW DECAL/STICKER, To remove:

- Apply hot white vinegar with a soft cloth. Let it soak for a few minutes and gently scrape off, adding more vinegar and scraping until the decal is gone.
- Spray with petroleum-based prewash spray. Let it sit for a short while, then scrub off.
- Cover with a piece of wet plastic cling wrap to keep the sticker moist until it can be lifted off.
- Apply vegetable or baby oil, let it sit for a while, then rub off with a rag or scraper.
- Rub with a wad of cotton soaked in rubbing alcohol.

AUTOMOBILE WINDOWS, To clean:

- Avoid washing the windows in direct sunlight.
- Rub on cola, which gets grease and film off car windows and windshields. Avoid getting it on the paint.
- Wash with a cloth soaked in white vinegar, then polish clean.
- Add ¼ cup ammonia or white vinegar to 1 quart or half a bucket water. Wash the windows using a sponge. Dry with paper towels or a clean lint-free cloth. See also HELPFUL HINTS, A TO Z, "Windows, To wash."
- Wash the car windows at the gas station every time you put gas in your car.

AUTOMOBILE WINDSHIELD, DIRTY FILM ON, To remove:

- Mix 1 cup white vinegar and 3 cups water. Put in a spray bottle or apply with a sponge or cloth. Polish clean with another cloth or paper towels.

- Sprinkle baking soda on a wet rag, wipe on the wet windshield and wash off.
- Fill a spray bottle with equal parts of rubbing alcohol and water. Spray and wipe clean with a soft cloth or paper towels.
- Wipe away stubborn spots with a cloth moistened with undiluted rubbing alcohol or mineral spirits.
- Remove really grimy film by mixing 1 cup nonsudsy ammonia and 3 cups water and proceeding as above.

AUTOMOBILE WINDSHIELD WIPER BLADES, To clean:

- Wash with a solution of ¼ cup ammonia to 1 quart cold water. Apply with a rag or paper towel saturated with the solution, then dry each blade with a fresh paper towel. You also can use this solution to wash the windshield.
- Clean away the dirt and grime with equal parts white vinegar and water.
- Use rubbing alcohol to clean the wipers.

AUTOMOBILE WORK, AFTER, To clean hands:

- Wet your hands and rub with dry baking soda.
- Massage your hands vigorously with vegetable oil or laundry prewash. Wipe dry with paper towels, then wash as usual.
- Add a little sugar to the soapy lather when you wash your hands, rub in well, then rinse.
- Clean your nails with baking soda on a damp nail brush or soak your fingers in lemon juice for 15 minutes.
- Rub salt on to remove any gasoline smell.
- Ease cleanup before beginning the work by rubbing on a light coat of petroleum jelly, undiluted liquid soap, or shaving cream, then rubbing your fingernails over a bar of soap.

Bathrooms

BATH PILLOW SUBSTITUTE:
- Fill a hot water bottle with warm water, and use it to relax your neck when soaking in the bathtub.
- Roll up a bath towel.

BATHROOM AIR, To keep fresh:
- Put a bowl of potpourri on top of the toilet tank for fragrance.
- Keep a bowl of vinegar in the corner of the vanity to absorb odors.

BATHROOM CABINET WITH MILDEW, To remedy:
- Tie several pieces of blackboard chalk together and hang them up to reduce dampness.
- Line shelves with a double layer of blotting paper and renew from time to time.
- Dissolve ¼ cup borax in 2 cups hot water and mix thoroughly. Saturate a sponge with the mixture and wash the mildewed areas. Leave the solution on for a couple of hours or overnight, then rinse well. If the mildew has penetrated the walls, leave the solution on until it is completely dry. Then sweep or vacuum up the powder.
- Use a commercial product such as silica gel or activated alumina, which work well in closets.

BATHROOM FLOOR, To wash:
- Add ½ cup ammonia to 1 gallon warm water to clean tile, linoleum, and ceramic floors (not unsealed wood). No rinsing is needed, and it will not leave a residue. See also HELPFUL HINTS, A TO Z, "Floors," various headings.

BATHTUB APPLIQUÉS, ADHESIVES, DECALS, To remove:
- Pry off with an old credit card or cuticle stick dipped in soapy water.
- Lift the edges and saturate the adhesive with prewash spray, WD-40, or cooking oil, and leave for a couple of hours. Remove remaining adhesive with cooking oil and a coarse cloth or nylon scrubber.
- Use alcohol or nail polish remover to remove the adhesive.
- Clean the tub thoroughly after removing the appliqué and adhesive.

BATHTUB, PORCELAIN, To clean:

- Use a nylon scrubber and a little liquid detergent.
- Sprinkle baking soda, borax, or washing soda on a damp sponge, piece of terry cloth, or long-handled toilet-bowl brush reserved for the bathtub. Scrub, then rinse thoroughly.

BATHTUB, PORCELAIN, COPPER STAINS (GREEN), To remove:

- Use soapy water containing ammonia. If stubborn, use oxalic acid as described for iron rust stains. Dripping faucets cause these stains. (Obtain oxalic acid from a paint store.)

BATHTUB, PORCELAIN, IRON RUST STAINS, To remove:

- Rub with a cut lemon if the stain is light.
- Pour hydrogen peroxide on the stain, then sprinkle with cream of tartar. Leave for 30 minutes before scrubbing. Bad stains may require two or three applications.
- Make a paste of borax and lemon juice, and rub on the rust stains.
- Soak a rag or a few layers of paper towels in vinegar and place them over the stain. Check the stain after 3 or 4 hours. If it's gone, remove the towels and rinse the area with clear water. If the stain remains, rewet the towels with vinegar and leave on overnight.
- Use a dry-cleaning solution if the stain remains.

BATHTUB, PORCELAIN, STAINS/DISCOLORATION, To remove:

- Sprinkle dishwasher detergent and water on the stain and scour. Wear rubber gloves.
- Use a mixture of cream of tartar and hydrogen peroxide. Stir in enough peroxide to make a paste and scrub the tub vigorously, using a small stiff brush.
- Moisten 1 tablespoon salt with a little turpentine and scour the stains with the mixture. Use a soft rag. Wash afterward with warm soapy water.
- Dampen the stain lightly with water, then sprinkle on 2 tablespoons cream of tartar and 2 tablespoons alum. Let sit for a few hours, then rub with a sponge and rinse.
- Sprinkle a few drops of turpentine on a cloth and rub the stains.
- Cover hard-water calcium deposits with vinegar-soaked paper towels. Put the paper towels on the deposits and pour on the vinegar. Let sit for 1 or 2 hours, or overnight if necessary. Remove the towels when the deposits are dissolved. If the deposits remain, sprinkle cream of tartar on the stain and scrub with a dampened plastic scrubber.

BATHTUB PLUG SUBSTITUTE:

- Use a golf ball. It stays in place and rolls back if dislodged.

BATHTUB/SHOWER ENCLOSURE, ACRYLIC OR FIBERGLASS, To clean:

- Wipe down the walls of the shower stall with a small towel or squeegee after each shower. This prevents soap scum from accumulating.
- Clean with 1 tablespoon mild dishwashing liquid and 2 quarts warm water.
- Sprinkle borax on a damp sponge or soft cloth and use it like any powdered cleanser. Rinse thoroughly. Borax will not scratch fiberglass. Do not use washing soda, which does scratch fiberglass.
- Make a thin paste of baking soda and water. Apply with a sponge and rub until clean. Rinse thoroughly.
- Moisten borax with vinegar until the borax is damp. Apply with a sponge and rub until clean. Rinse thoroughly.
- Remove heavy soap scrum with a solution of ¼ cup baking soda, ½ cup white vinegar, 1 cup ammonia, and 1 gallon warm water. Mix the solution well and provide adequate ventilation. Apply with a sponge or sponge mop, wearing rubber gloves, then rinse thoroughly.
- Maintain after cleaning by applying a thin coat of paste wax. Buff to a high shine with a soft cloth. Do not wax where you stand; it will be slippery.
- Restore dull or scratched surfaces by applying a white automobile polishing compound with a soft cotton cloth. Vigorously rub scratches and dull areas. Wipe off residue. Follow with a coat of white automotive paste wax. Do not wax areas where you walk or stand.

CAULKING, SILICONE, To clean:

- Apply rubbing alcohol with a clean soft cloth.

CHROME, To clean:

- Rub with a damp sponge sprinkled with baking soda. Rinse and wipe dry.
- Clean with leftover club soda.
- Moisten a cloth or sponge with vinegar and use it to polish the chrome. No rinsing is necessary.
- Shine quickly with a soft cloth moistened with rubbing alcohol.
- Polish with automobile chrome cleaner, if necessary.

CHROME, To remove rust:

- Remove the spots by rubbing with crumpled aluminum foil dipped in cola. Rub the rust area only, as the foil will scratch the chrome.

DRAINS, To keep free-flowing:

- Pour 1 cup of chlorine bleach down the drains occasionally to keep them sanitary and free-flowing. Let the bleach sit in the drains overnight.
- Unclog a sluggish drain by pouring 1 cup baking soda, 1 cup salt, and ½ cup white vinegar into the drain and letting it sit for 15 minutes. Then pour 2 quarts boiling water in the drain followed by hot tap water for 1 minute.

FAUCET, DRIPPING, To silence:

- Tie a piece of string to the faucet until you can fix it. The water will roll down the string.

FAUCET MINERAL DEPOSITS, To remove:

- Mix ¼ cup white vinegar with ¼ cup water and apply to the areas coated with the calcium deposits. Or soak a cloth in the solution and lay it over the area for 10 minutes, then wash with clear water.
- Dissolve 2 teaspoons salt in ¼ cup white vinegar. Wash the faucets and handles with a sponge or soft cloth. Rinse thoroughly and polish dry with a clean cloth.
- Dissolve 1 teaspoon alum in ¼ cup vinegar or lemon juice. Soak a cloth in the mixture and leave it on the area for a few hours before rinsing. (Obtain alum from a drugstore or the spice section of a supermarket.)

GROUT, STAINED/MILDEWED, To clean:

- Use a grout brush available at hardware stores, a nail brush, or old toothbrush.
- Mix 1 cup baking soda and ⅓ cup warm water to a smooth paste, and then scrub it into the grout. Rinse thoroughly afterward.
- Scrub with wet powdered cleanser. Leave it on for a few moments, then rinse off.
- Clean with full-strength white vinegar. Leave it on for a while, then rinse off.
- Brush with an old toothbrush dipped in chlorine bleach. Make sure the area is well ventilated any time you work with bleach.
- Soak cotton balls with bleach and put them on the discolored or mildewed areas. Let them sit for a few hours before removing.
- Remove mold and hard-water deposits from the tile grout with lemon oil.
- Camouflage stained grout with white shoe polish applied with a cotton swab, or use a white fingernail pencil.

MEDICINE CABINET, To prevent rust rings:

- Avoid rust rings from shaving cream and other metal containers by putting them in Styrofoam or foam rubber soft drink can insulators.
- Stick plastic lids from other containers to the bottom of the metal containers, or place the containers on plastic lids kept in the cabinet.
- Switch the plastic cover from the top of a can to the bottom.
- Line the metal shelf with self-adhesive paper.

MILDEW, To inhibit:

- Dissolve 1 cup table salt in 2 quarts hot water and wipe the tile walls with the solution after cleaning mildew stains. Let dry. Soak the shower curtain or wipe it down with the salt water and let dry without rinsing.
- Spray areas with a fungicide to inhibit mildew.

MINERAL DEPOSITS: See "Faucet Mineral Deposits, To remove," and "Shower Head Mineral Deposits, To remove."

MIRROR, To clean:

- Wet the mirror with a cold wet tea bag, then wipe it with a paper towel.
- Add a little laundry starch to cool water. Rub on with a sponge, allow to dry, then rub with a soft cloth.
- Mix 1 tablespoon ammonia, 1 cup rubbing alcohol, and 2 cups water. Pour into a spray bottle. Spray and polish dry.
- Polish with a cloth dipped in rubbing alcohol. Wipe dry and shine with a cloth, newspaper, or paper towel.
- Rub on white vinegar with a sponge cloth and wipe off with crumpled newspaper.
- Spray with a mixture of 1 tablespoon ammonia to 1 quart water, and wipe with a clean cloth.

MIRROR, FOGGED, To dry in a hurry:

- Blow hot air from a hair dryer on the mirror.

MIRROR, FOGGED, To prevent:

- Spray a thin coat of shaving cream onto a dry mirror, then rub with a lint-free cloth until the cream disappears. The mirror won't fog up when you're taking a shower.
- Put a bit of shampoo on a dry cloth and wipe the mirror with it before taking a shower or bath.
- Smear ½ teaspoon glycerin over a thoroughly wet sponge or cloth, and rub the sponge over the mirror before taking a shower.

- Keep candles lit while you take a bath or shower.
- Cover the mirror completely with liquid soap, then polish dry with another cloth. This lasts for a long time.
- Rub with dry soap and polish briskly with a dry clean cloth until the soap is removed.
- Apply a thin coating of reconstituted lemon juice, then rub dry.
- Put 1 cup strong black tea and 3 tablespoons vinegar in a spray bottle and spray on the mirror, then wipe clean.
- Spray with an antifog product sold for the purpose.

MOUTHWASH, Containers for:
- Put into small individual containers for each member of the family so you don't have to use so many cups. Save the trial size, identify, and refill as necessary from the economy-size bottle.

MOUTHWASH, To make:
- Add ¼ cup apple cider vinegar to 2 cups boiling water, then let cool. Store in a clean, used mouthwash container.

RUST ON FIXTURES AND SINK, To remove:
- Mix lemon juice and salt to make a paste and rub it on the rust area.
- Add enough lemon juice to borax to make a paste, then apply it to the stain.
- Sprinkle on citric acid or Kool-Aid. Leave for 1 hour, then brush. (Obtain citric acid in drug stores, and spice section or canning section of supermarkets.)
- Try a little glycerin or olive oil.
- Use a commercial rust cleaner.
- See "Bathtub, Porcelain, Iron Rust Stains, To remove" and "Chrome, To remove rust."

SHOWER, To save time and water:
- Fix the running water to your liking, then apply a line of colored nail polish across the faucet and connecting fixture.

SHOWER CURTAIN, PLASTIC, To clean:
- Remove water spots and soap film by spraying full-strength white vinegar on both sides of the curtain, or apply vinegar with a sponge. Leave on for at least 30 minutes. Scrub persistent spots with a brush. Vinegar also helps kill mold and mildew.
- Wash in the washing machine with warm water, ¼ cup detergent, and

½ cup baking soda. Put some towels in the machine along with the shower curtain. Add 1 cup white vinegar to the rinse cycle to make the plastic soft and pliable, then hang up and let air-dry. If wrinkles remain, put the curtain in the dryer for a few minutes with a couple of dry towels.

- Wash the curtain in the washing machine with ½ cup borax in warm water.

SHOWER CURTAIN, PLASTIC, To prevent mildew:
- Soak the curtain in the bathtub for an hour or so in warm water and 1 cup of borax. Don't rinse.

SHOWER CURTAIN, PLASTIC, To remove mildew:
- Take the curtain outside and brush off excess mildew, then wash in the washing machine with warm water, ¼ cup detergent, and ½ cup baking soda. Add 1 cup white vinegar to the rinse cycle to make the plastic soft and pliable and to prevent further mildewing. Hang to dry. If mildew still is visible, lay the curtain flat and rub gently with a brush.
- Launder in the washing machine with warm water, ½ cup detergent, and ½ cup liquid chlorine bleach. Let the machine run for a few minutes to mix the bleach and detergent, then put in the curtain along with a couple of bath towels and run through the complete cycle. Put the shower curtain in the dryer with a few bath towels for a few minutes, then rehang immediately.

SHOWER CURTAIN, PLASTIC, To remove new-plastic smell:
- Put the curtain in the sun and turn it every few hours.

SHOWER DOOR, GLASS, To clean:
- Wipe down the lower portion of the shower door after each use to avoid frequent cleaning.
- Apply baby oil on a moist cloth to remove dried soap residue.
- Wipe with a soft cloth or sponge saturated with white vinegar or water softener solution, then shine with a dry cloth.
- Spray with prewash spray, let it sit for a few moments, then wipe with a sponge, nylon net, or plastic scrubber.
- Use a window-washing solution.
- Use a wax floor cleaner, then polish with a dry cloth.
- Rub on lemon oil furniture polish to soften residue. Leave on for a few minutes, then polish with a clean soft cloth. Use nylon mesh or a plastic scrubber if the film is heavy.

- Remove stubborn lime deposits with a single-edge razor blade, taking care not to scratch the glass.
- Give the door a coat of wax or lemon oil after cleaning.

SHOWER DOOR TRACKING, To clean:
- Remove the door by lifting it up, then clean the track with a foam rubber brush sold in paint stores.
- Leave door in place and pour full-strength white vinegar into the track, let it soak for a few minutes, then rinse or wipe out with cotton balls.
- Clean the track with a toothbrush or paint scraper wrapped in a cloth and dipped in a cleaning solution.

SHOWER HEAD MINERAL DEPOSITS, To remove:
- Remove the shower head, take it apart, and soak it in white vinegar for several hours, then brush deposits loose with a toothbrush. Clean the holes with a pin, toothpick, or ice pick. If that doesn't work, boil the shower head in ½ cup white vinegar mixed with 1 quart water for 15 minutes. Do not use vinegar on brass or brass-plated fixtures. Soak plastic shower heads in the hot vinegar and water solution instead of boiling them.
- Unable to remove the shower head? Then wrap a small towel or washcloth soaked in white vinegar around it, and attach a plastic sandwich bag to the shower head tightly with a thick rubber band. Leave on several hours or overnight, then wipe away the softened mineral deposits. If necessary repeat the procedure.

SHOWER MAT, RUBBER OR VINYL, To clean:
- Wash it in the washing machine with a couple of heavy bath towels, then air-dry, preferably in the sun.
- Spray it with bathroom cleaner, let it sit for a few moments, then scrub and rinse with very hot water.
- Soak it in a solution ⅛ cup chlorine bleach to 1 gallon water for a couple of hours to remove grime and stains.
- Keep it aired by sticking it on the tile wall in between showers. The suction cups make it stick.

SHOWER MAT SUBSTITUTE:
- Spread a wet terry hand towel on the shower floor.

SINKS: See "Bathtub, Porcelain."

SOAP DISH, To clean:
- Use an old toothbrush for cleaning out a built-in soap dish.

- Use a nail brush for the plastic free-standing kind. Scrub the container under running water.
- Put a small sponge in the soap dish to make cleanup easier.

TILES, To clean:
- Dissolve ¼ cup baking soda in 1 gallon warm water. Then add ¼ cup white vinegar and 1 cup ammonia, mixing well. Wear rubber gloves and apply with a scrub brush or sponge. Rinse well.
- Use washing soda on a damp sponge. Rinse well.
- Spray generously with laundry prewash spray. Wait a couple of minutes, then rub with a damp sponge. Rinse well.
- Rub with an old washcloth or piece of terry cloth wrung out in rubbing alcohol.
- Polish with lemon oil to keep the shine longer and prevent water stains from accumulating so fast.
- Apply self-polishing wax to the wall tiles to prevent water spots.

TOILET, To clean:
- Sprinkle in ¼ cup borax, then scrub with the toilet bowl brush and leave for at least 30 minutes. Flush to rinse.
- Pour ½ cup borax and ⅛ cup white vinegar into the bowl. Let it sit for a few hours, then scrub with the toilet bowl brush. Flush to rinse.
- Sprinkle ½ cup baking soda into the toilet bowl, then add ½ cup white vinegar and scour with a toilet brush.
- Pour in flat cola, let it sit for 1 hour or more, then scrub and flush. Cola will get a toilet clean.
- Pour ½ cup chlorine bleach into the bowl. Brush the inside of the bowl thoroughly. Let it sit for 10 to 45 minutes to sanitize and disinfect. Flush to rinse. Do not use this method if your water contains iron.
- Pour in 1 cup ammonia, scrub, then flush.
- Use a toothbrush and cleaning solution to clean the hinges and plastic caps near the floor.

TOILET, To conserve water when flushing:
- Raise the water level in the tank with a plastic bottle or jar filled with either water or sand or half filled with pebbles and water. Seal tightly. Experiment with different size bottles so you can save water yet still get a good flush.
- Use a foil-covered brick. Place the brick in the tank so that it is clear of the toilet mechanism.

- See if your flush mechanism allows you to lower the float ball by turning a screw.

TOILET LEAKING, To correct:
- Check if water is spilling over the overflow tube inside the tank when you hear the water leaking. If so, readjust or bend the float downward so the water shuts off at a lower level.
- Check the toilet for silent leaks by putting several drops of food coloring in the toilet tank. If the water in the bowl is colored after 15 minutes, there is a leak. Usually a bad flush-valve ball or corroded flush-valve seat is the reason. Buy a replacement kit.

TOILET LIME DEPOSITS, To remove:
- Pour full-strength white vinegar in the bowl, let it sit for several hours, then brush away. If that doesn't work, pour a bucket of water quickly into the bowl to empty it, then cover the lime marks with paper towels soaked in vinegar. Let stand for several hours, then scrub with a brush or plastic scrubber.
- Pour a pail of water down the toilet to empty it, then apply a paste made of borax and lemon juice to the ring or deposit. Let it sit for about 2 hours, then scrub well.
- Sprinkle ½ cup water softener around the bowl (above the water line) immediately after flushing.
- Remove old stubborn rings with pumice or wet-dry sandpaper. (Obtain pumice or wet-dry sandpaper at a hardware store.)

TOILET OVERFLOWING, To halt:
- Raise the ball float arm and tie it to a wooden spoon. Position the spoon over the top of the tank until you can get a new float arm installed.

TOILET RUST STAINS UNDER RIM, To remove:
- Use extra-fine (000 grade) steel wool or wet-dry sandpaper.
- Unclog the holes in the inside rim with the end of a coat hanger that's been bent for the job.
- Use a commercial rust remover.

TOILET, STAINED, To clean:
- Pour a bucket of water into the bowl so it will empty without refilling, then lightly scrub the stains with powdered cleanser.
- Pour 1 cup borax into the bowl before retiring for the night. In the morning the stains will be gone.

- Pour in flat cola, and let it sit for 1 hour or more.
- Use several denture cleaning tablets. Let them foam, scrub and brush, then flush.
- Pour a bucket of water into the bowl so it will empty without refilling. Wet a pumice stick until it is saturated. Holding one end of the stick, gently rub on the stains. Keep the pumice stick wet at all times to prevent scratching. When the stains are gone, flush the toilet to rinse.
- Pour a bucket of water into the bowl so it will empty without refilling. Squirt in a bowl cleaner and let it sit for 2 to 3 hours, then flush to rinse.

TOOTHBRUSH HOLDER, To clean:
- Run a cleaning cloth up and down in each hole or use cotton swabs with a cleaning solution.
- Sterilize it with full-strength white vinegar or a few drops of chlorine bleach added to ½ cup of water.

TOOTHPASTE SUBSTITUTE:
- Combine baking soda with a few drops of hydrogen peroxide.

TOWEL RACK, LOOSE, To tighten:
- Remove the screws, wrap a piece of a cotton ball around them, and dip them into glue or fingernail polish. Screw the screws back in the holes and wait until the glue is completely dry before using the rack.
- Insert wooden toothpicks or match sticks in the holes to give the threads something to grip.
- Put plastic plugs of the correct size into the screw holes.

WASHCLOTH SUBSTITUTE:
- Put on a jersey cotton glove and use in place of a washcloth when showering.
- Use a household sponge reserved for the purpose.

WINDOWS, To make opaque:
- Brush on a mixture of 4 tablespoons Epsom salts and 1 cup stale beer and allow to dry.
- Apply a commercial pressurized spray that frosts glass windows. It allows full light to enter but ensures privacy.
- Glue on wax paper.

WINDOWS, To prevent steaming: See "Mirror, Fogged, To prevent."

Carpets

CARPET, To clean:
- Sprinkle baking soda, borax, or cornmeal on a dry carpet. Rub or brush it in and leave for 30 minutes to 24 hours, then vacuum thoroughly.

CARPET, BRAIDED, To mend:
- Sew the carpet with fishing line or dental floss.
- Use fabric glue instead of sewing the rug.

CARPET BURN, To mend:
- Cut out the burned section, then cut some strands from another area and glue them in the hole with fabric glue. Place a piece of paper over the mended spot, weigh it down with a book, then allow the glue to dry.

CARPET, MATTED/INDENTED, To restore:
- Brush the carpet back into place with a stiff brush that's been moistened slightly with warm water.
- Hold a steam iron over the area for a few seconds, then brush the nap with a stiff brush or work it up gently with a coin. Repeat a couple of times if necessary.
- Put an ice cube on each indentation and let it sit overnight. In the morning blot up any moisture with paper towels and fluff up the carpet fibers carefully with a stiff brush or comb.

CARPET, PET ACCIDENT ON, To treat:
- Blot the stain quickly with paper towels or facial tissues to absorb all moisture. Then use one of the following:
- Blot with club soda, then cover with a dry white towel and weigh it down with a weight so the towel can absorb the moisture from the rug. If the towel becomes damp, replace it with another one.
- Rub the spot in a circular motion with a terry-cloth towel dipped in white vinegar. When dry, fluff the nap with a soft brush.
- Apply an enzyme product made for the purpose, such as Nature's Miracle (sold in pet stores), and follow directions.

- Avoid using ammonia. It smells like urine.
- Sprinkle baking soda over the carpet to get rid of a lingering smell. Apply it to the dry carpet and leave for at least 24 hours, then vacuum up. The smell should be gone.

CARPET, SMELLY, To freshen:
- Sprinkle baking soda over the carpet with a flour sifter, leave on for 30 minutes or overnight, then vacuum.
- Sponge the area with white vinegar, then rinse with clear water.
- Put a few drops of perfume, oil of peppermint, or other pleasant-smelling liquid on a tissue. Vacuum the tissue into the cleaner before vacuuming the carpet.

CARPET, SOOT ON, To remove:
- Cover with salt, then vacuum or sweep it up carefully. If this is done quickly, no trace of the soot will be left.

CARPET SPILLS, GREASY, To remove:
- Cover immediately with an absorbent such as fuller's earth, cornmeal, cornstarch, baking soda, talcum powder, or baby powder. Lightly brush into the carpeting, leave on overnight, then vacuum up the next day. Use fuller's earth on dark-colored carpets and cornmeal on light-colored ones.
- Dampen a cloth with cleaning fluid and rub toward the center of the stain. (If you rub outward, you'll spread the stain.) Repeat until the grease is removed.
- Mix fuller's earth with boiling water to form a paste. Spread it thickly over the stain and let it sit for 24 hours. Then vacuum up the dried paste or brush it off with a whisk.

CARPET SPILLS, NONGREASY, To remove:
- Blot up as much of the liquid as possible with white paper towels, tissues, napkins, or white absorbent cloths or towels. Don't rub. Rubbing forces the stain deeper into the carpet fibers. Blot and lift. Pour a little club soda over the stain and let it sit for a few seconds, then sponge it up. Repeat until no more seems to be coming up. If any stain remains, treat it later with a spot remover. Club soda is especially effective on food and beverage spills.
- Stir ½ teaspoon mild dishwashing liquid and ½ teaspoon white vinegar into 1 cup warm water. After blotting up as much liquid from the stain as possible, gently sponge the stain with the solution with a

press-and-lift motion. Do not rub. Rinse with a cloth or sponge rinsed in clean water and wrung out well. Repeat if necessary until the spot disappears.

CARPET STAIN, Blood:

- Cover the spot immediately with an absorbent such as fuller's earth or cornstarch mixed with cold water to form a paste. Spread the paste thickly on the stain, let it dry, then brush it off. Repeat until the stain is gone.

CARPET STAIN, Coffee:

- Blot quickly and dilute with plain water.

CARPET STAIN, Glue:

- Use a cloth dipped in white vinegar.

CARPET STAIN, Lipstick:

- Rub the spot with glycerin first, then with undiluted lighter or cleaning fluid.

CARPET STAIN, Shoe polish:

- Rub with a rag dampened in rubbing alcohol or turpentine.

CARPET STAIN, To remove:

- Pour a little club soda onto the stain, allow it to sit for a few seconds, then sponge up.
- Combine ¼ cup white vinegar and ¼ cup water, and apply it to the stain with a sponge. Rinse well with water.
- Spray on foamy shaving cream, allow it to sit for few seconds, then rinse using a damp sponge.
- Rub cornstarch into lightly soiled spots before vacuuming. It will clean the carpet while freshening it.
- Use an enzyme product sold in pet stores for pet accidents. It also works well on other stains.

CARPET STATIC ELECTRICITY, To eliminate:

- Mix ½ cup liquid fabric softener with 1 quart water in a spray bottle. Spray on to the area where you want to eliminate static electricity, then let dry. The area will remain static free for several months.

CARPET, TAR ON, To remove:

- Scrape off as much as possible with a dull knife, then sponge with a cloth soaked with cleaning fluid. Use a light upward brushing motion so that the stain will be rubbed out of the rug rather than into it. Change the cloth when it becomes soiled and continue brushing until the stain is gone.

CARPET TEAR, To mend:

- Place a strip of carpet tape beneath the tear and press down.

Food and Cooking

APPLES, To prevent browning after peeling:
- Place the apples as you pare them into a pan of cold water containing a few drops of lemon juice.
- Add the apples last when making fruit salad.

APPLES, To ripen:
- Place one mellow-ripe apple in a basket of barely ripe ones to speed up the ripening.

APPLES, To store:
- Place them in plastic bags in the refrigerator and mist them once a week with cool water. When stored this way, apples will keep from 4 to 6 weeks.

ASPARAGUS, LIMP, To crisp:
- Cut ¼ inch off the bottom of the stalks, then stand them upright in a couple of inches of ice water. Cover with a plastic bag and refrigerate for 2 hours.

AVOCADOS, To ripen:
- Put them into a brown paper bag with a tomato, then put the bag in the warmest part of the house. Or cover the bag with a towel.
- Put the avocado in a plastic bag with a banana peel and put in a warm place.

BACON, To avoid drying out while storing:
- Wrap in foil or put the package in a plastic bag.
- Flash freeze cooked bacon on a cookie sheet, then store in a heavy-duty freezer bag.

BACON, To avoid shrinking and curling:
- Start in a cold pan and periodically prick the strips with a fork while cooking.
- Dip the strips in milk and roll in flour before cooking.
- Rinse the strips in cold water before cooking.
- Sprinkle the strips with flour before cooking.

- Bake on a rack with a drip pan underneath in a preheated 325°F oven until crisp. Or bake them on a jelly-roll pan in a preheated 400°F oven for 10 to 15 minutes.

BACON STRIPS, To separate:

- Store the package rolled and secured with a rubber band.
- Remove the bacon from the refrigerator at least 30 minutes before cooking.
- Microwave the bacon on high for 30 seconds.

BAGELS, STALE, Hints on:

- Wet them and put them in a paper bag. Put the bag in the microwave for 30 to 60 seconds to steam them. Then, either toast the bagels or make bagel chips by cutting them into ⅛-inch slices and drying them in a 275°F oven. Or brush the slices lightly with olive oil, sprinkle with garlic or seasoning salt, herbs, or sesame seeds, and toast for 5 minutes on each side (or until brown) in a 350°F oven.

BAKING, To organize:

- Place all the ingredients on the counter on one side of the mixing bowl, then after using an ingredient put it on the other side of the bowl. This way you will know what you added and what you have not if you are interrupted.
- Measure dry ingredients first, then use the same spoons or cups for liquids. This will cut down on the cleanup.
- Fill the sink with hot sudsy water before starting, then slip each utensil into the water when finished. Soaking makes cleanup easier.

BAKING PANS, To substitute:

Recommended	Alternate
1 (11 × 7 × 2½-inch) rectangle	1 (9 × ½-inch) round layer
	1 (8 × 2-inch) round layer
	1 (8 × 8 × 1½-inch) square pan
	1 (7½ × 3-inch) Bundt pan
	1 (8½ × 4½ × 2½-inch) loaf pan
2 (8 × 1½-inch) round layers	1 (9 × 5 × 3-inch) loaf pan
	1 (9 × 2-inch) deep-dish pie pan
	1 (9 × 2-inch) round layer
	1 (8 × 8 × 2-inch) square pan
	1 (9 × 9 × 1½-inch) round layer
	1½ to 2 dozen cupcakes

2 (9 × 1½-inch) round layers	1 (13 × 9 × 2-inch) rectangle
	1 (15½ × 10½-inch) jelly-roll pan
	1 (9-inch) tube pan
	2 (8 × 8 × 2-inch) square pans
	2½ dozen cupcakes
1 (13 × 9 × 2-inch) rectangle	1 (10-inch) tube pan
	2 (8 × 8 × 2-inch) square pans
	2 (9 × 1½-inch) round layers
	2 (1½ × 10½-inch) jelly-roll pans
	2 (9 × 5 × 3-inch) loaf pans
	2½ dozen cupcakes
1 (9 × 5 × 3-inch) loaf pan	1 (9 × 9 × 1½-inch) square pan
	1 (9 × 2-inch) round layer
	1 (8 × 8 × 2-inch) square pan
	1 (9 × 3-inch) Bundt pan
	1 (8 × 3-inch) tube pan
	1 to 1½ dozen cupcakes
1 (10 × 3½-inch) Bundt	1 (9 × 3-inch) tube pan
	1 (10 × 2½-inch) springform pan
	2 (9 × 5 × 3-inch) loaf pans
	2 (7½ × 3-inch) Bundt pans
1 (10 × 4-inch) tube	2 (9 × 5 × 3-inch) loaf pans
	2 (9 × 2-inch) round layers
	2 (8 × 8 × 2-inch) square pans
	2 (9 × 9 × 1½-inch) square pans

BAKING POWDER, To determine if fresh:

- Check the powder. Soft lumps indicate slight deterioration; a hard caked condition indicates advanced deterioration. Baking powder keeps for about 2 years under ideal conditions.
- Pour ¼ cup hot tap water over ½ teaspoon baking powder. If the mixture doesn't bubble up almost at once, it's too old to use.

BAKING SODA, To determine if fresh:

- Add 1 teaspoon white vinegar or lemon juice to a pinch of baking soda. If it bubbles, the soda is still effective.

BANANAS, To avoid turning brown when used in fruit salad:

- Rinse them them in cold tap water or coat them with lemon juice.

BANANAS, To ripen:

- Put them in a brown paper bag or a large plastic bag with either an apple or pear.

BANANAS, *To store:*

- Put them unpeeled in a tightly closed jar, then refrigerate. To use only a portion of the banana, cut off the amount needed and put the unused, unpeeled portion back in the jar. It will keep for several days without turning brown.
- Peel and stand them upright in a tightly capped jar in the refrigerator. They will stay fresh for a week or so.
- Keep ripe bananas in the refrigerator. The skins will darken, but the fruit will be good for about 2 weeks.
- Keep them in a closed plastic bag. They will keep at least 2 weeks at room temperature. Once the bag is opened and left open, the bananas ripen faster.

BARBECUE RIBS OR CHICKEN PIECES, *To tenderize:*

- Simmer for 45 minutes before barbecuing. Drain them and marinate in barbecue sauce for 15 minutes to overnight, then barbecue.

BASTING, *To make easier:*

- Use a paintbrush instead of a pastry brush.

BEANS, GREEN, *To cook:*

- Drop the prepared beans into a large pan of slightly salted, rapidly boiling water. When the water returns to the boil, cook for 2 to 3 minutes for small or cut beans and 5 minutes for whole beans. Drain and season. If using them for salad, run cold water over the beans to stop further cooking. When prepared this way, the beans retain their bright green color.

BEANS, PEAS, ETC., DRIED, *To fast-cook:*

- Add to fast-boiling water or stock if making soup. The peas or beans will become pulpy in 20 to 30 minutes.

BEETS, *To store:*

- Cut tops off about 2 ½ inches from the beets. Once root vegetables are out of the soil, food material in the roots starts flowing back into the leaves.

BERRIES, *To freeze:*

- Arrange in a single layer on a jelly-roll pan and freeze. When frozen, pack into a plastic freezer bag.

BISCUITS/SCONES, STALE, *To freshen:*

- Sprinkle or spray the biscuits lightly with cold water, then place

in a brown paper bag or wrap in foil. Heat in a 375°F to 400°F oven for about 5 minutes, or until hot. They will taste freshly baked.
- Dip in milk and put in a 450°F oven for a few minutes.
- Wet the biscuits with milk or water, then put them in a paper towel and microwave on high for 5 to 10 seconds.

BISCUITS/SCONES, Hints on:
- Use hot milk instead of cold to make them lighter and have them rise better.
- Melt the butter or shortening in the milk or water instead of cutting it into the dough. The biscuits or scones will be fluffier.
- Substitute 1 teaspoon each baking soda and ascorbic acid powder (vitamin C) for the baking powder. The biscuits will have a yeasty taste.

BRAISE, Explanation of:
- Brown the food in fat over moderate heat.

BREAD, To keep fresh:
- Keep a large washed and dried potato in the bottom of the bread box.
- Freeze the bread. Cut the loaf in half or quarters, then bring out part at a time.
- Keep bread at room temperature to keep it fresh longer, rather than in the refrigerator.
- Freeze sliced rye bread but not sliced white bread. The individual slices of white bread will get soggy when thawed. Frozen day-old bread will be as good as fresh bread when thawed.

BREAD, To slice paper thin:
- Freeze the unsliced loaf until it is firm but not solid, then slice.

BREAD CRUMBS, To make:
- Put pieces of stale bread in the blender. If you don't have stale bread, put fresh bread slices in the oven to dry out, then blend.
- Put the bread in a paper bag before rolling with a rolling pin so the crumbs will not scatter. Or grate frozen bread.
- Substitute prepared stuffing crumbs or crushed packaged croutons for any dish calling for bread crumbs.

BREAD CRUMBS, BUTTERED, To make:
- Melt 2 to 3 tablespoons butter in a skillet. Add ½ cup dry bread crumbs and stir over moderate heat until crumbs are all coated and slightly toasted.

BREAD, ITALIAN OR FRENCH, To freshen:

- Sprinkle it with water and put in a 300°F oven uncovered for about 6 to 8 minutes, until hot and crispy.
- Wet it and wrap in a paper towel. Microwave on high for 5 to 10 seconds.
- Wrap it in a damp cloth and keep it in the refrigerator for 24 hours. Cut off what you want for one meal and warm in the oven.

BREAD, YEAST, Hints on making:

- Warm all ingredients, including flour and mixing bowl, in a warm oven if the kitchen is cold. The dough will rise higher.
- Wear disposable plastic gloves while kneading the dough or knead it inside a large plastic bag. The dough will not stick to the plastic and cleanup is easy.
- Add some unbleached flour or gluten flour when making whole wheat bread. It will make the dough easier to knead and develops the gluten.
- Try using potato water for added moisture, volume, and texture. It also acts as a natural preservative. (Save the unsalted water in which you've boiled potatoes.)
- Apply a thin coating of vegetable oil to the mixer dough hook or food processor blade or squirt with nonstick vegetable spray. This will prevent the dough from climbing up the hook or blade during kneading.
- Rise the bread dough at 70° to 75°F. A slower rising makes for a better product.
- Determine if the dough is risen sufficiently by sticking your finger into it up to the first knuckle. If the mark remains, the dough has done all the rising it's going to do.
- Prevent the crust from cracking by making 4 or 5 shallow, diagonal slashes across the top of the loaf before putting it in the oven.
- Obtain a shiny crust by brushing before baking with either beaten whole egg or egg white beaten with a little water.
- Guarantee a soft tender crust by brushing with butter, margarine, or milk before baking. Or brush with oil after baking.
- Get a tough chewy crust by brushing or spraying the bread with water before baking and again 15 minutes before removing the bread from the oven.
- Remove the bread from the pan 5 to 10 minutes before it's done and place it on the oven rack if you want the sides and bottom crust to be brown. Or bake in an anodized aluminum or darkened metal pan.

- Place a pan of hot water on the shelf below the bread during baking for a really crispy crust. Or bake the bread on an unglazed terra-cotta tile for a crispy bottom crust. (Buy the tile in a tile store or masonry supply outlet.)
- Cut the bread with a long, thin sharp blade with a serrated edge to avoid crumbs.

BREAD, YEAST, Hints on rising:
- Fill the rising bowl with boiling water and let it stand while you knead the dough. Then pour the water out of the bowl, dry it, and put the dough into the warm bowl to rise.
- Put the container of dough on a heating pad set to medium with a towel placed between the bowl and the pad.
- Position the bowl on a rack over a pan of warm water.
- Put the dough in an unheated oven with a pan of hot water on the oven floor. Or put it in a gas oven that has a pilot light and keep the door ajar. Or turn an electric oven on for 1 minute, no longer. Turn it off, then place the bowl of dough in the oven to rise.
- Bring 2 cups of water to a boil in the microwave. Turn off the microwave, remove the water, put the bowl of dough inside, and close the door.
- Run the clothes dryer for 1 minute, turn it off, and put the bowl of dough inside to rise.

BREADING FOOD, Hints on:
- Use stale crushed crackers, crushed croutons, or crushed potato chips in place of bread crumbs.
- Cover and refrigerate breaded food for 20 to 30 minutes before cooking to set the coating.

BROILING, Hint on:
- Place a slice of dry bread in the broiler pan to soak up the dripping fat. This will prevent splatters and keep the fat from catching fire.

BROTH, CANNED, To improve the flavor of:
- Simmer uncovered for 15 to 20 minutes with some chopped onion, carrot, celery, and a little wine.

BROWN SUGAR, To prevent drying out:
- Keep it in an airtight container with a piece of fresh bread.
- Store tightly closed in its original box in the refrigerator and it will not get hard.

BROWN SUGAR, To soften when dried out:

- Put in a tightly closed jar with a piece of apple, lemon, orange, or fresh bread. It should soften in a day or two.
- Grate it or put a small amount at a time through the blender or food processor until it is soft and fine.
- Sprinkle it with water and place in a covered shallow pan (or wrap in aluminum foil) and heat in a 250°F oven for about 5 minutes or until soft. Then loosen it with a fork or put in the blender for a second or two.
- Microwave in a covered dish on high heat for 30 to 60 seconds per cup.

BROWN SUGAR SUBSTITUTE:

- Mix together 1 cup granulated sugar with 2 or 4 tablespoons dark molasses, depending if the sugar is light or dark brown. Mix with a fork to distribute the molasses thoroughly. It won't have the same consistency but will serve in a pinch.

BRUSHING WITH SHORTENING, To make more appetizing:

- Add a few drops of yellow food coloring to the shortening.

BUTTER, Hints on:

- Keep it firm without refrigeration by wrapping it in a cloth dipped in cold salted water, then wrung out.
- Keep it ready for spreading by storing it at room temperature in a small crock that once held cheese spread.
- Soften butter that is too hard by cutting it into a couple of pieces and microwaving it on the defrost cycle for a second or two. (Be careful it doesn't melt.) Or grate the butter and let it sit for a couple of minutes at room temperature.
- Make your own soft spread by blending equal parts of softened butter and mild-flavored vegetable oil (such as safflower) in the blender until combined, then pour into containers and refrigerate.

BUTTERMILK SUBSTITUTE:

- Add 1 tablespoon lemon juice or 2 tablespoons white vinegar to 1 cup milk. Let it stand for 10 minutes.
- Mix ½ cup plain nonfat yogurt with ½ cup skim milk.
- Substitute buttermilk for regular milk in most baking recipes by adding ½ teaspoon baking soda for each cup of buttermilk.

CABBAGE, Hints on:

- Add a slice of lemon or a little white vinegar to the cooking water. It will cut down on the cooking odor and help the cabbage retain its natural color. A slice of bread added also will cut down on the cooking odor.

- Freeze cabbage leaves overnight when making stuffed cabbage. The leaves will be as limp and easy to roll as if they were cooked.

CAJUN SPICE SUBSTITUTE:
- Combine 1 teaspoon black pepper, 1 teaspoon paprika, ¼ teaspoon ground allspice, and ½ teaspoon garlic salt.

CAKE, To beat egg yolks and sugar:
- Set the bowl in a pan of hot water for the first 4 to 5 minutes of beating or until the mixture is warm to the touch, then remove from the water and continue beating for another 8 to 10 minutes until thick and light.

CAKE, To cool:
- Put the cake rack on top of a colander to speed the cooling process.

CAKE, To cream the butter and sugar:
- Heat electric mixer beaters in boiling water before use to keep shortening or butter from sticking to them.
- Bring the butter to room temperature. Or cut the butter in a few pieces and microwave on the defrost cycle for a few seconds. Watch it carefully so it doesn't melt. Or shred the butter with a potato peeler.
- Add 2 tablespoons boiling water or 2 to 3 tablespoons of milk a teaspoon at a time while you are creaming the butter and sugar. Keep creaming the mixture while adding the liquid.
- Use superfine sugar instead of granulated. (See "Sugar, Superfine, Substitute.")

CAKE, To cut:
- Use unflavored dental floss or silk thread to avoid squashing the cake or frosting.
- Soak the knife blade in very hot water for a few minutes.

CAKE, To fold in the egg whites:
- Stir in a quarter of the egg whites before folding in the balance. Doing so will make incorporating the egg whites easier and thus avoid losing too much air.

CAKE, To freeze individual servings:
- Cut the cake into serving pieces and place in the freezer unwrapped. When frozen, wrap each section individually in heavy-duty aluminum

foil. Prior to serving, unwrap while frozen so the icing doesn't stick to the foil, then defrost.

CAKE, To lighten:
- Substitute buttermilk for regular milk. Add ¼ teaspoon baking soda for each ½ cup buttermilk. Buttermilk makes for a very light cake.
- Separate the eggs. Add the yolks to the butter-and-sugar mixture and fold the beaten egg whites into the batter after adding the other ingredients. If the batter is heavy, stir in about a quarter of the egg whites to moisten it, then fold in the rest.

CAKE, To prevent dried fruit from sinking to the bottom:
- Toss the fruit in a little of the flour called for in the recipe before adding it to the batter, or mix it with the dry ingredients before adding them to the rest of the batter.

CAKE, To prevent nuts from sinking or browning:
- Heat them in the oven and then dust them with flour before adding to the batter. This will stop them from sinking to the bottom. Brush nuts with milk if they are to be placed on top of a cake while baking. This will stop them from browning.

CAKE, To remove from a tube pan:
- Use a small knitting needle or poultry skewer instead of a knife to slip around the ring of the center tube without tearing the edge of the cake.

CAKE, To test for doneness:
- Use a toothpick, poultry skewer, or piece of uncooked spaghetti.

CAKE, LAYER, To keep fresh longer when cut:
- Cut the cake in half and take a large diagonal slice from the middle, then press the two halves together. The cake will stay moist. Or put a piece of plastic wrap on the cut edge. Or place a slice of fresh bread against the cut edge. Keep the bread in place with toothpicks.

CAKE LAYERS, To cut:
- Make a shallow vertical notch in the side before splitting the cake, then, after filling, realign the sides using the notches as a guide.
- Cut the layers with a long thin serrated knife such as a ham knife.
- Wrap a long piece of thread or unflavored dental floss around the area to be cut, cross the ends, then slowly but firmly pull on each end.

CAKE MIXES, Hints on:
- Crack the eggs in the measuring cup first and then pour them into the mixing bowl. The eggs coat the cup so that when you measure the oil, it will slide out easily.
- Put the water in the bowl before putting in the cake mix. You won't have unincorporated dry mix on the bottom of the bowl.
- Put the mixing bowl in the sink on a damp cloth to prevent it from moving around while you use the beaters.
- Dust the pan of a chocolate cake with cocoa instead of flour.

CAKE, PLAIN, To keep fresh longer:
- Put half an apple in the cake container.

CAKE, SPONGE, To make light:
- Put 1 tablespoon lukewarm water in the cake mixture directly after pouring in the eggs. This gives a light and spongy cake.

CAKE, SPONGE, WITH JAM FILLING, To avoid getting soggy:
- Prevent the jam from soaking in by lightly buttering the cake before spreading the jam.

CAKE, STALE, To use up for a trifle or tipsy pudding:
- Cut plain stale cake, preferably sponge or pound, into slices or pieces. Sandwich together with jam, and sprinkle with sherry or orange juice. Cover with boiled custard and let sit in the refrigerator for a couple of hours, then top with whipped cream.

CAKE STUCK IN THE PAN, To remove:
- Place the hot pan on a wet towel.
- Prevent cake from sticking by lining the bottom of the cake pan with wax paper.

CANDY, To prevent from becoming sugary:
- Add 1 teaspoon white vinegar to the ingredients before cooking.

CANDY, To prevent from boiling over:
- Coat the edge of the pan with butter.

CANNED FOOD SIZE NUMBERS:

No. 1 can	10 to 12 ounces
No. 300 can	14 to 16 ounces
No. 1½ can	1 pound 17 ounces
No. 303 can	1 pound 17 ounces (same as No. 1½ can)
No. 2 can	1 pound 12 ounces to 1 pound 14 ounces

| *No. 3 can* | 3 pounds 3 ounces or 1 quart 14 ounces |
| *No. 10 can* | 6 pounds 2 ounces or 7 pounds 5 ounces. |

CANS, To open:
- Rinse the can first before opening, and open from the bottom of the can to make the contents easier to remove.

CARROTS, Hints on:
- Cut the tops off close to the carrot. Once root vegetables are out of the soil, food material in the roots starts flowing back into the leaves.
- Avoid storing apples in the same crisper as carrots. Apples give off ethylene gas and make the carrots taste bitter.
- Skin carrots by dropping them into boiling water for 3 to 4 minutes and then plunging them into ice water. The skins will slip right off when cool.
- Revive limp carrots by soaking them in ice water for 30 minutes in the refrigerator.

CARROTS, COOKING, Hints on:
- Add a dash of sugar when cooking. Or add 1 teaspoon lemon juice for every 1 cup carrots. The sugar will enhance the flavor and the lemon juice will keep the color.
- Leave carrots unpeeled if boiling them whole. The skins will slip off easily when cooked.
- Grate the carrots and sauté with a little butter or oil, then add a small amount of water, cover, and steam for about 5 minutes, or until tender. This will give you carrots in a hurry with less loss of nutrients.

CASSEROLES, Hints on:
- Grate a cold stick of butter on the surface of an au gratin dish rather than dotting it with butter. The results will be more uniform.
- Line the casserole dish to be frozen with foil before cooking, then when frozen solid, remove the casserole from the dish, wrap, label, and refreeze. Or freeze the casserole without the foil, then, when frozen, unmold and wrap in freezer wrap. When ready to serve, unwrap, place the frozen casserole in the original dish, and warm in the oven or microwave. Add crumb or cheese toppings just before you warm the casserole.

CAULIFLOWER, To cook:
- Snap off the florets and peel the stems. Make a 1-inch slit through the stems of any large pieces. Doing so will make the cauliflower cook faster and thus retain more of the nutrients.

- Add 1 teaspoon of white vinegar or lemon juice, or a little milk, or ½ teaspoon cream of tartar to the cooking water to keep the cauliflower white.

CELERY, WILTED, To restore:
- Pour cold or ice water over the celery stalks to cover, then put them in the refrigerator for 1 hour to crisp them up again.

CEREAL, DRY, Hints on:
- Pour it into a gallon-size zip-closing bag if the cereal isn't in a resealable bag.
- Crisp and freshen it by pouring it on a cookie sheet and heating it in a 275°F oven for 8 to 10 minutes. Let cool, then package.

CEREALS, WHOLE GRAIN, Hints on:
- Refrigerate whole-grain cereals because of their fat content.
- Have breakfast ready the next morning by putting ¾ cup cereal into a preheated pint-size Thermos and filling it up with boiling water. Seal and let stand overnight.

CHEESE, To cook:
- Cook at a low temperature or for a very short time at a high temperature. Cheese cooked too long or at too high a temperature becomes rubbery and stringy.
- Prevent cheese from separating while cooking by dusting it with cornstarch before adding it to the sauce. This will help thicken the sauce and absorb the melting fat.
- Rescue a sauce that has separated or turned stringy by whisking in drops of lemon juice or dry white wine while it is simmering.

CHEESE, To cut:
- Use unflavored, unwaxed dental floss or a heated knife.

CHEESE, To freeze:
- Freeze in small amounts of 1 pound or less and not more than 1 inch thick. Cheddar, Camembert, Edam, Gouda, mozzarella, Muenster, provolone, and Swiss are cheeses that can be frozen.
- Grate mozzarella, provolone, or cheddar and spread it on baking pans to fast-freeze, then put in self-sealing bags and use as needed.

CHEESE, To grate:
- Place cheddar cheese in the freezer for 10 to 15 minutes to make it easier to grate.
- Check out the salad bar for grated cheddar cheese. Sometimes it's cheaper than buying and grating it yourself.

CHEESE, To keep from drying out:
- Wrap it in a cloth dampened in white vinegar, then put into an airtight container. Or wrap the cheese in plastic wrap to keep the air out.
- Rub butter or margarine over the cut portion.

CHEESE, To prevent and remove mold:
- Prevent mold by keeping the cheese in an airtight container with 2 lumps of sugar. The sugar will absorb any moisture.
- Use a potato peeler to remove the mold. Dip it in white vinegar and slice the mold off. Or dip a knife in white vinegar and after each slice of the knife, dip it in white vinegar again. The white vinegar kills the mold and keeps it from returning.

CHEESE, To serve:
- Take ripened cheese out of the refrigerator 2 hours before serving to bring it to room temperature and bring out the full flavor.

CHICKEN, To tenderize:
- Use salt sparingly; it draws out the juices. Season or marinate chicken the day before cooking so the flavors will permeate the bird completely.
- Marinate chicken breasts in buttermilk, cream, or plain milk for 3 hours in the refrigerator before baking.
- Use 1 teaspoon cornstarch in the marinade for stir-fry. It keeps the chicken moist.

CHICKEN BREASTS, To cook with minimum shrinking:
- Cut out the white tendon that runs lengthwise through the underside of the meat. The breasts will shrink less.

CHICKEN, FRIED, Hints on:
- Refrigerate the coated chicken uncovered for 30 minutes to 1 hour before cooking to make the coating adhere better.
- Get a crispier coating by using half flour, half cornstarch, plus ½ teaspoon baking powder instead of all flour.
- Fry the chicken pieces until nicely browned, then finish in a 350°F oven. To reduce the fat, place the chicken on a rack set on top of another pan.

CHICKEN, POACHING, Hint on:
- Let the chicken cool in the poaching liquid for 1 hour before cutting it. The chicken will have more flavor and a better texture.

CHICKEN, ROASTED, Hints on:

- Coat with oil and bake on a greased V-shaped rack in a baking pan at 450°F until done. Put the pan on the lowest oven rack.
- Rub regular or imitation mayonnaise over the chicken for a crisp, golden-brown skin.

CHINESE COOKING, Hint on:

- Cut meat and chicken more easily by slicing when partially frozen.
- Add 1 teaspoon cornstarch to the marinade to keep chicken moist and tender.

CHIVES SUBSTITUTE:

- Use the sprouted tips of onions.

CHOCOLATE, To melt:

- Cut the chocolate into small pieces (unless they are chocolate chips) so it will melt faster and not scorch.
- Melt it in a cup made from aluminum foil in the top of a double boiler to avoid cleanup.
- Microwave it on the defrost cycle on a piece of wax paper. Or put it in a microwave container or custard cup and microwave on low for 1 minute. (Spray the container with nonstick vegetable spray so the chocolate will slip right out.) Stir and rotate the container, then microwave for another minute. Stir again. If not nearly melted after 2 minutes, heat it in 30-second intervals. Remove the chocolate before it's completely melted and let stand awhile.
- Put the chocolate on a piece of wax paper or on the original wrapping if it's a 1-ounce cube, and let it sit on top of a hot stove. Sometimes the surface heat will melt the chocolate. Or cover it and put in a 100°F oven.
- Place it in a small, sealable plastic bag. Set the bag, tightly closed, in very hot or simmering water. When the chocolate is melted, dry the bag and let the chocolate cool for a moment. Cut off a corner of the bag and squeeze out the chocolate. Or set the bag upright in a small bowl and microwave it on low heat until the chocolate is almost melted, then let stand 5 minutes until it is completely melted.
- Stir in 1 to 2 tablespoons vegetable shortening (not butter or oil) if the chocolate becomes a hard lump while melting. Beat well.

CHOCOLATE, BAKING, SUBSTITUTE:

- Use 3 tablespoons cocoa powder plus 1 tablespoon shortening or unsalted butter for each 1 ounce chocolate.

CHOCOLATE FROSTING, To make darker:
- Add a few drops of blue food coloring to the frosting.

CITRUS, To extract more juice from:
- Roll the fruit in your hands or on the countertop until it becomes soft and pliable.
- Microwave it for 30 to 60 seconds on medium.
- Heat it for 5 minutes in boiling water if it is quite dried up.
- Avoid having to strain the juice by wrapping a piece of cheesecloth around the cut side of the fruit so the juice strains as you squeeze it.

COCONUT, To crack:
- Put it in a cold oven for 20 minutes at 300°F or a preheated 425°F oven for 12 to 15 minutes. When it cools it will usually crack open by itself. If not, tap it lightly with a hammer. Putting it in the oven makes the meat easier to remove from the shell.

COCONUT, DRIED OUT, To restore:
- Put it in a tightly closed container with a slice of fresh bread. The moisture will be restored in a few days. Or soak it in a little milk. To prevent coconut from drying out, keep it in the freezer.

COFFEE, To economize on:
- Buy extra-fine grind and regrind it to a powder so as to use less.
- Make your own gourmet coffee at half the price. Break cinnamon sticks or vanilla beans into dry coffee grounds, then brew as usual.

COFFEE, To make without a coffee maker:
- Measure coffee into an old-fashioned 1-quart coffeepot or 2-quart pan and fill with cold water. Bring to a boil and boil for 2 minutes. Remove from the heat and add 1 cup cold water to settle the grounds.

COFFEE, To store:
- Transfer it to a dry glass or tin container with a tight-fitting lid if purchased in a paper sack. Keep the container stored upside down in the freezer or refrigerator.

COFFEE FILTER SUBSTITUTE:
- Use a double thickness of paper towels.

CONFECTIONER'S SUGAR SUBSTITUTE:
- Blend 1 cup granulated sugar and 1 tablespoon cornstarch for several minutes at high speed. It does not have the same consistency but will serve in an emergency.

COOKIES, To bake in bulk:

- Place the first two batches of cookies on foil-lined cookie sheets. While they are baking, cut two more pieces of foil the size of the pans and arrange the cookie dough on them. When the first two batches are done, remove the foil and the cookies, allow the pans to cool (or run them under cold water to speed up the process), then slide the two other batches onto the sheets. After removing the cookies, wipe off the foil and reuse it for consecutive batches.

COOKIES, When giving away:

- Use disposable foam meat trays covered with foil. Cover the cookies with plastic wrap and add a bow for a festive touch.

COOKIES, BAR, Hint on:

- Line the pan with foil or wax paper, leaving a 2- to 3-inch overhang on two sides. Tuck the foil or paper down on the sides of the pan. When the cookie bar has cooled, run a knife around the sides and lift it from the pan by the overhang. Remove the lining and cut the cookie into bars or slices.

COOKIES, OATMEAL, To improve the flavor:

- Toast the oatmeal first. Sprinkle it evenly in a jelly-roll pan and bake in a 300°F oven for 10 to 12 minutes. Or roast the oatmeal in a dry skillet over medium heat until golden brown. Cool before adding to the recipe.

COOKIES, ROLLED, Hints on:

- Roll between sheets of wax paper. The dough won't stick to the rolling pin.
- Roll dough into balls or use a melon ball cutter, then flatten the balls with a glass dipped in water or flour.

COOKIES ROLLED INTO BALLS, Hint on:

- Use a large melon ball cutter. All the cookies will be of uniform size.

COOKIES, STALE, Hints on:

- Restore crispness by putting them on a cookie sheet and baking them in the oven at 350°F for 5 to 10 minutes. Or put them in the microwave for a minute or so. Cool on a wire rack.
- Make crumbs out of the cookies, crisped in the oven or not, and freeze them in a plastic bag. Use the crumbs to make a cookie crust or as a topping for ice cream.

COOKING OIL DISPENSER:
- Use a well-washed squirt bottle such as a used mustard container.

CORN CHIPS, POTATO CHIPS, STALE, To freshen:
- Bake them on a cookie sheet in the oven for 5 minutes at 350°F, or put them in the microwave for a minute or so.
- Save any crumbs from crisping the chips to top a casserole, or crush them up and use in place of bread crumbs in a meatloaf or meatballs or to bread foods. (Reduce the salt accordingly.)

CORN ON THE COB, Hints on:
- Use the day you purchase it, before the sugar starts converting to starch.
- Remove the husks when the water for the corn is boiling. Dampen a paper towel and brush downward on the ear of corn to remove the silk. Place the corn in the boiling unsalted water. When it returns to the boil, cook the ears for exactly 3 minutes, then remove or drain. Butter the corn immediately after removing it from the pot to stop the kernels from shrinking, or wrap each ear individually in a napkin to keep it hot and moist.
- Intensify the flavor of the corn by adding a few well-washed husks to the cooking water.
- Grill it on the barbecue by removing the silk but leaving the husks intact. Fasten the husks at the top with a twist tie and soak the corn in cold water for 15 minutes. Or proceed as above and roast in a 325°F oven about 45 minutes.

CORN SYRUP, To measure: See "Measuring Corn Syrup, Honey, Molasses, Hints on."

CORNBREAD, Hints on:
- Experiment until you find the version you like. Add more buttermilk for a moister one; add another egg for a richer one with a more tender crumb. For a crispy crust, bake it in a preheated, oiled cast-iron skillet.

CORNMEAL, To store:
- Keep it refrigerated, as recommended by the Food and Drug Administration. Or freeze it along with other whole-grain flours.

COTTAGE CHEESE, To keep fresh longer:
- Refrigerate it upside down in its original container.

CRACKERS AND COOKIES, To freshen:
- Dry them out in a 350°F oven for 5 to 6 minutes, then cool on cooling racks.

CRANBERRIES, To chop:
- Freeze them first to make the job easier.

CREAM, To avoid splattering when whipping:
- Cut the center out of a piece of wax paper and fit it around the electric mixer beaters so it acts like a tent.
- Whip cream with a hand-held beater in a 1-pound coffee can. Store in the can and put the lid back on.

CREAM, To whip:
- Chill the beaters and containers before whipping the cream.
- Whip half a pint (1 cup) at a time, rather than a full pint. It will be fluffier.
- Use a mug and only one beater of the electric mixer for small amounts.
- Add 2 or 3 drops lemon juice to the cream to make it whip more readily. A pinch of salt also works for cream that won't whip up.

CREAM, WHIPPED, To freeze leftover:
- Drop mounds on a wax-paper-lined cookie sheet and freeze until solid, then pack in plastic bags and store in the freezer.

CREAM, WHIPPED, To make it hold up longer:
- Sprinkle ½ teaspoon unflavored gelatin over 1 tablespoon cold water in a custard cup, then set the cup over simmering water to melt the gelatin. Whip 1 cup heavy cream until almost stiff, then add the cooled gelatin and continue beating until the cream is stiff.

CREAMED SOUPS, CANNED, Hint on:
- Shake the can well before opening. The milk or water will blend in easier and you will avoid lumps.

CRÊPES, Hints on:
- Obtain a lighter crêpe by using 1 part water to 3 parts skim milk as the liquid instead of cream or milk.
- Use instant flour instead of all-purpose flour if you're in a hurry. It requires only 10 minutes resting time; regular flour needs to rest at least 1 hour in the refrigerator before using.

CUPCAKES, To fill the paper liners:
- Use a small soup or gravy ladle or a well-washed cardboard milk or cream carton.

CUPCAKES, To make heart-shaped for Valentine's Day:
- Put a marble between the paper liner and the cupcake tin.

CUPCAKES, To pack for lunches:
- Put the frosting in the middle instead of on the top.

DATES, DRIED OUT OR STUCK TOGETHER, Hints on:
- Moisten the dates by putting a slice of apple in with them for a day or so.
- Separate the dates by putting them in a 300°F oven for a few minutes or in the microwave on medium for 30 to 60 seconds. Let them sit for a minute before separating.

DECORATING BAG SUBSTITUTE:
- Use a plastic sandwich or small storage bag. Cut a corner out of the bottom of the bag, slip in the decorating tip, and close the bag. If you don't have a decorating tip, use the bag without it.
- Make one by twisting aluminum foil into a cone shape and cutting off a tiny piece at the point.

DOUBLE BOILER, Hints on:
- Add some salt to the water in the bottom pot and the food in the top section will cook faster.
- Put a few marbles or a small metal lid in the lower section to alert you if the water boils away.

DOUGHNUTS, STALE, To use up:
- Slice them in half, dip them in egg, then fry them like french toast.

DRIED FRUIT, To dice or mince:
- Spray scissors with nonstick cooking spray before cutting.
- Dip a knife or scissors into hot water frequently while cutting the fruit.
- Add lemon juice to the fruit before dicing or mincing.
- Freeze the fruit for 1 hour before chopping or cutting.

DRIED FRUIT, To plump:
- Sprinkle 1 cup fruit lightly with juice or water, then cover and microwave on full power for 1 minute, stirring after about 30 seconds. Cool before use in baking.
- Steam in a covered steamer for 5 minutes or until plump.
- Cover with boiling water and let sit for about 15 minutes. Drain, then blot dry before using.

EGG STUCK IN CARTON, To remove:
- Wet the bottom of a cardboard carton. Or fill the indentation of a Styrofoam carton with a little water and let it stand for about 5 minutes until you can remove the egg.

EGG SUBSTITUTE IN BAKING:
- Use 2 tablespoons mayonnaise if the recipe calls for 2 eggs and you have only 1. Or add 1 teaspoon white vinegar in place of a missing egg in a recipe.

EGG WHITES, To beat:
- Make certain no trace of grease is in the container used to beat the whites and no particle of egg yolk is in the whites.
- Use a glass or metal container, if possible. Copper is the ideal container.
- Have the whites at room temperature.
- Add 1 teaspoon cold water while beating to increase the volume.
- Avoid tapping the beater on the bowl. This causes the whites to lose air.

EGG WHITES, To freeze:
- Put each egg white in an individual section of a plastic ice-cube tray. Freeze, then put in a plastic freezer bag.

EGG WHITES, To use up:
- Use them for macaroons, angel pie, baked Alaska, Pavlova, meringues, meringue toppings, white mountain frosting, divinity fudge, white cake, angel food cake, snow pudding, marshmallow pudding, 7-minute frosting, marzipan, French bread for airy, crunchy loaves, or use 2 to equal 1 whole egg in a cake recipe.

EGG WHITES SUBSTITUTING FOR WHOLE EGGS:
- Use 2 egg whites when substituting for 1 whole egg.
- Add 1 tablespoon oil and 1⅓ tablespoons liquid for each 2 egg whites in the recipe to make up for the fat in the egg yolk.

EGG YOLKS, To store:
- Put them in a glass container or custard cup and pour a thin layer of cold water over the surface. Cover and refrigerate. Use within 2 or 3 days.

EGG YOLKS, To use up:
- Use them for mayonnaise, hollandaise or béarnaise sauce, flan, custard sauce, baked custard dishes, custard pie, flaky French pastry, spritz cookies, duchess potatoes, croissants, lemon filling, vanilla pastry cream, butter icing, painting the top of pastry to make it glossy, thickening soups and sauces. Or use 2 yolks to equal 1 whole egg in a cake recipe, or 1 egg yolk plus 1 tablespoon milk.

EGGS, To bring to room temperature for baking:

- Put them in a bowl of hot water for several minutes or in the microwave on the defrost cycle for a few seconds.

EGGS, To determine if fresh:

- Place in a bowl of salted cold water. Discard any that float to the top or turn broad end up.

EGGS, To freeze:

- Mix together lightly 1 cup raw eggs (about 5 large ones) with either ½ teaspoon table salt or ½ teaspoon sugar or corn syrup and store in an airtight freezer container. Thaw overnight in the refrigerator. Will keep up to 6 months. Three tablespoons of egg mixture is equivalent to 1 large egg.

EGGS, To hard-boil:

- Prick the large end with a pin, going in ¼ inch.
- Cover the eggs with cold water, bring the water to a boil, cover, and let sit for 17 minutes, then immediately put the eggs into very cold water.
- Add to the water in which you boil the eggs 1 teaspoon salt, lemon juice, or white vinegar, or a small piece of lemon. The eggshells will peel off easier, and if the eggs crack, the whites will not seep out.
- Stir eggs gently for the first 2 minutes if hard-boiling them for stuffing. This sets the whites and the yolks will be in the center.

EGGS, To poach:

- Put 1 tablespoon white vinegar or a few drops of lemon juice in the poaching water before bringing it to a simmer. This will keep the eggs firm and whole. Make sure the water is simmering gently before adding the eggs.
- Use cans from deviled ham, tuna, or pet food for rings. Remove the bottoms and sterilize the clean washed cans in boiling water.

EGGS, To separate:

- Separate them when chilled; they separate better, but they have more volume when beaten at room temperature.
- Use a small funnel. The white will run through, leaving the yolk in the funnel.
- Break the egg into a saucer and place a small glass over the yolk. Hold the glass and saucer together firmly and pour the egg white into the container.

EGGS, To store:

- Store eggs big end up, just as they come in the carton. Keep them in the closed carton, as the shells can absorb odors.

EGGS, HARD-BOILED, To identify:

- Mark them with a pencil to distinguish them from uncooked eggs or add a little yellow food coloring to the water.

EGGSHELL IN BATTER, To remove:

- Scoop out the piece of shell with another larger piece or with the end of a paper towel.

EMERGENCY COOKING, Hints on:

- Use a chafing dish, cast-iron cookware over a fire in the fireplace, a charcoal grill or hibachi placed in the fireplace (don't use indoors unless you have a fireplace), or a camp stove.

ENGLISH MUFFINS, Hints on:

- Split the muffins with a fork to avoid flattening the crumb.
- Split the muffins before freezing and have all the cut edges facing the same way. This makes them defrost faster and is handy if you want only half a muffin.
- Freshen a stale muffin by holding it under the cold water tap to wet it. Shake off the excess water from the muffin, then place it in a paper towel and microwave on high for 5 to 10 seconds.

EVAPORATED MILK, To whip:

- Chill milk in an ice-cube tray or shallow container until ice crystals form around the edges. Turn into a chilled bowl and whip with a rotary beater or with an electric mixer on high speed until milk is stiff.

FAT, To drain from browned ground meat:

- Use a bulb-syringe turkey baster.

FAT, To remove from soups and stews:

- Place a piece of wax paper directly on the surface of the liquid, then refrigerate it. When cool, congealed grease will come off with the paper.
- Put an ice cube on the surface. The fat will congeal around the ice cube. Remove the cube before it melts.

FISH, To cook:

- Soak in milk an hour or so before cooking. Or add 1 tablespoon vinegar to the water when poaching. The fish will be firmer.

- Marinate in ¼ cup vinegar, wine, or lemon juice for about 20 minutes before cooking. This will make the fish more tender and prevent it from drying out.
- Measure the fish at its thickest part, then cook it 10 minutes for every inch of thickness. This pertains to every method: baking, broiling, pan frying, and poaching.

FISH, To freeze:

- Place the fish on a jelly-roll pan and put in the freezer. When frozen, put it in ice water for 2 minutes, then freeze on the pan again. Repeat once more, then wrap, label, and freeze. Or put the fish in a well-rinsed cardboard milk carton, fill with water, seal, and freeze.

FISH, CANNED, Hints on:

- Put a little vinegar (preferably apple cider) in an opened can of sardines or tuna and let sit for a few minutes. It will remove the oil taste.
- Soak canned shrimp in a little sherry and 2 tablespoons vinegar for about 15 minutes to improve the flavor.
- Prechill canned shrimp and rinse well in ice-cold water before using to remove the salty taste.

FISH, FRIED, For a crisp batter:

- Roll the fish in self-raising flour, dip into a well-beaten egg, then roll again in the flour.
- Use 1 part white vinegar to 3 parts water as the liquid called for in the batter recipe.
- Use 1 teaspoon baking powder for every 1 cup flour.

FLOUR, To have on hand for small jobs:

- Save a plastic spice bottle with a shaker top and fill with flour to have on hand for dusting cake pans, coating fish or cutlets, and so on. Or store seasoned flour in the same kind of container. Keep it in the freezer.

FLOUR AND GRAINS, To store in bulk:

- Freeze flour or other dry staples for 24 hours after purchase. Freeze in plastic freezer bags or plastic wrap. Freezing destroys any eggs that may hatch into worms or bugs. After 24 hours, remove the items from the freezer and store at room temperature in a tightly closed container. Flours, meals, and grains can be stored in the freezer permanently. However, don't store wheat germ in the freezer; freezing destroys the vitamin E content.

FLOUR SIFTER, Hint on:
- Keep in a plastic food bag to avoid washing after each use and to protect it from dust.

FLOUR SIFTER SUBSTITUTE:
- Press the flour through a kitchen sieve with a spoon. Turn and stir the flour as you press it down. Or aerate the flour with your hands.

FOOD COLORING, To measure:
- Use a dropper.

FOOD SALE, Contributing to:
- Give the recipe with the food you are contributing. It will sell faster because it's a two-for-one-deal.

FROSTING, Hints on:
- Add a pinch of baking powder to powdered sugar icing to keep it moist and prevent hardening.
- Use powdered milk if the frosting is too thin and you have used up all the confectioner's sugar.
- Stir in ¼ to ½ teaspoon white vinegar or lemon juice if a cooked frosting starts to turn granular.
- Dust the cake surface with cornstarch before frosting to prevent the frosting from running off.
- Dip the knife in hot water frequently when spreading the frosting on the cake. Doing so makes it easier to spread.

FRUITS, To ripen:
- Put them in a brown paper bag with holes poked in it. Add an apple or banana if you have one to speed the ripening process.

FRYING, DEEP FAT, Hints on:
- Add 1 tablespoon white vinegar to the fat before heating or 1 teaspoon vinegar to the batter to keep the food from absorbing too much fat and to eliminate the greasy taste.

FRYING SPLATTERS, To prevent:
- Place an inverted metal colander over the frying pan. The colander lets the steam escape and the meat browns without splattering fat.

FUDGE, To cut:
- Use a pizza cutter.
- Pour it into a pan lined with buttered foil. Allow enough foil to serve as an overhang so you can lift the fudge out and cut it on a board.

FUNNEL SUBSTITUTE:
- Cut the corner off an envelope to fill small spice jars.
- Cut an empty plastic milk or bleach bottle in half and use the half containing the spout for the funnel. Make sure it is well washed out and thoroughly dried.

GARLIC, To peel:
- Cut the garlic cloves in half and gently press a knife blade against each half of the peel side. The skin will come right off.
- Soak them in warm water before peeling. The skins will slip right off. Or drop them into boiling water, wait for 30 seconds, and lift them out using a slotted spoon. Drain and run cold water over them, then slip off the skins.
- Place a whole head of garlic on a paper plate and microwave on high for 1 minute. Rotate the plate halfway through. Let the garlic stand for 1 minute and peel when cool.
- Put the cloves on a piece of wax paper and fold it over to cover, then hit the cloves with a meat pounder or edge of a heavy can.

GARLIC, To store:
- Peel the cloves, put them in a small container or self-closing bag, and keep them in the freezer. They will keep indefinitely.
- Store unpeeled garlic in the crisper section of the refrigerator.
- Keep garlic in oil for no longer than 12 hours. According to the Garlic Information Line of Cornell University, botulism can develop in garlic kept in oil.

GARLIC, TOO MUCH ADDED BY MISTAKE, To correct:
- Add some parsley or parsley flakes to neutralize the taste. Or put the parsley in a tea ball or a cheesecloth bag and let it simmer in the mixture for about 10 minutes.

GELATIN, Hints on:
- Mix the gelatin with the sugar and add the liquid if the recipe calls for 1 tablespoon or more sugar. It is not necessary to soften the gelatin beforehand.
- Add 1 teaspoon of apple cider vinegar to any recipe for molded salad or dessert to keep the mold from melting too rapidly.
- Fold the gelatin mixture into the egg whites when a recipe calls for both. The mixture will be fluffier.
- Boil fresh or frozen pineapple juice for 2 minutes before combining

with gelatin. This kills the enzymes that prevent the gelatin from setting. Never use fresh pineapple in gelatin.

GELATIN, Molds for:

- Use any type of dish or pan as a mold, such as muffin pans, cake pans, ice-cube trays, coffee cans, custard cups, mixing bowls, or jars. Use a 1-pint jar for a small package and 1-quart jar for a large package. Jars take up less room in the refrigerator and can be unmolded and served on their side.

GELATIN, To quick-set:

- Soften and dissolve the gelatin in hot liquid, then add frozen juices, fruits, ice cream, or ice cubes as part of the liquid to have the gelatin gel in about 30 minutes.
- Set the bowl of gelatin in a container of ice and water and stir for about 5 minutes, or until it thickens. Or place the container in the freezer for about 10 minutes, stirring occasionally so it will chill uniformly.
- Use smaller molds.

GELATIN, To unmold:

- Loosen around the edge with the tip of a paring knife and dip the mold in warm (not hot) water to the depth of the gelatin. Place a serving dish rinsed in cold water on top of the mold, and invert plate and mold together. Shake gently, holding the serving dish lightly to the mold. If the gelatin does not unmold, repeat. If the mold is off-center on the plate, slide it into position.
- Loosen around the edge of the mold, then place it on the serving plate. Wrap a tea towel wrung out in warm water over the mold and leave for a second or two, then tap the mold gently. Or use a hair dryer to apply heat to the mold. Be careful you don't melt the gelatin.

GINGER ROOT, To keep:

- Peel and cut in pieces, then put in a small jar with sherry, vodka, or a mild vinegar such as rice vinegar.
- Peel and place in a plastic bag and store in the freezer. Grate the amount you need and return the rest to the freezer.

GRAPEFRUIT, To peel for salad:

- Place fruit in a hot oven for 2 to 3 minutes or in hot water for 5 minutes before peeling. The white fiber will come off with the peel.

GRAPES, To freeze:

- Wash, dry, then place on a cookie sheet or in a shallow plastic container and freeze until solid. Pop them into a self-closing freezer bag and serve them frozen for a warm-weather treat (do not defrost), or use in place of ice cubes in a cold drink.

GRAVY, To avoid lumps:

- Add a little salt to the flour before putting in the water.
- Avoid lumps by using instant flour instead of all-purpose.

GRAVY, To get rid of lumps:

- Push the gravy through a fine sieve.
- Beat it vigorously with a wire whisk, or use the electric mixer.
- Whirl it in the blender, although this will thin the gravy.

GREASING A PAN, Hint on:

- Put a small sandwich bag over your hand, dip it into the shortening or butter, and spread it on the pan. When using oil, pour it on the pan first. When finished, turn the bag inside out and discard.

GREEN PEPPER, To freeze:

- Wash and dice, then spread the pieces on a cookie sheet and freeze. Once frozen, pour the pieces into a plastic bag. Take what you need out of the bag and return to the freezer.

GREEN PEPPER, STUFFED, Hint on:

- Bypass the preboiling and just bake the peppers longer. Rub vegetable oil over the skins to keep them supple.

HAM, CANNED, Hints on:

- Heat the ham thoroughly in the oven even if you plan to serve it cold. Heating will greatly improve the flavor.
- Run hot tap water over the canned ham before opening. The gelatin will melt and the ham will slide right out.

HAM OR CORNED BEEF, To cook:

- Add a little apple cider or white vinegar to the water used for boiling ham. It will remove some of the saltiness and improve the taste.
- Cool and freeze the liquid used for cooking the ham. Use later for cooking vegetables and for making split pea, lentil, or bean soup.
- Let corned beef cool in the liquid it was cooked in. It will be much juicier.

HAMBURGER, Hints on:

- Avoid handling the meat excessively. Overhandling toughens it.
- Get juicier hamburgers by adding either 1 grated raw potato to each pound of ground meat or 2 to 3 tablespoons vegetable juice, broth, or water.
- Cook hamburgers faster by making several holes in each patty or one large hole in the middle of each patty.

HERBS AND SPICES, Hints on:

- Keep ground ginger, chili powder, and paprika in the refrigerator. Once opened, they lose their flavor quickly.
- Crumble dried herbs between the palms of your hands before adding to a recipe. They will release their flavor better during cooking.
- Avoid sprinkling spices directly from the can or jar into cooking food. Steam rising from food causes powdered spices to cake and lose their potency. Sprinkle some in your hand instead, or scoop from the can with a measuring spoon.
- Put whole spices and bay leaves in a tea ball to make them easy to remove.
- Use minced parsley, dried or fresh, with other herbs to enhance their taste.
- Soften the herbs for 10 to 20 minutes with a little hot water or in the liquid called for in the recipe when using them in a quickly cooked dish or sauce. Or boil them for a minute or so in a small amount of water, then drain.
- Save money by buying dried herbs and spices at ethnic markets or the ethnic section of the supermarket. Or buy them at import stores such as Cost Plus. Look for them in cellophane or plastic bags.

HERBS, FRESH, Hints on:

- Preserve by chopping them, then place in plastic ice-cube trays, add a little water, and freeze. Transfer to a plastic bag when frozen and return to the freezer. Drop frozen into soups, sauces, and stews.
- Rinse and thoroughly dry the leaves, then seal in small plastic bags, pressing out any air, and freeze. Do not thaw; simply take out what you need and snip or chop them while frozen.
- Cut fresh herbs with scissors to avoid crushing them with a dull blade, which can alter their flavor.

HERBS, FRESH, To dry:

- Arrange fresh washed and dried leaves in a single layer on shallow trays, cover with cheesecloth, and place in a dry shady place to dry. Or stretch cheesecloth over a container, put the leaves or sprigs on the cheesecloth, then cover with another layer of cheesecloth. When dry, the herbs will crumble when handled.

- Put the washed and dried herb leaves on a cookie sheet with a double thickness of paper towels and leave in a gas oven for 4 hours with only the pilot light on or in an electric oven on the lowest possible setting. Leave until dry (from a couple of hours, overnight, to a day or two). Pack loosely in clean dry jars with tight-fitting lids and store in a cool, dark, dry place. When ready to use, crumble between the fingers or rub through a fine sieve.
- Place rinsed and completely dry leaves on paper towels and microwave uncovered for 1 minute at full power. If still damp, reset for another minute. Continue on 1-minute settings until completely dry. Pack and store as above.

HONEY, To measure: See "Measuring Corn Syrup, Honey, Molasses, Hints on."

HONEY, To ungranulate:
- Place the jar in a pan of hot water for a few minutes. Or microwave the jar for a few seconds on the defrost cycle.

ICE CREAM, To keep:
- Press plastic wrap onto the surface of the ice cream to prevent crystals from forming.

ICE CUBES, To make quickly:
- Use cooled boiled water. It contains less oxygen.
- Leave a couple of cubes in the tray when you refill it.

ICED DRINKS, Hint on:
- Freeze coffee, tea, lemonade, or punch in ice-cube trays to add to the specific drink instead of ice cubes. This prevents the drink from becoming diluted when the ice cubes melt.

JAM, MAKING, Hints on:
- Add the juice of 1 lemon to almost any jam recipe when cooking. This improves the color and makes for faster jelling.
- Melt paraffin to seal the jelly jars in the top section of a double boiler lined with foil. If there is leftover paraffin, cool it and fold the foil around it so it's ready to unfold and use again. Or put the paraffin in a clean tin can, set the can in a pan of water, and bring to the boil. Or melt the paraffin in a microwave set to 50 percent power, and stir fre-

quently. Use a microwave bowl to heat the paraffin and remove the paraffin from the oven before it is completely melted. It will continue to melt after removal.

JARS, To open:
- Take an ice pick or can opener and make a little hole in the top of the jar lid. This releases the pressure and the jar will open easily.
- Twist the lid with a piece of sandpaper, sand side down.
- Wrap rubber bands or a thick broccoli band around the lid.
- Twist the lid off small bottle caps with a nutcracker.
- Use a damp cloth or rubber glove.
- Hold the lid under hot tap water and rotate the jar slowly. If the jar has been refrigerated, begin with warm water and gradually work up to hot water so the glass won't crack.
- Buy a jar opener that accommodates all sizes of jar lids from a kitchen supply store.

KETCHUP, To start flowing:
- Turn the bottle upside down and shake vigorously before opening.
- Push a straw, wooden skewer, or long thin knife blade all the way to the bottom of the bottle, then remove.
- Run a knife around the inside of the bottle neck.

LEMONS, To extract more juice: See "Citrus, To extract more juice from."

LEMONS, To preserve the juice:
- Freeze in plastic ice-cube trays, then remove from trays and store in plastic freezer bags.

LEMONS, To preserve the rind:
- Wrap and freeze the rind after squeezing the juice. It is easier to grate frozen rind than rind at room temperature.
- Put the grated rind in a small screw-top jar and cover with vodka. It will keep for months stored in the refrigerator.
- Dry the grated zest on an ungreased baking sheet in a 200°F oven for 15 to 20 minutes, stirring occasionally. Cool and store in an airtight container at room temperature.

LEMONS, To store:
- Keep lemons and limes in an egg carton in the refrigerator.
- Poke a hole in one end of the lemon with a toothpick. Squeeze out the amount you need, insert the toothpick, then store the lemon in a plastic bag in the refrigerator.

- Place lemons in a jar of cold water and change the water every day.
- Seal them in a plastic freezer bag and freeze. When needed, take them out of the bag and microwave for a few minutes, then let stand on the counter for 10 more minutes before using.

LETTUCE, Hints on:

- Add a few drops of lemon juice to the water in which you wash the lettuce. Doing so will make it crisp and remove all sand and slugs. Do not use salt; salt makes lettuce flabby.
- Wash head lettuce when you are ready to use it, not in advance. Then wash only what is to be used at the time. Return the unwashed portion to the refrigerator with 2 or 3 unwashed outer leaves wrapped snugly around the cut part. This will retard discoloration.
- Restore wilted lettuce by washing it in hot water, then plunging it into ice water that has 1 tablespoon apple cider or white vinegar added.

LETTUCE, To cook:

- Cook with a small amount of water until crisp tender. Boston, leaf, escarole, or romaine are good choices.

LIQUID, To measure when reducing:

- Stand the handle of a wooden spoon upright in the liquid. Take it out and mark the level of the liquid with a pencil. Check the depth of the liquid periodically with the marked spoon handle.

MARSHMALLOWS, Hints on:

- One large marshmallow is equal to 10 small ones.
- Store them in the freezer to keep them fresh and prevent them from drying out.
- Soften dried-out marshmallows by putting them in a self-closing plastic bag with 2 to 3 slices fresh white bread and letting them sit for 3 days.

MEASURING CORN SYRUP, HONEY, MOLASSES, Hints on:

- Measure the oil in the cup first; then the corn syrup, honey, or molasses will slide right out.
- Spray cups and spoons with nonstick cooking spray before measuring.
- Rub the cup or spoon with margarine, shortening, or vegetable oil.
- Dip the spoon in flour first, and the ingredient will not stick to it.
- Rinse the cup in hot water, then pour the contents into the center of the measuring cup, not down the sides.

MEAT, To braise, sauté, or fry:

- Snip the edges of steaks and chops before cooking to prevent them from curling up when cooking.
- Have the meat at room temperature, dried with a paper towel, and lightly dusted with flour (to help it brown) or brushed with a light film of olive oil. Lightly brush the bottom of the pan with oil (if you haven't brushed the meat with oil), and make sure it is very hot but not smoking before adding the meat. Avoid poking the meat with a fork or cutting into it to test for doneness. This releases the juices.

MEAT, To defrost:

- Coat all sides with oil before defrosting. No juices will be lost from the meat as it defrosts.
- Let the meat defrost in the marinade if you plan to marinate it before cooking.

MEAT, To keep fresh:

- Remove the original wrapping and wrap the meat loosely in wax paper to allow air to circulate around it.
- Preserve meats temporarily by covering them with salt.
- Salt fresh chicken or ground meat immediately if you are unable to cook it right away. This will prevent spoiling and enables you to keep them a day or two longer before cooking.

MEAT, To marinate:

- Use a self-closing bag. You use less liquid and there is no mess when you turn the meat. Just turn the bag.

MEAT, To slice thinly:

- Pop it into the freezer for an hour to let it harden slightly.

MEAT, To tenderize:

- Add a little vinegar (any kind) or lemon juice to the cooking water of stews and pot roasts. Or add a few tomatoes for their acid content.
- Cook it in strong tea or beer instead of water.
- Marinate the meat in 2 cups cold water and 1 tablespoon vinegar for 30 minutes. Turn the meat after 15 minutes.
- Marinate it in lemon juice for several hours in the refrigerator.
- Rub a little oil and vinegar on both sides and let it stand for 2 hours before cooking.
- Rub it well with baking soda and let stand a few hours, then wash it thoroughly before cooking.
- Soak in ¼ cup vinegar and 2 cups water for 12 hours.

MEAT BRAISING TIMETABLE:

Beef pot roast (3–5 lbs.) 2 hours and 30 minutes to 3 hours and 30 minutes.
Cubes (1 inch)   1 hour to 1 hour and 30 minutes.
Cubes (2 inch)   1 hour and 30 minutes to 2 hours and 30 minutes.
Short ribs (pieces)   1 hour and 30 minutes to 2 hours and 30 minutes.

MEAT, GROUND, To freeze:

- Form gently into flat disks so they will freeze and defrost faster.

MEAT, POT ROASTED, To add flavor and color:

- Stir 1 teaspoon or more paprika into the liquid. It will not affect the taste. Or add 1 teaspoon instant coffee for a dark rich color.

MEAT POUNDER SUBSTITUTE:

- Use the edge of a saucer or an unopened tin can to pound meat or chicken.

MEATBALLS, Hints on:

- Dip your fingers into water before rolling. The meat will not stick to your fingers.
- Add 2 to 3 tablespoons broth, vegetable juice, or water to each pound of meat to keep it moist.
- Refrigerate meatballs for about 20 minutes before frying. They won't fall apart so easily.
- Place on shallow baking pan and bake at 350°F for 10 to 20 minutes, depending on size. Or place meatballs on a rack or cake cooler inside another pan to catch the grease.
- Keep meatballs on hand in the freezer. Place freshly mixed meat-balls on a cookie sheet covered in wax paper, and place in the freezer for 1 hour until nearly frozen. Then store in freezer bags in the freezer.

MELON, To store:

- Put a piece of wax paper over the cut surface, then place in a large plastic bag or wrap securely in aluminum foil.
- Store in a paper bag on the top shelf of the refrigerator.

MERINGUE, Hints on:

- Add ½ teaspoon baking powder to the room-temperature egg whites before beating for a high, fluffy meringue.
- Add ¼ teaspoon white vinegar to 3 egg whites to make the meringue fluffy.
- Sprinkle ½ cup sugar gradually over 3 egg whites while beating for a meringue that is higher and has more body.

- Obtain a crisp crust by sprinkling the top with confectioner's sugar just before baking, then bake up to 30 minutes. Cook the meringue slowly so it won't split or crack. After the meringue turns brown, shut off the oven, open the oven door slightly, and leave the pie for several minutes before removing.

MILK, To freeze:

- Freeze whole containers. They take 2 days to defrost in the refrigerator or 6 hours at room temperature. Shake well before using.

MILK, To keep cold:

- Put the milk in a clean screw-top bottle, such as a mayonnaise or pickle jar. Cut a piece of wool blanket and sew it so it will cover the bottle. Dip the blanket-covered bottle in cold water and hang it in the shade out of doors. The milk will keep icy cold. Be sure to keep the blanket wet.

MILK, When heating:

- Rinse the pot in cold water before heating the milk to keep it from sticking to the bottom.

MINT, Hints on:

- Dip mint in vinegar before chopping and it will retain its bright green color.
- Store it upside down in a sealed jar. Mint will remain fresh a long time. Both the mint and jar must be dry.

MIXING/CREAMING, Hint on:

- Heat electric mixer beaters in boiling water before use to keep shortening or butter from sticking to them.

MUFFINS, Hints on:

- Substitute buttermilk or yogurt for milk for lighter, more tender muffins. Use ½ teaspoon baking soda for each cup of buttermilk or yogurt used.
- Separate the eggs. Mix in the yolks, then fold in the beaten egg whites last. If the batter is stiff, stir in a quarter of the whites, then fold in the remainder. This will make the muffins much lighter.

MUFFINS, STALE, To freshen:

- Sprinkle or spray the muffins lightly with cold water, place in a brown paper bag and close snugly, or wrap in foil. Heat in a 375° to 400°F oven for about 5 minutes or a 300°F oven for 15 minutes or until hot.
- Sprinkle the muffins with water, place in a paper towel, and microwave them on high for 5 to 10 seconds.

MUFFINS/CUPCAKES STUCK IN THE PAN, To remove:
- Place the hot pan on a wet tea towel.

MUSHROOMS, To cook:
- Sauté in butter before adding them to a stew or braised dish. They will have a better flavor and texture.

MUSHROOMS, To store:
- Store in a brown paper bag in the refrigerator crisper. They also can be kept in the freezer in a brown paper bag. Cook straight from the freezer without thawing. Storing in brown paper prevents sweating, which causes them to turn brown.

NONSTICK COOKING SPRAY, To make:
- Wash a used spray bottle in hot soapy water, then rinse well and dry thoroughly. Pour vegetable oil into the bottle and use it the same way you would a commercial aerosol spray.
- Combine equal parts of vegetable oil and liquid lecithin in a pump bottle. (Buy the liquid lecithin in the health food store.)
- Combine 5 ounces vegetable oil and 1 ounce vodka in a spray bottle.

NUTS, Hint on:
- Soak nuts in water for a few hours or overnight to increase protein and vitamin content and to aid in digestion.
- Toast or roast nuts before using in recipes to intensify their flavor. Toast them in an ungreased skillet over medium heat, stirring frequently until golden, or roast them in the oven at 350°F, stirring occasionally, for 10 to 15 minutes. Or microwave 1 cup chopped nuts on a paper plate uncovered on high for 3 to 4 minutes until the nuts smell toasted. Rotate the plate halfway through.

NUTS, To blanch:
- Drop almonds, walnuts, or pistachios into boiling water for 30 seconds or so, then drain and slip the skins off.

NUTS, To shell:
- Place in a covered dish with enough water to cover them. Micro-wave on high for 4 to 5 minutes or until the water boils, then let sit covered for 1 minute. Or cover with water and bring to a boil on the stove, then let sit for 15 minutes or so. Turn into a colander to drain, then spread over a towel to cool for several minutes before cracking. Let the nutmeats dry on paper towels overnight before using.

- Avoid getting shells in with the nuts by putting the nuts in a bowl of cool water. The shells will float. Drain and dry nuts before using. This is handy if you have a lot of nuts to shell.
- **Brazil nuts:** Freeze before cracking. Or cover with water, bring to a boil, then boil for 3 minutes. Drain off the water and cover with ice water. Let stand for 2 minutes, then drain and crack.
- **Chestnuts:** Cut an X on the flat side, then microwave a handful uncovered on high for about 45 seconds. Or cover with cold water and bring to a boil. Cook for 4 minutes, then peel while still warm.
- **Walnuts:** Cover with water, bring to a boil, remove from heat, put a lid on the pan, and let sit for at least 15 minutes. Dry, then crack. Soak overnight in salt water before you crack them if you need whole nuts. Let dry before using.

NUTS, SHELLED, To chop, dice, or sliver:
- Heat for 5 minutes in a 325°F oven or in the microwave on high for 2 to 3 minutes. This makes them easier to chop or sliver.
- Sliver almonds on a board with a single-edge razor blade.
- Put walnuts in a plastic bag, seal it tightly, then roll it lightly with a rolling pin. Make sure to use a light touch.
- Chop small loads in the blender and use quick on/off surges until the nuts are chopped or diced.

OIL AND VINEGAR DRESSING, HOMEMADE, Hints on:
- Combine the ingredients in a screw-top jar, add an ice cube and shake, then discard what's left of the cube. The dressing will be smooth and thoroughly mixed.
- Add 1 teaspoon water to the oil and vinegar.
- Allow the dressing to warm up to room temperature before using. It mixes better when shaken, spreads farther, and coats the salad greens evenly.

OIL, SUBSTITUTING FOR BUTTER/SHORTENING:
- Use one third less vegetable oil when substituting oil for butter or shortening in recipes other than bread or baked desserts. For example, substitute 2 teaspoons vegetable oil for 1 tablespoon solid shortening, or ⅔ cup oil for 1 cup solid shortening.

OIL, To avoid staining shelf surfaces:
- Place the bottle in the cut-off bottom of a box of salt or Parmesan cheese, or set it on a plastic margarine or coffee can lid. This will pro-

tect cabinet and refrigerator shelves from oil running down the side of the bottle.

OMELETS, Hints on:
- Take eggs from the refrigerator 30 minutes before using.
- Do not overbeat the eggs, just incorporate the whites and yolks, and don't add the salt before beating.
- Use water instead of milk to make the omelet more tender.
- Heat the pan before adding butter or oil, and make sure the butter is bubbling and beginning to brown before adding the eggs. Cook 1 minute, then remove from heat.
- Cook in the oven for a high fluffy omelet. Separate eggs and beat the whites till fluffy, then fold into beaten yolks. Add a pinch of cornstarch or baking powder to the egg mixture to keep it from collapsing, then put into a 350°F oven for 2 minutes.

ONIONS, To obtain a few slices for a sandwich:
- Slice through the middle of the onion, cut off the slices, then put the two parts back together. Wrap or seal in a plastic bag and refrigerate.
- Make extra-thin slices by leaving the skin on the onion while cutting. You can peel the skin off easily afterward.

ONIONS, To peel without tears:
- Breathe through your mouth.
- Peel the onion under cool running water.
- Hold a kitchen match in your mouth (sulfur side out) while working with the onions.
- Chill the onion well before peeling or put it in the freezer for 20 minutes.
- Use a diver's mask, snorkel, or safety goggles if you have many onions to peel.

ONIONS, To store:
- Arrange onions in a single layer on racks.
- Store in a plastic bag in the vegetable compartment of the refrigerator.
- Place onions in the legs of clean sheer pantyhose, tying a knot between each one. When you want one, cut below the knot.

ONIONS, FRIED, To cook:
- Soak sliced onions in milk for 15 minutes before frying to give them a brown, appetizing color.

ORANGES, To peel:
- Place fruit in a hot oven for 2 to 3 minutes or in hot water for 5 minutes before peeling. The white fiber will come off with the peel.

ORGANIC PRODUCE, To clean:
- Soak for a few minutes in water to which you have added 1 or 2 teaspoons table salt. This will kill any bugs lurking in the produce. Salt makes lettuce flabby, so use white vinegar or lemon juice instead.

PANCAKES, Hints on:
- Stop mixing the ingredients just before all the tiny lumps of flour dissolve, then let the batter sit for 1 hour in the refrigerator before cooking. The batter will smooth out.
- Use 2 eggs instead of 1 and separate. Beat the whites until fluffy, then fold them into the batter. This will produce lighter pancakes.
- Rub a slice of raw potato over the griddle before cooking the pancakes to keep them from sticking.
- Replace the liquid in the batter with club soda. Mix just before you cook the pancakes, as this batter will not keep. Freeze any extra pancakes.
- Use buttermilk to produce the lightest pancakes. They rise higher than baking powder pancakes.

PAPAYAS, To select:
- Buy firm, pale green or pale yellow fruit and ripen at room temperature.

PARSLEY, To dry:
- Dip a bunch in boiling water, holding it by the stems, until it is a vivid green. Put it in a 450°F oven to dry, then rub between your hands or through a coarse sieve. Pack in a clean dry jar with a tight-fitting lid.
- Place washed and drained parsley on paper towels and microwave uncovered on high for 1 minute.
- Rinse the parsley, pat it dry, and put the leaves minus the stems in a small brown paper bag. Close the bag and put it in the refrigerator. Turn the bag over once a day. The parsley will dry in 3 to 4 weeks.

PARSLEY, To store:
- Wash and drain and place loosely in a clean jar with a wet paper towel in the bottom. Cover and refrigerate.
- Freeze it. It retains its full flavor and can be mixed while frozen and crisp. It is also easier to chop when frozen.
- Revive wilted parsley by cutting one-half inch off the stems, then

standing the parsley in a glass of ice water and refrigerating it for at least 1 hour.

PASTRY, To make crisp or flaky:

- Cut in shortening and refrigerate before adding ice water. Or chill the shortening for 15 to 20 minutes before using.
- Put butter or margarine in the freezer for 15 to 20 minutes before combining with shortening. Shortening produces a flaky texture but does not have much flavor.
- Add 1 tablespoon powdered milk to the flour and use ice-cold water and a squeeze of lemon juice.
- Substitute 1 tablespoon white vinegar or lemon juice for 1 tablespoon ice water.
- Substitute ice-cold sour cream, yogurt, or whipping cream for the water. This makes the pastry extra flaky.
- Use oil, although the crust will have a mealy texture.
- Allow chilled dough to stand at room temperature until it's pliable enough to roll out easily, usually about 1 hour.

PASTRY, To prevent edges browning too fast:

- Cover the edges with aluminum foil strips.
- Make a reusable crust cover by cutting out the center of a foil pie pan to within an inch or so of the edge, leaving the rim on the pan. Place the ring upside down on the crust. Keep on hand for pie baking.

PASTRY, To roll out:

- Avoid excess flour by using a pastry cloth and rolling pin cover.
- Chill the rolling pin in the freezer before flouring to prevent pastry dough from clinging to it.
- Roll out on freezer paper placed waxed-side up or on wax paper. Moisten the counter with a sponge to prevent the paper from slipping.
- Use cornstarch instead of flour to keep the dough from sticking.

PASTRY BAG, To fill:

- Place the bag inside a large jar for support, then turn the top of the bag down over the top of the jar rim and secure with a rubber band.

PASTRY BAG SUBSTITUTE:

- Cut a small hole in one corner of a small heavy plastic bag. Fill with whipped cream or other mixture, and pipe.

PASTRY DOUGH, LEFT OVER, To use:
- Wrap and freeze. Grate it on top of fruit, then bake. It makes a handy instant topping.

PASTRY, SHORT-CRUST, To keep crisp:
- Use milk for moistening if it is to be served cold. The pastry will keep crisp longer than if mixed with water.

PASTRY TARTS, JAM, To prevent becoming soggy:
- Heat the jam almost to boiling before filling the tarts. The pastry will be crisp and never soggy.

PÂTÉ À CHOUX PUFFS, Hints on:
- Beat in the eggs with a portable mixer or wire whisk for lighter puffs, and bake as soon as possible after the pastry is made.
- Store in a closed container for several days before filling. Then crisp them in a 350°F oven before filling.
- Freeze them. Then heat them without defrosting in a 400°F oven for a few minutes. Cool before filling.

PEACHES, To peel:
- Dip in boiling water for 15 seconds, then plunge into ice water. Put them in a mesh bag or a large wire mesh strainer for easy removal.
- Microwave them on high for 20 seconds and let cool. The skins should slip off.

PEACHES, To ripen:
- Put them in a cardboard box, then cover with newspaper to seal in the gases.

PEANUT BUTTER, HARDENED, To soften:
- Add 1 tablespoon liquid honey and stir in well.

PEANUT BUTTER, NATURAL, To incorporate the oil:
- Place the jar upside down or on its side for a day or so. That way the fat on the top sinks to the bottom or side and makes it easier to mix. Stir well and keep refrigerated.

PEPPER SHAKER, To keep free-flowing:
- Put some whole peppers in the pepper shaker.

PEPPERS, BELL AND CHILIES, To remove the skins:
- Arrange the peppers or chilies on a baking sheet and place under a preheated broiler. Turn as needed until the skins are evenly blackened and blistered on all sides. Remove from the heat and cover with a tea

towel or place in a paper bag until cool enough to handle, about 10 minutes. With your fingers or a small knife, peel off the blackened skins and remove the stems and seeds. Will keep in an airtight container in the refrigerator for up to 3 days.

PERSIMMON, Hints on:

- Buy firm persimmons and ripen them for several days at room temperature.
- Eat when the skin is shriveled.
- Freeze. When defrosted they will be ripe and edible.

PICKLE JUICE, Uses for:

- Make mild homemade pickles by submerging cucumber slices, cauliflower, or other vegetables in the pickle jar containing the leftover juice. Refrigerate for 4 days.
- Use to season deviled eggs, egg or potato salad, or coleslaw.
- Combine with mayonnaise and ketchup for French dressing.

PIE, To dot with butter:

- Grate very cold butter over the surface instead, using a coarse grater.

PIE, To freeze:

- **Baked:** Let it cool to room temperature, then place an aluminum pie plate on top of the pie and tape the two plates together. Label and freeze.
- **Unbaked:** Freeze the whole unbaked pie. Bake at the regular temperature but for 15 to 20 minutes more than the usual 50 to 60 minutes. Freezing keeps the pie bottom crispy.

PIE, To prevent filling from boiling over:

- Insert a piece of tube-type macaroni in the center of the pie before baking. Or put a few pieces of a paper straw in the center.

PIE, To prevent filling from soaking bottom crust:

- Brush the crust lightly with egg white or melted butter or give it a light sprinkling of flour before adding the filling.
- Pierce a single-crust pie all over and brush the inside with 1 egg white lightly beaten with 1 teaspoon cold water. Chill for 30 minutes, then bake at 450°F for 5 minutes. Allow the crust to cool, then pour in the cooled filling and bake.
- Bake an unfilled pie shell in the middle of an upper shelf and bake a double-crust pie on a lower shelf.
- Place a baking sheet under the pie if using aluminum or tin, or set the pie on top of an upside-down cast-iron skillet.

- Bake in an aluminum pie pan with holes in the bottom. Or use a foil pie pan saved from a pie purchased from a pie shop. These pans usually have holes in the bottom.
- Butter the pie pan before putting in the pastry.

PIE CRUST, To give it a shine or glaze:
- Brush the crust before baking with milk, beaten egg, or lightly beaten egg mixed with 1 or 2 teaspoons water.
- Dissolve 1 teaspoon sugar in 1 teaspoon hot water and brush on the pastry before baking.
- Whip an egg white until frothy, brush it over the pie crust, then sprinkle with sugar. This will produce a lightly browned crispy crust.
- Take the pie out of the oven when it is almost baked and brush the top with vinegar, then place back in the oven for a few minutes. There will be no vinegar taste.

PIE PLATE SUBSTITUTE:
- Invert the flat top of a 2-quart ovenproof casserole dish and use for an 8-inch pie plate.

PIMIENTOS, To keep:
- Prevent them from spoiling once you've opened the jar by covering the remaining pimientos with vinegar, then refrigerate.

POPCORN, Hints on:
- Store unpopped corn in the freezer. Bring to room temperature before popping.
- Remoisten too-dry popcorn kernels by sprinkling with water and putting in a glass jar or plastic container for a few days. (Don't use too much water or the corn might mold.) Store in the refrigerator or freezer. If the corn is too moist, it won't pop well; if it is too dry, you'll have some burned kernels.
- Allow the oil to heat up until it barely starts to smoke. Corn pops much more quickly when the pan and oil are preheated.
- Add flavoring to the melted butter before pouring on the popcorn. Use minced garlic, onion salt, Parmesan cheese, blue cheese, etc.

POPOVERS, Hints on:
- Bring the milk and eggs to room temperature before mixing. Let the batter stand at room temperature for 30 to 60 minutes, then stir well before pouring it into the cups.

PORK CHOPS, BREADED, To reduce the fat:
- Bake them on a wire cake rack in a baking pan.

POT WATCHING, Hints on:
- Use a Pyrex pie plate for a cover so you can check the contents of the pot without having to lift up the lid constantly. This is a handy way to determine if the contents are simmering and not boiling.

POTATOES, To store:
- Keep them in a dark, dry, cool place. Don't put them in the refrigerator; the cold makes the starch change to sugar. Also don't store potatoes with onions; moisture from potatoes can cause onions to sprout. Store a few apples with extra potatoes to keep them from sprouting.

POTATOES, BAKED, To cook faster:
- Soak for 15 to 20 minutes in hot water. Add salt to the water, if desired.
- Bake potatoes on the floor of the oven instead of on a rack.
- Use potato nails so the heat is conducted quicker.
- Place the potatoes on the oven rack and invert a cast-iron pan or pot over them. This will cut baking time almost in half.
- Prick potatoes before cooking or as soon as they are soft inside to allow steam to escape and prevent them from becoming soggy.

POTATOES, BOILED, Hints on:
- Add 1 teaspoon white vinegar or fresh lemon juice to the cooking water, and the potatoes will always stay white. Or add a little milk to the water.
- Test for doneness with a toothpick or poultry skewer. It doesn't break up the potatoes as a knife does.

POTATOES, MASHED: Hints on:
- Warm the butter and milk before adding to the potatoes to keep them light and fluffy.
- Add ¼ teaspoon baking powder to the potatoes while mashing and beating to make them much lighter.
- Add some powdered milk to overcooked potatoes that are soggy after mashing.
- Keep them on hold before serving by placing a cotton or linen napkin over the pot, then putting a pan lid on the top of the napkin. The napkin will absorb the steam.

POTATOES, ROASTED, To make crisp and crusty:

- Parboil for about 5 minutes, dry, then roll in seasoned flour and bake as usual with the roast.
- Parboil and dry, then scratch a crisscross pattern with a fork into the potatoes before putting them into the hot fat in the oven.

POULTRY, To keep fresh:

- Remove the original wrapping and wrap the poultry loosely in wax paper to allow air to circulate around it.
- Salt fresh chicken immediately if you cannot cook it right away. This will prevent spoiling and enables you to keep it a day or two longer before cooking.
- Place a large peeled onion inside a bird that is not to be used or cooked for a day or two.

POULTRY, To truss:

- Use unwaxed, unflavored dental floss.
- Cover the cavity with a piece of bread to keep the dressing in place.
- Use one or two pieces of raw potato to seal the cavity.

POULTRY RACK/HOLDER SUBSTITUTE:

- Tear off two strips of heavy-duty foil about 4 inches wide. Fold each piece lengthwise to measure ½ inch. Lay the strips in the baking pan, positioned where the weight of the bird will be placed, then place the bird on top. When the bird is cooked, lift it from the pan using the foil strips as holders, then slide them out.
- Place the bird on a bed of washed celery stalks, which will serve as a rack and keep it from sticking.

PRESSURE COOKER, To reduce cooking time:

- Boil the water before adding it to the ingredients in the cooker to reduce the time necessary to bring the cooker to the pressure point.

PRICKLY PEARS, To select:

- Buy them large and ripen at room temperature, then refrigerate.

PUDDING, SUET, To lighten:

- Use equal amounts of stale bread, soaked in cold water and thoroughly squeezed, and suet. The pudding will be much lighter.

PUMPKIN, Hint on:

- Use an electric mixer to beat fresh pumpkin. The strings will wind around the beaters and be easy to remove.

PUMPKIN PIE SPICE, To make:

- Mix together 4 teaspoons cinnamon, 2 teaspoons ginger, 2 teaspoons nutmeg, 1 teaspoon allspice, and 1 teaspoon cloves.

PUNCH, Hint on:

- Mix a small batch of punch beforehand and freeze in ice-cube trays, a tube pan, or any other suitable container. Using these prevents the punch from getting diluted while standing. Put pieces of fruit in the mold for a decorative effect.

RECIPE CARD, To keep handy:

- Slip it between the tines of a fork and stand the fork in a glass.

RICE, Hints on:

- Add 1 tablespoon butter or oil to the water before adding the rice. Doing so will prevent it from becoming gummy or sticking to the pan.
- Add ½ teaspoon lemon juice to the water when cooking to make rice whiter and fluffier.
- Keep it on hold by covering the pot with a dish towel, then the pan lid. Or place it in a 250°F oven to keep warm.
- Freeze leftover rice in small portions in freezer bags. To serve, heat the rice (without defrosting) in the microwave on high for 2 minutes per 1 cup. Toss after 1 minute.

ROLLING PIN SUBSTITUTE:

- Fill a wine bottle or other glass bottle with ice water.

ROLLS, To keep warm longer:

- Heat a piece of ceramic tile in the oven at the same time you're baking or warming the rolls, then wrap the tile in a napkin and put in the bottom of the bread basket. Be sure to set the basket on a trivet. Or set the hot tile on a trivet and put the bread basket on top.
- Line the bread basket with heavy-duty foil, and put a napkin on top of the foil, then fold it over the rolls.

ROLLS, STALE, To freshen:

- Sprinkle or spray the rolls lightly with cold water, then place them in a brown paper bag or wrap in foil. Heat in a 300°F oven for 15 minutes or a 375° or 400°F oven for about 5 minutes. They will taste freshly baked.
- Place them in a wet paper bag and put in a 450°F oven until the bag is dry.

- Sprinkle the rolls with cold water, then wrap them in paper towels and microwave on high for 5 to 10 seconds.

SALAD DRESSING: See "Oil and Vinegar Dressing, Homemade, Hints on."

SALT, Hint on:
- Add a pinch of salt to sweet dishes to bring out the flavor.

SALT, To keep free-flowing:
- Keep uncooked rice inside the salt shaker. Or keep a small jelly glass inverted over the shaker top.

SALTED FOOD, To remove excess salt:
- Add 1 teaspoon sugar mixed with 1 tablespoon white vinegar to the food.
- Add several slices of raw potato and let them cook in the mixture for 6 or 7 minutes, then remove the potato slices. The potato slices will absorb the excess salt.

SANDWICHES, Hints on:
- Use salad dressing instead of mayonnaise when freezing. Mayonnaise tends to separate after freezing.
- Use 2 thin slices of meat instead of 1 thick one. Then spread the lettuce, tomatoes, and mayonnaise in the middle to keep the bread from getting soggy.
- Carry the lettuce, tomatoes, and pickles separately, then add to the sandwich when ready to eat.

SAUSAGES, LINK, To prevent cracking and curling:
- Roll link sausages in flour before cooking to prevent them from cracking open when frying.
- Join together small sausage links with toothpicks to prevent curling when you fry them and make turning them easier. Use poultry skewers for larger sausages when broiling them.

SAUTÉ, Explanation of:
- Brown food quickly or cook food in a small amount of fat.

SCALLOPS, To prevent shrinking:
- Soak in beer for 1 hour before cooking to prevent them from shrinking.

SEASONED SALT, To make:
- Mix together 4 tablespoons salt, 1 tablespoon pepper, 1 tablespoon paprika, 1 teaspoon onion powder, and 1 teaspoon garlic powder. Store in a spice shaker.

SESAME SEEDS, To make more digestible:
* Toast them in the oven.

SHORTENING, To measure:
* Beat or drop the eggs in the measuring cup first. Empty into the bowl, then measure the shortening in the same cup. The shortening will slip out easily.
* Use the displacement method. If you need ½ cup shortening, fill a measuring cup with ½ cup water, then add solid shortening until water level reaches 1 cup. Drain off water and the shortening will come right out without scraping.

SHORTENING, To reuse:
* Keep shortening clean after deep-fat frying by pouring 1 tablespoon boiling water into the container of hot fat. The water will sink to the bottom carrying the impurities with it.

SIFTER SUBSTITUTE:
* Use a sieve and push the flour or confectioner's sugar through it with the back of a spoon.

SHRIMP, FROZEN, Hint on:
* Soak frozen shrimp in ice-cold salted water for 10 minutes before using to improve the flavor.
* Soak completely thawed shrimp in lemon juice for 10 minutes.

SODA DRINKS, To keep after opening:
* Put the cap on loosely and squeeze the plastic bottle until the liquid comes as close to the top as possible, then quickly tighten the cap. Excluding the air helps to keep the fizz.

SOUP, To thicken:
* Add mashed potatoes or instant mashed potato flakes.
* Use more vegetables than called for and puree them in the blender with some of the soup. Return the puree to the soup.

SOUP BONES, To cook:
* Add vinegar to the water when cooking bones for soup. It will draw out calcium from the bones into the soup broth. Add 1 ounce vinegar to 1 quart water, or up to 4 ounces vinegar. No vinegar taste will remain in the final product.
* Brown the bones in the oven for maximum flavor before adding to the soup.

SPICES AND HERBS, See "Herbs and Spices, Hints on."

SPINACH, Hint on:
- Revive ready-to-cook spinach sold in a plastic bag by soaking it in cold water for 20 minutes before cooking. Doing so will allow it to swell up.

SQUASH, WINTER, Hints on:
- Poke holes in the squash and microwave it on high for a couple of minutes, then let stand for a few minutes before cutting.
- Grate the squash and sauté it with a cover for 3 to 5 minutes if you are short of time.

STEAMER SUBSTITUTE:
- Use an aluminum pie tin with holes poked in it. Pour ¼ to ½ inch water into a pan with a slightly large diameter, put the pie tin in the pot, rim side down, and put the vegetables on top of the pie tin.
- Use a footed metal colander set in a large pan.

STOCK, VEGETABLE, To make:
- Save time by not peeling garlic, onions, and vegetables if stock is to be strained later. Just wash and cut them into large chunks.
- Cook stock no more than 1 hour. It will look and taste light, which is what vegetable stock is supposed to be like; cooking longer will extract bitter flavors.
- Save all well-washed vegetable peelings and trimmings in a jar or plastic bag in the refrigerator. When you have enough, put them in a pan, cover with cold water, add salt, and bring to a boil. Cover and simmer for 20 minutes, then strain immediately and cool.

STRAWBERRIES, Hint on:
- Wash before serving, not before storing, and wash prior to removing the stems so the juice will not run out. Serve at room temperature for a more intense flavor; however, the flavor deteriorates if strawberries are allowed to stand at room temperature for more than 30 minutes after preparing.

STRAWBERRY HULLER SUBSTITUTE:
- Remove the stems with the end of a vegetable peeler.

SUGAR, GRANULATED, To keep from lumping:
- Put a few soda crackers in the container.

SUGAR, SUPERFINE, SUBSTITUTE:
- Blend regular sugar in small batches at high speed.

SWEET POTATOES, COOKING, Hints on:
- Scrub, pierce with a fork, and bake on a foil-lined jelly-roll pan at 400°F for 30 to 60 minutes until tender. Or wrap each potato individually in foil, then bake.
- Peel, cut in chunks, and boil for 10 to 15 minutes until tender.

TACO SEASONING MIX, To make:
- Mix 3 teaspoons chili powder, 2 teaspoons cumin, 2 teaspoons paprika, ½ teaspoon onion powder, 1 teaspoon garlic powder, and ¼ teaspoon cayenne pepper. Use half as much as the commercial mix, or season to taste.

TEA LEAVES, USED, To recycle:
- Save them in the refrigerator, and when you have enough, pour boiling water on them and leave for 1 hour. Use the liquid to clean mirrors and windows, wash varnished surfaces, or fertilize plants, especially ferns.

TOMATO PASTE, LEFTOVER, To store:
- Place in a small container or babyfood jar and pour vegetable oil over the top, then refrigerate. When ready to use, pour the oil off.
- Flash-freeze in 1-tablespoon portions, then place in a small container or freezer bag. This makes measuring easy and no defrosting is necessary.
- Consider buying tomato paste in a tube. It will keep for months in the refrigerator after opening, and you can squeeze out just the amount you need.

TOMATO SAUCE, LEFTOVER, To store:
- Freeze the sauce in ice-cube trays, then put them in a freezer bag.

TOMATOES, To freeze for cooking:
- Core tomatoes. Put a few in a large wire-mesh strainer and dip in boiling water for 2 to 3 minutes, depending on size. Remove the strainer and immediately put the tomatoes into ice water to stop the cooking. When the tomatoes are cool enough to handle, peel them and pack into freezer containers or bags. They will keep for up to a year.
- Place whole unblanched tomatoes on baking sheets and freeze. When frozen, store in plastic bags. When ready to use, the skins will have cracked and be easy to remove. Or hold the frozen tomatoes under hot water for a few seconds. The skins will slip right off.

TOMATOES, To peel:
- Dip 2 or 3 at a time in boiling water for 5 to 30 seconds (depending on ripeness), then into ice water. For easy removal put the tomatoes in a mesh bag or a large wire-mesh strainer for dipping.
- Microwave them on high for 15 to 20 seconds, then let them cool so you can handle them.
- Impale a tomato on a cooking fork and hold it over the flame of the stove's gas jet until the skin bursts.

TOMATOES, GREEN, To ripen:
- Wrap tomatoes individually in newspaper and store in a cool dark place; they will ripen uniformly.
- Seal them in a plastic bag or container with a couple of ripe apples.

TURKEY GIBLETS, To cook conserving energy:
- Cook in the oven along with the turkey. Place the giblets, neck, and ingredients used to make the stock in a casserole barely covered with water. Cover the dish, place it in the oven, and cook at the same time as the turkey.

TURKEY RACK/HOLDER SUBSTITUTE: See "Poultry Rack/Holder Substitute."

TURNIPS, COOKING, Hints on:
- Avoid cooking in aluminum or iron pots as the turnips will discolor.
- Slice turnips and steam until tender. Or shred them and sauté in a little butter, then add a little water and steam them for 3 to 5 minutes or until tender.
- Put turnip slices in a shallow baking dish. Sprinkle with a little water, cover, and bake in a 350°F oven about 30 to 45 minutes until tender.

VEGETABLE DIP DISH, To make:
- Use a red, green, or yellow bell pepper. Cut the top off the pepper, and remove the seeds and inner fibers. Stand it on end in the middle of a vegetable platter to hold the dip. Trim the bottom end if necessary so it will stand erect.
- Use a hollowed-out small red or green cabbage, a hollowed-out head of bib lettuce, or a large beefsteak tomato.

VEGETABLE NONSTICK SPRAY, To make: See "Nonstick Cooking Spray, To make."

VEGETABLES, To cook:
- Start those that grow underground in cold water and cook without a cover or covered loosely.
- Start anything that grows aboveground in boiling water and with a cover.
- Try cooking strong-flavored vegetables in milk. Greens, cabbage, turnips, chard, kale, spinach, brussels spouts, cauliflower, and broccoli. Doing so will reduce the cooking smell and make the vegetables milder tasting. Use the cooking milk to make a white or cheese sauce.

VEGETABLES, GREEN, Hints on:
- Perk up slightly wilted vegetables by soaking them facedown in cold or ice water to which 1 teaspoon white vinegar or lemon juice has been added.
- Add 1 teaspoon lemon juice or white vinegar when cooking to help them retain their color. Or blanch them in a large pot of slightly salted, rapidly boiling water, which will accomplish the same thing.

VEGETABLES, ROOT, Hint on:
- Peel, grate, or shred, then sauté them in a little oil or butter. Add a small amount of water and cover, then steam them for 3 to 5 minutes or until tender.

VEGETABLES, STEAMED, Timetable:

Asparagus:	8 minutes
Beets, medium:	40–45 minutes
Brussels sprouts:	8–10 minutes
Broccoli:	10–12 minutes
Carrots, sliced:	20 minutes
Cauliflower, florets:	6–10 minutes
Corn on the cob:	6–10 minutes
Green beans, whole:	20–25 minutes
Onions, small white:	15 minutes
Peas:	15 minutes
Potatoes, new:	20–25 minutes
Spinach:	5 minutes
Squash, summer, sliced:	10 minutes

- Cut vegetables that require longer cooking times into thinner pieces when you are steaming mixed vegetables and don't want to keep an eye on the clock or let the steam escape by removing the lid often.

WAX PAPER LINERS OF CEREAL BOXES, Uses for:
- Save for crushing cracker crumbs; shaking chicken, cutlets, or fish in coating; microwaving vegetables; packing sandwiches for a picnic lunch; mixing ingredients for a meatloaf; or open up to roll small amounts of dough.

WHEAT, Substitutes for:
Substitute 1 cup wheat flour for one of the following if you are allergic to wheat.

1 cup barley flour
1 cup corn flour
¾ cup coarse cornmeal
1 cup fine cornmeal
1⅓ cups oat flour
⅝ cup potato starch flour
⅞ cup rice flour
1¼ cups rye flour

WHITE SAUCE, To avoid lumps:
- Add 1 tablespoon cold water to the butter and flour before adding the milk, and the sauce will not become lumpy.

WINE, To chill faster:
- Put the bottle in a bucket filled with ice and water instead of just ice. It will cool much faster.
- Put the bottle in a bucket, lay the ice around the bottom, and sprinkle it with a few tablespoons of table salt. Keep adding salt and ice until it reaches the neck of the bottle, then fill the container with tepid water. The bottle will be chilled in 10 minutes.

WINE, LEFTOVER, To keep:
- Pour into the smallest jar possible and cover it with an airtight lid.
- Save it for future cooking needs by pouring a little vegetable oil into the bottle. The oil floats and seals out the air that can turn wine into vinegar. Pour off the oil when ready to use the wine.
- Freeze less-then-full bottles of wine in their original containers. There must be enough space for the wine to expand. After thawing, decant the wine before serving, as the sediment may have increased slightly. Storing wine in the refrigerator hurts its quality.

YEAST, To prove:
- Dissolve 1 tablespoon or 1 package yeast in 3 tablespoons warm water

(110°F), then add 1 tablespoon flour or ¼ teaspoon sugar. If in 5 minutes it begins to foam, the yeast is alive..

YEAST, To store:
- Store it in the refrigerator and bring it to room temperature before using. Or to prolong its life almost indefinitely, keep it in the freezer in a well-sealed, moisture-proof container.

YOGURT MAKING, Hints on:
- Thicken and enrich yogurt made from low-fat milk by adding powdered milk. Usually ½ cup to 1 quart liquid is sufficient.
- Firm it by adding 1 teaspoon carrot or tomato juice to every 1 cup milk. Add the juice to the prewarmed milk when you add the yogurt starter.
- Buy yogurt culture as a starter or use pure yogurt that does not contain a stabilizer. Ask at your health food store for suggestions. The Continental brand is a pure yogurt.
- Incubate yogurt in an insulted picnic cooler filled with crumpled newspaper, in a gas oven with just the pilot light burning, in an electric oven with the oven light on (preheat the oven to the lowest setting first, then turn it off before putting the yogurt in), on a heating pad and covered with a towel and newspapers (or put a large inverted pot on top of the towel instead of newspapers), or in a wide-mouth Thermos bottle.
- Avoid disturbing the yogurt during the incubating period and while it is cooling.

YORKSHIRE PUDDING, Hints on:
- Let the batter sit for 1 hour or so before baking.
- Add 1 tablespoon hot water to the batter before putting it into the hot fat.
- Use hot milk for a light, crispy pudding. Heat half the milk until very hot, then add it last to the beaten flour, egg(s) and milk.
- Use small round tins. The pudding will puff and be very light.

ZIPPER FREEZER BAGS, Hint on:
- Prevent freezer burn by expelling all the air. Remove as much air as possible and close the bag, but leave enough space to insert a straw. Suck out any remaining air, then remove the straw and quickly zip the bag closed.

SUBSTITUTIONS FOR COMMON INGREDIENTS

Allspice: 1 teaspoon = 1 teaspoon cinnamon plus ⅛ teaspoon ground cloves

Arrowroot: 1 tablespoon = 2 tablespoons all-purpose flour or 1 tablespoon cornstarch

Baking powder: 1 teaspoon = ¼ teaspoon baking soda plus ½ teaspoon cream of tartar

Baking powder, double acting: 1 teaspoon = 1¼ teaspoons tartrate or phosphate baking powder

Beef stock: 1 cup = 1 cup water plus 2 teaspoons tamari, OR soy sauce, OR 1 cup water plus a bouillon cube or instant bouillon

Bread crumbs: 1 cup = 1 cup crushed cornflakes or ¾ cup cracker crumbs

Broth, chicken or beef: 1 cup = 1 bouillon cube or 1 envelope instant broth dissolved in 1 cup boiling water

Brown sugar, light: 1 cup = ½ cup dark brown plus ½ cup granulated sugar

Butter: 1 cup = 1 cup vegetable shortening plus ½ teaspoon salt

Buttermilk: 1 cup = 1 cup plain yogurt, OR 1 cup whole milk plus 1 tablespoon lemon juice or white vinegar (let stand 5 minutes for lemon juice and 10 minutes for vinegar), OR ½ cup plain nonfat yogurt mixed with ½ cup skim milk

Cayenne: ⅛ teaspoon = 3 to 4 drops of pepper sauce or Tabasco sauce

Celery seed substitute: Use finely chopped celery leaves

Chocolate (unsweetened): 1 square (1 ounce) = 3 tablespoons cocoa plus 1 tablespoon butter or shortening

Corn syrup, dark: 1 cup = ¾ cup light corn syrup plus ¼ cup light molasses, OR 1¼ cups packed brown sugar plus ¼ cup water

Corn syrup, light: 1 cup = 1¼ cups granulated sugar plus ¼ cup water

Cornstarch for thickening: 1 tablespoon = 2 tablespoons all-purpose flour or 1 tablespoon arrowroot

Cracker crumbs, fine: ¾ cup = 1 cup fine dry bread crumbs

Cream, heavy (not for whipping): 1 cup = ¾ cup milk plus ⅓ cup melted butter

Cream, light:	1 cup = ⅞ cup milk plus 3 tablespoons melted butter
Cream, sour:	1 cup = ⅞ cup buttermilk or plain yogurt plus 3 tablespoons melted butter
Cream, sour, for dip:	1 cup = 1 cup plain nonfat yogurt
Cream, whipping:	1 cup = ⅔ cup well-chilled evaporated milk, whipped, OR 1 cup nonfat dry milk powder whipped with 1 cup ice water
Creamer for tea or coffee:	Use instant nonfat powdered milk
Egg, whole for baking:	1 = 2 egg whites plus 1 tablespoon cooking oil and 1⅓ tablespoons liquid to make up for the fat in the egg yolk, OR 1 heaping tablespoon soy flour and 1 tablespoon water. OR for baking cookies 2 egg yolks plus 1 tablespoon water
Flour, all-purpose:	1 cup = 1⅛ cups cake flour, OR ⅝ cup potato flour, OR 1 cup fine cornmeal, OR 1 cup barley flour
Flour, self-rising:	1 cup = 1 cup all-purpose flour plus ⅓ teaspoon baking powder plus ¼ teaspoon salt, OR 1 cup all-purpose flour plus 1 teaspoon baking soda plus 2 teaspoons cream of tartar
Fruit juice:	1 cup for cooking = 1 cup brewed spicy herb tea
Garlic:	1 small clove = ⅛ teaspoon garlic powder or instant minced garlic
Gravy browner:	Use strong coffee or instant coffee granules
Half and half:	1 cup = ⅞ cup milk plus 1½ tablespoons melted butter
Herbs, dried:	1 teaspoon = 1 tablespoon fresh, minced and packed
Herbs, fresh:	1 tablespoon = 1 teaspoon dried herbs
Honey:	1 cup = 1¼ cup granulated sugar plus ½ cup liquid, OR ¾ cup sugar plus ¼ cup liquid

Ketchup/chili sauce: 1 cup = 1 cup tomato sauce plus
2 tablespoons granulated sugar,
1 tablespoon vinegar, and ⅛ teaspoon
ground cloves

Lemon juice: 1 teaspoon = 2 teaspoons vinegar
Lemon rind, grated: 1 teaspoon = ½ teaspoon lemon extract
Mace substitute: Nutmeg
Marshmallows: 1 large one = 10 small ones
Milk, skim: 1 cup = ⅓ cup instant nonfat dry milk
plus about ¾ cup water

Milk, whole: 1 cup = ½ cup evaporated milk plus
½ cup water, OR 1 cup water, ⅓ cup
instant nonfat dry milk, and 2 teaspoons
melted butter, OR 1 cup skim milk plus
2 teaspoons melted butter

Mustard, prepared: 1 teaspoon = ¼ teaspoon dry mustard plus
¾ teaspoon vinegar

Nonstick cooking spray: Mix 5 ounces vegetable oil and 1 ounce
vodka in a spray bottle.

Oil for baking: Substitute an equal amount of applesauce
for oil

Onion, chopped: 1 small = 1 tablespoon instant minced
onion, OR 1 teaspoon onion powder,
OR ¼ cup frozen chopped onions

Parsley substitute: Celery leaves
Red pepper sauce: 3 to 4 drops = ⅛ teaspoon cayenne pepper
Saffron substitute: Turmeric
Shortening: 1 cup = 1 cup plus 2 tablespoons butter or
margarine, OR ⅔ cup oil for baking

Sour cream for dip: 1 cup = 1 cup plain nonfat yogurt
Steak sauce: Mix equal parts of Worcestershire sauce
and ketchup

Sugar: 1 cup = 1 cup firmly packed brown sugar,
OR 1¾ cups confectioner's sugar (do
not substitute in baking), OR 2 cups
corn syrup, OR 1 cup superfine sugar

Sugar, brown: 1 cup = 1 cup granulated sugar mixed with
2 to 4 tablespoons dark molasses,
depending if the sugar called for is light
or dark brown (mix thoroughly with a
fork to distribute molasses)

Sugar, confectioner's: 1 cup = 1 cup granulated sugar plus 1 tablespoon cornstarch. Blend several minutes at high speed.

Sugar, refined or superfine, for baking: 1 cup = ⅔ cup honey or pure maple syrup plus 3 tablespoons extra flour, OR blend small batches of granulated sugar in a blender at high speed

Tabasco sauce: 3 to 4 drops = ⅛ teaspoon cayenne pepper

Tomato juice: 1 cup = ½ cup tomato sauce plus ½ cup water plus dash each salt and sugar, OR ¼ cup tomato paste plus ¾ cup water plus dash each salt and sugar

Tomato ketchup: 1 cup = 1 cup tomato sauce plus 2 tablespoons sugar, 1 tablespoon vinegar, and ⅛ teaspoon ground gloves

Tomato paste: 1 tablespoon = 1 tablespoon ketchup, OR stir and heat to the bubbly stage 1 teaspoon flour mixed with 6 tablespoons tomato sauce

Tomato puree: 1 cup = ½ cup tomato paste plus ½ cup water

Tomato soup: 1 can (10½ ounce) = 1 cup tomato sauce plus ¼ cup water

Tomatoes, canned: 1 cup = ½ cup tomato sauce plus ½ cup water, OR 1⅓ cups chopped fresh tomatoes, simmered

Vanilla: 1-inch bean = 1 teaspoon vanilla extract

Vinegar, white: 1 teaspoon = 2 teaspoons lemon juice

Wine, dry white: ¼ cup = ⅓ cup dry white vermouth, OR use chicken broth for savory dishes and apple, pineapple, or orange juice for sweet foods or desserts

Worcestershire sauce: Diluted steak sauce (half and half with water) or plain soy sauce

Yeast: 1 cake (¾ ounce) = 1 package active dried yeast, OR 2 teaspoons granulated baking yeast

Furniture

ALUMINUM, CHROME, STAINLESS STEEL, WROUGHT IRON, To clean:
- Wash with mild liquid detergent and water, then rinse and dry thoroughly. Once a year, apply a coat of automobile wax.
- Clean stainless steel with a little ammonia and water, a spray glass cleaner, or a commercial product made for the purpose.
- Clean dirty aluminum frames with extra-fine (000) steel wool and a little kerosene. Or use aluminum cleaner.
- Cover scratches on wrought iron with matching exterior paint applied with a small artist's brush or cotton-tipped swab.

BAMBOO, CANE, REED, Care of:
- Wash with warm soapy water. When dry, apply a little linseed oil.
- Wash with ¼ cup salt and 1 tablespoon washing soda per quart of water, then dry and apply linseed oil.
- Wet and dry in the sun to shrink sagging seats back to normal.
- Protect with a coat of clear shellac.

CARVED FURNITURE, To dust:
- Dust with a clean dry paintbrush or a baby's hair brush or other soft brush.

FURNITURE POLISH, To make:
- Add 1 tablespoon lemon oil to 1 quart bottle mineral oil. Shake to mix.
- Mix 1 cup olive oil and ⅓ cup white vinegar until well blended. Apply to the furniture with a clean, soft cloth.
- Mix equal parts raw linseed oil and turpentine and store in a sealed jar or bottle. Use by applying a thin film with a soft cloth and buffing to a shine with a clean cloth.

GARDEN FURNITURE, ACRYLIC MESH, To clean:
- Wash with sudsy lukewarm water. Rinse thoroughly, then air-dry.

GARDEN FURNITURE, METAL, To prevent rust:
- Melt ¼ cup lanolin and 1 cup petroleum jelly in a double boiler or con-

tainer set in a pan of hot water. Stir until melted, then remove from the heat and let it cool slightly. Use while still warm and let it dry on the furniture.

GARDEN FURNITURE, PLASTIC MESH, To clean:
- Wash with a mild detergent, chlorine bleach, and lukewarm water. Use ⅓ cup bleach to each 1 gallon water. Rinse thoroughly and let air-dry.

GARDEN FURNITURE, WOODEN, To maintain:
- Rub with linseed oil periodically to prevent the wood from cracking.

HEAVY FURNITURE, To move on bare floors:
- Put small, thick rugs or bath mats under the two back legs, then tilt the furniture back and slide to the new location.
- Slip an old heavy sock over each leg, then slide or pull it across the floor.
- Slide scraps of old carpeting, facedown, under the furniture legs.

LACQUERED FURNITURE, To clean without removing lacquer:
- Stir ¼ cup flour and ¼ cup olive oil into a paste. Smooth on the wood with a soft cloth, then wipe off with a clean cloth. Buff to a gloss with a dry clean cloth.
- Wipe the entire surface with a cloth dampened in lemon oil. Remoisten the cloth as necessary.

LEATHER-COVERED FURNITURE, FADED, To renew:
- Mix 2 parts linseed oil and 1 part white vinegar in a jar and wipe it on with a soft cloth.

OIL FINISH AND FRENCH POLISH FURNITURE, To clean:
- Rub the surface with a cloth lightly sprinkled with boiled linseed oil.

PAINTED FURNITURE, DECALS ON, To remove:
- Lay a sponge saturated with white vinegar on the decal. Leave on until the decal has softened, then peel or scrape off the decal with a plastic scrubber.

PAPER STUCK ON POLISHED TABLE, To remove:
- Saturate the paper with cooking oil or mayonnaise. Leave until the paper is softened, then wipe off.
- Paint the paper with white vinegar and let it soak in, then scrape it off gently.
- Wet it with boiled linseed oil and let soak awhile, then peel it up gently. Clean with a mild soap and water solution, then rewax.

PLASTIC AND VINYL FURNITURE, Ballpoint pen ink, To remove:

- Dip a cotton swab in rubbing alcohol and gently dab at the stain. Wipe with a damp sponge after removal, then recondition the vinyl.

PLASTIC AND VINYL FURNITURE, To maintain:

- Dust and wipe up spills regularly. Wash with mild detergent and warm water. Rinse and dry.
- Dissolve ¼ cup washing soda thoroughly in 1 cup boiling water. Let it cool, then, while wearing rubber gloves, saturate a sponge with the mixture and rub it over the upholstery. Rinse thoroughly with clean water.
- Do not use chemical cleaners or acids on plastic furniture.

UPHOLSTERED FURNITURE, To maintain:

- Remove all dust and dirt with the upholstery attachment of the vacuum cleaner or a soft brush or whisk broom, depending on the finish. Then clean the soiled pieces by one of the methods listed below:
- Heat some bran and rub well into the soiled parts. When all the dirt has been removed, brush off all traces of bran.
- Wash with a sponge dipped in the suds of a mild detergent and water. (Whip up the suds in a blender.) Rub the foam in gently on a small area using a circular motion. Work on one area at a time and overlap the areas. Scrape the suds off with a spatula and wipe the spatula on a paper towel. Wet the sponge in clean rinse water, wring it out well, then wipe the area. Dry with an electric fan.
- Clean as above but use shaving cream instead of suds.
- Use a spray-on dry-cleaning product made for cars. Coral Dri-Clean Upholstery and Carpet Cleaner is good for small jobs. Purchase it at automotive stores.

UPHOLSTERED FURNITURE ARM COVERS, To keep in place:

- Lay a sheet of art foam between the arm covers and the armrest. (Buy the foam at art supply stores.)

UPHOLSTERED FURNITURE, CAT-CLAWED, To fix:

- Shave the area with a single-edge razor blade or snip it smooth with manicure scissors.

UPHOLSTERED FURNITURE, STAINS ON, To remove:

- Spray shaving cream on the stain as an emergency measure, then rinse and blot dry. Or dab with club soda and blot up.
- **Alcohol:** Blot with a clean cloth, then sponge with cold water. Finally,

sponge the fabric with a mixture of 1 part white vinegar and 4 parts water, and let dry.

- **Blood stain:** Cover the spot with a paste of cornstarch and water. Rub it on and allow to dry. When dry, brush off the cornstarch and repeat if needed. Or use a cleaner that contains natural enzymes, such as Nature's Miracle, sold in pet stores.
- **Coffee, tea, fruit juice, or soft drinks:** Blot up, then sponge with a solution of 1 teaspoon liquid dishwashing detergent and 1 cup cool water. Squeeze the sponge well to avoid overwetting the fabric. Finally, sponge with clean water and let dry. If the stain persists, sponge with a mixture of 1 part white vinegar and 4 parts water and let dry.
- **Grease marks:** Rub gently with a cloth and dry-cleaning fluid. Work from the outer edge of the stain inward. Repeat with another cloth wrung out in a solution of warm water and liquid detergent. Rinse well. This works well for sofa or chair headrests and arms.

VARNISHED FURNITURE, To clean:
- Rub with a cloth dipped in cool tea. Tea does not impair the gloss as soap and water does.
- Use ½ cup white vinegar to 1 quart water.
- Use a commercial oil soap and follow directions on the label.
- Wipe with a cloth dampened in lemon oil, remoistening as necessary.

VELVET FURNITURE, To clean:
- Brush with a piece of crumpled nylon net.

WICKER FURNITURE, Care of:
- Dust with a clean, dry paintbrush or scrub brush.
- Prevent it from drying out by applying lemon oil occasionally.
- Prevent white wicker from turning yellow by washing it with a solution of warm salt water.

WOOD FURNITURE, To clean:
- Wet a washcloth and wring out as much water as possible. Wipe the furniture surface with the damp washcloth. Dry immediately with a clean, soft dry cloth. You can remove sticky fingerprints and dust safely from wood surfaces using this method, but furniture with an oil finish needs an oil-based cleaner.
- Sprinkle a soft absorbent cloth lightly with water and then sprinkle lightly with furniture polish. Roll it up and let it sit a few minutes before using. This will remove finger marks and smudges.
- Add 1 teaspoon olive oil to ¼ cup white vinegar. Saturate a soft cloth

in the solution and wring out well. The white vinegar cleans and the oil feeds the wood. You can use the vinegar-and-oil cloth repeatedly as a dusting cloth. Use less vinegar if furniture is highly waxed.
- See also "Wood Furniture, Dirty, Grimy, To clean."

WOOD FURNITURE, ADHESIVE LABELS ON, To remove:
- Rub with a cloth dipped in cooking oil.

WOOD FURNITURE, ALCOHOL STAIN ON, To remove:
- Wipe up spilled alcohol, medicines, perfumes, and lotions instantly and rub the spot with any of the following: olive oil, oil polish, paste wax, linseed oil. Or dip a damp cloth in ammonia and quickly pass it over the stain. Don't rub.
- Polish as usual after the stain is removed.

WOOD FURNITURE, ALCOHOL STAIN, OLD, To remove:
- Mix rottenstone or powdered pumice to a thin paste with raw or boiled linseed oil, mineral oil, or cooking oil. Rub lightly in the direction of the grain, then wipe with another cloth dampened with plain linseed oil. Repeat as many times as necessary, then polish. Do not use on highly polished furniture. (Obtain rottenstone, powdered pumice, and raw and boiled linseed oil from a hardware or paint supply store.)

WOOD FURNITURE, BURN MARK ON, To remove:
- Rub the burn stain with silver polish.
- Rub it with a paste made of fine fireplace ash and lemon juice, then wipe the area clean.
- Sand out the burn by wrapping sandpaper around the eraser end of a pencil and rolling the sandpaper in the burned area until it is removed. Or scrape away the discoloration with a small dull knife. Fill in the depression with a wax filler stick or crayon or stain the area with an appropriate stain. Next, either varnish the spot, then feather the edges of the touch-up with super-fine steel wool (grade 0000), or apply clear fingernail polish and let it harden. Repeat the application of nail polish until the depression is filled. Let harden, then wax as usual.
- Use rottenstone or finely powdered pumice, mixed to a thin paste with raw or boiled linseed oil. Rub in the direction of the grain. Wipe with another cloth moistened with plain linseed oil. Repeat, if necessary, then polish. (See also "Wood Furniture, Scratches on, To conceal.")

WOOD FURNITURE, CANDLE WAX ON, To remove:
- Scrape away as much of the wax as you can with a credit card or plastic spatula. Wash off the remainder with a cloth dipped in mild, warm

soapsuds, and wrung out, or wipe with a cloth moistened with a cleaning fluid, then polish.

- Harden the wax with an ice cube, remove as much wax as you can, then rub the spot with liquid wax and wipe dry. Repeat until the spot is removed.
- Blow warm air from a hair dryer on the wax. Remove the softened wax with paper towels, then rub with a mixture of white vinegar and water.

WOOD FURNITURE, DENTS IN, To remove:

- Pour a little hot water into the depression, wait 5 minutes, then wipe with a clean cloth.
- Place either a heavy damp cloth or a piece of brown paper folded 5 or 6 times and saturated with hot water on the dented part. Hold a medium-hot iron on the cloth or paper until it begins to dry. Repeat by dampening the cloth or paper until the dent is raised.

WOOD FURNITURE, DIRTY, GRIMY, To clean:

- Combine 3 tablespoons boiled linseed oil, 1 tablespoon turpentine and 1 quart warm water. Apply with a cloth dipped in the solution and well wrung out, then quickly go over it with a clean, dry cloth. Remove any residue with a cloth dipped in ¼ teaspoon dishwashing detergent and 1 quart cool water and well wrung out. Dry well and rewax.
- Mix equal parts of boiled linseed oil and mineral spirits. Warm the mixture slightly by standing the container in a pan of hot water, then rub it on with a cloth.
- Wash with any good commercial oil soap following directions.

WOOD FURNITURE, GREASE SPOTS ON, To remove:

- Wipe with a cloth moistened with cleaning fluid, then polish.

WOOD FURNITURE, NAIL POLISH SPILLED ON, To remove:

- Let dry, then gently scrape off the nail polish with a credit card. Wax the surface with olive oil or furniture polish using superfine (No. 0000) steel wool, then polish dry.

WOOD FURNITURE, OLD, To recondition:

- Mix 2 parts turpentine to 1 part linseed oil and apply with a soft cloth. Rub in the solution, then polish with a dry cloth.
- Mix equal parts of turpentine, linseed oil, and white vinegar. Rub in the solution, then polish with a soft dry cloth.
- Coat the item with linseed oil and leave it on for at least a week to feed the wood. Then polish with beeswax.

WOOD FURNITURE, OLD, MUSTY SMELL IN, To eliminate:
- Spray the drawers with 2 teaspoons Australian tea tree oil mixed with 2 cups water. Don't rinse. (Obtain tea tree oil from a health food store.)
- Stick some cloves in a green apple and place in the drawer.
- Put zeolite in the drawer. Zeolite absorbs odors. (See USEFUL ADDRESSES AND PHONE NUMBERS, "Toxin-Free/Low-Toxin Products" for sources for zeolite.)

WOOD FURNITURE, PAINT SPLATTERS ON, To remove:
- **Water-based, fresh:** Rub with a cloth dampened in water.
- **Oil-based, fresh:** Rub gently with fine steel wool (No. 000) dipped in paste wax.
- **Dried and old:** Saturate the spot with boiled linseed oil and let it sit for a while, then wipe off. Remove any remaining paint with a paste made of pumice powder and mineral oil.

WOOD FURNITURE, SCRATCHES ON, To conceal:
- Rub an extra amount of polish into the scratch or apply paste wax and buff.
- Use a cotton swab or artist's brush to apply any stain treatment directly into the scratch so as not to darken the surrounding wood.
- Rub with cod-liver oil. Leave on for 24 hours before wiping off.
- Match the wood with liquid or paste shoe polish. Rub in well, allow to dry, then polish. Repeat as often as necessary. If the color is too dark, use mineral spirits to remove the polish.
- Paint the scratch with a little turpentine. Avoid using too much so as not to darken the wood. Let dry, then polish.
- Use wax sticks or crayons. Soften them first by warming them.
- Mix 1 teaspoon instant coffee and 2 teaspoons water, and use as a stain.
- Rub lightly with olive oil and methylated spirits. Use sparingly so as not to soften the finish.
- Mix 1 tablespoon finely ground pecans with 1 teaspoon mineral oil in a small container. Rub mixture into the scratches with a soft cloth. Remove excess with a clean soft cloth.
- **Light wood:** Rub the scratch with a piece of fresh pecan.
- **Light and dark wood:** Rub with camphor oil applied with a soft cloth and rubbed in the direction of the grain. The darker the wood, the more oil you need to apply. Or fill the scratch with a brown crayon or eyebrow pencil of the appropriate shade.

- **Cherry or mahogany:** Apply iodine with a cotton swab or rub with a dark brown crayon.
- **Walnut:** Rub with a piece of fresh, unsalted walnut. Let it dry, then polish.

WOOD FURNITURE, WHITE MARKS FROM HEAT/LIQUID ON, To remove:
- Rub vigorously with vegetable oil, mineral, or baby oil.
- Rub petroleum jelly into the spot and leave for 48 hours.
- Brush the stain quickly and lightly with a wet, well-wrung-out cloth to which has been added a few drops of rubbing alcohol, ammonia, peppermint oil, camphor oil, or turpentine. Don't rub.
- Rub with toothpaste on a damp cloth.
- Mix together a little baking soda and nongel toothpaste. Rub the mixture into the stained area with a damp cloth, working with the grain of the wood until the ring disappears, then wash with an oil soap, such as Murphy's Oil Soap, and polish. Repeat if the stain persists.
- Rub on metal polish with a soft cloth in the direction of the grain.
- Rub with mineral or cooking oil and a sprinkling of salt.
- Put a little fine wood ash or cigarette ash on the stain, then pour a little olive oil on top and rub gently.
- Apply a paste made of butter, mayonnaise, or vegetable oil and very fine wood ash or cigarette ash. Buff gently with a damp cloth. Let sit for an hour or so, then wipe off.
- Rub well with a soft cloth that has been dipped in a solution of 1 cup warm water to 1 tablespoon white vinegar. Dry with a soft cloth, then polish.
- Wipe with equal parts of linseed oil and methylated spirits.
- Rub the stain with rottenstone, or finely powdered pumice, or very fine ashes, mixed to a thin paste with lemon oil or linseed oil. Rub lightly in the direction of the grain, wipe with a cloth moistened with plain linseed oil, then polish. Don't use on a highly polished finish. (Obtain rottenstone or powdered pumice from a hardware or paint store.)

WOOD FURNITURE, WHITE MARKS FROM HEAT/LIQUID ON HIGHLY POLISHED TABLE, To remove:
- Pour a little mineral or olive oil on the stain and rub it in. Dry with a clean cloth and rewax with paste wax.
- Dampen a small cloth and add a few drops of ammonia. Brush it quickly over the surface. Don't rub.

- Go over the surface with extra-fine (000) or superfine (0000) steel wool, then rewax. Never use pumice or rottenstone.

WOOD FURNITURE, WORMS IN, To get rid of:

- Insert paraffin into the largest holes with a knitting needle daily for 10 days.

Gardens

ANIMALS, To repel:

- Scatter naphthalene (mothball flakes) in the garden area. (Don't use mothballs.) This does not harm plants or grass. Flakes will settle into the grass and last for several days. Animals may stay away from the area even after you've ceased putting out the flakes.
- Repel dogs, raccoons, and opossums from trash cans by sprinkling or spraying ammonia around each can or spraying the cans with hot sauce. Soak garbage bags with full-strength ammonia for extra protection.
- Mix 2 cups rubbing alcohol and 1 teaspoon lemongrass oil. Brush or spray the liquid on areas you want dogs and cats to avoid.
- Put down used coffee grounds to keep cats away from an area.
- Sprinkle chili powder or cayenne pepper around vegetables and flowers you want animals to avoid. Buy the spice in large quantities in an Asian or Hispanic food market or a food warehouse that sells institutional-size containers.

ANNUALS, To encourage growth:

- Pinch the top off the plants when they are 3 to 4 inches tall.
- Deadhead spent blooms to prolong the blooming time.

APHIDS: See "Insects, Plant, To control."

APPLE TREES, Hints on:

- Sprinkle 1 pound borax under a tree that refuses to bear fruit. Fruit trees need a trace of boron in the soil to produce fruit.
- To prevent worms in the fruit: Put 1 cup white vinegar and 1 cup sugar in 1 gallon milk or bleach plastic jug. Fill with water, shake well, and add the peel from 1 banana. Hang the jug in the tree (with the cap off) before the blossoms open.

BIRD BATH, Hints on:

- Place a few colored marbles in the water to attract the birds.
- Hose out the bath daily and wash it with hot, soapy water at least once

a week. Add liquid chlorine bleach to the soapy water to help kill algae and bacteria, then rinse thoroughly.

- Remove algae by placing bleach-soaked paper towels on the birdbath and letting them sit for 30 minutes to 1 hour, then remove, rinse thoroughly, and let dry.

BIRD FEEDER, HUMMINGBIRD, Care of:

- Mix 4 parts water to 1 part sugar. Boil the water first, then add the sugar and let the solution cool before pouring it into the feeder. Be sure to clean the dispenser in very hot water and refill it with fresh syrup every 3 to 4 days. Don't use honey to make the syrup; it can cause a fungal growth on hummingbirds' beaks.
- Keep ants off the hummingbird feeder by spreading a little olive oil on the tip that dispenses the sweet water. It won't hurt the hummingbirds.
- Attract hummingbirds by planting deep tubular flowers in red or orange.

BIRDS, To keep away from fruit trees:

- Hang several disposable foil pie tins or the tops and bottoms of frozen juice tops in the tree branches so they can spin in the wind. Punch them with a nail and thread them on a string.
- Cut an old garden hose into 4-foot-long pieces. Drape the pieces among the branches of the tree to act as fake snakes. Or cut mylar balloons into ribbons about 1 inch wide and tie them to the tree branches.
- Cover the trees with nylon netting or cheesecloth.

BIRDS, To keep from eating grapes:

- Cut the tops off old pantyhose and slip one leg over each bunch of grapes. Or slip each bunch into a plastic bag to ripen.

BIRDS, To keep from eating strawberries:

- Cover plants with opened-up mesh bags that onions or fruit are sold in. String them together to make a larger covering.

BIRDS, To keep off newly seeded areas:

- Put nylon netting or old sheer curtains over the areas.

BIRDS, Treats for:

- Mix suet with seeds.
- Fill a paper cup half full of birdseed, then add any fat left in the frying pan or skimmed from meat dishes. When the cup is full, put it in

the refrigerator until hard. Peel off the paper cup and put out for the meat-eating birds. It's a great winter treat for them.

- Tie the bones from a roast or steak and hang them on a tree. Or attach uncooked fat rinds to tree twigs. Woodpeckers, starlings, blue jays, and grackles love them.
- Put out leftover popped popcorn.
- Form peanut butter and seeds into little balls.
- Save the seeds from watermelons, squash, sunflowers, and pumpkins and put out.
- Spread a thin layer of peanut butter or honey onto a pinecone, roll it in birdseed, and tie it to a tree.
- Cover a pinecone with bacon grease, chicken or meat fat, then roll in bread crumbs, rolled oats, or birdseed.
- Use sunflower seeds in the bird feeder. Most seed-eating birds favor it.
- Add crushed eggshells to the feeder, particularly in winter and spring. Birds have no teeth to grind their foods. The dirt, sand, pebbles, and grit they eat sits in their crop and helps grind up their food. Eggshells do the same thing and in the spring have an added benefit—they provide extra calcium during nesting season.

BROWN SPOTS ON LEAVES, Trimming hints:
- Leave about one-half inch between the brown and green, otherwise the leaf will bruise and brown more. And cut in the angle in which the leaves grow, an inverted V, not straight across.

BULBS, Hints on:
- Force the bulbs in a pot of vermiculite, sand, or gravel with the tops sticking out. Keep in a dry, cool place and water. When shoots appear, place the pots in the sun or a sunny window.
- Store bulbs in an old nylon stocking or a mesh bag that onions come in. Hang them high to dry.

CAMELLIA AND GARDENIA BLOOMS, To stop turning brown:
- Sprinkle a little table salt in the center of the blossoms.

COMPANION PLANTING, Hints on:
- Plant basil near tomatoes to repel hornworms and flies. Or chop and scatter basil leaves to repel aphids, mosquitoes, and mites in the vegetable and flower beds.
- Plant blue sage with lettuce, spinach, and leaf crops.
- Plant catnip by eggplant to deter flea beetles and near cabbage to deter cabbage pests.

- Plant French marigolds in among the vegetables. The odor repels many pests, such as tomato hornworms, whiteflies, and nematodes.
- Plant garlic near corn, carrots, lettuce, tomatoes, and peas to repel many pests. And plant with roses to repel aphids and Japanese beetles.
- Plant horseradish by potatoes to repel potato bugs.
- Plant mint by cabbage and broccoli to reduce white cabbage butterfly, with radishes to discourage flea beetles, and with tomatoes to repel tomato hornworms.
- Plant nasturtium to repel aphids.
- Plant onions next to beets and carrots to keep bugs away.
- Crush a leaf of the companion plant occasionally in order to release the aroma.

COMPOST ALTERNATIVE, Hints on:

- Dig a little trench in the garden and use it to put in your kitchen scraps—potato peelings, green matter, coffee grounds, tea bags, eggshells (crushed first), fruit and vegetables (no meat or bones) plus any garden refuse. Cover with a little soil each time you add to the trench to keep it sanitary. When the trench is filled, start another one. You also can chop kitchen scraps in the blender or puree them with water. Put the mixture in the trench, dig it in the soil, or add it to the compost to speed up the composting process.

COMPOST MATERIALS, To acquire:

- Explore local facilities for compost materials: riding stables; sheep, goat, hog, or dairy farms; egg ranches (contact a feed store to find out where they are located); racetracks; zoos or petting zoos; wildlife reserves; or circuses for manure; poultry farms for feathers; lumber- yards, firewood lots, cabinet makers, or high school woodshops for sawdust; mushroom growers for mushroom compost; neighbors for grass clippings and leaves; the utility company and tree care/tree removal companies for ground-up leaves and bark. Include kitchen scraps, coffee grounds, tea leaves, crushed eggshells, leaves (shredded are better), pine needles (although they take awhile to break down), hay, shredded newspaper (no colored or glossy ads), and dust from the vacuum cleaner. Do not include dog/cat feces, weeds (unless the com- post pile has heated up sufficiently), fat, or meat scraps.
- Call the county or municipal Department of public works to inquire if free compost is available in your area.

COMPOSTING, Information on:

- Contact your local municipal solid waste agency, the local U.S.

Department of Agriculture Cooperative Extension Office, or write the Composting Council or the American Horticultural Society (AHS). See USEFUL ADDRESSES AND PHONE NUMBERS, "Gardens, Composting Information."

COMPOSTING, Quick trick:

• Put all the compost materials in a heavy-duty trash bag, add a spadeful of soil and ¼ cup of 10-10-10 fertilizer, then moisten the mixture thoroughly. Seal the bag and set it in a sunny area. Roll it over carefully twice a week for 2 months.

CUTTINGS, To propagate:

• Propagate coleus, pothos, ivy, and willow by placing cuttings in a jar two-thirds filled with water. If you like, put in a few pieces of activated charcoal to keep the water clean. Cover the jar with plastic wrap or aluminum foil, poke small holes in the cover, and stick the cuttings through the holes. Keep in a warm, light place but out of direct sunlight. Remove the cover every few days and stir well to incorporate more air. Check the cuttings frequently. Plant the cuttings in soil while the roots are still small so they can adjust easier.

• Propagate impatiens, geraniums, begonias, and fuchsias and other softwood cuttings of perennials and shrubs in August during active growth. They should snap, not bend. If they bend, they are too old. Cut off stem sections 3 to 5 inches long, making the cut one-half inch below a leaf node with a single-edge razor blade. Remove flowers and all leaves except for a few leaves on top. Place the cuttings in moist vermiculite, perlite, or coarse sand, cover with a plastic bag propped up inside with a plastic straw so the plastic isn't touching the plant, and then keep out of direct sunlight. When established and new growth appears, pinch it back to encourage bushiness.

• Propagate a rose cutting by sticking it in the ground in the spring. Cover it with a 1-quart glass jar. Or put it in a glass jar filled halfway with soil. Water well and cover the top with a piece of clear plastic wrap. Remove the plastic periodically to allow the cutting to dry so it doesn't mildew.

• Propagate African violets, gloxinias, rex begonias, and other fleshy-leafed plants by placing a leaf with about 2 inches of stalk on top of moist sand and anchoring it with a few toothpicks. Keep moist, shaded, and at a constant temperature.

• Maintain the humidity when planting in a pot by inverting a drinking glass over the soil. Or set the pot in a plastic bag, making several small holes in it for air. Put sand or gravel in the bottom of the pot.

DEER, To repel:

- Hang bags of human hair on trees 3 feet above the ground and 3 feet apart. Use net, mesh, cheesecloth, or old nylons for the bags. Ask your barber or beauty shop to save you the hair clippings.
- String bars of strongly scented soap about 3 feet from the ground in every tree. Replace every 2 months.
- Spray shrubs and trees with a mixture of 1 teaspoon dishwashing detergent, 1 egg, and 1 quart water.
- Scatter dried blood meal around the perimeter of the property. Buy the blood meal at a slaughterhouse, where it's sold cheaply in 5-gallon cans.
- String small blinking Christmas-tree lights around the perimeter of the property and keep on from dusk to dawn.

DELPHINIUMS, Hint on:

- Cut them back for a second growth.

DISEASE, PLANT: See "Mildew, Black Spot, Rust, To control," and "Roses, Fungi, To control."

DISEASE ON PLANTS, To avoid spreading:

- Wash your hands after touching a diseased plant. Sanitize the tools in a solution of ½ cup chlorine bleach and 1 quart water. Let them air-dry, then wipe them with a little oil to prevent rust. Or wipe the tools with alcohol and let them air dry.

EARWIGS, To get rid of:

- Dampen newspaper, roll it into a tight cylinder, then place it where earwigs appear. It should be full of earwigs the next morning. Empty the earwigs into a bucket of water, or put the newspaper into a plastic bag, seal, and put it in the garbage. Continue until no more earwigs appear in the paper. Corrugated cardboard will also work.
- Tie together a couple of short lengths of old garden hose. Place them between the vegetable rows or the base of shrubs. Next morning empty the tube traps by knocking the earwigs into a bucket of water. Continue until earwigs no longer appear.
- Grease the inside of a tin can with bacon grease from the top to about one-third down and fill with water up to the grease. Cover with brown paper and put out where the earwigs appear. Dispose of the can when it is filled with earwigs.

- Put out small cans (tuna or cat food size) filled with ½ inch vegetable oil, then dispose of them as they fill with earwigs.

FERNS, To feed:
- Save used tea bags and leftover tea to feed the ferns.

FERTILIZER, LIQUID, To measure:
- Mix the fertilizer in a washed-out 1-gallon bleach bottle. No measuring is necessary with the gallon container.

FERTILIZING, Hints on:
- Apply fertilizer to damp soil, never to dry soil.
- Mow the grass about a week after you fertilize and let the clippings remain on the lawn for the nitrogen content.
- Mix some flour with the dry fertilizer before you spread it. It will indicate what areas have been covered and will water in without harming the lawn.
- Enrich the soil and add humus with kitchen scraps and food past its prime (no meat or fat, though). For instance, raw wheat bran contains 2.65 percent nitrogen, 2.90 percent phosphorus, and 1.60 percent potash; banana peels provide 41.76 percent potash and 3.25 percent phosphorus. Chop the peels into small pieces and bury them around roses, tomatoes, peppers, and eggplants. (See also "Compost Alternative, Hints on.")
- Use the water from the aquarium to water vegetable plants or roses. It is rich in minerals.

FLOWERPOTS: See entries for "Planter" and "Planters" in this chapter.

FLOWERS, To dry:
- Gather the flowers right before their prime when they are not quite fully opened on a warm, dry day. Work in a warm, dry, dimly lit area. (Sunlight fades the colors of dried flowers.) Flowers to be dried in silica gel (obtainable from a hardware store or craft shop) must be completely dry, with absolutely no moisture. Silica will cling to any dampness and discolor the flowers. Flowers dry faster in gel but must be removed as soon as they're dry, or they become brittle and discolored. The less gel used, the faster the flowers will dry. After drying, you may spray the flowers with acrylic matte sealer to make them less fragile. Dry out wet silica gel for reuse by placing it in a shallow container and heating it in a 250°F oven for 30 minutes, or until the crystals turn from pink to bright blue. Or place under a lit 60-watt light bulb. You can renew silica gel this way many

times. Store silica tightly sealed, as it draws moisture from the air.

- Dry small flowers for 1 minute in the microwave, up to 3 minutes for larger flowers using silica gel. Let stand for 10 minutes before pouring out the gel and removing the flowers, then let the gel cool before reusing.
- Dry everlasting flowers in the microwave without silica gel. Put them inside a paper towel or napkin, then dry for 2 minutes on high. If flowers are dry and crisp, they are done. If not, dry for another minute or so. Dry leaves in the same way. Place some inside a folded paper towel and put a microwave-safe container on top to prevent the leaves from curling.

FLOWERS, CUT, Longest-lasting:
- Plant asters, chrysanthemums, freesias, gerberas, gladioli, hydrangeas, lilies, mullein, or orchids if you want the longest-lasting cut flowers.

FLOWERS, CUT, To make last longer:
- Pick them early in the morning and don't take any more leaves than necessary. After picking, use a sharp knife to cut a 2-inch slit running from the stem up, then cut across the bottom at a 45-degree angle. On woody plants, scrape the bark from the last 2 inches of the stem base until green shows, then cut across the bottom at an angle. Put in tepid water for 1 hour, then in deep cold water. Keep out of direct sunlight.
- Cut the flowers when half open, and submerge them in warm water at about 100°F for 30 minutes, then arrange them in a vase with cool water and let them air dry.
- Recut roses under water by taking ¼ inch off the stems, then put them into hot tap water (110°F) containing 2 to 3 drops chlorine bleach per 1 quart water. Let the water come to room temperature in a cool dim area before arranging the flowers.
- Recut the stems of flowers from the florist under water, at an angle, and just before placing them in a vase of tepid water.
- Recut flower stems every few days.
- Refrigerate cut flowers at night to nearly double their life. Make sure there is no fruit in the refrigerator when you do this. Fresh fruit gives off a gas that is detrimental to cut flowers.
- Add Floralife (available from a florist) to the water, or any of the following:
  Add a pinch of baking soda to the water to keep it fresh.
  Add an aspirin to the water.

Add 2 tablespoons white vinegar and 3 tablespoons sugar per 1 quart of warm water.

Add ⅛ teaspoon chlorine bleach and 1 teaspoon sugar per 1 quart water. Do not use bleach if the container is silver or pewter.

Add 1 tablespoon white Karo syrup and 1 teaspoon chlorine bleach to 1 quart water. Mix well.

Add ½ teaspoon of medicinal-type mouthwash per 1 quart water.

- For carnations, add a touch of boric acid to the water. It makes them last longer.
- When arranging cut tulips, add a few drops of vodka to the water. It keeps them standing straight instead of drooping.
- Singe the cut ends of daffodils, hollyhocks, poinsettias, milkweed, and Oriental poppies by passing them briefly through the flame of a match. Repeat every time you recut the stems. This breaks the milky seal the flowers secrete.
- For roses and snapdragons, add 2 tablespoons table salt to 1 quart water.
- For marigolds, add 2 tablespoons sugar and 2 tablespoons table salt to 1 quart water.

FROST CONDITIONS, To protect plants:
- Use buckets, baskets, or plastic containers.
- Apply protective covers of old bed sheets, tablecloths, or blankets. Anchor them by fastening them to sturdy lower branches with clothespins.
- Hose off any frost on the plants early in the morning to remove the ice.

FUNGI: See "Mildew, Black Spot, Rust, To control," and "Roses, Fungi, To control."

FUNNEL SUBSTITUTE:
- Cut the spout and neck off a plastic bottle. Different sizes of bottles will make different-size funnels.

GARDEN EQUIPMENT, Hint on:
- Check whether a garden center or nursery will lend you the equipment you need for free. For example, if you are planting a lawn, ask if you can borrow a seed spreader when you buy your seed; if you are installing sprinklers, see if you can borrow the necessary tools.

GARDEN FURNITURE, Hints on:
- Spray metal furniture with a rust preventive.

- Clean white plastic patio furniture with a product for cleaning vinyl car tops.
- Use Simple Green. It's nontoxic and biodegradable and will get the dirtiest furniture clean.

GARDEN HOSE, Hints on:

- Coil the garden hose while the water is still running through it so it doesn't kink up, and turn the water on before pulling the hose to the garden area.
- Buy an inexpensive hose hanger, which will prevent the hose from crimping and cracking.

GARDEN HOSE, To recycle:

- Turn it into a soaker hose. Punch holes with an ice pick, sharp knife, or screwdriver at regular intervals along the length of the hose on one side. When using, lay the hose on the ground with the hole-side down. You can shorten it with a pants hanger peg, a C-clamp, or just leave a nozzle on the end, shut off.
- Use a piece of the hose to wrap around and anchor a newly planted sapling.
- Cut it into pieces and hang the pieces in fruit trees to scare birds away. Painting them with yellow stripes makes for more authentic-looking snakes.

GARDEN HOSE, To repair:

- Sand the surface of a rubber patch and the area around the hole very lightly with fine sandpaper. Apply contact cement to both surfaces and wait until the cement dries. Then firmly press the patch over the hole and wrap the patched area with either electrical tape or duct tape.

GARDENING CLOTHES, Hints on:

- Buy a pair of army fatigue pants from an army surplus store. They are roomy, have drawstrings at the bottom, a reinforced seat and knees, and lots of big outside pockets to hold seeds and tools.
- Pick up a cloth nail apron from the hardware store and wear it when planting. The many pockets will hold seed packages and tools.

GARDENING GLOVES, Hint on:

- Use oven mitts for pruning and cutting roses. They offer more protection for the hands.
- Switch hands and wear the gloves backward when holes wear through.

GRASS, Hints on:

- Buy seed recommended for your area. Purchase it at a farm supply store or home improvement store to save money.
- Mow the grass in the morning before the sun is up; cut off no more than a third of the blade. Let the grass grow 2 or 3 inches before cutting. (Longer grass prevents sunlight from reaching weed seeds, and the grass is better able to resist wind, sun, and drought.) Leave the clippings on the lawn to provide nitrogen.
- Avoid fertilizing during the middle of summer; doing so stimulates the weeds.
- Apply vegetable oil to the blades of a hand mower when the ground is damp and you have to mow. Or spray on nonstick cooking spray. The grass won't stick to the blades.
- Wear golf shoes while working in the garden. The cleats go into the ground and aerate the lawn.

GRASS AND WEEDS IN WALKWAYS, To remove:

- Pour boiling water from a teakettle on grass and weeds that grow in driveways, concrete pavements, and between patio stones.
- Pour on white vinegar; it's safe and nontoxic.
- Pour table salt in cracks to kill unwanted grass.
- Mix 1 pound table salt or rock salt in 1 gallon boiling water, and pour the solution on the grass and weeds.
- Sprinkle borax in cracks along walkways in the early spring to help prevent weeds from sprouting.
- Pour chlorine bleach in the cracks. The vegetation dies and is easily pulled out, and the bleach prevents it from growing back.

GRASSHOPPERS, To get rid of:

- Fill old jars with a solution of water mixed with several tablespoons of honey or molasses and place in the garden.

HAND CARE WHEN GARDENING, Hints on:

- Rub a thin coat of petroleum jelly on your hands before starting a messy job.
- Scrape your fingernails over a bar of soap before you begin gardening. This makes nail cleaning easier.

HANDS STAINED FROM GARDENING, To clean:

- Add a little sugar to the soapy lather when you wash them.
- Put a generous amount of hand lotion or cooking oil in your palms, add a little sugar, and rub hands well, then wash with soap and warm water.

- Moisten a couple of tablespoons of dry oatmeal with milk and vigorously massage into the hands, then rinse. This should leave your hands smooth and remove stains.
- Wet your hands and scrub with a dampened nail brush sprinkled with baking soda.
- Make a paste with a couple of tablespoons of cornmeal, 1 tablespoon water, and a little apple cider vinegar. Rub the paste into your hands until they are clean, then rinse. This will also soften the hands.

HEDGES, To trim in a straight line:
- Tie a string to a branch at one end and run it across to the other end, making sure the string is straight. Or stick two broom or mop handles in the soil at either end of the hedge and tie the string from one to the other.

HERBS, Hints on:
- Cut them just before they flower when their oils are at peak, at mid-morning on a sunny day.
- Store them by freezing, drying, or putting them in oil or vinegar.
- Obtain the most flavor from dried herbs by storing them with their leaves whole. Crumble the leaves when you are ready to use them.
- See also FOOD AND COOKING chapter, "Herbs, Fresh, To dry."

INSECTICIDAL SOAP, To make:
- Add 4 tablespoons of liquid dishwashing soap or a nontoxic, organic, biodegradable household cleaning solution to each 1 gallon water.

INSECTICIDE/PESTICIDE, Information on:
- Neem oil is easy on beneficial insects and of very low toxicity to mammals.
- Rotenone is prepared from roots of various South American legumes. It is less toxic than other insecticides and loses its effectiveness within a week.
- Pyrethrin is the least toxic for diseases.

INSECTS, PLANT, To control:
- Remove aphids, whiteflies, mealy bugs, cabbage worms, red spider mites, and young scale with a strong spray of water from the garden hose, hitting both sides of the leaves. Do it every few days. Or mix a solution of 1 tablespoon dishwashing detergent, 2 or 3 drops Tabasco sauce and 2 quarts water and spray it on the plants. Or use insecticidal soap, but not in hot weather.
- Hose off adult whiteflies, hitting both sides of the leaves. Do it every

few days. Or suck up the insects early in the morning with a small hand vacuum. Or place next to plants yellow cards, stakes, or plastic lids from food or coffee containers smeared with honey, mineral oil, motor oil, or petroleum jelly. They will attract whiteflies and aphids. Wash the traps periodically and reapply the sticky stuff.

- Spray red spider mites with leftover coffee.
- Boil 2 quarts water with a couple of large chopped onions and plenty of garlic for about 45 minutes. (There is no need to peel the vegetables.) When the solution is cool, spray the plants with it. It doesn't smell and won't hurt vegetables.
- Combine 1 teaspoon garlic powder, 1 teaspoon liquid hand soap, and 1 cup hot water. Microwave on high for 1 to 2 minutes, then add to 2 quarts cold water. Mix well, then spray.
- Apply dormant-oil spray before leaf growth begins. Read the instructions on the package regarding temperature conditions.
- Investigate biological controls—beneficial insects you release in the garden.
- Add 1 ounce molasses to 1 gallon water, and use half the amount of insecticide the label calls for. Mix and apply as usual. The molasses increases the adhesiveness and is used effectively by gardeners at Disney World in Florida.
- Strengthen the plant's resistance by adding ¼ to ½ teaspoon vitamin C (ascorbic acid powder) per 1 quart watering solution every week or so. According to Dale Norris, a professor of entomology and neurobiology at the University of Wisconsin/Madison, who tested the vitamin therapy on some 50 species of vegetables, flowers, and trees, this helps the plant withstand stresses such as drought, transplantation, and insect depredation.

IRON FOR THE PLANTS, Hint on:
- Put old nails, old tools, and anything rusted beyond repair in a can and fill it with water. Let the items sit until they are thoroughly rusted, then use the rust water for a mineral boost for the plants. Add ¼ to ½ cup to 1 gallon water.

KNEELING PAD, To make:
- Wrap a piece of foam rubber or Styrofoam in a plastic bag.
- Stuff an old hot water bottle with discarded nylon hose, rags, or Styrofoam pellets. Cut the top off and seal with sturdy tape.
- Wrap an old pillow in plastic and seal with sturdy tape.

LAWN: See "Grass, Hints on."

LEAF VEGETABLES, To gain several harvests from:
- Cut spinach, lettuce, and chard back to 2 inches instead of uprooting the plant. They will grow back again and again. Or cut off the outer leaves as needed.

LEAVES TO RAKE, Hint on:
- Lay an old plastic shower curtain liner or plastic tablecloth on the ground and rake the leaves onto the top of it, then gather up the four corners and drag it to the compost pile. Use an opened-up large plastic garbage bag for smaller amounts of leaves.

MILDEW, BLACK SPOT, RUST, To control:
- Mix together 1 tablespoon baking soda, 1 teaspoon dishwashing detergent, and 1 gallon water. Spray the plant, paying special attention to the underside. Do this in the morning so the foliage has a chance to dry.

MOLES, To get rid of:
- Place pinwheels at intervals on the lawn to scare them away.
- Flood their tunnels. This works but may take awhile.
- Mix 3 tablespoons castor oil and 1 tablespoon dishwashing detergent. Add to 1 gallon water, then soak the tunnels and the entrances.

MOSS ON WALKWAYS, To remove:
- Sprinkle a solution of half water and half chlorine bleach onto the moss. Do it on a sunny day and keep off it for 24 hours.
- Paint the moss with methylated spirits.
- Mix equal parts of white vinegar and methylated spirits, and apply with a scrubbing brush. Leave for 15 minutes, then scrub the surface again with the mixture. Leave for another 15 minutes, then hose and sweep away the moss with a broom.

MUDDY CONDITIONS IN THE GARDEN, Hint on:
- Avoid working in the garden when the soil is wet. If you absolutely have to do something, such as harvesting, stay off the grass so as not to compact the soil.
- Cover your shoes with plastic bags, such as the ones newspapers are delivered in. Secure at the top with rubber bands.
- Use a plastic kneeling pad. See "Kneeling Pad, To make."

MULCH, Materials for:
- Use sheets of aluminum foil for mulch to double your yields of squash,

cucumbers, and corn. The reflected light repels insects while encouraging plant growth.

- Use black plastic. The plastic absorbs the heat, which warms the soil and protects fruits, such as cucumbers or strawberries.
- Use newspapers. Layer several sheets between the flower or vegetable beds and anchor them with rocks or weigh them down with soil. Or take the Sunday's newspaper intact, wet it thoroughly, then put it in place dripping wet. Or shred the newspaper and incorporate it into the soil. Newspaper is a cheap, water-conserving, biodegradable mulch that decomposes rapidly. Avoid the glossy or colored advertising.
- Use seaweed washed up on the beach. Rinse it first to remove the salt.
- Use fresh or spoiled hay. Decomposed hay can be turned under at the end of the season and will enrich the soil. Buy a bale of hay from feed stores and spoiled hay from farmers.
- Use autumn leaves. Run the power mower over them to chop them up. Do not use the leaves of acacia, walnut, eucalyptus, California bay, juniper, camphor, cypress, and pittosporum for mulch. When decomposing, they release chemicals toxic to plants.
- Use sawdust or shredded bark, but don't add more than 2 inches a year. Also add a high-nitrogen fertilizer, blood meal, or cottonseed meal to offset the nitrogen lost as the sawdust decomposes. Avoid cedar sawdust, which is toxic to some seedlings.
- Call the county or municipal Department of Public Works to inquire if free compost is available in your area.
- Inquire at a tree care company or the utility company if wood chips are available free or for a nominal price.
- Ask at a local brewery for used "spent" hops.

MULCH, WOOD CHIP, Hints on:
- Avoid mulching vegetables and annuals with wood chips. Instead use grass clippings under flower and vegetable beds.
- Fertilize first with a high-nitrogen fertilizer before using wood chips. As the chips decay, nitrogen is temporarily depleted from the soil.

PLANT MARKERS, To make:
- Cut into 1-inch strips bleach or plastic milk bottles, waxed milk cartons, aluminum TV dinner containers, or other foil containers and use as markers. Use an indelible marker, crayon, or grease pencil to write the names of the seeds and the planting dates.

- Save Popsicle or ice cream sticks and disposable plastic knives. Mark them with a permanent marking pen.
- Cut pieces of old miniblinds with scissors so that one end is pointed and slides into the ground or seed tray.
- Coat markers with clear fingernail polish to make them more weatherproof.

PLANT TIES, To make:

- Cut lengthwise strips from old pantyhose, and use the strips to tie tomato and other plants to poles. The pantyhose stretches so it won't cut into the stalks as they grow.
- Tie up plants with double-knit material instead of cotton; there is more give to it.
- Save the plastic ties that bind the newspaper, especially the Sunday edition.
- Slice up strips of dry-cleaning bags. They make almost invisible ties.

PLANTER AND FLOWERPOT DRAINAGE HOLES, To cover:

- Use old sponges cut into squares, activated charcoal, pebbles, marbles, stones, Styrofoam packing popcorn, broken pieces of clay pottery, nylon net or mosquito netting folded into several layers, well-washed fruit pits, crushed eggshells, cracked walnut shells, or a piece of old screen. (Obtain activated charcoal at health food stores and aquarium supply stores.)

PLANTER WITHOUT DRAINAGE HOLES, Hint on:

- Line the bottom of the container with 1 inch or more of gravel or pebbles. Or use Styrofoam packing pellets or chips, which don't add extra weight. Use more material for taller containers.

PLANTERS, Sinking them into the soil:

- Wrap them in a double thickness of old nylon hose to keep slugs and insects from entering through the drainage holes.

PLANTERS, To disinfect for reuse:

- Scrub moss or algae off clay planters with a stiff brush or nylon scrubber. Use steel wool for mineral deposits.
- Wash them in hot sudsy water and then disinfect with a solution of 1 part chlorine bleach to 9 parts water. Rinse the pots and let them air-dry. If possible, soak the pots overnight in the bleach and water solution.
- Immerse them in boiling water or heat them briefly in a 180°F oven. Allow them to cool, then store in a clean, dry place.

- Soak clay pots in water for a few hours before putting in plants; otherwise they will draw water out of the potting mix.

PLASTIC AND METAL CONTAINERS, To make holes in the bottom:

- Hold a heavy plastic container upside down over a candle until the spot softens, then lay the container on a board right side up and use a hammer and chisel to cut a hole in the softened area.
- Heat the point of an icepick, metal knitting needle, or straightened-out wire coat hanger over the flame of a gas stove or candle, and use it to melt holes in the bottom of a plastic container.
- Freeze water in a metal container (such as a 3-pound coffee can), then turn the can upside down and poke holes in the bottom with a nail and hammer.
- Set the container on a piece of wood (right side up), and hammer holes in the bottom with a large nail or Phillips head screwdriver.

POINSETTIAS, To make bloom longer:

- Clip the yellow flowers from the centers to have the blooms last up to a month longer.

PRUNING, To protect your hands:

- Use a spring-type clothespin, pliers, or barbecue tongs to hold on to the thorny/prickly stems of roses and berries.
- Wear a pair of oven mitts for those small tough jobs.

RABBITS, To repel:

- Put naphthalene crystals (mothball flakes) around each plant the rabbits especially like. For plants in rows, arrange the mothball crystals in the rows along both sides.
- Scatter human hair cuttings around or put them in bags made of cheesecloth or old pantyhose.
- Sprinkle red pepper on the plants or put red pepper or dried blood meal around the plants. (See "Animals, to repel.")
- Plant horseradish or strongly scented herbs in among the vegetables and plants.
- Spray the plants with a solution of 3 ounces Epsom salts in 1 gallon water or 1 teaspoon Lysol in 1 gallon water.

RACCOONS, To repel: See "Animals, To repel."

ROOF DRAIN SPOUT, Hint on:

- Place a large flat stone or garden stepping stone beneath the drain spout to avoid soil erosion when it rains.

- Buy a Rain-Drain that automatically unwinds when it rains and gently releases water away from the house.

ROSES, Hints on:
- Plant Rugosa for the least work and pick Fragrant Cloud for the most fragrance. Most people consider Fragrant Cloud the most fragrant rose every hybridized.
- Place a dead fish in the bottom of the hole when planting or dig it into the soil close to an established rosebush. (Ask your fish merchant for free fish scraps instead.)
- Bury 3 or 4 garlic cloves 2 inches deep around each rosebush. They will act as natural "systemics" against rose pests. Garlic is a known accumulator of sulphur, which is effective against black spot.
- Fertilize with time-released banana skins by laying them on the soil at the base of the rosebush. Renew every few weeks. Or bury an old brown banana at the base of each rosebush. Banana skins are rich in calcium, magnesium, sulfur, and phosphates, on which roses thrive.
- Cut roses just above a leaf with five leaflets.
- Cut roses in the late afternoon, when their sugar content is high, rather than in the early morning. Recent studies show that doing so prolongs the life of the flower.

ROSES, FUNGI, To control:
- Combine 2 tablespoons baking soda, 2 tablespoons light horticultural oil or canola oil, 2 drops liquid dishwashing detergent, and 1 gallon water. Spray the whole plant, paying special attention to the underside of the leaves. (See also "Mildew, Black Spot, Rust, To control.")

SCOOP, To make:
- Cut off the bottom and cut out one side (up to the handle) of an empty washed-out plastic bleach, milk, or orange juice bottle. Use the top with the lid attached for scooping compost, peat moss, potting soil, and other soil amendments.

SEED GERMINATION, Light requirements:
- Read package directions. Some seeds, such as begonias, snapdragons, petunias, and sweet alyssum, should not be covered. Sow those seeds on the surface and don't cover with soil mix.

SEEDLINGS IN THE GARDEN, To protect:
- Make hot caps from clear plastic 1-gallon milk jugs or 2-liter soda or water bottles. Remove the labels and cut the bottoms off. Place over

each transplant and leave on at night. During the day remove either the caps or the entire bottle, depending on weather conditions.

- Use milk cartons with the tops and bottoms cut off to protect plants from cutworm. Place the cartons over the plants and press them into the soil.
- Use Styrofoam cups for cutworm collars. Cut the bottom section off the cups and leave 1 inch or so of the cup above ground.
- Cut cardboard tubes from toilet paper, wrapping paper, or paper towels into 2-inch lengths. Slip one section over each small seedling, pressing it lightly into the soil.
- Cut both ends off juice cans and place over the plant, pressing them firmly into the soil.
- Make an aluminum-foil sleeve from a 4- to 5-inch length of foil, folded into two thicknesses. Slip the sleeve into the soil about 1 inch below ground level.
- Split drinking straws up one side, and cut them into sections. Slip individual sections around the stems of transplants for cutworm protection.
- Dig around a plant destroyed by cutworms; usually the cutworms are just under the soil nearby.
- Put berry baskets over newly transplanted seedlings to protect them from the sun.

SEEDLINGS IN THE GARDEN, To water:
- Spray with a fine mist from the garden hose.
- Place a canvas soil soaker next to the seedlings. (Canvas soil soakers can be purchased from a garden supply store.)
- Punch small holes in a plastic garden hose and lay it on the soil between the rows, holes down.
- Slip a cotton glove over the nozzle of the hose and fasten the wrist securely with wire, twine, or a rubber band. Turn on the water and lay the gloved nozzle of the hose in areas to be soaked.

SEEDS, To hasten germination:
- Soak flower seeds in water for a couple of days before planting them. Change the water frequently.

SEEDS, To set in rows:
- Use a broom or rake handle to form a ¼-inch trench, or use a piece of string to position the row.
- Use the perforated edges of computer paper as a guide to sowing the seeds. The holes are spaced half an inch apart, so you can use the spacing you need.

- Mark the rows by planting radishes as row markers for slow-germinating crops. Plant a few of these fast growing seeds in the same row with the other seeds.

SEEDS, To sow in hot weather:

- Put wet burlap, a piece of carpet, boards, or a piece of plywood over the seedbed. Remove when the seeds start to germinate.

SEEDS, To start indoors:

- Check seed instructions for those seeds that require stratification (prechilling) before being sown, scarification (nicking the seed coat), low germination temperatures, a presoaking in warm water, and light or darkness requirements for germination.
- Sprout seeds first by placing them between two pieces of wet paper towels set on Styrofoam meat trays, aluminum pie pans, or plates. Keep them moist at all times by covering the container with plastic wrap to seal in the moisture, or put in a plastic bag. Set the seed trays on top of the refrigerator, on a board over a radiator, or on top of the hot water heater. Check every day and keep the toweling moist. After a few days when the seeds sprout, plant them in containers containing fine potting soil, vermiculite, or perlite. Put the container(s) on the windowsill or where there is plenty of light, and mist the seedlings every day. Turn the seed container(s) every day if on the windowsill.
- Start the seeds in containers with the bottoms pierced for drainage or in flats with the bottom lined with a layer of paper towels or newspaper. Fill with a mixture of ½ potting soil, ¼ perlite, and ¼ peat moss or vermiculite. Or use a soilless seed starting mix. If the container is too deep, you can put a layer of gravel or Styrofoam in the bottom to reduce the amount of soil required.
- Set the seed trays on top of the refrigerator, on a board over a radiator, on top of the hot water heater, or in any warm spot in the house. Put clear plastic over the trays to maintain a humid atmosphere, or put them in a plastic bag. Those that newspapers arrive in on a rainy day are ideal. Keep the containers or flats moist but not wet. Ventilate for 1 hour or so several times a week by opening the lid or bag or removing the plastic wrap. Once the seeds sprout, remove the plastic or covers and move the containers to a slightly cooler area with plenty of light. If you choose the windowsill, turn the containers every day. Gradually expose the seedlings to outdoor conditions before planting them in the garden. Two weeks before outdoor planting, stop feeding them if you have been and

reduce the water. About a week before, put them outdoors in a protected area out of direct sun and wind. Leave outdoors for only 2 hours at first; increase by 2 hours daily until they are used to a full day outside. Water frequently. When it is time to plant, wait for an overcast day or plant in the late afternoon. Handle the seedlings by a leaf, not the stem. When thinning the seedlings, snip the unwanted ones off with scissors at soil level so as not to disturb the roots of neighboring seedlings. After planting, put berry baskets over the seedlings to protect them from the sun, or use other protection against cutworms or cold nights. (See "Seedlings in the Garden, To protect.")

SEEDS, To store:

- Store them in old prescription bottles, plastic film containers, or small jars with screw-top lids and keep dry at room temperature.
- Keep the packages in a PC diskette storage box made for 3½-inch disks. They come with dividers.
- Keep them in the refrigerator in a plastic bag. They will keep and still germinate several years after the expiration date (except for short-lived seeds such as delphiniums, larkspurs, the onion family, and parsnips).
- Freeze them in heat-sealable foil packages, or freeze several seed packages all together in a screw-top jar.

SEEDS SAVED FROM PREVIOUS CROPS, To test:

- Test a few weeks before planting to determine their germination rate. Place 10 to 20 seeds on a wet paper towel on a Styrofoam meat tray and cover with another paper towel, or place the seeds on one side of a paper towel and fold over the other side to cover. Place the seeds in a plastic bag to keep moist, then put them in a warm place. Record the date and check the seeds regularly. Germination may take a few days to a few weeks. If at least 7 out of 10 seeds sprout, the seeds are viable. If only a few seeds sprout, either throw them away or sow them extra generously.

SEEDS, SMALL, To sow:

- Pour them onto a plate, pick up a seed with a moistened toothpick, and drop it onto the soil surface. Use tweezers to place larger seeds.
- Add a few teaspoons of clean white sand or dried coffee grounds to the seed packets. Hold the packet closed and shake it to mix the sand or coffee grounds and seed. Spread the mixture evenly over the soil surface.

- Sift a light layer of sand or flour over the surface of the seedling trays. You will be able to see where the seeds are placed.
- Pour seeds into an old salt or spice shaker, put the lid on, and sprinkle over the soil surface or garden row to distribute the seeds evenly.
- Put the seeds in a clean shaker container and add dry unflavored gelatin. Sprinkle the mixture evenly over the soil surface. The gelatin will provide water and protein to the germinating seeds.
- Mix the seeds with the contents of a packet of unflavored gelatin and add water according to package directions. During the jelling process, make sure the seeds are evenly distributed. After the mixture gels, lay spoonfuls on the soil, cover lightly with more soil, then water.
- Roll out white toilet paper, sow the seeds on it, cover with another layer of toilet paper, then cover with sifted soil.

SEEDS STARTED INDOORS, Containers for:

- Use a cardboard or Styrofoam egg carton with the top cut off. Poke holes in the bottom and put a little eggshell in the bottom to make removal easier. Use the lid as a drain tray underneath the container. Or use eggshells set in the egg carton. Poke a small hole in the bottom end for drainage. When transplanting, crush the shells so that the roots can get out.
- Use small paper or Styrofoam drinking cups, tin cans, pint ice cream containers made of plastic, plastic yogurt cups, cottage cheese or sour cream containers, 1-pound cardboard mushroom or vegetable containers, cut-off bottoms of plastic mineral water or soda bottles, half-pint milk cartons with the tops cut off, and hollowed-out orange or grapefruit halves. Poke holes in the bottom for drainage, then fill with potting soil to ¼ inch from the top.
- Cut the upper half off a quart or half-gallon milk carton and use the base for a container by stapling or taping the open end shut. Poke several holes in the bottom for drainage, line with newspaper cut to fit, then fill with seed starter mix to within ¼ to ½ inch from the rim.
- Completely line a cardboard box with aluminum foil. Poke holes in the bottom and fill with the seed starter mix. The light off the foil will keep the plants growing straight.
- Use a disposable foil container. Punch holes in the bottom for drainage, line with newspaper cut to fit, then fill with potting mix to within ¼ to ½ inch from the top.
- Use clear plastic food containers, such as carry-out salad containers. Poke a few drainage holes in the bottom half and fill to ½ inch from the rim with seed starter mix. Plant the seeds and close the lid with a

rubber band, if necessary, This will provide a humid, greenhouselike atmosphere.

- Make individual pots from cardboard. Cut tubes from paper towels, wrapping paper, or toilet rolls into 1½- to 2-inch sections. Stand the cylinders upright side by side in a container, then fill with dampened potting mix and water until the cardboard is saturated or turns dark. Plant one seed in each container. When ready to plant, sow directly in the ground. These are good for plants that don't like their roots disturbed.

- Make individual pots from newspaper. Wrap several sheets around a bottle to form a cylinder. Fasten them with a little paste, and, when dry, cut the cylinder into sections. Place the rings in a container and fill them with potting soil. The containers can be transplanted without disturbing the roots.

- Buy peat pots, which expand in water and make good starting containers. They can be planted directly into the ground or into a larger container and are also good for plants that don't like their roots disturbed.

- Reuse plastic containers a few times by washing them thoroughly with soap and water and disinfecting them in a solution of 1 part chlorine bleach to 8 parts water. Cardboard milk cartons are good only for one use.

- See "Plastic and Metal Containers, To make holes in the bottom."

SEEDS STARTED INDOORS, Starter mix:

- Use fine potting soil, vermiculite, perlite, or a mixture of all. Put whatever you choose in a plastic bag, filling the bag half full, then dampen the starter mix with warm water at the rate of 1 part water to 4 parts starter mix. Mix well by squeezing the bag gently until the water is evenly distributed.

SEEDS STARTED INDOORS, To boost the lighting:

- Line the shelf or windowsill with aluminum foil, or surround the seedlings on the windowsill with sheets of foil-covered cardboard.
- Prop up an old mirror behind the seedlings.

SEEDS STARTED INDOORS, To water:

- Mist gently with a spray bottle. Or place the pot or flat in a shallow pan containing water or a nutrient solution. Let the seedling pot soak up water until the top of the soil is moist. Then remove and let drain.

SEEDS, TREE, To plant:

- Gather the seeds when they are ripe and ready to fall from the tree.

For fruit trees, gather the seeds when the fruit is ripe. Wash orange seeds in lukewarm water and dry before planting. Stick the seed just under the soil surface and give a good watering. Then let the soil dry out before the next watering. If you plant the seeds in a pot, cover it with a plastic bag with breathing holes. Place the pot in a warm, bright location and occasionally spray the top soil with warm water to keep the humidity level high. Remove the plastic when the seed sprouts.

SLUGS AND SNAILS, To get rid of:

- Use a flashlight to find the slugs at night. Pick them up with a stick or wear rubber gloves. Drop them into a container of soapy water or put them in a bag, seal it and put it in the garbage.
- Put out a board or shingle or inverted flowerpots at night where they are likely to be. Or place lettuce, spinach, or cabbage leaves or upside-down grapefruit rinds around the garden. In the morning, lift the traps and scrape the snails into a bucket of soapy water.
- Put down a mulch of used coffee grounds. Besides keeping the slugs away, the grounds make great food for earthworms. They contain 4.0 percent nitrogen, 2.2 percent phosphorus, 3.0 percent potassium, and even help to repel some insects.
- Dry and finely crush eggshells and put them where slugs are bothering plants.
- Sprinkle sawdust around the plants or lay sandpaper around them. (Ask for sawdust and used sandpaper at lumberyards, firewood lots, cabinetmakers, or high school woodshops.)
- Put coarse sand, gravel, cinder, or garden-variety diatomaceous earth around each plant. (Obtain diatomaceous earth from a garden or pool supply store.)
- Cut the bottoms off milk cartons to make shallow dishes 1½ inches deep. Bury them below the surface of the soil, and put in a little beer, or a mixture of equal parts beer and water sweetened with 1 teaspoon sugar to 1 cup water. Or bury a nearly empty beer can in the soil with the can top level with the surface of the ground.
- Dissolve 2 teaspoons sugar and ¼ cup baking yeast in 2 cups water. Dig shallow depressions into the soil, and set a shallow container into the soil with the top edges flush with the surface. Pour ½ cup yeast mixture into each container. Or cut 1-inch holes, 1 inch up from the bottom around a plastic bleach bottle. Bury the bottle in the soil up to the bottom, edge of the holes, and fill to the same level with the bait.
- Edge the garden beds with copper-based strips. Make sure there are no snails in the area before putting up the strips.

SNAPDRAGONS, Hint on:
- Cut off the top half when the plants are 4 to 5 inches tall to have them grow sturdy instead of lanky.

SOIL, To acidify:
- Add dampened acid peat moss to the soil. (Pour a little boiling water on the peat moss, then add cold water to dampen it thoroughly, and leave for several hours before adding it to the soil.) Or add tea leaves, coffee grounds (inquire at local coffeehouses or espresso bars whether you can pick up their used grounds), cottonseed meal, oak sawdust (add high-nitrogen fertilizer at the same time), or mulch with pine needles or oak leaves.
- Water gardenias and other acid-loving plants with leftover tea or coffee or with a solution of ½ teaspoon white vinegar in 1 quart warm water.
- Put a pinch of Epsom salts in the hole when planting acid-loving vegetables such as tomatoes, peppers, or eggplant. The magnesium helps set blossoms, and the sulfur adds acid.

SOIL, To make more alkaline:
- Add wood ashes, pulverized eggshells, clam shells, oyster shells, bonemeal, or most animal manures.

SOIL, To sterilize for potting:
- Sterilize it in the microwave by half filling a plastic bag with moistened garden soil. Use 1 part water to 4 parts soil. The soil should be damp but not wet. Mix well in the bag. Seal it and make a hole in the top. Heat on full power for 3 minutes per 1 quart soil (or until it is steaming), then let the soil cool.
- Sterilize it in the oven by spreading the moistened soil in a shallow pan and baking it at 200°F for at least 30 minutes. Cool before using. (Be prepared for the aroma of baking soil; it's not pleasant.)

SOIL, To test:
- Call your local Department of Agriculture Cooperative Extension Service for information on where to send your soil for testing, or if they will do it for you.
- Test the soil pH quickly and inexpensively with blue litmus paper (obtainable at a pharmacy). Water the area, wait a few minutes, then press the paper to the damp earth. Repeat the procedure wherever you want to test for acidity. If the paper turns pink, the soil is acid.

SOWBUGS, To get rid of:
- Place a clay flowerpot upside down wherever sowbugs are appearing. Let the pot sit for a couple of days, then remove the sowbugs from inside the pot and drop them into a container of soapy water. Or pour boiling water on them if they are on concrete and away from the grass.

SPRAYER, CLOGGED, To unclog:
- Remove the nozzle and rinse it. Use a toothpick to clean out the holes. If the nozzle is still clogged, soak it in white vinegar for 1 hour. Rinse before using.

TOMATOES, Hints on:
- Trench tomato transplants by laying them sideways and pinching off the lower leaves below the soil level. Have only the top third showing. This makes for a sturdier plant.
- Mix 1 teaspoon Epsom salts or 2 teaspoons bonemeal in with the dirt at the bottom of the hole when transplanting. When the plants have blossoms, dissolve 1 tablespoon Epsom salts in 1 quart warm water and spray the solution on the leaves and blossoms, then pour the remainder in a ring around the plant at the drip line. Repeat several times during the blossoming period. Or for a one-time boost, add ¼ cup Epsom salts to the soil around each plant when blossoms appear. Epsom salts consists of magnesium sulfate, which will improve the soil.
- Mulch with black plastic or aluminum foil before the weather gets too hot. It warms the soil and increases the yield. Aluminum foil also will repel flea beetles and aphids.
- Ensure better pollination by gently shaking the plant during the driest part of the day or by gently flicking each blossom or by dabbing each blossom with a soft artist's paintbrush.

TOMATOES, GREEN, To ripen:
- Wrap each one in three thicknesses of newspaper and store in a cool place, not the refrigerator. Wrapping the tomatoes in newspaper absorbs moisture, lets them ripen slowly, and prevents one spoiled one from spoiling the others.

TOOLS, To locate quickly:
- Paint a band of bright paint on the handles of your garden tools. This makes them easy to find if they are left in the garden. Naturally, don't use green paint.

TOOLS, To make a caddie for:
- Use a 1-gallon plastic bleach bottle. Cut away the upper side opposite the handle and use it for gardening gloves, shears, clippers, etc.
- Buy a child's red wagon at a garage sale and use it to cart heavy items around the garden.

TOOLS, To prevent rusting:
- Clean them after each use with a stiff-bristle brush and rub them with an oily rag before putting them away.
- Clean and lubricate the tools in a mixture of sand and motor oil. Fill a pail with sand and pour in 1 quart oil (used motor oil is fine), then mix together. Keep the container in the garage or tool shed, and after each use push the tools into the oily sand a few times. Or keep a pail of plain clean dry sand, and store the tools in the sand when not using them.
- Rub the lawn mower with an oily rag after each use.

TOOLS, To remove rust:
- Clean metal parts with a wire brush, emery cloth, or steel wool. Apply a protective coating of oil or petroleum jelly with a clean rag.
- Rub them with a soap-filled steel wool pad dipped in turpentine, then rub with a wadded piece of aluminum foil.
- Put a tool that is rusted beyond repair to good use. Cover it with water and let it sit until the water turns brown, then pour the water around the plants to give them an iron-mineral boost.

TRANSPLANTING FROM PEAT POTS, Hint on:
- Slit the sides and remove the bottom of the peat pot, unless roots have already penetrated the pot, and tear off the rim above the soil.

TREES, STAKING, Hint on:
- Secure the tree to the stake with a slice of old inner tube from a ten-speed bike.

TRELLIS, To make:
- Tie together the rings that hold beverage six-packs.

VEGETABLE PLANTING, Hints on:
- Rotate your vegetables. Never plant the same crop in the same area two years in a row.
- Avoid planting peppers where tomatoes grew previously. They are subject to similar diseases and pests.
- Do not purchase vegetable transplants that are already flowering.

- Put several matches in the bottom of the holes dug for eggplant or pepper transplants. The matches are a good source of sulfur that acid-loving plants need. (Save matches that restaurants give away as advertising.)

WASPS, To get rid of:
- Put 2 inches white vinegar in a long-neck bottle and leave out.

WATER CONSERVATION, Information on:
- Send away for "How to Xeriscape" from the Texas Water Development Board. (See USEFUL ADDRESSES AND PHONE NUMBERS, "Gardens.") Xeriscape (from the Greek *xeros* for "dry") relies on garden designs that retain rainwater, soil improvement to increase its water-holding abilities, mulches that keep the soil moist, groundcover that is drought tolerant, and mature plants suitable to an area's rainfall.

WATERING A SPECIFIC AREA, Hint on:
- Bend a coat hanger into a V. Place the hose in the V and position it to water the shrub or tree.

WATERING A YOUNG TREE/SHRUB OR WATER-LOVING PLANTS, Hints on:
- Poke a tiny hole in the bottom of a 1-gallon plastic milk or bleach bottle, put it next to the plant, and fill it with water. The water will drip out slowly and seep down to the roots. Fill the jugs early in the morning and at night during dry spells.
- Cut off the bottom of the jug and sink the neck of the jug deeply into the ground, then fill the jug with water.
- Punch holes in the bottom of a 3-pound coffee can and sink it at ground level next to the tree. Fill it with water. The water will get below the root level.
- Drive PVC pipes into the ground close to the plants, then pour the water into the pipes so it will be directed closer to the roots.

WEED KILLER, Hint on:
- Spray the weed killer through an empty paper-towel or toilet-paper cylinder to avoid harming surrounding vegetation. Or make a funnel from a cut-off bleach bottle or plastic soft drink bottle.

WINDOW BOXES, Hints on:
- Line the bases of the boxes with several layers of newspaper before adding the soil. The paper prevents the soil from drying out too quickly after each watering.

- Place a layer of gravel on the top of the boxes to prevent the soil from splattering when it rains and a layer of gravel or charcoal on the bottom so drainage holes won't clog.

WHITEFLIES: See "Insects, Plant, To control."

Kitchens

APPLIANCES, To clean:
- Scrub with undiluted white vinegar to remove grease and grime.
- Rub with a cloth moistened with rubbing alcohol.
- See HELPFUL HINTS, A TO Z, "Cleaners, All-Purpose, To make."

APPLIANCES, Too heavy to move:
- Put a piece of linoleum cut to size under the appliance. When time to clean, pull the linoleum out and wash it, then slide it back under again.
- Squirt liquid dishwashing detergent around the base of the appliance. The appliance will glide on the detergent when you push it.

BASTER SUBSTITUTE:
- Use a clean plastic squeeze bottle, such as a mustard or ketchup container, with the tip on top. Squeeze and draw in the juice and squirt. Make sure the top is on tight and the container is very clean.

BLENDER, To clean:
- Put a drop of liquid dishwashing detergent in the jar, half fill with water, cover, and run for a few seconds on low speed. Rinse and let dry. Periodically remove the blade and bottom assembly from the jar to wash out food particles.

BOWL, To prevent slipping when using:
- Place the bowl on a folded damp towel on the counter or in the sink.

BREAD BOARD, DISCOLORED, To clean:
- Dip a slice of lemon into a little table salt and rub the board well with the cut side of the lemon. Rinse with clear water and let air-dry. It will whiten as it dries.
- See "Butcher Block, To clean" and "Cutting Board, Wood, To avoid odors."

BROILER PAN, To clean:
- Pour off fat while the pan is still hot, then fill it with hot water and replace the grid. Sprinkle the grid with dishwasher or laundry detergent, or table salt, and cover with wet paper towels or newspaper. Then put the pan back into the warm oven for about 20 minutes.

BROILER PAN, To make cleanup easier:
- Put about ¼ inch water or a piece of bread in the bottom section when broiling.
- Line the bottom of the broiler pan with foil.

BROILER PAN, To prevent food from sticking:
- Spray the grid with nonstick cooking spray or grease it with oil.

BUTCHER BLOCK, To clean:
- Pour on straight white vinegar. Scrub, then rinse with plain water.
- Scrub the block with baking soda applied with a damp sponge, then rinse.
- See "Bread Board, Discolored, To clean" and "Cutting Board, Wood, To avoid odors."

CABINETS, PAINTED, GREASY, To clean:
- Mix 1 cup ammonia and ¼ cup washing soda mixed with 1 gallon warm water. While wearing rubber gloves, sponge the solution onto the cabinets, then rinse with clear water.

CABINETS, WOOD, To clean:
- Clean the dirt around the handles with dishwashing detergent first, then wash the entire cabinet with a solution of Murphy's Oil Soap and water. Wipe the solution on lightly without saturating the wood. Dry promptly with terry cloth in the direction of the grain.
- See HELPFUL HINTS, A TO Z, "Wood Paneling/Cabinets, Dirty, Greasy, To clean."

CAN OPENER, To clean:
- Spray the cutter assembly with rubbing alcohol and wipe dry.
- Run a paper towel through the cutting process.
- Brush with an old clean toothbrush to loosen the grime.

CANS, To remove contents:
- Place the opened can upside down on a plate. Puncture the other end with a can opener and the ingredients will slide right out. If not, remove the end and push the ingredients out.

CASSEROLE DISH, BURNED, To clean:
- Sprinkle with automatic dishwasher detergent, dampen slightly, and let sit for a while to soften the burned-on food.
- Cover with baking soda, moisten, and leave for a couple of hours or overnight.

CASSEROLES AND SERVING CONTAINERS, Hint on:
- Measure the volume of each container and mark it on the outside bottom. Scratch the information into metal, and use a waterproof marking pen or nail polish on glass or ceramic containers.

CERAMIC WARE, METALLIC MARKS ON, To remove:
- Rub gently with steel wool to remove the marks caused by something metal rubbing against it in the dishwasher.

CHINA, SELDOM USED, To store:
- Wrap in clear plastic wrap to keep it clean. Wrap stacks of plates together.

CHINA, STAINED, To clean:
- Remove tea and coffee stains by rubbing the china with a soft wet cloth that has been dipped into baking soda or table salt.
- Use equal amounts of table salt and white vinegar to clean the coffee and tea stains.
- Soak china overnight in automatic dishwasher detergent and hot water.
- Soak china in a mild solution of chlorine bleach and water until the stains are removed.

CLEANING HARD-TO-REACH PLACES, Hint on:
- Tie an old sock over the end of a yardstick or flyswatter and use to clean crevices beneath the refrigerator, washer, or dryer.

COFFEE MAKER, AUTOMATIC DRIP, To clean:
- Remove mineral deposits by running 1 quart white vinegar through the brewing cycle, then pouring the white vinegar back in and letting it sit for 30 minutes, then running it through the brewing cycle again. Finally, run fresh water through the brewing cycle twice.

COFFEE PERCOLATORS: To clean:
- Remove mineral deposits by filling the percolator with white vinegar and leaving for 30 minutes. Rinse thoroughly with clear water. Clean the tubes with a small piece of cotton saturated with sudsy water. Poke it through with a pencil or straw.

COFFEEPOT, GLASS, BURNED, To clean:
- Pour table salt into the pot and let it sit until the burned crust comes loose, then wash the pot clean.

COLANDER SUBSTITUTE:
- Punch holes in an aluminum pie plate and bend it to the shape required.

COOKING OIL, To make easier to pour:
- Store in a small well-washed-out bottle that has a squirt top or a well-washed-out squeeze-type mustard or ketchup container. No excess will be poured out by mistake.

COPPER KETTLE, To clean:
- Fill the kettle with hot water and polish the outside with a cloth dipped in buttermilk or sour milk.
- Fill the kettle with boiling water before cleaning. It will polish more quickly.

COPPERWARE, To clean: See "Pots and Pans, Copper, Care of," and HELP-FUL HINTS, A TO Z, "Copper, Unlacquered, To clean."

COUNTERTOPS, PLASTIC LAMINATES, FORMICA, Care of:
- Wipe work surfaces with a sudsy sponge. Soap or detergent kills most household bacteria and leaves behind an alkaline pH in which germs do not thrive.
- Wash with straight white vinegar. No rinsing is necessary.
- Scrub with baking soda applied on a damp cloth, then rinse. For stubborn spots, scrub with a paste of baking soda and water and let sit for half an hour, then wipe up and rinse.
- Remove stains such as grape juice, Jell-O, and Kool-Aid by squeezing on lemon juice. Let it sit for a while, then rinse.
- Remove ink stains from meat labels and packaging with rubbing alcohol.
- Rub with car wax or a silicone sealer to spruce up dull or scratched countertops.
- Cover up scratches with a matching permanent felt-tip marker, automobile touch-up paint applied with an artist's brush, or a melted crayon tip.

CROCK POT, BURNED, To clean:
- Fill the crock pot with a hot soapy solution and cook on high for 1 hour or so.
- Sprinkle on baking soda and moisten. Let it sit for a couple of hours.

CUTTING BOARD, Best kind to use:
- Use wood. Researchers at the University of Wisconsin's Food Re-

search Institute have found that wooden cutting boards kill off bacteria that live for hours on plastic boards. Scientists Dean Cliver and Nese Ak discovered that food-poisoning bacteria lived for only 3 three minutes on the wooden board they contaminated but did not die on the plastic boards.

CUTTING BOARD, WOOD, To avoid odors:
- Rub the board with a slice of freshly cut lemon or lime after cutting onions or garlic, then rinse and wipe dry.
- Rub table salt into the board to eliminate odors as well as stains.
- Make a paste of baking soda and water and rub it into the surface. Rinse off.
- See "Bread Board, Discolored, To clean" and "Butcher Block, To clean."

DISHES, BROKEN, To replace:
- Look for the manufacturer and call 800 directory assistance.
- See also USEFUL ADDRESSES AND PHONE NUMBERS, "China and Ceramic Makers."

DISHES, CRACKED, To repair:
- Put the item in a pan of milk and boil it for 45 minutes. The crack will disappear due to the protein in the milk.

DISHES, GREASY-SMELLING, To remove odor:
- Put a few tablespoons of white vinegar in the dishwasher or dishwashing water to cut down the grease and help remove the odor.

DISHWASHER, To clean periodically:
- Set a bowl of white vinegar (about 2 cups) in the bottom rack of the dishwasher and run it through a complete cycle.

DISHWASHER, To remove iron stains:
- Use a commercial iron stain cleaner, such as Iron-Out or Rover.

DISHWASHER, To remove mineral deposits:
- Put 1 tablespoon citric acid or 2 tablespoons Tang (the orange drink) in each section of the detergent dispensers, and run the empty machine through the entire cycle without detergent. (Obtain citric acid in a drugstore or the spice or canning section of a supermarket.)

DISHWASHER, To remove odor:
- Place an uncovered bowl of baking soda in the dishwasher, or sprinkle baking soda in the bottom. Close the dishwasher and leave for 24

hours. Remove the bowl of baking soda before using the machine. The baking soda in the bottom can remain.

DISHWASHER PRONGS, To repair the coating:
- Slide a white silicone caulking tube over the prong.
- Buy a dishwasher rack patch product made for the purpose.

DISHWASHING LIQUID SUBSTITUTE:
- Use mild shampoo.

DOUBLE BOILER, Hint on:
- Place a small jar lid or a few marbles into the bottom section with the water. The rattling sound will tell you that the water is getting low.

DRAIN STOPPER, Hint on:
- Put a piece of plastic wrap under the drain stopper for a tight seal. If you tie the bag at the top, there will be no chance of it accidentally going down the drain.

EGG, DROPPED, To make it easier to wipe up:
- Pour table salt on the egg immediately and let sit for 15 to 20 minutes, then sweep it up. Also use salt to remove egg from dishes or egg cups.

ELECTRIC CORDS, To store:
- Keep detachable appliance cords in empty cardboard cylinders from toilet paper or paper towels. Indicate the contents on the outside of the container.

FAUCET LIME DEPOSITS, To remove:
- Cover with white-vinegar-soaked paper towels for 1 hour. The vinegar will soften the deposits.

FIRE, To extinguish:
- Extinguish fires in a pan by putting the lid on. The lack of oxygen will put out the fire.
- Use baking soda for a small electrical fire. Use salt or baking soda for a small grease fire. Don't use flour; it can explode.

FISH ODOR ON HANDS, To remove:
- Rub with a piece of lemon dipped in table salt, then rinse with water.

FLOOR, To remove black heel marks:
- Scrub the spots with a damp sponge sprinkled with baking soda. Or make a paste of baking soda and water and scrub the spots until gone, then rinse.

- Put a dab of nongel toothpaste on a moist paper towel and rub the spots gently. Rinse with water.

FLOOR, To remove cooking-grease particles:
- Add a little white vinegar to the water used to clean the kitchen floor.

FLOOR, To remove dull film:
- Rinse after washing no-wax floors. To restore shine, add 1 cup white vinegar to a bucket of water and mop.

FLOOR, To remove old wax:
- Mop with a solution of 3 parts water to 1 part rubbing alcohol.

FLOOR, To remove spilled grease:
- Sprinkle with water to stop the grease from spreading, then wipe up with newspaper or paper towels.

FLOOR, To shine between waxings:
- Put a piece of wax paper under the mop and slide it around the floor.

FLOOR, VINYL, To remove asphalt, tar, glue:
- Lift the spot with a soft cloth dipped in alcohol or lighter fluid, then wash with a mild detergent solution.

FLOOR, VINYL, To remove food stains:
- Rub the stains lightly with a little rubbing alcohol, then rinse.

FLOUR SIFTER, To store :
- Keep in a plastic bag. You won't have to wash it between uses.

FOOD SCALE, To determine accuracy:
- Place nine one-cent coins on the scale. They should weigh 1 ounce. A stick of butter or margarine should weigh 4 ounces.

FOOD SPILL, CAKED ON, To remove:
- Place on the spill a soapy dishcloth that has been heated in the microwave. After the food is loosened, wipe up and rinse.

FORMICA SCRATCHES, To cover up:
- Use a matching permanent felt-tip marker, automobile touch-up paint, or melted crayon.

FREEZER, Hints on:
- Fill the freezer just over three-quarters full for optimum efficiency. Packing the freezer impedes the flow of air needed for cooling, and understocking the freezer wastes energy.

- Put plastic milk or juice cartons filled with water in the freezer if it's understocked. Fill the containers three-quarters full. You'll also have water on hand in an emergency.
- Keep a roll of masking tape in the kitchen to date and label anything to be stored.
- Cut the labels off original meat packages and tape them to rewrapped packages. The labels have the type of meat, date of purchase, and weight.

FREEZER, To defrost:
- Blow on the ice with a hair dryer set to high.
- Put a pan of boiling water in the freezing unit and several thicknesses of newspaper on the top shelf of the refrigerator. The paper will absorb the ice and water, making cleanup easier.

FREEZER, To remove odors: (See "Refrigerator Odors, To eliminate.")

FRYING, To avoid splatters:
- Invert a metal colander over the frying pan to prevent splatters.

FRYING PAN, ELECTRIC, To clean:
- Cover the bottom of the frying pan with an ammonia-soaked cloth and put into a plastic bag. Close the bag tightly and let it sit overnight.

GARBAGE CAN, To sanitize:
- Wash with soapy water, then wipe with a solution of 2 tablespoons chlorine bleach and 1 quart water. Leave for 10 minutes, then rinse.

GARBAGE DISPOSAL, To keep clean and sanitary:
- Run the disposal using cold water. This solidifies the grease and washes it out without clogging the drain.
- Grind up citrus rinds in the disposal.
- Mix 1 cup water and 1 cup white vinegar and freeze in ice cube trays. Grind the frozen cubes through the disposal with cold water. This will also sharpen the blades.
- Pour in ½ cup baking soda or a couple of tablespoons of borax and let stand for 1 hour, then flush with hot water with the disposal running.

GARBAGE DISPOSAL, LOCKED, To unjam the motor:
- Press the red restart button. If that doesn't work, turn off the disposal and place the handle of a broom or plunger down the disposal and turn it counterclockwise. Then remove the broom or plunger and push the restart button.

GARLIC AND ONION ODOR ON COUNTERS, *To remove:*
- Wet the area and sprinkle on baking soda. Rub in, then rinse with clear water.
- Add 1 tablespoon chlorine bleach to 1 cup water and wipe the area. Leave for 5 minutes, then rinse thoroughly.

GARLIC AND ONION ODOR ON HANDS, *To remove:*
- Rinse hands in a solution of 1 tablespoon vinegar to 1 cup of warm water, then dust with baking soda. Rinse again thoroughly with cool water.
- Rub with a piece of cut lemon or lemon juice, getting it under the nails and around the cuticles.
- Rinse hands with mouthwash or scrub with toothpaste.
- Rub with baking soda or a paste of baking soda and water.
- Rub with an unpeeled raw potato.
- Rub hands over a stainless-steel spoon under running water.
- Wash hands in milk, followed by a cold-water rinse. The milk absorbs the odor.

GLASSES, TWO, STUCK TOGETHER, *To separate:*
- Put cold water in the top glass and dip the bottom one in fairly warm water. Gently pull the glasses apart.
- Pour some baby oil or mineral oil between the glasses, allow to set for a while, and then gently pull them apart. Wash in hot soapy water and rinse.

GRATER, *To clean:*
- Spray with a nonstick cooking spray before use.
- Rub a raw potato over the surface after grating cheese to make it easier to clean.

GREASE SPOTS BEHIND THE STOVE, *To remove:*
- Tackle the spots when they occur with a spray of water and vinegar or water and ammonia.
- Make a paste of baking soda and water, leave on for 1 hour, and rinse.
- Let a pot or kettle of water steam until the walls are moist, then wipe dry with paper towels. Or after steaming, wipe with an all-purpose cleaner.
- Remove brown spots with a mixture of 1 ounce each milk, chlorine bleach, and water. Saturate a paper towel with the mixture and place over the stain for 1 minute, then rinse.

- Make a paste of powdered cleanser and chlorine bleach. Leave it on the brown spot for 5 minutes, then rinse it off.
- Make cleanup of a painted wall easier by applying furniture polish and buffing it well.

ICE-CUBE TRAYS, To avoid sticking:
- Wipe the trays dry and rub the outside with glycerin.
- Line the freezer shelf with wax paper.

JARS AND CONTAINERS, To open:
- Take an ice pick or can opener and make a little hole in the top of the jar lid. This releases the pressure and the jar will open easily.
- Twist the lid with a piece of sandpaper, sand side down.
- Wrap rubber bands around or use a thick broccoli band.
- Twist the lid off small bottle caps with a nutcracker.
- Use a damp cloth or rubber glove.
- Hold the lid under hot tap water and rotate the jar slowly. If the jar has been refrigerated, begin with warm water and gradually work up to hot water so the glass won't crack.
- Place the jar in a shallow drawer and hold firmly in place with your hip while unscrewing the lid.

JARS AND CONTAINERS, To remove odors from:
- Rinse the jars with white vinegar before reusing them.
- Put a little dry mustard and water in the containers, and let them sit awhile.
- Fill jars with warm water, 1 tablespoon tea leaves, and 1 tablespoon white vinegar. Let stand 3 to 4 hours, then shake out and rinse.

KETTLE, ELECTRIC, To clean:
- Wipe exterior with a damp cloth. Do not immerse in water. Half fill the inside with equal parts of white vinegar and water, and boil for 10 to 15 minutes. Prop the spout cover open on an automatic kettle so that it will not switch off. Empty the kettle and rinse a number of times to remove mineral particles. If particles remain, repeat the procedure with undiluted vinegar.

KETTLE LIME SCALE, To remove:
- Boil equal parts of white vinegar and water in the kettle. Let it sit for several hours or overnight, then scrape out the deposit with steel wool. If necessary, repeat the process. Rinse thoroughly.
- Heat white vinegar in the kettle and let it stand overnight. Rinse thoroughly the next day.

- Boil 2 teaspoons cream of tartar in 4 ounces water in the kettle for a few minutes. Add a few clean pebbles, marbles, or oyster shells during the boiling to break up thick deposits. Rinse thoroughly afterward.
- Fill the kettle with water and refrigerate for several hours.
- Fill the kettle with water and 2 teaspoons borax, and boil for 20 minutes. Scrape off any remaining deposit and rinse out thoroughly.

MICROWAVE CONTAINER, To test if safe:
- Put the container in the microwave along with a glass measuring cup containing 1 cup water. Turn on high for 1 minute. If the dish is hot, it is not microwave-safe.

MICROWAVE OVEN, To clean:
- Put 1 cup water in a 2-quart glass measuring cup or a microwave-safe cup and bring to a boil in the microwave. After the water boils, turn off the microwave and keep the door closed for a few minutes. The steam will soften the cooked-on food and make it easy to wipe down. Then dissolve 2 tablespoons baking soda in 2 cups warm water and wash the interior with a sponge or cloth.
- Remove smells from the oven by adding lemon juice to 1 cup water and heating it on high for 1 minute. Turn off the microwave and keep the door closed for a few minutes, then wipe the interior dry.
- Remove spills by covering them with wet paper towels and turning the oven on high for a few seconds. Wipe up.

MIXING BOWL SPLATTERS, To avoid:
- Cut the bottom out of a large paper shopping bag and slip it over the bowl and mixer. Or put a plastic bag or plastic wrap over the mixing bowl and make a hole for the beaters to fit through.

MOP HEAD REPLACEMENT, CLAMP TYPE, To make:
- Stitch or tie together strips of old socks and clamp as many strips in the mop as it will hold.

ODOR FROM ONIONS OR GARLIC ON HANDS: See "Garlic and Onion Odor on Hands, To remove."

ODOR OF FISH IN PAN AFTER COOKING, To remove:
- Sprinkle the pan with table salt, pour hot water in it, and let it stand for a while, then wash as usual.
- Boil 1 to 2 tablespoons white vinegar in water in the pan before washing it.
- Wash it with a mixture of baking soda and water.

- Put used tea leaves into the pan, cover with water for a few minutes, then rinse out. Any taste or smell of fish will have disappeared.

ODOR OF FISH OR VEGETABLES COOKING, To minimize:
- Place a saucer filled with white vinegar on a nearby counter.
- Bake orange peels in a 350°F oven directly on the oven racks.
- Boil white vinegar in an uncovered pan.

OVEN, To clean:
- Warm the oven to 150°F, then turn it off. Plug vent holes in the oven with paper towels and extinguish the pilot light in a gas oven. Place a small glass or pottery bowl containing ½ cup ammonia on the top shelf and a large pan of boiling water on the bottom shelf. Close the door, and leave the ammonia and water in the oven overnight. The next day, open the oven and let it air before washing off the surfaces with the ammonia and a little dishwashing detergent added to a small pail of warm water. Scrub the loosened grease from the oven and rinse with clear water.
- Warm the oven to 150°F, turn it off, then thoroughly spray the interior with an all-purpose spray cleaner. Wait 15 minutes, then rub the grease off. Put a paper cup over the oven bulb to protect it from the spray cleaner.
- Sprinkle the bottom of the oven with automatic dishwasher detergent and cover it with wet paper towels. Let it stand a few hours, then wipe it up.
- Wet the bottom of the oven with water, then cover it with baking soda. Sprinkle some more water on top of the baking soda. Let it sit overnight, then scrub and rinse.
- Use 1 cup baking soda and ¼ cup washing soda for stubborn burned-on areas. Proceed as above.
- Use a commercial oven cleaner according to directions, then wipe up with a short-handled window squeegee or newspaper. Rinse with clean water, then spray the surface with a solution of equal parts of white vinegar and water. Wipe down with a damp sponge. The vinegar and water will eliminate any smell the first time you use the oven after cleaning. Or bake orange peels at 350°F to remove the smell of the cleaning solution.
- Lay sheets of newspaper on the countertop, then put the oven racks on the newspaper. Position the racks, slightly overlapping, so you can scrub them all at one time. When finished with one side, turn the racks over and scrub the other side, then rinse.

- Put the racks in the bathtub on top of an old towel. Put in enough hot water to cover, then sprinkle 1 cup automatic dishwasher detergent over the racks and allow to soak clean, then rinse.
- Wipe away grease and spills in the oven after each use, or put a liner on the oven bottom to catch spills and reduce the need for frequent cleaning.

OVEN DOOR, GLASS, To clean:
- Sprinkle with baking soda, then rub with a damp cloth. Allow to dry for a few minutes, then wipe with a soft dry cloth.
- Wipe on ammonia and let it set for a few minutes, then rinse.

OVEN DOOR, SQUEAKY, To silence:
- Rub the point of a soft lead pencil across the hinges.

OVEN FOOD SPILL/FOOD CATCHING FIRE, To take care of:
- Pour table salt immediately on the spilled food, grease, or juice to absorb it and prevent smoking. When the oven cools, brush up the residue and wipe with a damp sponge.
- Extinguish flame and smoke by pouring on either table salt or baking soda.

OVEN USE, Hints on:
- Avoid preheating the oven except for baking or unless the recipe specifically calls for it.
- Use oblong or oval dishes. They use oven space more economically than round ones.

PAPER PLATES, To store:
- Put them in a cake carrier to keep them clean and out of the way.

PAPER TOWELS, To economize on:
- Have your paper towels do double duty. Once you've used one to wipe your clean wet hands, reuse the towel to wipe up a spot on the counter or floor.
- Drain fried food on layers of newspaper or with only one layer of paper towels on the top.
- Keep the old phone book and tear off a page or two to mop up greasy pans.
- Use crumpled newspaper to wipe out greasy pans, wipe off oven cleaner, and polish windows.
- Cut the roll in half so you'll have smaller sheets. If you need more, simply use more sheets.

- Use Handy Wipes, cotton tea towels, or cotton diapers, which can be washed.

PEPPER SHAKER, CLOGGED, To prevent:
- Place a dried pea in the pepper container.
- Put a few peppercorns in the container.

PIPES, To keep sanitary:
- Fill the sink with 1 gallon water and ⅔ cup chlorine bleach, then drain and let the tap run for a minute.

PLASTIC CONTAINERS, To remove lettering:
- Use nail polish remover to remove lettering on margarine lids and other containers intended for reuse.

PLASTIC CONTAINERS, To remove stains:
- Fill the containers with water, then drop in 1 or 2 foaming denture cleaning tablets. Let the articles soak for 15 to 20 minutes, then rinse.
- Rub the surface vigorously with a damp cloth dipped in baking soda, then rinse.
- Put them outside in the sun; even tomato stains disappear.
- Pack with crumpled-up newspaper, then cover and leave overnight.

PLASTIC FOOD BAGS, To dry:
- Stick them on top of a soda bottle or wire whisk propped up in the dish drainer, or stuff with crumpled paper towels.

PLASTIC GROCERY BAGS, To store:
- Keep them in an empty tissue box to dispense them one at a time and save space.
- Stuff them in an empty cardboard paper towel or gift wrap cylinder.

PLASTIC MELTED ON AN APPLIANCE, To remove:
- Wipe off with a piece of terry cloth while the surface is still warm.
- Heat the appliance to soften the plastic, then scrape off as much as possible with a hard plastic spatula or credit card. Remove any residue on the cold appliance with a cloth dipped in rubbing alcohol.
- Hold a hair dryer set to high 6 to 8 inches away from the melted plastic. As the plastic softens, scrape it with a hard plastic spatula or paper towel soaked in white vinegar.
- Use rubbing alcohol, lighter fluid, or nail polish remover.

PLASTIC UTENSILS ROUGH OR RAGGED, To restore:
- File them down with a fresh emery board or cut away the edges with scissors.

PLASTIC WRAP, To make easier to handle:
- Wet hands with warm water before touching plastic wrap.
- Store it in the freezer to keep it from tangling.
- Moisten the rim of the bowl you are covering and the plastic will cling better.

POT AND PAN SCRUBBER SUBSTITUTE:
- Use a crumpled ball of aluminum foil.

POTS AND PANS, ALUMINUM, Hint on:
- Prevent aluminum from leaching out of a new pot or pan by washing it with hot sudsy water and rinsing well. Then fill it with water and boil for 3 or 4 minutes. Rinse again.

POTS AND PANS, ALUMINUM, DISCOLORED, To brighten:
- Do not use baking or washing soda on aluminum. It darkens the metal.
- Boil 2 teaspoons lemon juice or white vinegar with 1 quart water in the pan until brightened.
- Dissolve 1 tablespoon cream of tartar in 1 quart hot water. Either soak the stained aluminum in it or boil the solution in the discolored pan for 5 minutes. After stains are removed, wash the pan in hot soapy water and rinse.
- Mix 2 tablespoons cream of tartar with enough white vinegar to make a stiff paste. Rub on the aluminum with a sponge, let dry, then wash off the paste with hot water.
- Mix 1 tablespoon alum, 1 tablespoon cornstarch, and enough water to make a paste. Rub on the aluminum with a damp sponge, then let the paste dry. Rinse in hot water and polish dry with a clean cloth.

POTS AND PANS, BURNED, To clean:
- Coat the food generously with baking soda and barely moisten it with water. Leave the paste on for several hours or overnight, then wash the pan as usual. (Not for aluminum.)
- Pour baking soda over the burned area and add a little cold water. Let it stand for 1 hour, then heat the water slowly and allow it to simmer for a few minutes. The burned particles will come off quite easily. (Not for aluminum.)
- Cover the burned area with table salt, moisten, and leave in the sun for 2 or 3 days. Repeat until the pan is clean.

- Fill the pan with water, drop in 1 or 2 fabric softening sheets, and let stand for 1 hour or more.
- Spray glass and porcelain baking pans with oven cleaner and let stand for about 30 minutes to remove burned-on grease.
- Place a pan with burned-on grease in a plastic bag along with an ammonia-soaked paper towel. Close the bag tightly and leave the pan in the bag overnight. The next day the grease will wash off easily.

POTS AND PANS, CAST IRON, To clean:

- Scrub with a vegetable brush or nylon scrubber and rinse it with boiling water, then dry thoroughly. To ensure thorough drying, put the pan in a 250°F oven for a few minutes. Avoid using soap or detergent.
- Prevent rust by rubbing the inside of the pan with a piece of wax paper or a little oil while it is still warm after washing.
- Clean a badly crusted outside with a commercial oven cleaner and let sit for 2 hours. Then wash with a solution of half white vinegar and half water. Or put the pan on the grill to burn off the baked-on residue.

POTS AND PANS, CAST IRON, To season:

- Wipe the pan lightly with vegetable oil and put it in a 250°F oven for a couple of hours. Wipe it with more oil every half hour.

POTS AND PANS, COPPER, Care of:

- Do not overheat the pans; overheating will shorten the life of the tin lining.
- Avoid using an abrasive cleaner or steel wool, which can erode the lining. After washing, coat with a nonstick cooking spray to keep moisture out of the tin lining and to prevent the copper from tarnishing. Wash off the coating before using.
- See HELPFUL HINTS, A TO Z, "Copper, Unlacquered, To clean."

POTS AND PANS, GLASS/PORCELAIN, DISCOLORED, To clean:

- Boil a solution of half white vinegar and water in the pan, then wash in hot soapy water, and rinse.
- Put enough water in the pot to cover the stain, then add 2 tablespoons powdered dishwasher detergent and boil for 15 to 30 minutes. Or bring to a boil and let soak overnight, then scrub with a plastic scrubber.

POTS AND PANS, GREASY, To clean:
- Boil equal parts of water and white vinegar in the pot for a few minutes.

POTS AND PANS, NONSTICK, STAINED, To clean:
- Simmer 3 tablespoons dishwasher detergent and 1 cup water in the pan for 15 to 20 minutes. Wash the pan thoroughly, rinse, and dry. Recondition the pan with oil before using.
- Place in the pan 3 tablespoons baking soda, 2 or 3 lemon slices, and enough water to cover the stains. Simmer until clean. Or put the item to be cleaned in a large pan containing the solution and simmer until clean.
- Put 2 tablespoons baking powder, ½ cup chlorine bleach, and 1 cup water in the stained pot and boil for about 10 minutes. Wash the pan well with soap and water and dry. Recondition the pan with cooking oil or shortening before using.
- Use ¼ cup coffeepot cleaner in 1 quart of water. Simmer in the pot until clean.
- Put 3 tablespoons oxygen bleach, 1 teaspoon liquid dishwashing detergent, and 1 cup water in the pot and simmer until the stain is removed.

POTS AND PANS, STAINLESS STEEL, DISCOLORED, To brighten:
- Remove water spots with rubbing alcohol or white vinegar applied on a damp sponge.
- Warm the pan slightly in the oven, then spray on oven cleaner. (Protect the countertop with newspaper before spraying the pan.) Allow to sit for 5 to 10 minutes, then rinse off the cleaner and wash the pan in hot soapy water. Rinse well.

RECIPE CARD, To keep handy while cooking:
- Place the card in a long plastic spear that florists include in gift arrangements and put it in a mug or glass.
- Put the card in the tines of a fork and stand the fork, handle down, in a glass.

REFRIGERATOR, Care of:
- Wash the interior and door gaskets with a solution of ¼ cup baking soda and 1 quart warm water. Or wipe out the interior with a wet sponge sprinkled with baking soda, then rinse.

- Dust the condenser coils every 2 or 3 months with the crevice tool attachment of the vacuum cleaner, a long-handled brush designed for the purpose, or a cloth fastened to the end of a ruler.
- Empty, wash, rinse, and dry the drip pan several times a year.
- Clean and remove mold from the rubber door seal by scrubbing with a toothbrush dipped in warm sudsy water or a wet toothbrush dipped in baking soda. Rinse and dry.

REFRIGERATOR, Hints on:

- Keep a dry sponge in the vegetable crisper to absorb excess moisture and help keep vegetables fresh.
- Keep the crisper at least two-thirds full for better performance. If it is less full, vegetables keep better if they are put in plastic bags first.
- Line the crisper sections with bubble wrap to avoid bruises and make cleanup easier.
- Keep all the leftovers on the same shelf.
- Line each door shelf with wax paper to cut cleaning time. Replace when necessary.

REFRIGERATOR AFTER BEING IN STORAGE, To freshen:

- Wash out the interior of the refrigerator or freezer with equal parts of chlorine bleach and water. (Wear rubber gloves and provide adequate ventilation.) Include shelves and bins. Also remove and wash out the drip pan. Rinse with clear water and dry thoroughly. This will remove mold and kill any mold spores. Then spread 8 ounces activated charcoal in a shallow pan, place it in the refrigerator or freezer, close the door, and turn on the unit. Leave the charcoal in the unit for 1 week, then check to see if an odor persists. If an odor is still present, replace the charcoal with fresh activated charcoal and leave it another week to 10 days. (Obtain activated charcoal at a health food store or aquarium supply store.)

REFRIGERATOR GOING INTO STORAGE, To prevent odor:

- Put several charcoal briquettes in a nylon stocking and place inside the unit to absorb any odors, or fill the refrigerator or freezer with wadded-up newspapers. The paper will absorb any moisture and help prevent odors.

REFRIGERATOR ODORS, To eliminate:

- Put a couple of slices of white bread in the rear of the refrigerator.
- Keep an open 1-pound box baking soda in the back of a middle shelf.

Replace the box once a month, or as needed. To remove strong odors, pour baking soda into a shallow pan. The more baking soda exposed to air, the more odors are absorbed.

- Put a small breather bag of zeolite in the refrigerator. Zeolite also extends the shelf life of vegetables. (See USEFUL ADDRESSES AND PHONE NUMBERS, "Toxin-Free/Low-Toxin Products.")
- Wash the interior with ½ cup baking soda and 2 cups water.
- Place 1 teaspoon baking soda in a glass of water and stand it in the refrigerator. This will absorb odors and keep the refrigerator fresh. Replace every 2 weeks.
- Fill half a lemon or orange skin after the fruit has been removed with table salt, and place it in the refrigerator. This also will reduce moisture. To reuse, dry out the salt by placing the salt-filled lemon or orange skin on the back of the range when the oven is on, then put it back in the refrigerator.
- Keep 3 or 4 charcoal briquettes in the refrigerator door shelf for a month. Reuse by burning on the grill.
- Keep activated charcoal in a container on a shelf.
- Take a small cotton ball, dip it in vanilla, and place it in a small dish in the refrigerator.
- Eliminate the odor of spoiled food by washing out the interior of the refrigerator or freezer with a solution of 1 half white vinegar and 1 half water, then letting the interior air-dry.
- Put fresh dry coffee grounds on a couple of paper plates and set them on different shelves. The odor should go away in two or three days.
- Remove a persistent smell by taking everything out and sponging the inside with a solution of ¼ cup table salt and 2 cups water. Then sponge again with a solution of 3 tablespoons ammonia and 1 quart water.

REFRIGERATOR, PUDDLES IN, To correct:

- Check the drain if water collects on the floor of a frost-free refrigerator. It may be clogged. Remove the drain cup and wash it, then use a poultry baster to squirt hot water through the drain tube into the drain pan.

SALAD BOWLS, WOODEN, To clean:

- Keep the surface of the bowls sealed by rubbing them inside and out with wax paper after washing and drying.
- Rub with raw walnuts or pecan halves to remove sticky gummy residue.

SALAD SPINNER SUBSTITUTE:

- Use a plastic grocery bag that you've poked holes in, or a washed-out mesh bag that onions come in, or a large clean dishtowel or piece of cheesecloth gathered up at the corners. Wash and shake excess water from the greens, and put them in the bag. Swing the greens up and around several times, preferably outside.

SINK, PORCELAIN, DISCOLORED/STAINED, To clean:

- Sprinkle baking soda in the sink and scrub with a damp sponge.
- Mix 2 tablespoons baking soda with enough hydrogen peroxide to make a paste. Apply the solution and leave on overnight, then scrub.
- Sprinkle baking soda in the sink and pour a bit of white vinegar over it, then scrub with a brush and rinse well.
- Cover the bottom of the sink with paper towels saturated with chlorine bleach. Let sit for 30 minutes or so, then rinse.
- See also BATHROOMS chapter, "Bathtub, Porcelain, Iron Rust Stains, To remove," and "Bathtub Porcelain, Stains/Discoloration, To remove."

SINK, STAINLESS STEEL: See "Stainless Steel, To clean."

SPACE, EXTRA COUNTER, To improvise:

- Cover the sink with a cutting board.
- Turn a cookie sheet upside down and place it over the stove burners.
- Put a cookie sheet, cutting board, or tray over a pulled-out drawer.

SPONGES AND SCRUBBERS, To clean, deodorize, and sterilize:

- Soak in a solution of half white vinegar and half water for 24 hours. Rinse thoroughly several times in cold water and dry in the sun if possible.
- Soak overnight in a solution of 4 tablespoons baking soda to 1 quart water, then rinse and dry in the sun if possible.

STAINLESS STEEL, To clean:

- Use a solution of ¼ cup ammonia to 1 quart water. Rinse and dry. (Wear rubber gloves.)
- Wipe with white vinegar to remove hard-water spots and grease buildup, then rinse with water. Polish dry with a soft cloth.
- Apply baking soda or borax on a wet sponge or mix with enough water to make a paste, then apply. Rinse well with warm water and polish dry with a soft cloth.

- Use rubbing alcohol and baking soda on a sponge to remove stains, then wash thoroughly with detergent and hot water.
- Polish occasionally with glass cleaner.
- Make it sparkle by applying a touch of cooking oil on a cloth.

STEAMER SUBSTITUTE:

- Use an aluminum pie tin with holes poked in it. Pour ¼ to ½ inch water into a pan with a slightly larger diameter, put the pie tin in the pot, rim side down, and put the vegetables on top of the pie tin.
- Use a footed metal colander set in a large pan.

STEEL WOOL, To keep after using:

- Prevent rusting by wrapping it tightly in aluminum foil.

STOVE BURNERS, CAST-IRON AND ENAMELED, To clean:

- Boil them for 10 minutes in a large nonaluminum pot containing ¼ cup washing soda and 1 gallon water. Remove from the water with tongs and rinse. Scrub stubborn spots with a plastic mesh scrubber. Dry cast-iron burners in a 250° to 300°F oven for 10 minutes to prevent rust. Air-dry enamel burners.
- Place the burners in a plastic garbage bag. Pour 1 cup ammonia over them, then close the bag tightly and leave overnight. The next day rinse in clear water and remove loosened particles with a plastic mesh scrubber. Wash in hot sudsy water, then rinse. Dry cast iron in the oven for 10 minutes to avoid rust.

STOVE, ELECTRIC, CHROME RINGS, To clean:

- Boil for 20 to 25 minutes in a pan of water to which 2 tablespoons powdered dishwasher detergent have been added.
- Put them in a plastic bag with enough ammonia to cover them or with an ammonia-soaked paper towel. Seal the bag and leave for several hours. Then remove the rings from the bag and soak them for 20 to 30 minutes in hot water and some heavy-duty laundry detergent or all-purpose cleaner. Then wash, rinse, and dry.

STOVE, GAS, WITH A PILOT LIGHT, To conserve energy:

- Turn off the pilot light and use a flintless lighter. You will save money on your gas bill.

SUGAR, Handy containers for:

- Use a cream container with a flip-top lid for easy pouring.
- Use a big kitchen table salt shaker to sprinkle sugar on cereal.

- Keep sugar in a canister or storage jar that accommodates a scoop.

SUPPLIES, KITCHEN, SELDOM USED, To store:
- Keep rarely used items in a labeled box or container. Doing so allows you to put your hands on frequently used items more easily.

TEAPOT, SILVER, Hints on:
- Dry the inside of a plated or silver teapot with a cloth, then put a lump of sugar inside. It will soak up any remaining moisture and prevent the pot from becoming musty.
- Remove tannin stains by putting in 2 teaspoons washing soda and filling the pot three-quarters full of boiling water. Allow it to stand for 1 hour, then wrap a dishcloth around a wooden spoon and wipe the inside of the pot. Pour out the mixture and repeat the procedure, if necessary. Rinse a couple of times with boiling water, then wash the pot in detergent and water. Rinse throughly. Dry with a clean tea towel, then polish the outside with silver polish.

THERMOMETER, CANDY AND DEEP-FAT, To check accuracy:
- Place in boiling water for 3 minutes. It should register 212°F. If it doesn't, note the difference and make the necessary adjustments when using.

TINWARE, Care of:
- Put in the oven or on top of a hot stove for a couple of minutes after washing and towel-drying. Doing so will dry it completely and prevent rust.
- Remove rust by rubbing with superfine No. 0000 steel wool or a fine steelwool pad that has been dipped in a few drops of mineral or cooking oil. Or rub with a piece of peeled potato dipped in baking soda or mild abrasive powder. Wash, rinse, and dry in the oven.

TOASTER, To clean:
- Brush out the crumbs from the crumb tray and the interior with a half-inch paintbrush. Clean the exterior by rubbing with a damp sponge dipped in baking soda. Or spray glass cleaner or white vinegar on a sponge. Apply, then polish with a clean cloth or paper towel.

WAFFLE IRON, To clean:
- Clean the metal grids by placing an ammonia-soaked paper towel between them and leaving it on overnight. The next day remove stub-

born spots with a nylon mesh scrubber and wipe clean with clear water.

- Follow the manufacturer's instructions for nonstick grids.

WEEVILS, To get rid of:

- Wash, scald, and dry the containers in the sun before reusing any that contained weevils.
- Place bay leaves in cabinets and drawers, and put 1 bay leaf in each canister containing flour, cereal, beans, etc. The bay leaves will not impart an odor.

Laundry

BLACK LINGERIE, CLOTHING, NYLONS, FADED, To restore:
- Add bluing to the rinse water.
- Add 2 cups strong coffee or strong black tea to the rinse water.
- Preserve the color by adding 1 teaspoon malt vinegar to the rinse water. This will prevent items turning a rusty black or dingy brown.

DETERGENT CHEMICAL RESIDUE, To eliminate:
- Add ½ cup baking soda or white vinegar to the final rinse cycle.

COAT COLLAR, GREASY, To clean:
- Rub with a cloth dipped in ammonia.

COLOR BLEEDING, To resolve:
- Soak in an enzyme detergent or an oxygen bleach, then launder.
- Rewash immediately with chlorine bleach if the fabric is white or colorfast. Or soak in a solution of 2 tablespoons bleach to 1 quart water. Leave 5 to 15 minutes until the dye disappears. Rinse thoroughly.
- Use a commercial color remover.
- Keep the dye in new clothes from running by soaking first in 3 cups water, 1 cup white vinegar, and ¼ cup table salt for a couple of hours, then washing as usual.
- Prevent fabrics from bleeding by adding ¼ cup of table salt to the wash and rinse cycles.

DOWN-FILLED ITEM, To wash:
- Wash alone in cold water using the gentle cycle and mild detergent, then rinse until the water is clear. Machine-dry at very low heat with a pair of clean sneakers, clean tennis balls, or a large bath towel to help rotate the item.

DRIP DRYING INSIDE, To make easy:
- Put up a rod that has suction cups in the bathtub enclosure. Use the rod to hang wash-and-wear items or wet raincoats.
- Put a heavy rubber band around the shower arm and hang the hanger holding the garment over the top, then loop it into the rubber band so it won't slide off.

DRIP DRYING OUTSIDE, Hints on:

- Prevent the drip-dry hangers from blowing off the line by securing them to the line with twist ties or clothespins.
- Slip the item over two hangers, one hanger hook facing the other, then slip both over the line and button the garment.
- Attach a shower curtain hook to the line and hang wash-and-wear garments on a hanger from it.
- Put a length of chain on the end of one of the clotheslines and hook the hangers in the links.

DRYER CYCLES, To make easier to read:

- Mark the start of the cycle you normally use with colored nail polish or a piece of colored tape.

DRYING OUTSIDE IN FREEZING WEATHER, Hint on:

- Add 2 tablespoons or more of table salt to the rinse cycle to keep clothes from freezing stiff.

DYE TRANSFERS: See "Color Bleeding, To resolve."

ENERGY CONSERVATION, Hint on:

- Rinse clothes in cold water regardless of the wash water temperature. The temperature of the rinse cycle does not affect cleaning.

FABRIC BRIGHTENER, Hint on:

- Add 1 teaspoon borax to the last rinse water.
- Add ¼ teaspoon table salt to the laundry to keep colors bright.

FABRIC SOFTENER, To make:

- Mix 1 part baking soda, 1 part white vinegar, and 2 parts water. Use as you would a commercial fabric softener.

GREASY CLOTHES, To clean:

- Mix 1 tablespoon glycerin, 1 tablespoon liquid dishwashing detergent, and ½ cup water. Rub into the greasy or oily stains before laundering.
- Rub shortening or glycerin into grease-stained clothes, then launder.
- Pour a bottle of cola into the wash water. Cola loosens grease stains.
- Add ⅓ cup baking soda to the wash cycle.
- Rub in a thick coating of white chalk, allow to sit overnight, then launder as usual.
- Make a paste of washing soda and water. Rub it into the grease, then let it sit until dry. Launder as usual.

- Rub the grease with a dry bar of soap.
- Apply full-strength liquid laundry detergent and let it sit for a few hours or overnight.
- Soak for about 15 minutes in hot water containing ½ cup ammonia.

HAND-WASHING DELICATE FABRICS, Hints on:
- Use 1 teaspoon liquid dishwashing detergent per 1 quart of water. It will do the same job as products sold for delicate and woolen fabrics.
- Use a mild shampoo.

HEIRLOOM LINENS OR BABY CLOTHES, To wash for storage:
- Wash, rinse, then rinse in a solution of 2 tablespoons white vinegar to 1 gallon lukewarm water. Do not starch or iron. If possible dry in the sun. For long-term storage use acid-free paper. (See also HINTS, A TO Z, "Heirloom Clothing and Linens, To preserve.")

JEANS, NEW AND STIFF, To soften:
- Fill a bucket with warm water and put in about ½ cup water softener. Mix well and put the jeans into the mixture. Let it sit for several hours, then launder.
- Add ½ cup table salt to the laundry detergent, and launder as usual.

LINT ON DARK CLOTHING AND CORDUROY, To avoid:
- Turn the garments inside out before washing.
- Put a large piece of nylon net into the dryer when you put the clothes in.

MOHAIR GARMENTS, To maintain:
- Wash in shampoo to keep them soft and fluffy.

NYLONS AND PANTYHOSE, To wash:
- Stuff them inside a sock, or place in a pillowcase and close, then run through the regular cycle of the washing machine. This saves doing them by hand or putting them through the delicate cycle if you don't have enough items to make a full load.
- Buy a mesh bag specifically sold for washing delicate items.

NYLON AND RAYON ITEMS, WHITE, To prevent yellowing:
- Soak garments in warm water and 1 tablespoon baking soda. Then wash as usual.

PERFUME ON CLOTHES, To remove:
- Mix 1 tablespoon dry mustard with enough water to make a paste. Rub

onto the washable surfaces that smell of perfume and let dry. Rinse thoroughly.

PERSPIRATION ODOR IN WOOLENS, To remove:
- Soak the items in a solution of 4 tablespoons table salt and 1 quart cold water, then wash as usual.

PERSPIRATION STAINS, To remove:
- Launder the garment as soon as possible.
- Sponge with a solution of half ammonia and half water.
- Sponge with a solution of half white vinegar and half water.
- Use straight white vinegar on old stains. Rinse carefully with water.
- Dissolve a few aspirins in cold water and soak the stained areas until the stains disappear.
- Rub a thick paste of baking soda and water onto the stain. Let it sit from 15 minutes up to 1 hour or so, then launder as usual.
- Mix a little table salt and enough water to make a paste. Rub the paste into the cloth and let sit for 1 hour or so, then wash as usual. Or soak in a strong salt-water solution.
- Remove yellow stains with sodium perborate, or chlorine bleach, or hydrogen peroxide.

PILLOWS, FEATHER AND DOWN, To wash:
- Check that ticking and seams are firm or sew the pillow into a pillow case. Open the seams at corners, diagonally, about 1 inch, then pin the openings. Doing so will prevent the pillow from filling with air and bursting. Wash two pillows at a time or add a couple of bath towels to balance the load. Use warm water, all-purpose detergent, gentle cycle, and a short wash. Push pillows down when they float, and turn them over during washing and rinsing. Use warm water to rinse, and rinse until the water is clear. Shake after washing and dry on low heat in the dryer with a couple of clean sneakers or tennis balls to balance the load. Or hang them on the line out of direct strong sunlight so the rays can't draw out the natural oil and destroy feather resiliency. Rotate the pillows on the line a couple of times to evenly distribute the feathers or down.

PILLOWS, FOAM RUBBER, To wash:
- Place pillows in cloth pillowcases before washing to prevent fraying. Squeeze carefully in lukewarm sudsy water and rinse several times in cool clear water. Press between two terry cloth towels, then dry in a cool breezy spot. Do not dry foam rubber in the dryer.

PILLOWS, POLYESTER AND SYNTHETIC, To wash:

- Wash by hand, if necessary, but do not wash them in the washing machine unless the manufacturer advises it. Tests by du Pont show that the batt structure tends to break down and become lumpy after 4 or 5 machine washings. If you do wash in the machine, follow the instructions for feather and down pillows. Hang outside to dry by two corners in a breezy spot. Fluff and turn occasionally while drying.

PREWASH SOLUTIONS, To make:

- Put liquid detergent into a small squeeze bottle, such as an empty rinsed-out trial bottle of dishwashing detergent. Use an old toothbrush or piece of nylon net to rub the detergent into the fabric.
- Use full-strength shampoo for prespotting collars, stains, grease, blood, and grass.
- Mix 1 teaspoon liquid detergent and 2 tablespoons ammonia with 2 cups warm water. Pour into a clean spray bottle. Apply to stain and let stand for 15 minutes. Then wash as usual. (Do not use with chlorine bleach.)
- Combine ¼ cup each white vinegar, ammonia (sudsy or plain), liquid laundry detergent, and water. Put in a spray bottle. (Do not use with chlorine bleach.)
- Combine ½ cup each water, liquid detergent, and ammonia. Mix and store in a spray bottle. Shake before using, and use just before laundering. This is good for collars, spots, and resistant stains. (Do not use with chlorine bleach.)

RAIN SPOTS ON CLOTHING, To remove:

- Hold the spotted parts over the steam coming from the spout of a kettle of boiling water or from a steam iron. Shake the garment in the steam until moist, then continue to shake until it is dry.

RING AROUND THE COLLAR, To remove:

- Rub with shampoo, prewash solution, or liquid laundry detergent and let sit for a few minutes before adding the item to the wash.
- Rub white chalk on the collar and let sit for 30 minutes or more to absorb the grease, then launder as usual.
- Scrub with a paste made of 3 parts baking soda to 2 parts white vinegar.

SHOELACES, WHITE, To wash:

- Put the laces in a small jar and pour in water, detergent, and chlorine bleach. Shake vigorously, then rinse thoroughly.

SILK, Gentle bleach for:

- Use 1 part 3 percent hydrogen peroxide mixed in 8 parts water. Immerse the garment in the solution for 5 to 30 minutes, as needed. Rinse in clear water.

SILK, Rings from dry-cleaning solvents, to remove:

- Steam the item over the spout of a kettle of boiling water or over a steam iron. Hold the item at some distance and do not get the stain wet. Then rub the fabric against itself. This also works on wool.

SILK, To wash:

- Wash by hand in cool water with mild soap, shampoo, or dishwashing detergent. Air-dry away from direct heat or sunlight.

SOAP/DETERGENT, TOO MUCH ADDED, To correct:

- Reduce excess suds by adding 1 teaspoon Epsom salts to the water.
- Sprinkle some table salt on the superfluous suds.
- Sprinkle the suds with talcum powder.

SOAP RESIDUE ON CLOTHING, To get rid of:

- Add 1 cup white vinegar to the final rinse water. Use less, of course, for hand-washing.

SOILED GARMENTS, OVERLY, To get clean:

- Presoak for 10 to 20 minutes in lukewarm water containing a non-precipitating water softener such as Calgon. If clothes are greasy, add one-half cup ammonia to the soak water.

STAINED WHITE AND LIGHT-COLORED ITEMS, To restore:

- Soak in boiling water and cream of tartar. Use 1 tablespoon cream of tartar to 1 quart boiling water.
- Soak for 5 to 10 minutes in a solution of 2 tablespoons chlorine bleach to 1 quart water in a nonmetal container, then rinse in clear water. Repeat as necessary.
- Put 1 gallon very hot water into a plastic bucket. (Do not use enamel, stainless steel or aluminum.) Add ½ cup dishwasher detergent and ½ cup chlorine bleach. Stir well. Soak white cotton items for 2 hours, or overnight if heavily stained. For bleachable, colorfast items or synthetics, allow the mixture to cool first, then soak for 30 minutes, or overnight if heavily stained. Do not stir the mixture while the clothes are soaking, and do not reuse the mixture. After soaking, remove the clothes, spin dry, then wash as usual, adding 1 cup white vinegar to the final rinse water.

- Spread the washed wet items flat on an old sheet on the grass or a picnic table. Leave them out all day. If the stains remain, wet the stains with lemon juice, turn the garments over on the other side, and leave out overnight to catch the dew.
- Pour a little chlorine bleach into the bottle cap and dab a bit on the stain with a cotton-tipped swab. When the stain disappears, usually within 1 minute, immediately rinse out the bleach.
- See "Yellowed, Dingy, Gray Items, To whiten."

STARCH BUILDUP, To eliminate:
- Spray inside the garments to eliminate starch buildup on the ironing board and on the right side of the items.

STARCH, SPRAY, To make:
- Mix 1 tablespoon cornstarch and 2 cups warm water, and store in a spray bottle. Rinse the nozzle after use to prevent clogging. Add ½ cup cold black tea to the starch when starching dark clothes.
- Mix 2 tablespoons powdered starch with 2 cups hot water. Use a spray bottle and shake frequently.

STATIC ELECTRICITY, To remove:
- Add 1 tablespoon white vinegar to the final rinse water if you choose not to use water softener or fabric softener sheets.

SWEATERS, SYNTHETIC AND COTTON, To wash:
- Turn garments inside out to prevent friction and pilling.

TEA TOWELS, To wash:
- Add a little borax to the wash water. This disinfects them and removes dirt and grease.
- Sterilize newly washed wet tea towels by folding them and putting them in the microwave on high heat for 5 minutes.

TEA TOWELS, NEW, To treat:
- Soak in cold water with a little Epsom salts to remove the sizing and make them soft and absorbent.

TOWELS, STIFF, To soften:
- Wash the towels in very hot water with 1 cup baking soda, borax, or washing soda (do not add detergent), then add 1 cup or more of white vinegar to the rinse water. Repeat this procedure periodically to remove detergent buildup and keep towels soft and fluffy.

WASHING BY HAND, Hint on:
- Agitate the clothes with a rubber plunger.

WASHING MACHINE, To clean soap film from hoses:
- Add 1 quart white vinegar to the washing machine and run for a full cycle. Or run 2 cups vinegar through the rinse cycle.

WASHING MACHINE, To use:
- Separate white and colored items and delicate items.
- Wash delicate items on the delicate cycle or by hand or put in the washer at the last minute.
- Close all zippers, hooks, and buttons. Turn pockets inside out. Treat stains and ring around the collar with prewash spray or a little liquid laundry detergent.
- Mix small and large items in each load to circulate and distribute the load evenly around the wash basket. Don't overload the machine.
- Read the label on the detergent container, but add only enough to make a few suds, not billows of them. Usually it's ½ cup or a scoop for a full load of powdered detergent or a capful for the liquid.
- Use hot water for regular sheets and for white and colorfast items that won't shrink. To bleach a load, follow instructions below.
- Bleach clothes by adding liquid chlorine bleach diluted in 1 quart water a few minutes after the machine has been running (to give the detergent a chance to do its job). If the machine has an automatic bleach dispenser, follow the manufacturer's directions. Let the machine run for a few more minutes after adding the bleach, then turn the machine off and let the clothes soak for 10 minutes, then start the machine again and let it continue.
- Use cold wash and cold water rinse cycles for all other items.
- Avoid lint on clothes by turning dark-colored garments inside out before washing.
- Remove the wash as soon as it's done and either hang up to dry or put in the dryer.
- Shake the clothes out before putting in the dryer. If desired, add a fabric-softener sheet to a load if you didn't use liquid water softener. Don't overdry; this makes fabrics stiff and wrinkled and shortens their life. Remove garments as soon as dry and hang up immediately to avoid creases.

WHITE SOCKS, DISCOLORED, To restore whiteness:
- Boil the clean socks in water containing a lemon slice or a little white vinegar.

WOOLENS, To wash:

- Wash with a solution of 1 tablespoon mild detergent containing no additives, shampoo, or dishwashing detergent to 1 gallon lukewarm water. Lay the woolen items in the sudsy solution and let them soak for 3 to 5 minutes, turning them once or twice. Do not rub, scrub, or twist. Rinse them a couple of times in clear lukewarm water, or until the water shows no more suds. Squeeze the items gently to remove as much water as possible, then put them in a colander or a dish drainer to drain further. Roll the garments in heavy towels to absorb more water, then lay them on a couple of dry, heavy towels with a few layers of newspaper underneath. Reshape and let dry.
- Add 1 to 2 tablespoons glycerin to the lukewarm rinse water. This will keep woolens soft and prevent itching when worn. (Obtain glycerin from a drugstore.)
- Put 1 capful cream hair rinse in the rinse water to keep the woolens soft.
- Wash machine-washable wool on the delicate cycle in lukewarm water with a mild detergent. Dry it partly in the dryer, using towels to absorb the moisture and buffer the load, then finish air-drying on a towel. To speed a sweater's drying time, insert a folded bath towel between the front and back of the item.

WOOLENS, SHRUNKEN, To restore:

- Add 1 cup Epsom salts to 1 quart boiling water and stir to dissolve the salt. Add 3 more quarts cool water and soak garment in the lukewarm solution for 30 minutes. Remove, squeeze out excess water, and restretch the garment to its correct shape. Dry flat.
- Soak the item for 15 minutes in ½ cup hair conditioner and 1 gallon lukewarm water. Squeeze the item to remove excess solution and pull gently to reshape.
- Dissolve 2 tablespoons borax in a few tablespoons of hot water, then add the mixture to a gallon of lukewarm water. Immerse the garment and pull gently into shape, then rinse in 1 gallon of lukewarm water to which you have added 2 tablespoons of white vinegar.
- Dissolve 1 or 2 cups noniodized salt in enough hot water to cover the garment. Let cool, add the garment, and let it soak for 3 hours. Wash in mild suds, rinse three times, then roll in a large towel to remove excessive moisture. Reshape and dry on a flat surface.
- Add 2 tablespoons plain shampoo to 1 gallon lukewarm water. Squeeze the solution through the garment and do not rinse. Reshape on a flat surface and let dry.

WRINKLES FROM THE DRYER, To remove:
- Put the items back in the dryer with a large wet bath towel.

YELLOW STAINS ON ITEMS STORED IN PLASTIC, To remove:
- Soak items overnight in warm water containing a few denture tablets.
- Combine 1 tablespoon each white vinegar, table salt, and water softener with 2 cups water. Dip the stained area up and down in solution, then rinse well and launder.
- Rub white nongel toothpaste into the spots, then wash in cold water.
- Use bleach for whites and colorfast items.

YELLOWED, DINGY, GRAY ITEMS, To whiten:
- Soak the clothes in hot water for several hours with a nonprecipitating water softener such as Calgon, then rinse and rewash in hot water with chlorine bleach.
- Run the clean clothes through the entire washing machine cycle using hot water and 1 cup washing soda, TSP, or borax. Do not add detergent.
- Soak the yellowed fabrics in 2 tablespoons bleach to 1 quart of cool water for 10 minutes. Rinse well.
- See "Stained White and Light-Colored Items, To restore."

YELLOWED SILK OR WOOL, To restore:
- Sponge with acetic acid (10 percent) or white vinegar (5 percent), then rinse with water.

YELLOWED WHITE SWEATER, To whiten:
- Soak the sweater for 2 to 4 hours in a solution of ¼ cup hydrogen peroxide to 1 gallon of warm water, then wash and dry.

YELLOWING DUE TO CHLORINE BLEACH, To remove:
- Rinse fabrics with water, then soak 30 minutes or longer in a solution containing 1 teaspoon sodium thiosulfate to 1 quart hot water. (Sodium thiosulfate is available in drugstores or from photo supply stores.)

Organization

ORGANIZATION AROUND THE HOUSE:

- Save steps. Leave articles at the bottom of the staircase that have to be taken upstairs and at the top to be taken downstairs. Next time someone goes up or downstairs he or she need not go emptyhanded.
- Keep appliance instruction booklets together in a 1-gallon self-closing bag or loose-leaf organizer. Write the date and place of purchase on guarantees and warranties and keep records of the type and date of repairs and persons who did them.
- Weed out the catch-all drawer occasionally.
- Keep changes of bedding together. Fold the top sheet, then tuck in the pillowcases and bottom sheet so they are together in one package. Put the linen bundles in the rooms where they belong, if space permits.
- Put each person's possessions in his or her room to keep common areas clutter-free.
- Tackle one chore at a time and in small steps. Start by planning to sort one drawer only, and do it. This will produce a sense of accomplishment and might even motivate you to sort another drawer. Be easy on yourself. A little here and there is the trick. And when you are on a roll, keep going.
- Allocate yourself a certain amount of time to work on a chore or project, and set the timer if need be. Knowing you have to work only 15 minutes on that particular job makes it seem easier.
- Make and post a list of "To do" chores. It's a reminder when you have some free time and feel motivated. And, who knows, a family member might surprise you.
- Promise yourself a reward for tasks accomplished—time out, a book to read.
- Provide the impetus for cleaning by inviting someone over.
- Organize your books according to subject matter, if space on the shelves allow, and keep all reference books together.
- Designate one area in the house specifically for library books and video rentals to avoid overdue fines on misplaced books.
- Reserve a place to put items when you arrive home or those you plan to take with you when you leave home. Use it for keys, letters to be

mailed (if you don't have a spot for incoming and outgoing mail), sun-glasses, papers, or books.

- Keep all first-aid supplies together in a small cardboard box or other container.
- Keep a little tool kit in the kitchen so you can lay your hands on a tool in a hurry.
- Keep a list on the refrigerator for items to buy or replenish.
- Label cupboards and drawers with a little number or a colored dot. When anyone wants to know where to find an item or where it goes, you can specify, kitchen "yellow" or kitchen "6."
- Keep a list of where everything is in the house. This is especially handy when moving into a new house, for people with short memories, and for storage areas in attic and basement. Be sure also to mark the boxes indicating contents.

ORGANIZATION ON A PERSONAL BASIS

- Write down your burial or cremation arrangements; information on insurance policies, pensions, securities, safe deposit box (location, contents, number, and where the key is); names and addresses of attorney, insurance broker or agent, accountant who prepares your tax return, physician, those who owe you money (with amounts); location of ownership certificates for autos, deeds for property; list of valuable items, their value and location; and where documents are kept, including marriage license, birth certificate, social security card, active credit cards, etc. Keep with your Power of Attorney, Living Will, and copy of your will in a labeled file. Make sure family members know the name of the file and where it is located.
- Record numbers of license plates, driver's licenses, bank accounts, social security numbers, passport numbers, EE Savings Bonds, and other pertinent numbers.
- Keep your family records in a water- and fireproof container.
- Keep a copy of your will. Make sure it is identical to the original but clearly marked "copy." It should not be signed. Don't keep your will in a safe deposit box.
- Insure any valuables you are storing in a safe deposit box. Add them to your homeowner's/renter's policy. Banks do not insure a safe deposit box.
- Make a list of the contents of your wallet. Doing so will make replacing and canceling items easier.
- Keep a traveler's check in your wallet for emergencies and change in the car glove compartment.

- Keep supplies at work. Have a small emergency kit in a 3 × 5-inch cosmetic bag with Band-Aids, aspirin, small sewing kit, small and regular size safety pins, small comb, coiled-up tape measure, nail file, emery board, lip balm, and a dollar in change. Also keep a box of all-occasion cards and postage stamps for last-minute occasions.
- Carry something with you to read.

ORGANIZATION WITH THE PAPER FLOW:

- Designate a place for incoming and outgoing mail.
- Handle a piece of paper once. File it, throw it out, or put in your "To read" file.
- Keep correspondence needing a response in a file or manila envelope.
- Keep a package of all-occasion cards on hand.
- Type name and address labels of the persons you correspond with frequently. Or address envelopes ahead of time to have on hand.
- Designate one day for paying bills, and keep all bills in one spot.
- Make up your bills ahead of time but don't mail them until a certain date. Put the date where the stamp usually goes (the stamp will cover it), or put the date and amount of check on the back of the envelope on the gummed-down flap.
- Go through your redemption coupons regularly to weed out the expired ones and take note of those nearing expiration. Don't clip coupons you'll probably never use.
- Sort your paperwork in steps. Break the pile down first into a few broad categories, then take each category and break it down further.
- Fill in a health insurance claim form for each member of the family with information that never changes, then make photocopies. Fill in the necessary information at the time of submittal.
- Enter all important dates in the calendar at the beginning of the year: birthdays, anniversaries, holidays, special family occasions, the month for license renewals, property taxes, etc.
- Label a small three-hole-punch binder or divide a loose-leaf notebook into sections. Put a calendar in the front and record important dates for the year. Make one section for addresses and phone numbers, directions to the house, directions and timetables of bus routes. Make other sections for things to do, including phone calls to make and letters to write, books to read, or videos to rent. Have a section for items to include in correspondence or phone conversations. Keep a section or another notebook for personal reflections, great ideas, and flashes of insight. Keep it with you at all times. You never know when inspiration strikes. Make sure you also have a pen or pencil handy.

- Keep a container by the telephone filled with pens, pencils, a little ruler, and a pair of scissors along with a message pad, Post-it Notes, and a list of frequently called phone numbers along with emergency phone numbers. Include in the emergency section numbers for a hospital, doctor, dentist, health clinic, pharmacy, emergency ambulance, taxi, and any number you might need in a hurry.

- Designate a message center and make the recipient of the message responsible for disposing of it once it's received. This will avoid clutter. Provide Post-it Notes for messages, and have family members use them to let others know if they are going to be late or where they are going to be.

- Make a household instruction list. If you are called away on short notice, it will be handy to give to whoever is looking after your home. Include the telephone numbers of neighbors or a contact person, tradesmen, service repair numbers for appliances, veterinarian (if you have a pet), what your pet eats and when, plant watering guide, location of fuse box, turn-off switches for gas, water, etc., garbage pickup day, day to move the car for the street sweeper (if required), and anything else you can think of that would be helpful in the day-to-day running of your home.

Painting

ADHESIVE RESIDUE FROM MASKING TAPE, To remove:
- Use a little paint thinner, lighter fluid, or nail polish remover.

BANISTERS AND RAILINGS, To paint:
- Use a paint glove to make the chore go faster.

BRUSHES, To store:
- Keep in self-seal plastic bags. Add 1 teaspoon white vinegar for each brush used for latex or 1 teaspoon paint thinner for oil-based paint.

BRUSHES, HARDENED, To soften:
- Simmer them in white vinegar to soften the hardened paint.

BRUSHES, OIL-BASED PAINT AND VARNISH, To clean:
- Suspend brushes in a baby wipe container containing the necessary solvent. Push the brush handle up through the opening in the lid. Make sure the bristles are ½ inch from the bottom.
- Soak brushes in an empty coffee can with a plastic cover. Make two slits in the center of the plastic to form an X, then insert the handle up through the X and replace the lid. Make sure the bristles are submerged but not touching the bottom. When clean, remove the brushes and wipe dry.
- Pour the solvent for cleaning the brushes into a heavy-duty plastic bag. Put the brushes into the bag and work the solvent into the bristles.
- Remove excess thinner after cleaning by twirling the brush in the palms of your hand inside a paper grocery bag.
- Wrap the brush in plastic wrap, then foil, if you plan to continue painting. To store for longer periods, freeze the brushes in foil, then defrost for 45 minutes before using.

CANS, PAINT, To keep clean:
- Punch five or six holes in the groove around the edge. The lid will seal the holes when put back in place.
- Wrap a strong rubber band or heavy twine vertically around the paint can to catch excess paint from the brush. This keeps the side and rim

free of paint. Wipe the brush gently across the rubber band or twine after dipping it in the can.

- Lay a piece of string or twine around the rim of the paint can, then remove when finished painting.

CEILINGS AND HIGH PLACES, To paint:
- Wear a long rubber glove with the cuff turned up so the paint will drip into the turned-up cuff.
- Wrap an old washcloth or paper towel around the handle of the brush with a rubber band. This will absorb the drips.
- Wear a shower cap or something to protect your hair.
- Put plastic wrap over your eyeglass lenses to protect them.

CHAIRS, PAINTING, Hint on:
- Turn them upside down and do the legs first, then turn them right side up and finish. Place the legs on washers or jar caps, or press thumb-tacks in the bottoms of the legs.

DRIP CATCHERS FOR PAINT, To make:
- Set the paint container on an old metal or aluminum foil pie plate.

FURNITURE FINISHES, To remove:
- Cover the stripping solvent with aluminum foil, which will keep the air out and prevent quick drying. Let the piece stand a few hours or overnight, then scrape off the old finish. Remove all traces of solvent after stripping according to directions.

HARDWARE, UNABLE TO REMOVE WHEN PAINTING, Hint on:
- Coat hardware with petroleum jelly.
- Cover it with plastic wrap, aluminum foil crimped to fit, or plastic sandwich bags tied on with rubber bands or tape.

LATEX PAINT, Hints on:
- Remove small grease stains with rubbing alcohol before painting. Use stain-blocking sealer or primer for large stains.
- Wash the paint with a nonalkaline preparation such as a pine-based cleaner.
- Make the paint easier to clean by adding 1 quart interior semigloss latex to each 1 gallon flat latex, and mix thoroughly. The addition of the semigloss won't affect the finish.

ODOR OF PAINT IN ROOM, To remove:
- Put out a bowl of water containing chopped or sliced onion.
- Set out a saucer containing a few drops of vanilla extract.

PAINT STIRRER, To make:
- Bend two ends of a wire coat hanger until they meet.
- Use an old table fork for small cans.

REPAINTING OVER NAIL AND HOOK HOLES, Hint on:
- Insert a piece of toothpick or small headless nail in the hook holes and paint right over them. You'll be able to locate the holes to rehang whatever was there before.

ROLLER, To clean:
- Roll it on several sheets of newspaper to remove excess paint. Then remove the roller from its support with a plastic bag over your hand or by putting a plastic bag over the roller. Clean the roller, then dry it on end.

ROLLER PAN, Hint on:
- Line the roller pan with foil or plastic to avoid cleanup.

SANDING PAINT, Hint on:
- Wrap a piece of metal window screening (not fiberglass) around the sanding block to remove rough built-up paint. It will remove the paint quickly and won't damage the surface.

SAVING AND STORING PAINT, Hints on:
- Store the can upside down so the skin will be at the bottom.
- Spray a thin film of mineral spirits over the surface of oil-base paint (no more than 1 teaspoon to ½ gallon paint).
- Top it with melted paraffin to prevent a layer of skin forming.
- Lay wax paper directly on the paint, then put on the lid.
- Seal the can with a double layer of wax paper or plastic wrap before putting on the lid.
- Blow into the paint can before sealing to increase the carbon dioxide level, which keeps paint from skinning.
- Mark the can with a line of paint to indicate how much is left in it and the color of the paint inside.
- Save some paint in a small jar with a screw-type lid, such as a baby food or small olive jar. (It comes in handy for touch-ups.) Put plastic wrap or a double thickness of wax paper between the jar and the cap, close tightly, and turn upside down. Add a label indicating the brand name, color, what it was used for, and clean-up instructions.
- Clean a plastic container with a tight-fitting screw-on cap. Pour in leftover paint, apply petroleum jelly around the treads, squeeze the container until the paint reaches the top, and hold it steady until the cap

is screwed on tightly. Identify the container by taking the label from the paint can and writing the information on the back and then attach it to the new container with a rubber band.

- Pour paint into a resealable plastic freezer bag. Squeeze the air out before you seal the bag, then put the bag into the original paint can and close the lid.

SKIN, PAINT ON, To remove:

- Rub it with mineral, baby, or vegetable oil, then wash it with hot water and soap.
- Use nylon net or plastic scrubber with a little detergent.
- Remove with a cotton swab dipped in hydrogen peroxide or mineral spirits.

SMALL OBJECTS, PAINTING, Hint on:

- Keep them in place on cardboard with double-stick carpet tape or double-sided tape.

SPLATTERS, PAINT, IN HAIR, To remove:

- Rub the spots with baby oil or vegetable oil. Wear a shower cap in future to avoid getting paint in your hair.

STEPS, To paint:

- Paint every other step one day and the others the next day. Or paint just half a step one day and the other half the next day.

STRAINING PAINT, Hints on:

- Pour into a clean empty container covered with cheesecloth or a nylon stocking held in place with a rubber band or string.
- Cut a circle of window screen slightly smaller than the can lid. Stir the paint, and drop the screen into the can. As the screen settles, it will carry all the lumps to the bottom.

THINNER, PAINT, To reuse:

- Pour it into an empty coffee can, cover it tightly, and put in a safe place for several days. The residue will settle. Strain off the clean thinner into another can and store for reuse.

TOUCH-UPS, Hints on:

- Keep clean empty nail polish bottles or other containers with a brush inside for small amounts of touch-up paint.
- Use a cotton swab to avoid cleanups.

VARNISH, APPLYING, To avoid bubbles:

- Wipe off the brush in another can instead of the can you are using.

- Press the brush against the inside of the can you're using and not the rim.
- Varnish wood that is at room temperature, not cold.
- Stroke the brush with the grain first, then against it.

VARNISH, OLD, To remove:
- Apply denatured alcohol. Let it sit for 1 minute, then wipe off the dissolved finish with a rag or paint scraper.
- Use 3 tablespoons washing soda to 1 quart water. Apply with a rough cloth to wipe off the varnish. After removing all traces of the varnish, dry the wood with a hair dryer set on low.

VINYL FLOOR, PAINT SPOTS ON, To remove:
- Soften the spots with full-strength white vinegar, then scrub the spots with nylon netting or a plastic scrubber.

WHITE PAINT, To touch up:
- Use typewriter correction fluid to conceal scratches.

WHITE PAINT TURNING YELLOW, To prevent:
- Stir a drop of black paint into it.

WINDOW FRAMES, To paint:
- Cut newspaper into 2-inch strips and dip into clear water. Wipe off excess water and put the straight edge of each strip on the glass next to the frame. Remove after frame is painted.
- Coat the glass panes with undiluted liquid detergent and let dry for a day before painting. Wash off after painting.
- Rub soap, petroleum jelly, or lip balm around the edges next to the trim instead of using masking tape.
- Use an angled sash brush working from the glass edge outward.
- Bind the bristles of a large brush together with an elastic band if a small brush is not available. Use for painting corners of the window frames and other awkward spots.

WINDOW PANES, To remove paint:
- Rub on hot white vinegar or scrape off with a safety razor blade.

WIRE OR CHAIN LINK FENCE, To paint:
- Use a sponge or paint glove to apply the paint, and wear rubber gloves.

Pets

ACCIDENTS, PET, ON CARPET, To treat: See CARPETS chapter, "Carpet, Pet Accident on, To treat."

ANIMAL HAIRS ON UPHOLSTERY, To remove:
- Use an antistatic spray on the furniture the animal favors. It will make cleanup easy. Also coat the pet brush with antistatic spray before brushing the pet to prevent hair flying all over.
- Put on a rubber glove and brush it over the upholstery.
- Scrape the hairs off with a squeegee, lightly dampened sponge, or piece of terry cloth or chamois.
- Wrap a length of duct tape, adhesive tape, or masking tape around your hand, sticky side out, and brush over the area. The animal hair will stick to the tape.
- Rub the fabric with a fabric softener sheet.

BIRD OUT OF CAGE, To get back in:
- Turn off the lights and close the blinds or draperies. The bird will stay put until you catch it.
- Place a feather duster near the bird. Most likely it will nestle in the feathers. Then place the duster at the opening of the cage so the bird can fly in.
- Throw a light towel over the bird, gently pick it up, and put it back in the cage.

CAT, To feed:
- Feed the cat one meal a day and milk, if milk agrees with it. Make sure the food and milk are at room temperature. Give the cat vegetables in small doses, but no starchy, greasy, or highly seasoned ones. Have fresh water available at all times. Once a week add a raw egg to the cat's food, and once every 2 weeks mash half a clove of garlic into the cat's food as a worm preventive.

CAT CARRIER, To make:
- Use two large plastic laundry baskets. Fasten them together with 2 bolts or with rope in the back, then tie them securely in the front.
- Utilize an old wicker picnic basket with the lid securely shut.

CAT DISHES, To avoid sliding around:
- Put the dishes on a piece of foam rubber.
- Place self-adhesive rubber pads under the dishes.
- Glue rubber canning rings on the bottom.

CAT EAR MITES, To get rid of:
- Put a few drops of vegetable or vitamin E oil into the cat's ear and gently rub in. Then clean out the debris with a cotton ball. Repeat for 3 days.

CAT FLEAS, To get rid of:
- Buy a flea comb and comb the cat 4 times a day for 2 weeks. Continue until no fleas appear, then comb the cat once a day for maintenance.
- Add ½ teaspoon granular brewer's yeast or a crushed brewer's yeast tablet (7½ or 10 grains) to the cat's food once a day for 2 weeks. If that doesn't work, increase the daily amount until you notice an improvement. Or rub the granular brewer's yeast on the cat's coat; and it will lick it off. From then on, add ½ teaspoon to the food each day.
- See "Cats and Dogs, Fleas, To remove."

CAT HAIR BALLS, To treat:
- Groom regularly to help keep the cat free of hair balls. Brush short-haired cats daily; comb long-haired cats. Use a woman's hairbrush with round-tipped plastic or rubber bristles, which is better than the brushes sold for cats.
- Add 1 teaspoon vegetable oil to the cat's food daily, or use the oil from a can of sardines when you have them. Or put a dab of petroleum jelly on your finger or on the cat's nose about once a week and let the cat lick it off.
- Ask your veterinarian for a malt lubricant.

CAT JUMPING ON FORBIDDEN AREAS, To discourage:
- Cover the area temporarily with plastic or foil until the pet gets out of the habit.
- Touch the cat's lips very lightly with a cotton ball moistened with rubbing alcohol or vinegar each time it goes where it shouldn't, then leave the cotton ball at the area.
- Tie a few small, inflated balloons to the furniture it jumps on. Cats don't like loud noises.
- Discourage a cat from jumping onto the kitchen counter by leaving several aluminum baking pans near the edge so they'll clatter when the cat lands. Or place some two-sided tape on the countertops.

- Spray the cat with a water squirt gun whenever it goes where it shouldn't.

CAT LITTER BOX, Care of:

- Use a slotted metal spoon as a scoop, which is sturdier than the plastic kind sold for the purpose.
- Set the box on top of a piece of Astroturf so the litter doesn't get all over the place. Or put the Astroturf where the litter usually lands.
- Replace litter at least once every 2 weeks. Keep it sweet-smelling by mixing ½ cup borax to every 5 pounds cat litter or 1 cup baking soda.
- Wash the box with sudsy water and rinse. Then wash it with ½ cup white vinegar per 1 quart water. Soak 5 minutes and rinse thoroughly. Never use ammonia, bleach, or cleansers containing phenol or coal-tar derivatives such as Lysol.

CAT REFUSING MEDICINE, Hint on:

- Spill the medicine on its fur. The cat will lick it off.
- Coat tablets and capsules with butter or roll them in ground lean meat or liverwurst.
- Give a cat a pill by squeezing the cat's cheeks together so that it opens its mouth, then place the pill as far back in the throat as possible. Close the cat's mouth quickly and gently rub its throat to stimulate swallowing or gently blow into the cat's nose. If the cat scratches, put it in a pillowcase or a blanket, with its head sticking out before administering the pill.

CAT SCRATCHING POST, To encourage use:

- Rub a little catnip on the post or secure a toy to a string and hang it alongside the post to attract the cat. (Make sure the string is secure so the cat cannot swallow it.)
- Place an old sheet over the area the cat likes to scratch until it gets used to the scratching post.

CAT SPRAYING FURNITURE, Hints on:

- Squirt the cat with a squirt gun containing plain water when you catch it spraying.
- Wash the sprayed area with rubbing alcohol or white vinegar to kill the scent.

CAT, TALKING TO, Hint on:

- Talk to the cat in a high voice. Cats associate lower voices with scolding.

CAT TOYS, To make:
- Place a paper clip, pen top, coin, or anything that will rattle in an empty film canister. Or give the cat an empty thread spool or a crumpled-up piece of aluminum foil to bat around.

CAT WITH SCRATCHES OR CUTS, To treat:
- Clean the wound with lukewarm water or hydrogen peroxide, then apply vitamin E oil. Apply more as needed.

CAT WITH WORMS, To deworm:
- Mash 2 cloves garlic into the cat's food and add 1 tablespoon of vegetable oil. Repeat for 3 consecutive days and again a week later if needed.

CATS AND DOGS, Accident on the carpet: See CARPETS chapter,
"Carpet, Pet Accident on, To treat."

CATS AND DOGS, Bedding, To clean and deodorize between laundering:
- Sprinkle baking soda on the dry bedding and let it sit for 30 minutes, then shake out or vacuum up the soda.

CATS AND DOGS, Eye Secretions, To remove:
- Mix ¼ teaspoon table salt with 1 cup warm distilled water. Saturate soft gauze or cotton in the table salt solution and gently wipe the area surrounding the eyes to soften the secretions.

CATS AND DOGS, Fights, To break up:
- Spray with a water-filled spray gun or throw cold water on the fighters.

CATS AND DOGS, Fleas, To remove:
- Deflea an animal that you obtained from the pound before bringing it into the house. Usually it has fleas.
- Do not apply excessive amounts of flea powder to a cat or dog's coat, and brush all the excess off within 30 minutes of applying so the pet won't try to lick off the residue. Treat the animal outdoors since the fleas will try to leave the animal's coat within a few minutes. Powder the head thoroughly and carefully, then powder the animal's rear and tail the same way, then powder the back, underside, and between the toes on each foot. Clean out its ears with a half and half solution of rubbing alcohol and white vinegar.
- Give your pet brewer's yeast. Start out a dog with 1 level teaspoon brewer's yeast flakes. Continue to give ½ teaspoon every other day once the pet stops scratching. For cats, rub the yeast into the fur and

put the cat outside. The cat will clean its coat and acquire a taste for the yeast. From then on put ½ teaspoon on the side of the cat's food dish or mix with food.

- Give ½ clove fresh garlic to cats and ½ to 2 cloves to dogs. Mince or crush garlic and mix well into your pet's food. Try ½ clove to every 1 cup food. If the pet refuses, hide the garlic clove in a chunk of liverwurst and hand-feed.
- Spread some pennyroyal oil on the inside of the pet's collar and gently rub the coat with 1 teaspoon pennyroyal oil mixed with ½ cup water. Or rub the coat with a handful of pennyroyal leaves. Also boil up some leaves and add to the rinse water when bathing the pet.
- Boil for 1 hour in 1 quart water 2 unpeeled lemons cut into small pieces. Let sit overnight, then strain. Sponge or spray the pet with the liquid.
- Stuff a pillow with cedar chips or cedar sawdust and use as a dog bed.
- Put pine needles in the doghouse if the pet sleeps outside.
- Air out a flea collar for several days before putting it on your dog or cat, and trim the collar to fit the animal so that it can't chew on the end. Never put a flea collar on a puppy or kitten, and never put a flea collar on an animal that is wet or going to get wet.
- Make a dog flea collar by stuffing a roll of fabric with tansy or catnip or soaking it for 24 hours in pennyroyal oil.
- Keep the house well vacuumed and, after vacuuming, sprinkle diatomaceous earth in all the affected areas, especially dark corners, baseboards, and under the bed. (Obtain diatomaceous earth from a garden or pool supply store.)

CATS AND DOGS, Glossy coat hints:

- Add 1 teaspoon vegetable oil to the pet's food every day to make its coat glossy, stop dry skin scratching, and avoid hair balls in a cat.
- Clear up dry skin in a dog by adding 1 tablespoon olive oil to its food each day. It should take a week to see results.
- Mix 1 egg in with the pet's food once a week.
- Crush up an alfalfa tablet and add to the pet's food occasionally. Also sprinkle on a little brewer's yeast. Alfalfa and brewer's yeast will produce healthy coats and prevent skin disorders.
- Add 1 teaspoon dried rosemary to 1 cup boiling water. Let steep for 10 minutes. Strain out the rosemary and let the water cool to room temperature. Pour over your cat or dog after the final rinse.
- Put a few tablespoons baking soda into the dog's rinse water.

CATS AND DOGS, Grease spots, To remove from fur:
- Massage cornstarch or baking soda onto the area, then brush out.
- Rub a small amount of Murphy's Oil Soap and warm water onto the spot. Rinse thoroughly with warm water.

CATS AND DOGS, Injured:
- Throw a blanket over the injured animal to protect yourself. Animals become frightened and may bite.

CATS AND DOGS, Itch, To treat:
- Dab apple cider vinegar over the pet's coat.
- Mix 2 tablespoons colloidal oatmeal with 2 gallons cold water and wipe the solution over the pet's entire body. This will provide itch relief for 2 to 3 days. (Buy colloidal oatmeal at the health food store, or blend regular or quick-cooking oatmeal until very fine.)

CATS AND DOGS, Nose secretions, To remove:
- Wipe the nose with a gauze pad or soft cloth dipped in warm water. If the secretion is hard and difficult to remove, apply warm, damp cloths repeatedly, softening and removing small amounts at a time.

CATS AND DOGS, Poisoned:
- Make a very thick mixture of activated charcoal and water. (Obtain activated charcoal from a health supply store.) Give 2 tablespoons to a cat or small dog. For medium or large dogs, give 3 tablespoons to 2 cups, depending on size. A little too much won't harm the animal. If the pet won't drink this antidote, administer it with a spoon, a bulb syringe, or a bulb-type poultry baster. Do not force your pet to swallow a large amount at one time. *Do not give any poison antidote to an unconscious animal.* If you don't have activated charcoal, give your pet whole milk. Give 2 tablespoons to a cat or small dog, 3 tablespoons to 2 cups to a medium or large dog. Use water as a last resort if you have no milk. If the poison is on the pet's skin or coat, immediately bathe the animal—shampooing and rinsing with water until you can no longer see or smell the toxin.

CATS AND DOGS, Shampooing, dry:
- Give a dry shampoo, when necessary. Cornstarch absorbs oil between baths. Baking soda is an excellent deodorant for dogs or cats. Rub the powder in and brush it out.

CATS AND DOGS, Shedding:
- Brush them regularly.

- Hand-vacuum pets frequently using the upholstery attachment. Avoid the face and ears. Start vacuuming pets when they are little so they get used to it.
- Massage the coat with a little olive oil once a week to curtail excess shedding.

CATS AND DOGS, Skin treatment, To give:

- Apply medication right before meals or walks. Doing so will take the pet's mind off the problem and prevent it from licking the medication off.

CATS AND DOGS, Sprayed by skunk:

- Apply at once tomato juice, equal parts of water and white vinegar, or stale wine (all of which contain 5 percent acid), then follow with a warm soapy bath and rinse. Repeat if necessary to remove the odor.

CATS AND DOGS, Traveling with:

- Consider fasting (plenty of water but no solid food) for a susceptible pet. Begin fasting 24 hours before departure, particularly if going by public transit. Fasting also helps to prevent a pet traveling in a container from becoming soiled with its own excrement.
- Withhold food for 2 to 3 hours (some say 5 to 6 hours) just before a car trip. Withhold water for 2 hours. After the journey or after any strenuous exercise, let your pet rest at least 30 minutes before feeding it.
- Fill a bottle of water for the animal each morning and take along its water dish. Then you can stop anywhere without looking for water. Or take bottled water if your pet has a sensitive stomach and a change of water would affect it.
- Check out the hotel/motel chains. Many chains, including the Marriott, Holiday Inn, Days Inn, Howard Johnson, Residence Inn, and others, now accommodate pets.

DOG, Chewing on furniture or rugs:

- Put some oil of cloves on the wood being chewed. The smell and bitter taste will deter the animal.
- Make a solution of ¼ cup clove oil, 1 tablespoon paprika, and 1 teaspoon black pepper. Sponge the solution on the furniture and other areas being chewed. Reapply as needed.
- Make a paste of alum powder and water and apply to area being chewed. (Obtain alum from a drugstore or the spice section of a supermarket.)

DOG, Disciplining:

- Establish eye contact first when giving a command, and use one-word commands in a firm voice. Don't bend over to talk to an animal; stand up straight. In disciplining an animal, never call its name and then administer a punishment. Reserve calling its name for good things. Be generous with praise for good behavior.

DOG, Feeding:

- Avoid feeding a dog immediately before or after exercising.
- Put a few sticks of beef jerky in a bag of dry dog food when you open it. It will make the food smell more enticing.
- Perk up the dog's dry dog food on occasion. Use water saved from cooking vegetables (without table salt) and oil drained from tuna or sardines.

DOG, Fungus/ringworm on paw, To treat:

- Apply tea tree oil, a germicide and fungicide. The dog won't lick it off as it's repelled by the smell. Or wet a deodorant crystal and apply. (Both are available at health-food stores.) Fungus/ringworm is contagious so consult your veterinarian for treatment.

DOG, Hot spot relief:

- Dip a black or green tea bag briefly in hot water. Allow it to cool to lukewarm, then press it gently against the moist, highly inflamed eruption for a few minutes while holding and petting the animal. Or tie the tea bag in place with a strip of cloth and leave on for up to 1 hour. The tannic acid in the tea helps heal hot spots.
- See your veterinarian if no improvement occurs.

DOG, Leaving at kennel or away from home:

- Leave a familiar article of your clothing with the dog, such as a worn sock that still has your scent.
- Sleep with a towel for a couple of days to put your scent on it.
- Bring the pet's favorite toys.

DOG, Left alone for several hours:

- Leave the radio on low. The sound will reassure the animal and make it feel less abandoned.
- Put down a special toy when you leave and remove it as soon as you come home.

DOG, Mange, To Treat:

- Bathe the dog in a shallow tub of water with about ½ cup chlorine bleach.
- Add 1 thinly sliced lemon and 1 peeled and grated garlic clove to 2 cups boiling water, then cool to room temperature. Pour over the affected areas twice a day until the problem is resolved.
- Use the above if a veterinarian is not available or to provide additional relief.

DOG, Mats in fur:

- Shampoo, then use conditioner. When the fur is dry, rub talcum powder into mats and tease them apart.

DOG, Medicine, administering:

- Insert the pill in your dog's mouth, then quickly close its mouth and tap its nose with your finger. This causes the dog to lick and then swallow.
- Open the dog's mouth, place the pill at the back of the throat, and quickly close its mouth.
- Wrap the pill in cheese or coat it with peanut butter or liverwurst.
- Pulverize it and mix it with the pet's food.

DOG, Nail cut too short:

- Use a bar of soap to stop bleeding if you accidentally trim your pet's nail too short. Press the bleeding nail into a bar of soap. It stops the bleeding almost immediately.
- Use alum powder mixed with water to form a paste. (Obtain alum from a drugstore or the spice section of a supermarket.)

DOG, To deworm:

- Give the pet 2 to 3 cloves garlic a day. Give puppies 1 clove a day. Mince or crush the garlic and mix well into your pet's food.

DOG, To keep off furniture:

- Put a piece of aluminum foil on top of each cushion. The noise of the foil frightens the dog, and it will soon get out of the habit.
- Fill a coffee can with coins and rattle. The dog will associate the unpleasant noise with jumping up. Use this also to discourage other inappropriate behavior.

DOG, To relieve gas:

- Rub the pet's stomach with apple cider vinegar. It should relive gas within 30 minutes.

DOG, To shampoo:

- Brush before shampooing, then put a cotton ball in each ear and a drop of mineral oil in each eye. Place a lather of shampoo around the neck to stop fleas from running to its head while you wash the body. Work from tail to nose and use a shampoo made for pets, not humans.
- Place nylon net, a nylon kitchen scrubber, or an upside-down tea strainer over the drain if washing the dog in the bathtub. The hair will collect in the receptacle, and prevent it from blocking the drain.
- Add 1 tablespoon table salt to the water. It helps kill fleas and add freshness.
- Give the dog a dry shampoo by rubbing cornmeal into its coat, then brushing it out. Follow up with baking soda for a sweet-smelling coat.

DOG DISH, To avoid tipping over when outside:

- Put a stake in the ground and put the water in a large angel food cake pan over the stake.
- Use a galvanized bucket.
- Install a dog nozzle to the water line outside. This will provide a constant fresh supply of water at all times.

DOG WIRE BRUSH, To clean:

- Weave a toothpick back and forth through the wire rows to loosen up the hairs.
- Use an old comb reserved for the purpose.
- Wash the brush in hot sudsy water to which a little ammonia has been added.
- Sterilize it by soaking it in 2 tablespoons chlorine bleach to 1 quart water. Leave for 10 minutes, then rinse thoroughly.

FISH TANKS, To clean:

- Scrub the tank after emptying with a nylon scrubber and either white vinegar or noniodized table salt. Rinse well before refilling.

HAMSTER, Escaped, To catch:

- Make a hole in the lid of a box and place a paper towel over the hole, then put some food in the middle of the towel. When the hamster steps on the towel to get at the food, it will drop in the box.
- Oil the inside of a glass container and put some food in the bottom. When the hamster goes for the food, it won't be able to get out.

KITTEN, To housebreak:

- Prohibit the kitten from using the same area to relieve itself by clean-

ing it and covering the area with aluminum foil. Gradually reduce the size of the foil.
- Move the litter box to the area it previously used to relieve itself.

KITTEN OR CAT, To make feel at home:
- Touch its paws with juice from a can of tuna, or rub butter on.
- Put out bowls, toys, etc., before bringing the kitten or cat into the new quarters. When it enters, it will feel at home right away.

KITTEN WITH WORMS, To deworm:
- Mash 1 whole clove garlic into the kitten's food and stir in 1 teaspoon vegetable oil. Repeat for 3 consecutive days. Repeat if necessary. Thereafter, a little garlic once a week should keep it wormed.

PUPPIES, Hints on:
- Put several pieces of old sock or material in with the puppies and mother if giving the puppies away. When the puppies leave for their new home, give the new owner a piece of sock or material. It will smell just like the puppy's mother and give the pup a feeling of security.
- Put in with the puppy a piece of your old clothing or a sock you've worn, a ticking clock, and a hot water bottle filled with warm (not hot) water, and leave a radio playing softly nearby. This will soothe the puppy to sleep and give it a sense of security.

PUPPIES, To housebreak:
- Take the puppy outside within 15 minutes after feeding, as soon as it wakes from a nap, right after playing, and whenever it starts to circle and sniff. Never punish the animal even if you catch it in the act, which can make it afraid to relieve itself outside.
- Cover a generous eating area with newspaper.
- Confine the puppy to a small area.

RABBITS, Food For, Hints on:
- Supplement pellet rabbit foods with apples, cabbage, carrots, fresh clover, grass, alfalfa, or any leafy hay, stale bread, sweet potatoes, and turnips. Do not feed rabbits under 6 months fresh greens.
- Ask the produce manager at the supermarket for carrot tops and other produce refuse. Also ask at the farmers' market for unwanted greens. Most people prefer the tops removed from the carrots before they buy them.

Sewing, Knitting, Crocheting

BUTTONS, To save from old garments:
- Remove them by sliding a comb underneath, then cutting the thread with a single-edge razor blade or seam ripper.
- String the buttons on dental floss and tie the ends.
- Store on a large safety pin.
- Open up a hairpin, thread the buttons on, and twist the ends together.

BUTTONS, To sew on a garment:
- Use elastic thread to sew on buttons at the waistbands of skirts and pants or for other buttons requiring a little give.
- Use dental floss for heavy-duty buttons that take a lot a wear and tear.

CROCHET HOOKS AND KNITTING NEEDLES, Hints on:
- Store crochet hooks in plastic toothbrush tubes and knitting needles in cardboard mailing tubes.
- Slip a foam hair roller cut to the desired length or a piece of foam tubing onto the ends of crochet hooks or knitting needles to make them easier to grasp.

CROCHETING, To prevent from unraveling:
- Put a snap-type clothespin on the hook, the thread, and the item you are working on before you put it away. This keeps everything together right where you stopped and keeps it from unraveling.

DARNING, Hints on:
- Straighten the ends and iron between 2 pieces of wax paper before darning.
- Use a hard-boiled egg or a Leggs-shaped pantyhose container to slip under the area to be darned.

ELASTIC, To replace:
- Open the waist band enough to insert a safety pin and pin one end of the new elastic to the old elastic. Hold the free end of the old elastic and pull. The new elastic will slide in place as the old is removed.

HAND-KNITTED OR CROCHETED ITEM, To give as a gift:

- Include a label saved from a skein of the yarn if it contains the washing instructions and a few yards of the wool for repairs.

HEMMING, Hints on:

- Cut a thin strip of cardboard the size of the hem and use it as a guide. Turn the material over the cardboard and press the hem with a warm iron, holding it in place as you work. The hem is now creased and ready to be pinned in place.
- Remove an imprint from the old hem by pressing the crease with a dampened press cloth or sponging undiluted white vinegar on the line, then pressing with a hot iron using a dry press cloth. Or soak brown paper (part of a grocery bag is fine) in white vinegar, apply to the crease, and press with a hot iron.

HOOKS AND EYES, To sew on a garment:

- Tape them to the garment with transparent tape first so they'll be easier to sew and won't slip. When the hook or eye is sewn on, the tape can be pulled off.

KNITTING, To prevent dropped stitches:

- Put a cork on the ends of the needles.

KNITTING NEEDLES WITH NO SIZE INDICATED, To identify:

- Identify the size by marking them with nail polish or paint. Two dots would denote size 2, three dots size 3, etc.

KNITTING NEEDLES, WOODEN, To make easier to use:

- Rub them with a dry, soap-filled scouring pad. It makes the yarn glide over them much faster.

KNITTING, STITCH COUNTER SUBSTITUTE:

- Use bread tags as stitch counters.

KNITTING, STITCH HOLDER SUBSTITUTE:

- Use a plastic straw.

MENDING A GARMENT OF LOOSELY WOVEN FABRIC, Hint on:

- Pull some thread from the inside hem or side seam, and use that to mend the garment.

MENDING WITHOUT THE RIGHT COLOR THREAD, Hint on:

- Improvise by using two strands of thread that blend to the needed shade. Use light brown and white thread for ecru, use dark blue and light blue for medium blue.

- Keep a clear or neutral thread as a substitute when you do not have the right color.

NEEDLES, To make glide easier:

- Stick them through a fabric softener sheet a few times. Thread the needle and knot the thread before doing this.

NEEDLES, To store:

- Prevent rust and have the needles and pins slide easily by keeping them stuck in a bar of soap in your sewing box.
- Make a little fabric bag and fill it with dry, used coffee grounds. This pincushion also will prevent rust.
- Clean a lipstick case carefully, and use it to store your needles.
- Use a piece of cork as a pincushion.
- Use a candle. When needles are waxed, they slip through material more easily. Wipe the excess wax off before using.
- Keep needles in the center of a spool of thread by using the filter tip of a cigarette or a piece of cork cut to fit.

NEEDLES, To thread:

- Cut thread on an angle instead of breaking it.
- Put a small piece of white paper behind the eye of the needle before threading.
- Use a needle threader or a self-threading needle that has a tiny slot on the top so you can pull the thread down through it.

NEEDLES, DULL OR RUSTY, To clean:

- Rub off rust with a steel wool soap pad or plain steel wool.
- Rub the needle over your hair to make it glide easier.
- Push them in and out of a cake of soap.

ODDS AND ENDS, To store:

- Save plastic containers such as breath-mint boxes for holding needles, straight pins, hooks and eyes, snaps, and other small items.

QUILTING, Liner for:

- Use a white sheet as the lining. The quilt will be smooth and lump-free after washing.

SAFETY PINS, To store:
- Keep them all together on a pipe cleaner, a food bag twist tie or another safety pin.

SEWING MACHINE NEEDLES, To thread:
- Take it out of the machine and thread it.
- Hold a piece of white paper close to the needle, but on the opposite side of the needle's eye to bring the eye into focus.
- Use a needle threader.

SEWING MACHINE NEEDLES, BLUNT, To sharpen:
- Pull the fine side of the needle several times at an angle across an emery board.

SNAGGED THREAD ON GARMENT, To fix:
- Insert a thin wire needle threader through the fabric from the wrong side. Thread the snag through it, then pull it back to the wrong side.
- Pull through to the wrong side by inserting a needle and pushing just the eye through the top of the fabric.

SNAPS, To sew on a garment: See "Hooks and Eyes, To sew on a garment."

YARN, To identify if wool or synthetic:
- Test a small piece by burning it. If the yarn burns to ashes, it's wool. If it hardens into a dark lump, it's synthetic.

YARN, To recycle from a knitted item:
- Wind it loosely around a cake rack after unraveling, then dip the rack into water and let it dry out. This will remove the kinks so that you can rewind it.

YARN HOLDER SUBSTITUTES:
- Put the yarn in an old teapot and bring the yarn out of the spout.
- Put it in a tall canister or coffee can with a plastic lid. Cut a hole in the lid and pull the yarn through the hole.
- Put the ball of yarn in a plastic bag and draw out the yarn through a hole in the bottom of the bag. Tie off the top of the bag or seal it. The yarn will feed out as you knit or crochet but will not unwind or tangle.
- Run the thread through a plastic drinking straw to prevent it from getting tangles or knots.
- Use a washed-out bleach bottle cut so you can put the yarn in and draw it up through the spout as you work.

ZIPPER OFF TRACK, To fix:

- Slit through the metal bottom of the zipper with a single-edge razor blade. Slip each side of the tab back into the zipper track. Pull the zipper up, then sew the slit up, stitching across the teeth at the bottom.
- Loosen up a sticking zipper by rubbing the teeth on both sides with soap, paraffin, candle wax, or a lead pencil.

Stains

HINTS:

- Treat as soon as possible.
- Avoid hot water unless specified.
- Treat from the wrong side of the fabric.
- Work inward toward the stain, never the other way around. This avoids leaving a ring.
- Treat the nongreasy component of a stain first if it is part nongreasy and part greasy. Soak in cold water and wash with detergent. Let air-dry, and then treat the greasy stain.
- Rinse out one stain-removal agent before you apply another.
- Record what works for you and use it the next time.

STAINS, GREASY, NONWASHABLE FABRICS:

- Rub fresh stains with an absorbent such as chalk, fuller's earth, corn-starch, baking soda, or talcum powder. Let it sit until the grease is absorbed (several hours, if necessary), then brush off the powder.
- Sponge with rubbing alcohol.
- Use a dry-cleaning fluid.

STAINS, GREASY, WASHABLE FABRICS:

- Sprinkle baking soda, talcum power, or cornstarch over the stain and rub it in. When the grease is absorbed, brush the powder off. Apply a prewash or liquid shampoo and let sit for several minutes, then wash it in the hottest water the fabric can take.
- Use dry-cleaning fluid if washing does not remove the stain. Let the material dry and sponge it repeatedly if necessary. If a yellow stain remains on old or heat-set stains, use a nonchlorine bleach or hydro-gen peroxide.

STAINS, NONGREASY, WASHABLE FABRICS:

- Apply club soda immediately to the stain.
- Sponge stains promptly with cool water or soak for 30 minutes or overnight. After sponging or soaking, work undiluted liquid detergent, shampoo, or a prewash product into the stain and rinse. If the stain remains, try one of the following:

- Soak for several hours or overnight in a cold water and enzyme presoak following manufacturer's directions.
- Moisten the stain with ammonia and keep it wet until the stain is gone. Rinse the area with water. If colors seem changed by the ammonia, try moistening the item with white vinegar. Then rinse with water. (Dilute the ammonia with an equal amount of water for use on silk or wool and add a small amount of vinegar to the last rinse.)
- Remove stains from materials not damaged by chlorine bleach by dissolving 2 tablespoons liquid bleach in 1 quart cool water and applying to the stain with a medicine dropper or cotton swab. Or soak the stained material in this solution for 5 to 15 minutes. Rinse thoroughly with water and repeat if necessary. If the stain remains, try equal parts of bleach and water, applying as described above. For really stubborn stains on white fabrics, apply bleach full strength with a medicine dropper or a cotton swab. Watch it closely until the stain disappears. Then rinse it immediately and thoroughly.

ALCOHOLIC BEVERAGES:

- Soak fresh stains in cold water and a few tablespoons of glycerin. Rinse with half white vinegar and half water and wash as usual. Alcohol stains turn brown with age, so you should treat them immediately.

ANTIPERSPIRANT AND DEODORANT:

- Restore faded colors by sponging them with ammonia. (Dilute the ammonia with an equal amount of water for use on silk or wool.) Sponge or rinse thoroughly with plain water.
- Rub spots on washable material with white vinegar before laundering.

BALLPOINT PEN INK:

- Apply mineral oil or white petroleum jelly. Allow it to set and then remove the oil or jelly, along with the mark, with dry-cleaning fluid.
- Apply hair spray liberally to the stain. Then apply a few drops of white vinegar, blotting every 5 minutes with a clean cloth. Allow to dry and launder as usual.
- Sponge with milk, then launder as usual.
- Rub rubbing alcohol in the spot before laundering.
- Sponge with methylated spirits, then wash as usual.

BATTERY ACID:

- Rub a paste of baking soda and water into the spot immediately. Leave for 2 hours, then launder.

BEETROOT:

- Fill a saucer with milk, put the stained portion of the cloth in the milk, and put a slice of bread on top to absorb the stain. Leave for a few minutes, then wash as usual.

BLOOD STAINS:

Washable Materials:

- Soak for several hours or overnight in a solution of 1 cup table salt to 1 gallon water. Or use an enzyme cleaning product, such as Nature's Miracle (sold in pet stores), and follow directions.
- Soak or rub the material in cold water until the stain is almost gone. Then cover the spot with meat tenderizer to make a paste. Let set, then wash with warm water and detergent.
- Saturate old or stubborn bleachable stains with diluted ammonia, or apply the ammonia to the wet area. Use hydrogen peroxide instead of ammonia if colorfastness is questionable. Rinse in cold water.

Blood on Cushions:

- Cover the spot immediately with a paste of cornstarch and water. Rub it on and put the cushion in the sun to dry. The sun will draw the blood out into the cornstarch. Brush off the dry cornstarch. If the stain is not removed, repeat.

BURN/SCORCH STAIN ON CLOTHING:

- Sponge with hydrogen peroxide until the stain disappears, then launder as usual.

CANDLE WAX:

- Rub the wax with an ice cube to harden it, then scrape off the wax with a spatula. Place the stain between two pieces of white blotting paper or paper towels and press with a warm iron. Change the paper as the wax is absorbed. Dry, then remove any remaining stain with dry-cleaning solvent. If a colored stain remains, sponge it with 1 part rubbing alcohol diluted with 2 parts water.

CELLULOSE TAPE:

- Sponge with rubbing alcohol. Test colors first.

CHEWING GUM:

- Rub with a piece of ice and scrape the gum out of the fabric.
- Place the item in a plastic bag and put it in the freezer for 1 hour. Remove and scrape off the frozen gum with a metal spatula.
- Loosen by soaking in white vinegar or rubbing with egg white.

CHOCOLATE:

- Rinse in lukewarm water before soaking for 30 minutes in a solution of 2 tablespoons all-purpose bleach (nonchlorine) and 1 quart warm water. If the stain persists, rinse in cool water and apply a solution made from hydrogen peroxide and a few drops of ammonia.
- Sponge the stain with cold water, then sponge with a solution of 1 tablespoon borax to 1 cup warm water. Rinse well and wash as usual.

COFFEE AND TEA WITHOUT MILK OR CREAM:

Washable Fabrics:

- Stretch the stained portion over a bowl and secure it with a rubber band or string. Sprinkle table salt on the stain, then pour boiling water on it from a height of 1 to 3 feet. Don't use soap; it sets the stain. Wash in the hottest water that's safe for the fabric.

CURRY:

- Soak the stained area in a solution of half ammonia and half cool water.

DYE TRANSFER ON COLORED FABRICS: See LAUNDRY chapter, "Color Bleeding, To resolve."

FELT MARKER:

- Soak the area with rubbing alcohol.

FRUIT, BERRIES, FOOD COLORING:

- Lay the fabric, stain side down, over a colander and pour boiling water on the stain from a height of several feet.

GRASS, FLOWER, FOLIAGE:

- Sponge with rubbing alcohol before washing.
- Rub stains with methylated spirits, oil, or glycerin, leave on for 1 hour, then wash as usual. Treat old stains by saturating with glycerin or oil, then washing in hot sudsy water.
- Saturate the area with hydrogen peroxide. Let sit until the stain disappears, then launder as usual.
- Use 1 tablespoon chlorine or nonchlorine bleach to 2 cups water.

GRAVY AND CHOCOLATE ON TABLE LINENS:

- Use shaving cream or club soda as an emergency measure before washing.
- Soak in cold water to dissolve the starch, if any, then treat the stain with prewash solution before washing.

INK:

- Soak the spot in tomato juice for 20 minutes, then wash as usual.
- Treat with rubbing alcohol and rinse well. Next apply prewash or liquid laundry detergent, and wash in the hottest water the fabric can stand.

LIPSTICK:

- Sponge the spot with rubbing alcohol, then with dishwashing liquid, then launder as usual.

MILDEW:

- Test the fabric on a hidden seam first, then soak it in a solution of half hydrogen peroxide and cool water. Wash thoroughly, then rinse and dry.

MUSTARD:

Washable Fabrics:

- Rub with glycerin before washing. (Obtain glycerin from a drugstore.)
- Soak overnight in hot water and detergent. If the stain persists, use chlorine or non-chlorine bleach following manufacturer's directions.

Nonwashable Fabrics:

- Sponge the stain with rubbing alcohol. Test first for colorfastness.

PAINT, WATER-BASED:

- Rinse thoroughly with warm water, then apply enzyme presoak following manufacturer's directions. Rinse again and launder.
- Use equal parts of ammonia and turpentine for old spots. Saturate the spot several times, then launder as usual.

PENCIL MARKS:

- Erase the marks with a soft pencil eraser. If not erasable, work detergent into the stain and rinse. For stubborn marks, put a few drops of ammonia on the stain, follow with detergent, and repeat until the mark is gone.

PERSPIRATION:

- Sponge with a solution of half white vinegar and half water, especially on old stains. Rinse carefully with water.
- Remove yellow stains with sodium perborate, chlorine bleach, or hydrogen peroxide.
- Dissolve a few aspirins in cold water and soak the stained areas until the stains disappear.

- Rub a thick paste of baking soda and water onto the stain. Let it sit anywhere from 15 minutes up to 1 hour or so, then launder as usual.
- Mix a little table salt and enough water to make a paste. Rub the paste into the cloth and let sit for 1 hour or so, then wash as usual. Or soak the stains in a strong salt-water solution.

PET STAINS ON CARPETS: See CARPETS chapter, "Carpet, Pet Accident on, To treat."

RUST STAINS:

- Wet the stain with water, then apply lemon juice mixed with table salt. Hold the area over the spout of a boiling kettle for several minutes, then rinse. Repeat if necessary.
- Sprinkle table salt on the stain, add lemon juice, and dry in the sun. Repeat if necessary.
- Boil the stained article in a solution of 4 teaspoons cream of tartar to 2 cups water until the stain is removed, then rinse thoroughly.

SCORCH MARKS, LIGHT:
Washable Fabrics:

- Rub a lemon into the scorched part, leaving on the fabric as much juice and pith as possible. Place the material in the sun to dry, then wash as usual.
- Rub the scorched part with the cut side of an onion, making sure the skin is completely removed, then soak in cold water before laundering.
- Wet the item, and immerse it in a solution of half hydrogen peroxide and half water. Wait until the mark disappears, then wash as usual.

Nonwashable Fabrics:

- Sponge the fabric gently with a cotton ball soaked in hydrogen peroxide.
- Brush scorched spots on thick woolens lightly with emery cloth or superfine sandpaper (grade 0000).

SHOE POLISH:

- Scrape off excess polish with a dull knife, then clean with a solution of equal parts rubbing alcohol and water. Launder as usual. Use straight alcohol for white fabrics.
- Sponge with methylated spirits, then wash as usual.
- Wash with warm water with a little ammonia added.

SILK, DRY-CLEANING SOLVENT RINGS ON:

- Steam the item over a kettle but avoid getting it too wet, then rub the fabric briskly against itself. This also works on wool.

SOFT DRINKS:

- Sponge immediately with plain cool water. If these stains are allowed to dry they are sometimes invisible, but they turn yellow with age or when ironed and are difficult to remove.

STUBBORN STAINS, OLD:

- Apply eucalyptus oil with a cotton swab. Leave overnight, then try dry-cleaning fluid if necessary. (Buy eucalyptus oil in health food stores or pharmacies.)
- Soak in hydrogen peroxide for several hours, rinse, and launder as usual.
- Soak several hours or overnight in a solution of ¼ cup powdered dish-water detergent, ¼ cup chlorine bleach, and 5 quarts very hot tap water. Do not use on delicate or noncolorfast fabrics, and do not use a metal container to soak the items.

TAR, ASPHALT, AXLE GREASE:

- Scrape off as much as possible, then follow the directions for greasy stains. If traces remain, try one of the following:
- Sponge with turpentine, then launder as usual.
- Soak a piece of white cloth in eucalyptus oil and rub it on the affected part until quite clean. This method is suitable for even very delicate materials.
- Rub the stain with a little dry-cleaning fluid until it's gone, then wash with mild detergent and water.

TAR ON CARPETS:

- Scrape off as much as possible with a dull knife, then sponge with a cloth soaked in dry-cleaning fluid. Use a light upward brushing motion so that the stain will be rubbed out of the rug rather than into it. Change the cloth when it becomes soiled and continue sponging until the stain is gone.

TEA, WITHOUT MILK OR CREAM: See "Coffee and Tea Without Milk or Cream."

TRAVEL STAIN TIPS:

- Blot fresh wine or coffee spills with a cloth soaked in club soda.
- Rub white chalk into greasy stains.

WATER SPOTS:

- Dampen the entire garment by sponging it with water or by shaking it in steam from a boiling tea kettle. Press the garment while it is damp.

WAX ON TABLECLOTH:

- Warm a knife over a flame, then gently slip it under the wax and lift the wax off the surface.
- Put the tablecloth in the refrigerator (wax side out) until the wax hardens, then peel it off.

WINE:
Washable Fabrics:

- Stretch the stained portion over a bowl and secure it with a rubber band or string. Sprinkle table salt on the stain, then pour boiling water on it from a height of 1 to 3 feet.
- Treat red wine spills by sprinkling immediately with lots of table salt. Put the item into cold water and rub the stain out before washing.

Travel Tips

HINTS ON:

- Make photocopies of your driver's license, passport, travel tickets, serial numbers of traveler's checks, and other documents. Keep one copy at home and one in your luggage.
- Keep passports, jewelry, valuables, and medications with you, not in your suitcase.
- Make a list of everything you intend to take with you and cross it off as you pack.
- Put your name and address inside your luggage. Put your name outside.
- Carry your medical insurance identity card as well as a claim form (filled out in advance) and a medical alert card (available at most pharmacies) stating any special medical conditions, allergies, and your blood type. Or keep a written notice of any medical problem on your person or wear an ID bracelet.
- Keep some moist towelettes in packages for quick freshening up. Small packets of tissues are also handy.
- Conserve energy and grab every opportunity. Never stand when you can sit, never sit when you can lie down, and never pass up a chance to use the bathroom.
- Address or type labels beforehand to those you'll be sending postcards to. It will save time during the trip. You can just pop them on the postcard.
- Head off motion sickness by taking two capsules of ginger root powder (450 mg each) 10 minutes before setting out on a trip. The *Lancet* and other sources reported it to be twice as effective as 100 mg Dramamine. Plus ginger root does not make you drowsy.
- Save little jars and plastic bottles and fill with your usual toiletries. Or buy trial-size products.
- Remove wrinkles in clothing at your destination by hanging the garments in the bathroom while taking a shower. The steam will smooth them out.
- Take along a couple of spring-type clothespins for each skirt. You can turn a wire hanger into a skirt hanger with them.

- Take a plastic expandable clothesline to dry clothing in the bathtub/shower enclosure.
- Include a little emergency kit consisting of a small Swiss Army knife, Kiwi Shine Wipes, double-stick tape for hems, small scissors, individual packets of detergent or a small container filled with detergent, aspirins, Band-Aids, etc. (To avoid packing shoe polish or Shine Wipes, clean shoes with a little hand cream applied with a tissue, then buff with a clean tissue.)
- Take a little sewing kit or make your own from an empty matchbook folder. Stick the needles in the bottom and various colors of thread around the back of the folder. Put in a few safety pins of various sizes.
- Take along a water heater and small containers of instant coffee, sugar, and creamer if you are on a beer budget and don't stay at hotels/motels that provide such amenities.
- Hang the DO NOT DISTURB sign on your hotel door if you are leaving for the evening.
- Use a highlighter to mark your route on the road map when traveling by automobile. Doing so makes the map easier to read.

TRAVEL ABROAD, Before you leave:

- Inquire if a visa or any shots or medications are required for the country you are planning to visit.
- Make two copies of all your important documents and travel aids (passport identification page, tickets, birth certificate, driver's license, credit cards, serial numbers of traveler's checks, and visas), and try to get as many documents on one page as possible. Keep one copy in your luggage and one at home.
- Have two passport-size photos taken in case you need to replace a lost or stolen passport or visa.
- Find out about the international driver's license, available from most branches of the Automobile Association of America, and ask the Motor Vehicle Department about any restrictions on driving in the country of destination. The United Kingdom and Ireland, for example, restrict drivers over 70 years of age.
- Avoid international travel troubles. Get a U.S. State Department Consular Information Sheet on the country you will be visiting. The sheet includes data on crime, medical care, terrorism, medication needed and required shots, such as antimalaria. The information sheets are available for more than 200 countries. (See USEFUL ADDRESSES AND PHONE NUMBERS, "Travel, Information Sheets on More than 200 Countries.")

- Check the travel section of the Sunday newspaper for statistics on countries you'll be visiting: temperatures and precipitation, national and religious holidays, exchange rates, and places deemed unsafe for U.S. travelers.
- Obtain an International Student ID if you're a full-time student. This will entitle you to discounts abroad. Teachers also are entitled to discounts in many European countries.
- Ask your insurance or travel agent about health-care programs for travelers if your health insurance does not cover you while abroad. (See USEFUL ADDRESSES AND PHONE NUMBERS, "Travel, Health Care While Abroad.")
- Buy a language phrase book and learn as many phrases as you can before departure.
- Take along a generic prescription, one that uses the drug name rather than a brand name. Trade names are different in other countries. Also, carry a prescription for your eyeglasses and contact lenses or an extra set. Your medicine kit should include aspirin, cold tablets, vitamins, antacids, sunscreen, Band-Aids, antidiarrhea medicine, and moleskin or corn plasters.
- Buy one all-purpose travel paperback book on Europe if you are visiting various countries. Carefully pull it apart and staple together the pages for each country. Carry the appropriate section with you in each country, along with notes from other sources. Keep the other sections in your luggage.
- Take some American money for ground transportation home plus $50 in one-dollar bills for emergency use, a small amount of money in the currency of your first destination for initial expenses, traveler's checks, your ATM card, and a credit card such as VISA or MasterCard for large expenditures.
- Buy your traveler's checks in small denominations from a company that doesn't charge a commission.
- Utilize your ATM card. You pay no commission charge, plus you get the wholesale exchange rate. The only charge is the normal transaction fee charged to access your checking account back home (one or two dollars, depending on the bank). The Plus network owned by VISA now has more than 239,000 ATMs in 87 countries. Cirrus (owned by MasterCard) has more than 201,000 ATMs in 68

countries. Check the back of your ATM card to see which network yours is compatible with. In a recent survey sponsored by VISA, using a U.S.-issued card at a foreign ATM was found to be less expensive than changing money at a bank, 43 percent less expensive than changing money at a foreign airport and 53 percent less expensive than exchanging currency at hotels. Make sure you have a four-digit PIN. Call Plus at 800-491-1145 or Cirrus at 800-4-Cirrus to inquire about ATM locations around the world.

- Inquire about MasterCard and VISA check-card services called Maestro and Interlink. If you have one of these logos on your ATM card, you can make debit purchases at cooperating merchants by punching in your PIN.
- Take a spare set of batteries for your camera and more film than you'll think you need. It's much cheaper at home than abroad.
- Tuck some self-closing plastic sandwich bags in your odds-and-ends kit to hold currency from different countries. You may be left with some foreign coins. You also may travel through the country again and need them.
- Pack a transformer plug or converter for any electrical appliances you are taking with you.
- Pack a flat fabric or heavy nylon bag in the bottom of your suitcase for shopping while abroad. Put all your purchases in the bag when returning home; it will ease your way through customs.
- Put a plastic grocery bag in your luggage to keep laundry in until you can wash it.
- Declare any new expensive, foreign-make cameras, watches, or other items with U.S. customs before you leave to avoid paying duty when you return.

TRAVEL ABROAD, Being there:

- Reserve judgment on others' lifestyles and manners, and respect the traditions and customs of the country you are in.
- Avoid being conspicuous in jewelry and attire.
- Wear a money belt (a pouch under your clothing) and wear your shoulder purse strapped across your body, not hanging from your shoulder.
- Keep spending money in your pocket or purse and the bulk of your valuables in a money belt.
- Keep coins on hand for using public restrooms.
- Stop at the local tourist information office for free maps and information. Ask about public bus routes for points of interest, and get a map

of the bus and subway lines. Also inquire about hours or days museums and galleries are open for free and museum and shopping hours. Some museums are closed Mondays. European train stations have tourist offices with English-speaking personnel.

- Check whether public transportation offers economical day passes or if you can buy tickets in bulk, before you purchase your tickets.
- Get a map of the city and clearly mark your hotel or lodgings, and have someone write out the name and address on a piece of paper you can carry with you. This is important in countries such as Japan and China, where the alphabet is different from ours. Then show the written address to someone giving you directions. Or you can carry a hotel matchbook or business card with you. Also pick up picture postcards of where you want to go. Show one if you have to ask for directions.
- Seek medical help at the nearest university teaching-hospital emergency room, or call the U.S. Embassy or consulate for a recommendation.
- Contact the U.S. Embassy in the event of legal, medical, or financial emergencies.
- Keep a travel log or diary to record your observations. You think you'll remember, but memories fade with time. Also keep a log of all purchases.
- Place overseas calls from a local post office to avoid the high handling rate charged by hotels. Or call collect or use a telephone credit card. Ask for instructions on how to use the public phones and whether you need special coins or tokens.
- Tuck a plastic or string bag into your carryall or purse when shopping. Many countries expect customers to supply their own bag.
- Shop exchange rates for traveler's checks before cashing them. If possible, don't exchange them at an airport bank, hotel, or money-changing service. Look for a source that offers a favorable exchange rate and little or no fee, such as banks or American Express offices, which do not charge their customers a fee for exchanging traveler's checks. Exchange for no more cash than you need for a short time. That way you won't get stuck with extra cash when entering another country.
- Carry a small calculator to determine the exchange rate.
- Use American Express or Poste Restante for mail service if you have no destination address. Have the sender address mail to "Poste Restante 1" and the name of the city and country. The main post office of that city will hold it for you.
- Check your bill to determine if service has been included. In cafés and

bistros, where a bill is not presented, ask. Most European countries include service in the bill. If service has been outstanding, leave a 3 percent tip.

- Plan to receive a refund of value-added tax (VAT), which ranges from 8 to 33 percent of the purchase price, on purchases made for your personal use. Upon leaving the country where purchases were made, ask the customs official to stamp the receipt. After returning home, mail all receipts back to stores, enclosing your U.S. address so the purchases can qualify as exports.

- Drink only beverages made with boiled water or drink bottled water. Ice, too, should be made only from boiled water. To be doubly safe, drink carbonated bottled water. Carbonation helps kill infection-causing microbes that can cause diarrhea. Avoid produce sold by street vendors and raw shellfish, peel all fruit, and eat cooked foods while they are still hot.

- Cut costs by making your own lunch of rolls and cheese and deli items. (Keep some plastic utensils on hand or utilize your Swiss Army knife.) When ordering wine in restaurants, choose the house wine and look for the *prix-fixe* or daily specials. Choose cafeterias and check out department stores, some of which have inexpensive cafeterias with good food.

- Exchange any local currency before leaving the country; otherwise you'll be left with coins as souvenirs. Coins cannot be exchanged.

- Prevent *turista*, or bacterial dysentery, when traveling to countries where hygienic conditions and bacterial flora are different by taking 2 tablets of betaine hydrochloride after each meal. Hydrochloric acid kills bacteria in the stomach and prevents infection. (Obtain betaine hydrochloride tablets from a health food store.) Straight lemon or lime juice, taken on an empty stomach, also has an antiseptic sterilizing effect.

TRAVEL BY AIR, Hints on:

- Know the difference between nonstop and direct: Nonstop flights do not stop, whereas direct may stop but you don't have to change planes at the stopover.

- Avoid flying within 12 hours after dental work. The change in atmospheric pressure can cause severe pain.

- Take a decongestant before the flight if you have a cold. It will help clear ears and sinus passages. If the cold is severe, continue taking decongestants as prescribed on the label.

- Take a pair of ear plugs and an eyeshade with you if you can't sleep on planes.

- Reconfirm your reservations and time of departure before leaving and returning.

- Get to the airport early; be prepared to show a photo ID; and do not wrap any gifts you are taking with you. If your seat was not booked ahead of time, get to the airport extra early so you'll have your choice of seating.

- Ask for rows 11 through 18 for best visibility and smoother ride on a 747. A seat over the wing makes for the smoothest ride. Seats up front are the quietest, and seats near the galleys the noisiest, plus they are usually last on the meal serving order. Request a seat in the first row of a section or just in back of exits for extra leg room. The July 1993 issue of *Consumer Reports* has a comprehensive seat comfort chart for every major airline.

- Consider a left aisle seat for a meal flight if you are right-handed and vice versa if you are left-handed.

- Book an aisle and window seat when traveling with another person. Often the middle seat will remain unsold.

- Put in your request for a special on-flight meal (kosher, vegetarian, severe hypoglycemia) when you book your flight. Remind the chief flight attendant about the special meal you ordered when boarding.

- Attach a piece of yarn to the handle of your luggage or some other means of quick identification.

- Don't check your luggage with the curbside baggage checking service. Doing so increases the odds of luggage being delayed or lost.

- Hand your film and camera (if it's loaded) to the airport guard for a manual inspection if you don't have a film shield bag. Also hand a laptop computer to the guard.

- Ask the flight attendant for a blanket and a pillow as soon as you are seated, unless they are already on your seat.

- To all men: Remove your wallet from your back pocket. Sitting on the wallet on a long flight could put your back out of kilter.

- Take a sweater in your carry-on bag to wear on the plane in case it gets cold, as it often does, and a pair of slipper socks to slip into. Include in your carry-on bag all essential toiletries, prescription drugs or medication, reading material, and a change of clothes.

- Dress comfortably with loose clothing, move around frequently, drink lots of fluids, curtail alcohol, and eat lightly the day before the flight to minimize jet lag.

- Try the Feast Fast Jet Lag Diet if you suffer from jet lag. Developed at a U.S. Department of Energy laboratory, it is available with a self-addressed, stamped envelope from Argonne National Laboratory, 9700 South Cass Avenue, Argonne, IL 60439. Or consult the library for books on overcoming jet lag.
- Put your feet up on your tote on a long flight to avoid swollen feet and ankles, place a pillow behind the small of your back to improve your comfort, and mist your face frequently to counteract cabin dryness.
- Keep a written notice of any medical problems on your person and keep a watch set to the home time if taking medication on schedule and crossing many time zones.
- Check your airline policy. Some airlines have a policy that lost luggage must be reported within 4 hours of arrival.

TRAVEL PACKING, Hints on:

- Buy lightweight luggage, such as heavy-duty nylon, so you don't have to depend on porters. While luggage with wheels has its place, consider stairs abroad that you might have to climb.
- Make a list of travel documents and clothing, and check off each item while packing.
- Coordinate your wardrobe around a single color or have lots of things that mix and match. Use separates, and choose clothes that can be layered. Include one good outfit and be prepared for unseasonable weather.
- Lay out everything to be packed, then pack half the items. Walk around with the bag for a few minutes to see if it's manageable. If it's too heavy, take out what you can do without. If packing the night before, leave the bag open; the air will keep things from wrinkling.
- Take only the basics you'll need, and wash as you go so you don't cart around dirty clothes.
- Utilize every inch of luggage space. Stuff hosiery and small items in shoes to conserve space, roll up sweaters and underwear to fit into corners of the suitcase. Place heavy items on the bottom, followed by layers of clothing that wrinkle more easily, keeping each layer as flat and even as possible. Place plastic cleaner's bags between layers to minimize wrinkles. Packing the bag very full helps keep the contents from sliding around. Or wrap garments lightly in tissue paper and then fold them around the paper or roll the garments. Pack items with buttons buttoned, folded as little as possible, and folded as close to the waist and seams as you can.

- Pack and repack articles in the same order each time so you can reach in and find things readily.
- Twist a cord or wire around all the hooks in a travel garment bag to keep the hangers from slipping off the rod.
- Avoid packing anything fragile or perishable. Don't pack money, jewelry, valuables, important documents, matches, cigarette lighters, or prescription items. Carry them with you.
- Transfer liquids to plastic containers, but don't fill them to the top. Compress the sides a bit as the tops are put on to create suction and make them leakproof. Then pack them, and cosmetics, in a resealable plastic bag.
- Take a comfortable pair of well-broken-in walking shoes with a ½ inch nonskid sole and a poncho or rain gear if sightseeing is on your itinerary.
- Wear your heaviest pair of shoes to save space in the suitcase. You can slip into a pair of slipper socks on the plane.
- Make everything do double duty. If weather necessitates a coat, take an all-purpose one with a zip-out lining so you can also use it as a raincoat or a housecoat for trips to the bathroom at a B&B or youth hostel. A pair of thongs will serve as slippers as well as footwear for going to the pool or beach.
- Remember the incidentals: bottle opener, corkscrew, paring knife, or a Swiss Army knife for a room snack and picnicking (pack in your suitcase, not on your person or in carry-on luggage), travel alarm clock, plastic bag for wet or dirty clothes, diary or log book to record your trip, binoculars, a couple of rubber bands to keep maps and literature together, a travel flashlight, small magnifying glass for less then optimum conditions, and a language phrase book if you're going abroad.
- Anticipate what's not available at your destination and include it.

TRAVEL PREPARATIONS:

- Call discount services that cut the cost of a room by as much as 40 percent. Quickbook and the Hotel Reservations Network each list lodgings in more than 20 large American cities. (See USEFUL ADDRESSES AND PHONE NUMBERS, "Travel, Hotel Room-rate Bargains.")
- Take advantage of frequent-flyer programs. Most major airlines are now affiliated with credit card companies that earn you mileage each time you charge. Long-distance telephone calls can also accumulate miles. AT&T, Sprint, and MCI have linked up with one or more major airlines.

- Inquire about hotel discounts through the airline. Carriers often negotiate special rates with certain hotels. In some cases, the airlines may even own the hotels or have a financial interest in them.

- Save up to 40 percent off regular coach fares if you are unable to fly on weekdays and can't take advantage of Saturday night stay-over discounts by purchasing two sets of discounted tickets, each with a Saturday-night stay-over, with one set originating in your home city, the other in your destination city. Use the first half of each pair to complete the round trip and cash in the other part of the ticket.

- Call the hotel directly and ask for special deals or discounts available. People calling 800 numbers are often quoted higher room rates than those who call the hotel itself.

- Check the travel section of a major city Sunday newspaper for airline consolidator ads—discount ticket firms that specialize in selling cheap tickets. You should be able to get a booking on a regularly scheduled flight at 20 percent to 50 percent savings. Or call Travel Avenue, 800-333-3335, Airhitch, 212-864-2000, or 800-FLY-4-LESS.

- Travel during off-peak periods, consider charter flights, and look to the no-frills airlines, such as Southwest, America West, American Eagle, and Shuttle by United to cut costs.

- Ask about senior citizen or student discounts when booking.

- Sign up for bargain flights at American's World Wide Web site (http://www2.amrcorp.com/cgi/bin/aans); these leave on Saturday and return Monday. Every Wednesday American Airlines lists tickets that cost 70 to 80 percent less than the already-discounted 21 advance-purchase fares on its NetSaver program. Northwest also sells last-minute weekend fares through its Web site (http://www.nwa.com) and CompuServe (go Northwest) that also average 70 percent off the airline's lowest advance-purchase fare.

- Call the American Automobile Association for maps and information and write to the tourist bureau or chamber of commerce for areas you plan to visit. Request information and ask for discount coupons for restaurants and attractions.

- Suspend your car insurance if you will be away for an extended period and won't be driving. If you will be driving while in Mexico or abroad, ask your insurance agent for the necessary coverage.

- Keep a handy bag packed with toothbrush, toothpaste, small brush or comb, and trial-size shampoo and other toiletries for spur-of-the-moment trips.

- Investigate your destination's conventions and visitors bureau for packages being offered.
- Read about your destination. Check out books from the library on the areas you plan to visit. Learn something about its history, culture, government, and people. Many libraries also have video travel cassettes of various countries, regions, and cities around the world that you can borrow.
- Notify police and neighbors before leaving. Leave your key with a neighbor or relative and ask him or her to check your home weekly.
- Maintain the appearance that the house is occupied. Have a neighbor park a car in your driveway if the neighbor customarily parks it in his or her driveway or on the street.
- Suspend all deliveries. Have the post office hold your mail and stop newspapers.
- Set up automatic timers that turn your lights off and on and play the TV or radio.
- Disconnect electric appliances, including the lead-in wires from your outdoor TV antenna, if you have one. This will prevent fires caused by lightning storms or surges in the electrical power lines. Turn off the hot water heater; turn down the thermostat; empty, clean, and defrost the refrigerator, and turn down the volume on the telephone, plus have the answering recording respond after a few rings.
- Arrange for the care of your lawn and garden and potted plants, or consider employing a house-sitting service.
- Leave an itinerary with friends, relatives, neighbors, or coworkers to let them know where to reach you in case of an emergency.
- Call before visiting popular tourist sites to inquire when the tour buses usually arrive and avoid the crowds and long lines.

Cleaning Products and Their Uses

The Ten Commandments on Handling Cleaning Products

1. Read labels.
2. Keep products in original containers or properly labeled.
3. Store flammable compounds in small amounts in metal safety containers away from heat sources.
4. Keep oily rags in a sealed metal or glass container.
5. Keep all cleaning products out of reach of children and pets.
6. Work in well-ventilated areas.
7. Wear rubber gloves when handling abrasive or poisonous compounds.
8. Avoid open flames, and do not smoke when handling flammable substances.
9. Never mix two cleaning compounds together, especially bleach with vinegar or ammonia. The fumes can be deadly.
10. Try the gentlest cleaning product first and choose the least environmentally harmful product you can get by with.

Product	Uses
Alcohol, rubbing	Disinfects; cleans glass, chrome, hard surfaces; removes resin stains on fabrics. Contains approximately 70 percent denatured ethyl or isopropanol alcohol. Toxic and flammable.
Alum	Removes rust and hard-water spots on porcelain. Especially effective when mixed with lemon juice or white vinegar.
Ammonia	Removes oil, grease, and stains. Cleans windows and glass. Breaks down burned-on food and grease in the oven. Not to be used on leather, soft plastic, varnished surfaces, wallpaper. Toxic.
Baking soda	Absorbs odors, deodorizes, mild abrasive.
Beeswax	Polishes furniture. Flammable.
Borax	Disinfects, deodorizes, inhibits mold, softens water.
Castor oil	Cleans and renews leather.
Chalk	Absorbs odors, removes grease stains. Mild nonabrasive cleaner.

Chlorine bleach	A stain remover for white enamel sinks and white or colorfast fabrics. A disinfectant for wood countertops or chopping blocks. Never mix with any other product except a laundry or dishwashing detergent.
Citric acid	Removes mineral deposits.
Cream of tartar	Cleans drains, metal, porcelain.
Detergent, mild	Gentle cleaner. Contains no washing soda or water softener.
Diatomaceous earth	Absorbs oil and water. Abrasive cleaner. Used as a filter.
Glycerin	Removes grease stains, helps oil mix with water.
Graphite	Loosens up locks.
Hydrogen peroxide	Removes stains. Acts as a penetrating oil. Mild antiseptic for cat and dog wounds
Kerosene	A volatile oil distilled from petroleum and other hydrocarbons found in many commercial cleaners. Toxic and highly flammable.
Lemon	Removes grease, tarnish, mineral buildup. Freshens air. Antimicrobial and antibacterial.
Linseed oil	Removes tar, restores leather. Used for furniture and wood because of its fast-drying property. An oil from flax seed. Highly flammable.
Linseed oil, boiled	Dries faster than plain linseed oil.
Mineral spirits	A petroleum distillate that thins paints and varnish. Removes adhesives. Highly flammable.
Murphy's Oil Soap	A cleaner for wood and soft plastics.
Neat's-foot oil	Conditions leather. Highly flammable.
Oxalic acid	Removes rust stains from porcelain, masonry and stone. Found in metal polishes, wood cleaners, paint, varnish, and rust removers. Poisonous. Use rubber gloves.
Pumice	Removes stains, polishes, absorbs water, increases the sudsing quality of soaps. Containing 60 to 75 percent silica, ground pumice stone comes in varying degrees of fineness and is found in many commercial scouring powders. Pumice is also available in stick form.
Rouge (iron oxide)	Cleans and polishes gems, glass, metal. Found in many cloths treated for polishing silver.

Salt	Inhibits bacteria, absorbs moisture. A mild non-scratching abrasive cleaner.
Shellac	Seals wood. Used on antiques because it is removable.
Soda, washing	Cleans dirt, grease, petroleum oils.
Sodium perborate or Sodium percarbonate	Bleaches fabrics. A natural alternative to chlorine bleach containing washing soda and hydrogen peroxide.
TSP	Containing sodium carbonate and sodium sesqui-carbonate, it cleans grease and dirt from porcelain, tile, and flat paint. (Originally TSP contained trisodium phosphate, which has now been replaced by non-phosphate ingredients.)
Turpentine	Solvent in varnishes and waxes, found in furniture polishes and washes. A resinous juice obtained from pine and fir trees. Flammable and poisonous.
Vinegar, white	Cuts grease and soap film, dissolves mineral deposits, inhibits mold growth, freshens the air.
Whiting	Used in cleaning powders, polishes, toothpaste. Gilder's whiting, the finest grade, is used for cleaning silver.
Zeolite	Absorbs pollutants from the air. A nontoxic mineral found near volcanic areas, it is the only mineral that is an ion exchanger in its natural state. Zeolite also desorbs after being put in the sun, which dissipates the absorbed fumes, so you can use it time and again.

Useful Addresses and Phone Numbers

- Look in your local phone book for the Agricultural Department listed in the County Government Offices section. Your local County Extension or Cooperative Agent of the U.S. Agricultural Department is an excellent source of information on just about anything connected to family, home, and garden. This branch of the Department of Agriculture offers advice, booklets, information over the phone, and sometimes tele-information services. All USDA publications currently in print are listed in a 185-page bulletin (#11). The publications are either free or nominal in price. Look for the bulletin on the reference shelf of the library.

- Call the information hotline at the library for information. Or ask for the reference desk if your local library does not have an information hotline.

- Obtain a catalog from the Consumer Information Center that lists more than 200 booklets with information on numerous subjects. The booklets are offered free or for a reasonable price, usually 50 cents. You can order up to 25 free booklets for a $1.00 service fee. Send your name and address requesting a current catalog to: Consumer Information Catalog Center, P.O. Box 100, Pueblo, CO 81002.

- Get in touch with your area's Food and Drug Administration's public affairs specialist. This branch of the government has public affairs specialists throughout the country who can respond to questions. Look for the Food and Drug Administration entry under the Department of Health and Human Services in the U.S. Government section of your local phone book or send requests for information to: FDA, Information and Outreach Staff, HFE-88, Room 16-63, 5600 Fishers Lane, Rockville, MD 29857, 301-443-3170.

AUTOMOBILES

AAA Gas Watcher's Guide
Mail Stop 150
1000 AAA Drive
Heathrow, FL 32746-5063
Enclose a stamped, self-addressed
business-size envelope. Members
can pick up a copy at their local
AAA office.

Buying a Safer Car
Charts that compare safety features
and identify vehicle theft rates.
Available free from
Consumer Information
Center
P.O. Box 100
Pueblo, CO 81002

Buying a Used Car
Available for 50 cents from
Consumer Information
Center
P.O. Box 100
Pueblo, CO 81002

Consumer Tire Guide
Information about tire mileage,
safety and pressure. Available
free from
Tire Industry Safety Council
P.O. Box 1801
Washington, DC 20013

Cost of Owning & Operating Automobiles, Vans & Light Trucks
Available for 50 cents from
Consumer Information Center
P.O. Box 100
Pueblo, CO 81002

Gas Mileage Guide
A publication that lists miles-per-
gallon estimates for city and
highway driving. Available free
from Consumer Information
Catalog
Consumer Information
Center
P.O. Box 100
Pueblo, CO 81002
Also available from the
U.S. Department of Energy
and Conservation by calling
800-523-2029

How to Deal with Motor Vehicle Emergencies
Available free from
General Services
Division/Distribution
National Highway Traffic
Safety Administration
400 7th Street SW
Washington, DC 20590

Motorist's Tire Care and Safety Guide
Send $4.00 for a handy and accu-
rate tire pressure gauge and tread
depth measurer, four valve caps,
and useful information about tire
care. Ask for the Tire Safety and
Mileage kit.
Tire Industry Safety Council
Box 1801
Washington, DC 20013

New Car Buying Guide
Available free from Consumer
Information Catalog

Consumer Information Center
P.O. Box 100
Pueblo, Colorado 81002

Prices of Autos by Telephone

Members of the AAA can use the
AAA Auto Pricing Service to
obtain information on new or used
car prices. The charge to members
for this information is $9.95 for
one vehicle, $17.95 for two, or
$25.95 for three. Nonmembers
also can use this service but at a
slightly higher price.

When calling, have your
credit card number ready.
800-933-7700

Shopping for a Safer Car

This booklet lists the safety features that come with many different 1996 car models. Free
with a self-addressed stamped
envelope from
Insurance Institute for
Highway Safety
P.O. Box 1420
Arlington, VA 22210
703-247-1500

Renew or Replace: RX for Making a Decision

Facts and figures to help you
decide whether to buy a new car
or fix up your old one. Free with
a business size self-addressed
stamped envelope from
Car Care Council
Department R
One Grand Lake Drive
Port Clinton, OH 43452

Tire Information

For a list of long-lasting tires and
the 1,800 tires rated by the
National Highway Traffic
Safety Administration, send a
stamped, self-addressed envelope to
The Center for Auto Safety
2001 South Street NW
Washington, DC 20009
800-424-9393

BARBECUE GRILL REPLACEMENT PARTS, To obtain:

Grill Parts Distributors
800-447-4557

CARPETS

Carpet Spot Removal Guide

Send $1.00 and a self-addressed,
stamped business envelope to
The Carpet and Rug Institute
Box 2048
Dalton, GA 30722

Protective Treatments for Upholstery Fabrics and Carpets

Available free from
Bureau of Home Furnishings
3485 Orange Grove Avenue
North Highlands, CA 95660

CHARITIES, TO CHECK OUT

Wise Giving Guide

A list of 200 charities. The
National Charities Information
Bureau evaluates national and
international charities and collects information on over 400
charities. To obtain a copy of this
free publication, write to

National Charities
   Information Bureau
19 Union Square West
New York, NY 10003
212-929-6300

Give, But Give Wisely
To obtain a copy of this free
   brochure, send a self-addressed,
   stamped envelope to
      Philanthropic Advisory
         Service of the Council of
         Better Business Bureaus
      4200 Wilson Boulevard
      Arlington, VA 22203

CHINA, DISCONTINUED, To replace:
China Traders Matching
   Service: 800-638-9955
Locators Inc.: 800-367-9690
Olympus Cove Antiques:
   800-564-8165
Replacements Ltd.:
   800-737-5223
White's Collectibles:
   800-618-2782

CHINA AND CERAMIC MAKERS
To inquire on sources for replacement or lead content of various
   patterns:
      Bernardland Limoges:
         212-737-7775
      Christian Dior: 212-686-5080
      Dansk: 914-666-2121
      Fitz and Floyd: 214-484-9494
      Franciscan: 800-955-1550
      Gorham: 914-666-2121
      Johnson Brothers:
         800-955-1550
      Lenox: 800-635-3669

Mikasa: 201-392-2501
Nikko: 201-633-5100
Noritake, Inc.: 210-319-0020
Pfalzgraff: 800-999-2811
Pickard: 708-395-3800
Portmeirion: 203-729-8255
Rosenthal USA:
   718-417-3400
Royal Doulton: 800-682-4462
Royal Worcester:
   212-683-7130
Sasaki: 212-686-5080
Spode Limited: 212-683-7130
Villeroy & Boch:
   800-223-1762
Wedgwood: 800-955-1550

COMPUTERS

How to Buy a Personal Computer
Available for 50 cents from
      Consumer Information
         Center
      P.O. Box 100
      Pueblo, CO 81002

CONSUMER RIGHTS

Consumer Complaints, To file:
Consult the following publications
   at the library to obtain the
   names, addresses, and phone
   numbers of corporations plus
   company presidents:
*Consumer's Sourcebook, National
Directory of Addresses and
Telephone Numbers, Standard
and Poor's Register of
Corporations, Directors and
Executives, Standard Directory of
Advertisers, Trade Names*

Directory, or *World Almanac*. Or call the library reference desk and ask them if someone can look up the information for you.

Consumer Fair Debt Collection

Describes what debt collectors may and may not do if you owe money. How and where to complain if you are harassed, threatened, or abused. Available for 50 cents from

> Consumer Information
> Center
> P.O. Box 100
> Pueblo, CO 81002

Consumer Federal Information Center

Lists telephone numbers across the country to call when you need assistance from the federal government. Available free from

> Consumer Information
> Catalog
> Consumer Information
> Center
> P.O. Box 100
> Pueblo, CO 81002

Consumer's Resource Handbook

Lists local, state, and federal agencies, corporate consumer contacts, Better Business Bureaus and trade associations. Available free from Consumer Information Catalog

> Consumer Information
> Center
> P.O. Box 100
> Pueblo, CO 81002

Getting Information from FDA

Covers drugs, foods, pesticides, medical devices, radiation safety, pet foods, and more. Available free from Consumer Information Catalog

> Consumer Information
> Center
> P.O. Box 100
> Pueblo, CO 81002

How to Write a Wrong

A guide for handling problems with door-to-door salesmen, mail-order firms, and regular businesses. Order Publication #D1128 from

> AARP Consumer Affairs
> Section
> Program Department
> 1909 K Street NW
> Washington, DC 20049

Protecting Your Privacy

How to check your credit file and medical records and how to keep them from falling into the wrong hands. Available free from Consumer Information Catalog

> Consumer Information
> Center
> P.O. Box 100
> Pueblo, CO 81002

To Investigate Fraud, Write to:

> Bureau of Consumer
> Protection
> Federal Trade Commission
> Pennsylvania Avenue & 6th
> Street NW
> Washington, DC 20580

CORNING WARE REPLACEMENT PARTS, To obtain:

800-999-3436

CREDIT CARDS

The Card You Pick Can Save You Money

Charts for 149 credit card plans help you compare annual percentage rates, types of pricing, grace periods, and annual fees. Available for 50 cents from

Consumer Information
Center
P.O. Box 100
Pueblo, CO 81002

CREDIT RECORDS

To receive a form for ordering a copy of your credit report to check for inaccuracies, contact any one of the three credit bureaus that operate on one of three national reporting systems. Some bureau systems charge for a copy of your report, but the law requires that if you have been denied credit within the last thirty days, the report is free from the bureau that supplied the report to the creditor.

Equifax Information Service
Center
P.O. Box 740241
Atlanta, GA 30374-0241
800-685-1111

Trans Union Consumer
Relations
P.O. Box 390
Springfield, PA 19064
800-851-2674

TRW Consumer Assistance
Center
P.O. Box 2016
Allen, TX 75002
800-422-4879

TRW will give you a free report once each year. Request it in writing with your name, address, social security number, date of birth, spouse's name, addresses for the past five years, and a copy of your driver's license or phone bill to:

TRW Consumer Assistance
P.O. Box 8030
Layton, UT 84041-8030
800-682-7654

CRYSTAL REPLACEMENT PARTS, To obtain:

White's Collectibles
800-618-2782

DIRECT MAIL RELIEF

Request that your name(s) be removed from all the direct mailing lists they service. It will take about three months to take effect.

Mail and Marketing
Association
6 East 43rd Street
New York, NY 10017

ELECTRONICS

Electronic educational booklets on computers, printers, telephone products, VCRs, camcorders, televisions, and audio equipment. Write for Consumer Publication List (which contains over twenty titles) to

Consumer Electronics Group
of the Electronic Industries
2001 Pennsylvania Avenue
NW
Washington, DC 20006
202-457-4929

EMERGENCY PREPAREDNESS

All-Purpose Emergency Preparedness Checklist

How to develop a family
emergency plan, what to keep
in a car emergency kit, and
other tips. Available for 50 cents
from
Consumer Information
Center
P.O. Box 100
Pueblo, CO 81002

Are You Ready?

Send for this emergency prepared-
ness checklist to
Federal Emergency
Management Agency
H-34, Item #8-0908
P.O. Box 70274
Washington, DC 20024

FINANCIAL PLANNING

How to Select a Certified Financial Planner

The Institute of Certified Financial
Planners has a free questionnaire
kit and booklet, which is a good
starting point in a search for a
planner. Contact
The Institute of Certified
Financial Planners
800-282-7526

Contact any of the following for
free financial planning information or a list of financial planners
in your area:
The International Association
for Financial Planning
800-945-4237

The Institute of Certified
Financial Planners
800-282-7526

The National Association of
Personal Financial Advisors
800-366-2732

To obtain free advice on handling
debts and debt management services for a nominal fee, contact
National Foundation for
Consumer Credit
1819 H Street NW
Washington, DC 20006

FIREWOOD PERMIT

For a permit to pick up downed
and dead trees, write to
USDA Forest Service
Public Affairs Department
14th Street and
Independence Avenue SW
Box 96090
Washington, DC 20090

FOODS AND COOKING

Canning and Jam-Making Information

A free newsletter published four
times a year. To request the
newsletter, send your name and
address to

Pantry
Kerr Glass Manufacturing
Corp.
Attn Department PRA
P.O. Box 76961
Los Angeles, CA 90067

Freezing Fish and Meat in the Home

Order a copy from
U.S. Department of
Agriculture
Washington, DC 20250
Their hotline number for questions
about freezing and wrapping food
for the freezer is 800-535-3455.

Food Label Close-Up

Describes the new food label
requirements, including nutrition
facts, ingredients, nutrient content, health claims, and what different dates on a package mean.
Free from Consumer Information Catalog
Consumer Information Center
P.O. Box 100
Pueblo, CO 81002

Pectin in Bulk for Making Jam

The Pantry
Dutch Valley Food
Distributors
P.O. Box 465
Meyerstown, PA 17067
800-733-4191

GARDENS

Backyard Bird Problems

How to control common problems,
such as destruction of garden
plants, nesting in gutters and

chimneys, and damage to your
home's exterior. Available free
from Consumer Information
Catalog
Consumer Information
Center
P.O. Box 100
Pueblo, CO 81002

Butterflies

To learn more about them, send a
self-addressed, stamped envelope
to
The Xerces Society
10 S.W. Ash Street
Portland, OR 97204

Citizen's Guide to Pesticides, The

The U.S. Environmental Protection
Agency's free booklet tells how to
choose and use pesticides and
how to handle an emergency.
Write or call
Environmental Protection
Agency
Office of Pesticide Programs
H7502C
401 M Street SW
Washington, DC 20460
800-858-7378

Composting Information

Send $1.00 and a self-addressed,
stamped envelope to
The American Horticultural
Society
AHS Education Department
7931 E. Boulevard Drive
Alexandria, VA 22308-1300

Composting information can be
obtained from your local munici-

pal solid waste agency, the local U.S. Department of Agriculture Cooperative Extension Office, or write to

> The Composting Council
> 114 S. Pitt Street
> Alexandria, VA 22314

Currants and Gooseberries

For information, write to

> The International Ribes
>   Association
> T.I.R.A.
> P.O. Box 130
> Booneville, CA 95415

Efficient Use of Water in the Garden and Landscape

Write for a copy to

> The Texas Water
>   Development Board
> P.O. Box 13231, Capital
>   Station
> Austin, TX 78711
> 512-445-1467

For the Birds

Three separate booklets describe how to attract different species of birds, feed them, and build or buy suitable homes. Available for 50 cents from

> Consumer Information
>   Center
> P.O. Box 100
> Pueblo, CO 81002

Garden Clubs or Garden Centers

> For information write to
> AGCA
> 325 Walnut Street
> Philadelphia, PA 19106

Grass Seed Recognition List

For recommended varieties of grass for your area, send a stamped, self-addressed business envelope to

> The Lawn Institute
> P.O. Box 108
> Pleasant Hill, TN 38578

Healthy Lawn, Healthy Environment

Preventive and practical tips on soil preparation, grasses, watering, mowing, pesticides, choosing a lawn care service, and more. Available for 50 cents from

> Consumer Information
>   Center
> P.O. Box 100
> Pueblo, CO 81002

Lawn Care Information

To obtain the Institute's eight free publications, send $1.00 for postage to

> The Lawn Institute
> 1501 Johnson Ferry Road,
>   NE, Suite 200
> Marietta, GA 30062-8122

Lawn Care Services

For information on lawn care services, send a stamped, self-addressed, business-size envelope to the

> Professional Lawn Care
>   Association
> Department FH
> 1225 Johnson Ferry Road,
>   NE, Suite B-220
> Marietta, GA 30067

Planting a Rose Garden

For information on roses and a free
publication, write to
> The American Rose Society
> P.O. Box 300
> Shreveport, LA 71130-0030

Potpourri from Roses

For complete instructions send
your request, along with a self-
addressed, stamped envelope, to
> Roses, Inc.
> P.O. Box 99
> Haslett, MI 48840

Raspberries and Blackberries

For information write to
> North American Bramble
> Growers Association
> 19060 Manning Tail North
> Maine, MN 55047-9723

Trees

To request free brochures on tree
care and preservation, write to
> International Society of
> Aboriculture
> P.O. Box GG
> Savory, IL 61874-9411

Vegetable Seeds Imported from Europe and Hard-to-Find Herbs

> The Cook's Garden
> P.O. Box 535
> Londonderry, VT 05148
> Catalog costs $1.00

> The Gourmet Gardener
> 8650 College Boulevard,
> Suite 205
> Overland Park, KS 66210
> Catalog costs $2.00

> Shepherd's Garden Seeds
> 6116 Highway 9
> Felton, CA 95018
> Catalog cost $1.00

GENEALOGICAL INFORMATION

To request genealogical information,
write to
> The Family History Library of
> the Church of Jesus Christ
> of Latter-day Saints
> 35 N.W. Temple
> Salt Lake City, UT 84150

It has the largest genealogical
library in the United States.

HOME AIR QUALITY

> Indoor Air Quality
> Information Clearinghouse
> P.O. Box 37133
> Washington, DC 20013-7133
> 800-438-4318

Distributes Environmental
Protection Agency publi-
cations, answers questions
on the phone, and makes
referrals to other nonprofit
and government organ-
izations.

The Inside Story. A Guide to Indoor Air Quality

For this free 30-page consumer
guide on how to keep your
home healthy, plus brochures
on specific hazards, call the
> Environmental Protection
> Agency's Indoor Air
> Clearing House
> 800-438-4318.

Home Guide

Copies of this free informative publication published by the National Association of Realtors are available from member agents and brokers.

How to Buy a Home with a Low Down Payment

Describes private and federal options for obtaining a low-down-payment mortgage, how to qualify, how to determine what you can afford, and much more. Free from Consumer Information Catalog

> Consumer Information
> Center
> P.O. Box 100
> Pueblo, CO 81002

The American Homeowners Foundation

This nonprofit educational and research organization offers a detailed how-to book on home buying, a model home-purchase contract, and other helpful publications. For a free catalog write to

> The American Homeowners
> Foundation
> 1724 S. Quincy Street
> Arlington, VA 22204

HOME ENERGY

> Conservation and Renewable
> Energy Inquiry and
> Referral Service
> P.O. Box 3048
> Merrifield, VA 22116
> 800-523-2929

This federal agency provides consumer information on conservation and renewable energy in residences.

Consumer Guide to Home Energy Savings by Alex Wilson

This guide lists and rates high-efficiency appliances and helps you pick the most economical. Borrow it from the library or order it from

> The American Council for an
> Energy-Efficient Economy
> 1001 Connecticut Avenue
> NW, Suite 801
> Washington, DC 20036

Low-Flow Shower Head, Source for
> Water Conservation Systems
> Damonmill Square
> Concord, MA 01742
> 800-462-3341

The Most Energy-Efficient Appliances

A booklet listing the top-rated appliances by type and size. To order this $5.00 publication, contact

> The American Council for an
> Energy-Efficient Economy
> 1001 Connecticut Avenue
> NW, Suite 801
> Washington, DC 20036
> 202-429-8873

Tankless Water Heater, Source for
> Real Goods Trading Co.
> 3041 Guildiville Road
> Ukiah, CA 95482
> 800-688-9288

Tips for Energy Savers
Available free from
> Technical Information Center
> U.S. Department of Energy
> Box 62
> Oak Ridge, TN 37831

HOME PRICE COMPARISON INDEX

Guide for comparing what a 2,200-square-foot home costs in 283 markets across North America. Gives average sales prices for homes in major cities within 50 states, Canada, and Puerto Rico. Request this free Home Price Comparison Index from
> Coldwell Banker Referral
> Network
> 27271 Las Ramblas
> Mission Viejo, CA 92691

INSURANCE INFORMATION

A Consumer's Guide to Life Insurance
Available free from
> The American Council of Life
> Insurance
> Community and Consumer
> Relations
> 1001 Pennsylvania Avenue
> NW
> Washington, DC 20004-2599
> 800-423-8000

Insurance Quotation Services

These companies will send to you at no charge complete price information from a range of companies on the plan of your choice.

InsuranceQuote
3200 North Dobson Road, Building C
Chandler, AZ 85224
800-792-1104

LifeQuote of America, Inc.
25 S.E. 2nd Avenue, Suite 1100
Miami, FL 33131
800-776-7873

Quotesmith has a database of 400 companies. If you specify the type of policy you're looking for, it will send you a list of the cheapest polices that meet your criteria.
> 800-556-9393

SelectQuote Insurance
Services
140 Second Street
San Francisco, CA 94105
800-343-1985

TermQuote Services, Inc.
3445 S. Dixie Drive, Suite 130
Dayton, OH 45439-2303
800-444-8376
TermQuote covers 75 companies and will furnish 3 to 5 quotes on either term or permanent insurance.

Insurance Helplines

The National Insurance Consumer Helpline answers consumer questions regarding automobile and home insurance questions. M–F, 8 A.M. to 8 P.M.

Insurance Information
Institute
110 William Street
New York, NY 10038
800-942-4242

Get free help analyzing or comparing insurance policies on property and liability insurance. Call or write
National Insurance
Consumer Organization
(NICO)
121 North Payne Street
Alexandria, VA 22314
800-942-4242

Twelve Ways to Lower Your Homeowners Insurance Costs
Practical tips on how to reduce your expenses. Lists phone numbers of state insurance departments for more information. Available for 50 cents from
Consumer Information
Center
P.O. Box 100
Pueblo, CO 81002

What You Should Know About Buying Life Insurance
Describes the advantages and disadvantages of various types; with tips on choosing a company and an agent and making sure a policy meets your needs. Free from
Consumer Information
Catalog
Consumer Information
Center
P.O. Box 100
Pueblo, CO 81002

IRA CALCULATOR
To find out what your IRA will be worth at retirement, the amount of interest earned, and how much you can withdraw per month for ten to twenty years without running out of money, request this free cardboard sliding scale from
Dean Witter Reynolds
401 North 31 Street, Suite 900
Billings, MT 95103
800-669-8913

KITCHEN APPLIANCES, SMALL, REPLACEMENT PARTS, To obtain:
Culinary Parts Unlimited:
800-543-7549
European Bazaar, Inc.:800-243-8540

LIVING WILL AND DURABLE HEALTH-CARE POWER OF ATTORNEY
Fill out your own Living Will and Durable Health-Care Power of Attorney without an attorney. For a free form send a business-size, self-addressed stamped envelope to
Choice in Dying
Box W
200 Varick Street
New York, NY 10014

MAIL-ORDER COMPANIES

Acid-free Tissue Paper
University Products, Inc.
P.O. Box 101
Holyoke, MA 01401
800-628-1912

Order it through the catalog that offers a full range of conservation supplies for family papers or memorabilia.

Antique Reproductions

Cohasset Colonials by Hagerty
Cohasset, MA 02025

The Bartley Collection Ltd.
3 Airpark Drive
Easton, MD 21601

Shaker Workshops
P.O. Box 1028
Concord, MA 01742

Sturbridge Yankee Workshops
Blueberry Road
Westbrook, ME 04092

Yield House
Department 6850
North Conway, NH 03860

Audio, Video, and Computer Equipment

Crutchfield: 800-955-3000 or 800-388-4656
J & R Computer World: 800-221-8180

Automobile Parts and Accessories

Don's of Tucson, Inc.
Nationwide Parts Locators: 800-221-2749
Marino's Auto Salvage: 800-273-5662
Pasco Auto Salvage: 800-548-4418

J. C. Whitney & Co.
2319 South Throop Street
Chicago, IL 60680
312-431-6102

Baby Products, Natural and Environmentally Safe

Baby Basics: 800-778-3887
The Natural Baby Company: 800-388-Baby

Bedding and Towels

Coming Home: 800-356-4444
Domestications: 800-746-2555
The Country Store: 800-285-3696

Books

Discounts up to 50 percent and even higher are offered on many of their listings:

Barnes & Noble
126 Fifth Avenue
New York, NY 10011
800-242-6657
Catalog available.

Daedalus Books
P.O. Box 9132
Hyattville, MD 20781
800-395-2665
Remainders. Catalog available.

Edward R. Hamilton, Bookseller
Falls Village, CT 06031
New hardcover publishers' overstock, closeouts, remainders.
Catalog available.

Publishers Central Bureau
Department 476
One Champion Avenue
Avenel, NJ 07001-2301

800-722-9800, extension 476
Catalog available.

Strand Book Store
828 Broadway
New York, NY 0003
800-366-3664
Current, rare, and secondhand
books. Catalog available.

Children's Clothing

After the Stork: 800-333-
KIDS
Lands' End: 800-356-4444
Olsen's Mill Direct: 800-537-
4979

Cleaning Supplies and Labor-saving Devices of All Kinds

The Clean Team
2264 Market Street
San Francisco, CA 94114
415-621-8444

Home Trends
1450 Lyell Avenue
Rochester, NY 14606-2184
716-254-6520

Fuller Brush: 800-732-1116

Clothing for the Handicapped

Wings of VGRS (Vocational
Guidance & Rehabilitation
Services)
2239 East 55th Street
Cleveland, OH 44102
216-431-7800

Clothing Made of Natural Fibers

Cool Designs
800-992-8924
Allergen-free cotton clothing.

The Cotton Place
800-451-8866
Clothing made of cotton, silk, and
wool.

Janice Corporation
800-526-4237
Allergen-free men's and women's
clothing. Household linens.

The Natural Baby Company
800-388-BABY
Cotton diapers and clothes for children and nursing mothers.

The Seventh Generation
800-456-1177
Untreated, unbleached cottons.

Computers, Accessories, and Software

CompuAdd
12203 Technology Boulevard
Austin, TX 78727
800-627-1967

CompUSA
15160 Marsh Lane
Dallas, TX 75234
800-451-7638

Computer Direct
22292 N. Pepper Road
Barrington, IL 60010
800-289-9473

Corporate Express
13800 East 39th Avenue
Aurora, CO 80011-1608
800-735-8700

Curtains

Curtains and Home:
800-228-7824

Down Comforters

The Company Store
500 Company Store Road
La Crosse, WI 54601-4477
800-356-9367

Down Comforters Refurbishing Service

The Company Store
2809 Losey Boulevard
La Crosse, WI 54601
Attn: Refurbishing Down
    Comforters
800-356-9367

Electronic and Audio Equipment

DAK: 800-325-0800

Flowers, Fresh

A Florist-Direct Co., Inc.:
    800-693-4732
All America Phillips Flower
    Shops: 800-356-7257
Calyx & Corolla:
    800-800-7788
Flower World:
    800-257-7880
Flowers Direct:
    800-874-7474
FTD Direct Access:
    800-736-3383
Jones the Florist:
    800-755-0528
Roses Only:
    800-927-6737

Food and Cooking

Chef's Catalog
3215 Commercial Avenue
Northbrook, IL 60062
800-967-2433

The King Arthur Flour Baker's
    Catalog
P.O. Box 876
Norwich, VT 05055-0876
800-827-6836

Vermont Country Stores
    Catalog
P.O. Box 3000
Manchester Center, VT
    05225-3000
802-362-2400

The Wooden Spoon Catalog
P.O. Box 931
Clinton, CT 06413
800-431-2207

Furniture and Accessories for the Home

The Bombay Company: 800-
    829-7789
Blair: 800-458-6057

Garden Supplies, Plants, and Seeds

Ames
P.O. Box 1774
Parkersburg, WV 26101
800-624-2654
Tools and other useful gadgets.

Bluestone Perennials, Inc.
7211 Middle Ridge Road
Madison, OH 44057
800-852-5243
216-428-7535
Live plants.

Brookstone Hard-to-Find
    Tools
1655 Bassford Drive
Mexico, MO 65265
800-926-7000

Hoses, water timers, doormats, outdoor furniture, and other items for the garden.

Burpee Company
300 Park Avenue
Warminster, PA 18974
800-888-1447
215-674-4900

Equipment, tools, seeds, herbs, fruit trees, plants, and shrubs.

The Cook's Garden
P.O. Box 535
Londonderry, VT 05148
802-824-3400

Untreated seeds, organic gardening supplies, and European vegetables.

Gardener's Eden
P.O. Box 7307
San Francisco, CA 94120
415-322-4707

Garden furniture, equipment, tools, plant containers.

Gardener's Supply Co.
128 Intervale Road
Burlington, VT 05401
800-955-3370

Equipment, tools, organic and environmentally sensitive gardening products.

Jackson & Perkins Co.
P.O. Box 1028
Medford, OR 97501
800-292-4769
Fax: 800-242-0329

Seeds, bulbs, plants, and a wide selection of roses including antique and David Austin roses.

Orol Ledden & Sons
P.O. Box 7
Sewell, NJ 08080-0007
800-783-7333

Plants, seeds, bulbs.

Park Seed Company
Cokesbury Road
Greenswood, SC 29647
800-845-3369
803-223-7333

Seeds, plants, bulbs, herbs.

Roses of Yesterday and Today
802 Brown's Valley Road
Watsonville, CA 95076
408-724-3537

Roses of all varieties.

Rowlands
7404 Menaul Boulevard, NE
Albuquerque, NM 87110
800-447-6177

Bulbs, herbs, seeds, plants.

Seeds Blum
HC 33, Idaho City Stage
Boise, ID 83706
800-528-3658
208-342-0858

A wide variety of heirloom seeds and collections.

Smith & Hawken
P.O. Box 6907
Florence, KY 41022
800-776-3336
415-383-4050

Garden supplies, furniture, tools, plant containers, bulbs.

Spring Hill Nurseries
110 West Elm Street
Tipp City, OH 45371
800-582-8527
Bare roots and plants.

Thompson & Morgan, Inc.
P.O. Box 1308
Jackson, NJ 08527
800-274-7333
An English mail-order catalog of
rare and unusual varieties of
annuals, bulbs, perennials,
vegetables, herbs, and grasses.

Van Bourgondien Bros.
P.O. Box 1000
245 Farmingdale Road,
Route 109
Babylon, NY 11702
800-622-9997
Bulbs of many kinds and a large
selection of perennials.

Van Dyck's Flower Farms, Inc.
P.O. Box 430
Brightwaters, NY 11718-0430
800-248-2852
Bulbs of many kinds.

Wayside Gardens
1 Garden Lane
Hodges, SC 29695
800-845-1124
Unusual and hard-to-find perennials, bulbs, grasses, shrubs, trees,
vines. Antique and David Austin
English roses.

Wildseed Farms, Inc.
1101 Campo Rosa Road
Eagle Lake, TX 77434
800-848-0078
Wildflowers.

Winterthur Museum and
Gardens
Winterthur, DE 19735
800-448-3883
Garden ornaments, statuary, foun-
tains, sundials, etc.

Gift Food Baskets
Harry & David: 800-547-3033
Hickory Farms: 800-332-4666

Health Appliances
Acme Equipment:
800-201-0706

Health-Related Products
Home Health Products, Inc.:
800-284-9123
Safety-Zone: 800-638-6366
SelfCare Catalog:
800-345-3371

Home Accessories of All Kinds
Alex & Ivy: 800-359-2539
Eddie Bauer Home:
800-426-8020
The Pottery Barn:
800-922-5507
This End Up: 800-627-5161

Home Safety
Perfectly Safe:
800-837-5437
The Safety Zone:
800-999-3030

Kitchen Supplies and Accessories
Colonial Garden Kitchens:
800-245-3399
Community Kitchens:
800-535-9901
Crate & Barrel:
800-829-7789

Rowe Pottery Works:
800-356-5003
Williams Sonoma:
800-541-1262

Lace
Linen & Lace: 800-332-Lace

Luggage, Leather Goods, and Travel-related Items
Luggage Gallery:
800-386-2247

Military Surplus Clothing and Supplies
U.S. Cavalary Catalog:
800-333-5102

Nontoxic/low-toxic products
See "Toxin-Free/Low-Toxin Products" on page 329.

Optical Supplies
Contact Lens Supply:
800-833-7525
Lens Direct: 800-325-5367
Lens Express: 800-442-5367
Lens for Less: 800-376-5367

Pantyhose
L'eggs Showcase of Savings
L'eggs Brands, Inc.
P.O. Box 1010
Rural Hall, NC 27098-1010

Rolane Direct Marketing
(No-Nonsense brand of pantyhose)
P.O. Box 23368
Chattanooga, TN 37422-9988

Pet Care Products
Cornucopia Natural Pet Products: 800-PET-8280

Doctors Foster & Smith:
800-323-4208
Harbingers of a New Age:
800-884-6262
Natural Animal:
800-274-7387
Natural Pet Care:
800-962-8266

Pharmacies
Call for brochures describing services and for price lists on prescription or over-the-counter medications, or call for a price quote.
Action Mail Order:
800-452-1976
Family Pharmaceuticals:
800-922-3444
Medi-Mail Inc.:
800-331-1358
Pharmail Corporation:
800-237-8937

Picture Frames
Exposures: 800-222-4947

Posters
United Communications
644 Merrick Road
Lynbrook, NY 11563
800-433-7523

Pottery
Pottery Barn: 800-922-3507
Rowe Pottery Works:
800-356-5003

Renewable Energy Systems
Real Goods: 800-762-7325
Solar energy, energy-saving light bulbs, water-saving devices, environmentally friendly cleaning products.

Sewing

Atlanta Thread and Supply
Co.: 800-847-1001
Home-Sew: 800-344-4739
Newark Dressmakers Supply:
800-736-4783
Oceans of Notions, Inc.:
800-626-8410

Shoes, Men's and Women's

Wissota Trader
1313 First Avenue
Chippewa Falls, WI
54729-1904
800-833-6421

Shoes, Women's, Hard to Find

Cinderella of Boston, Inc.:
800-274-3338
Has a 20-page catalog of women's
shoes from size 1½ to size 5 and
from AA width to D width.

Skin and Hair Care Products:

Beautiful Times:
800: 223-1216
The Body Shop, Inc.:
800-541-2535
Home Health Products:
800-284-9132
Self Care Catalog:
800-345-3371

Sponges, Natural

State Line Tack:
800-228-9208

Sports Clothing and Camping Equipment

Cabela: 800-237-4444
L. L. Bean: 800-221-4221

Mountain Gear:
800-829-2009
Patagonia: 800-336-9090
Sierra Designs: 800-635-0461

Storage Items

Anderson Storage:
800-782-4825
Hold Everything:
800-421-2264

Toxin-free/Low-toxin Household Products

See "Toxin-Free/Low Toxin
Products" on page 329.

Travel Supplies

HITEC Group International:
800-962-4943
Magellan's: 800-962-4943
TravelSmith: 800-950-1600

Videos

Critics' Choice Video (carries
movies): 800-367-7765

College Videos:
800-433-6769

VC.I.E.W. Video Inc.
34 E. 23 Street
New York, NY 10010
More than 200 special-interest and
award-winning titles.

Windo.w Treatments

Rue de France:
800-777-0998

Women's Clothing and Shoes in Large Sizes

Lane Bryant:
800-477-7070

MAIL-ORDER SHOPPING, INFORMATION ON

At-Home Shopping Rights

How to deal with late deliveries, unordered merchandise, billing errors, and much more when making purchases by mail or phone order. Available for 50 cents from

>   Consumer Information
>   Center
>   P.O. Box 100
>   Pueblo, CO 81002

Home Shoppers: Know Your Rights.

Request the free pamphlet from

>   Public Reference Branch
>   F.T.C. Room 130
>   Washington, DC 20580

How to Write a Wrong

A guide for handling problems with door-to-door salesmen, mail-order firms, and regular businesses. Order Publication #D1128 from

>   AARP Consumer Affairs
>   Section
>   Program Department
>   1909 K Street, NW
>   Washington, DC 20049

Shopping at Home Consumer Information Guides

"Guidelines for Telephone Shopping," "How Did They Get My Name," "Make Knowledge Your Partner in Mail Order Shopping" can be obtained free from

Direct Marketing Association
Consumer Services Department
11 West 42nd Street
P.O. Box 3861
New York, NY 10163-3861

If complaints to the company about the quality of goods, misrepresentation of the product, etc. go unanswered

>   Write to
>   Postal Inspection Service
>   475 L'Enfant Plaza West SW
>   Washington, DC 20260

MEDICAL

Medical and Allied Health Information and Complaint Guide

A brochure to assist consumers and consumer agencies with health-care complaints. For a free copy write to

>   Medical Guide
>   1430 Howe Avenue, Suite 86
>   Sacramento, CA 95825-3240

>   National Health Information
>   Clearinghouse
>   P.O. Box 1133
>   Washington, DC 20013
>   800-336-4797

This organization helps the general public find health-care information.

>   National Injuries Information
>   Clearinghouse
>   5401 Westbard Avenue,
>   Room 625
>   Washington, DC 20207
>   301-492-6462

This organization deals with injuries that people suffer as a result of consumer products. It will refer questions of a general nature to the Consumer Products Safety Commission.

National Institute of Mental Health
5600 Fishers Lane
Rockville, MD 20857

Write for literature on mental-health problems of all kinds.

Thinking About Having Surgery
National Second Surgical Opinion Program
Health Care Financing Administrative Office of Public Affairs
350 Independence Avenue SW
Washington, DC 20201
800-639-6833
800-492-6603

Call if you are planning nonemergency surgery and need information on getting a second opinion.

MEDICAL RECORDS

The Medical Information Bureau (MIB) is a data bank used by about 670 insurance companies. To obtain a copy of your records write to

Medical Information Bureau
P.O. Box 105, Essex Station
Boston, MA 02112
617-426-3660

The price is $8.00, but the report is free if you've been turned down for health or life insurance or charged more due to illness.

MILDEW
How to Prevent and Remove Mildew
Request Home and Garden Bulletin #68 from

Department of Agriculture
The U.S. Department of Agriculture
Washington, DC 20250

MOVING
Consumers Guide to Moving
Provides consumers with information to consider when choosing a moving company. Includes obtaining estimates, weighing your goods, and filing damage and loss claims.

Moving Fact Sheet
P.O. Box 310
Sacramento, CA 95802

Guide to a Satisfying Move
Send a self-addressed stamped envelope for this free booklet to

The American Movers Conference
1611 Duke Street
Alexandria, VA 22314-3482

PAPERS AND MEMORABILIA

University Products, Inc. offers a full range of conservation supplies for museums and libraries to preserve family papers or memorabilia. Write or call for their catalog to

University Products, Inc.
P.O. Box 101
Holyoke, MA 01401
800-628-1912

PESTS, HOUSEHOLD

Controlling Household Pests

Send for this U.S. Department of
Agriculture Home and Garden
Bulletin from
Superintendent of
Documents
U.S. Government Printing
Office
Washington, DC 20402

Questions and Answers Regarding Household Pests

Answers questions concerning general household pest inspections
and pesticides such as "What are
considered general household
pests," and "How can a consumer find out what pesticides
are used on his/her property?"
Structural Pest Control Board
1430 Howe Avenue
Sacramento, CA 95825

PETS

The Veterinarian's Way of Selecting a Proper Pet

To help you decide on the right pet,
write for the free brochure to
American Veterinary Medical
Association
Public Information
Department 1931
North Meecham Road.
Schaumburg, IL 60173

PURCHASING INFORMATION

Tips on Purchasing Feather and Down Products

Provides information on down and
feather-filled pillows, comforters,
sleeping bags, and upholstered
furniture and explains labeling
requirements for these products.
Write to
Bureau of Home Furnishings
3485 Orange Grove Avenue
North Highlands, CA 95660

Tips on Purchasing a Waterbed

Write to
Bureau of Home Furnishings
3485 Orange Grove Avenue
North Highlands, CA 95660

REPLACEMENT PARTS, To obtain:

See "Barbecue Grill," "China,"
"Corning Ware Replacement
Parts," Crystal Replacement
Parts," "Kitchen Appliances,
Small, Replacement Parts,"
"Revere Ware Replacement
Parts," "Silver, Sterling
Discontinued."

REVERE WARE REPLACEMENT PARTS, To obtain:

800-999-3436

SENIORS

Guide to Health Insurance for People With Medicare

Fill in gaps in Medicare coverage
and avoid paying for duplicate
benefits. Obtain this free 37-
page booklet from
Consumer Information
Catalog
Consumer Information
Center
P.O. Box 100
Pueblo, CO 81002

Legal Assistance Over the Phone

The Administration on Aging runs the Legal Counsel for the Elderly free legal hotline. Licensed attorneys answer your questions over the phone. (You must be over 60 to use this service.)

Florida:	800-252-5997
Michigan:	800-347-5297
Ohio:	800-248-6060
Pennsylvania:	800-262-5297
Texas:	800-622-2520

Pets for People

A program that pays humane societies to provide pets free of charge to persons 60 years and older. In addition to covering adoption fees, Pets for People pays for neutering, initial shots, feeding bowl, leash, collar, and pet-food coupons. Check your local Humane Society or write for the participating Humane Society nearest you to

Purina Pets for People
Checkerboard Square OCA
St. Louis, MO 63164

Senior Care and Assistance

Free information on senior care and assistance is available from the 670 Area Agencies on Aging across the country. To reach the National Association of Area Agencies on Aging's Eldercare Locator, call 800-677-1116. It will connect you with information and assistance on a wide range of programs.

State Tax Laws: A Guide for Investors Aged 50 and Over

Contains a breakdown of each state's tax structure. It includes current sales, property, and estate taxes; how each state treats retirement income, social security and pensions and cities' special state tax provisions for older taxpayers. Free from

AARP
Investment Program from
Scudder
Box 5014
Jonesville, WI 53547

Tax Assistance

The IRS offers free tax assistance to persons over 60.

Call 800-829-1040 for the location nearest you.

Thinking Ahead on Long-term Care

Answers key questions and includes a guide to organizations that help, financial worksheets, and more. For your free copy, write

Aetna Public Service Library
151 Farmington Ave, RE6H
Hartford, CT 06156

Tips on Continuing Care Retirement Communities

Characteristics, staff, services, contracts.

Send $2.00 with a business-size, self-addressed, stamped envelope to

Council of Better Business
Bureau, Inc.
Department 023
Washington, DC 20042

SILVER, STERLING, DISCONTINUED, To obtain:

Atlantic Silver: 800-288-6665
Locators Inc.: 800-367-9690
White's Collectibles:
800-618-2782

SMALL CLAIMS COURT PROCEDURE

Small Claims Handbook contains
information for defendants and
plaintiffs and covers topics such
as mediation, filing your claim,
preparing your case, court costs,
and what to expect on your day
in court. For a copy write to
Small Claims Handbook
P.O. Box 310
Sacramento, CA 95802

TELEMARKETING LISTS

To have your name removed from
many telemarketing lists, contact
Telephone Preference Service
P.O. Box 9014
Farmingdale, NY 11735-9014

TELEVISION NETWORKS

ABC Entertainment
2040 Avenue of the Stars
Los Angeles, CA 90067

CBS Entertainment
7800 Beverly Boulevard
Los Angeles, CA 90036

NBC Entertainment
3000 W Alameda Avenue
Burbank, CA 91505

TOXIN-FREE/LOW-TOXIN PRODUCTS

AFM Enterprises
350 W. Ash Street
San Diego, CA 92101
800-639-0231
Low-toxin cleaning products,
sealants, paints, mildew control
products, carpet sealant and
adhesives, etc.

Dasun Company
P.O. Box 668
Escondido, CA 92033
800-433-8929
A pure form of zeolite in loose
powder form or in breather bags.

The Ecology Box
425 East Washington #202
Ann Arbor, MI 48104
800-735-1371
Zeolite air fresheners called Non-
Scents and other items.

Environment Health
Foundation
8345 Walnut Hill Lane
Suite 225
Dallas, TX 75231
800-428-2343
Environmentally safe cleaning
materials and personal care
products.

The Living Source
3500 MacArthur Drive
Waco, Texas 76708
817-756-6341
Detergents, natural soaps, and
other items.

Natural Animal
1 North Street
St. Augustine, FL 32085
800-274-7387

Natural unprocessed diatomaceous earth, nontoxic pet-care products, and other items.

Natural Choice
1365 Rufina Circle
Santa Fe, NM 87501
800-621-2591

Low-toxin stains and paints, body care, linens, and other items.

NEEDS (National Ecological & Environmental Delivery Systems)
120 Julian Place
Syracuse, NY 13210
800-634-1380
315-446-1122

Household products for the chemically sensitive, air and water purifiers, and other items.

The Seventh Generation
49 The Meadow Park
Colchester, VT 05446
800-456-1177

Recycled paper products. Environmentally friendly, biodegradable household cleaners, personal-care products, clothing, and linens.

Sinan Company
P.O. Box 857
Davis, CA 95617-0857
916-753-3104

Natural building products and organic paints. Nontoxic, plant-derived, petroleum-free wood protectors, stains, paints, waxes, linseed oil, and furniture products.

TRAVEL

Air Travel with Your Dog or Cat

To help organize your animal's next flight, request the brochure from
The Air Transport Association of America
709 New York Avenue NW
Washington, DC 20006-5206

Airline Bargain Travel

800-FLY-ASAP offers bargains on last-minute airline travel in the United States, Canada, Mexico and Caribbean. The company's $6 fee for a filled order covers ticket delivery.

Cheap Tickets: 800-377-1000 sells international and domestic flights at 40 percent to 50 percent less than full fare.

Avoiding Travel Problems

Deals with scams and other potential travel troubles. Free with a business-size, self-addressed stamped envelope from
American Society of Travel Agents
1101 King Street
Alexandria, VA 22314

B&B Hotline

More than 14,000 U.S. bed and breakfasts priced from $35 to $350 a night are in this database. Call to request a free computer printout for your destination. The report will be mailed or faxed.

800-US-BAND8

Camping and the RV Lifestyle, Information Sources

Contacts for renting RVS, locating campgrounds, publications, and RV clubs. Free from

Recreation Vehicle Industry Association
P.O. Box 2999
Reston, VA 22090
800-477-8669

Camping Spots in National Parks

To reserve by phone call MISTIX, which handles the thirteen most popular parks.

800-365-CAMP

Camping Vacation Planner

Resources for locating campgrounds near your destination, a guide to different types of RVs, and sources for further information. Order the free *Go Camping America Camping Vacation Planner* from

Recreation Vehicle Industry Association
P.O. Box 2999
Reston, VA 22090
800-477-8669

Courier Firms

Air Facilities: 718-712-1769
East West Express:
718-656-6246
Halbart Express:
718-656-8189

International Bonded Couriers: 310-607-0125
Jupiter Air: 415-697-1773
Midnight Express:
310-672-1100.
Now Voyager: 212-431-1616
UTL Travel: 415-583-5074
Way to Go Travel:
213-466-1126
World Couriers, Inc.:
718-978-9552

For more information contact

The International Association of Air Travel Couriers (IAATC)
P.O. Box 1349
Lake Worth, FL 33460.

Cruise Bargains

Cruiseworld: 800-994-7447 offers average discounts of 40 to 50 percent on cruises anywhere in the world. (Off-season, you can save even more.)

World Wide Cruises of Florida: 800-882-9000 offers savings on most 7-day sailings. Call for up-to-the-minute information on discounts and cabin availability. No membership charges. No service fees. Discounts at 40 to 60 percent off normal rates.

Book a last-minute cruise for departures one week to three months after you call and save up to 60 percent. The service is free except for Moments' Notice, which charges $25.00 per year.

Encore Travel Club:
800-638-0930

Moments' Notice:
718-234-6295
Spur of the Moment Cruises:
800-343-1991

Discover America

A listing of state and territorial
travel offices of the United
States. Use this list to order
free vacation information,
including maps, calendars
of events, travel guides, and
more. Available for 50 cents
from
Consumer Information
Center
P.O. Box 100
Pueblo, CO 81002

Elderhostel

A nonprofit organization offering
one-and two-week educational
and travel vacations here and
abroad for persons 60 and over.
Obtain a catalog from
Elderhostel
75 Federal Street
Boston, MA 02110
617-426-8056

Fly-Rights

Practical advice for airline traveling
on how to get the best fares and
what to do when faced with lost
tickets and baggage, canceled or
overbooked flights, travel scams,
and much more. Available for
$1.75 from
Consumer Information
Center
P.O. Box 100
Pueblo, CO 81002

Fly Smart

Lists more than 30 things you can
do to help make your flight a
safe one. It includes a passenger
checklist. Available free from
The Consumer Information
Catalog
The Consumer Information
Center
P.O. Box 100
Pueblo, CO 81002

Handicapped or Disabled Travelers

Write for information to help you
plan your trip in the United
States and abroad to
Travel Information Service
Moss Rehabilitation Hospital
12th St. and Tabor Road
Philadelphia, PA 19141
215-329-5715

Exchange Visits
Mobility International is a clearinghouse for information on travel
in Europe, North America and
the Middle East. Mobility provides specific contact for
exchange visits. Write to
Mobility International
2 Colombo Street
London, SW1 8DP
England

House Swaps
Swap with someone with a similar
disability so that the home will
contain the same basic equipment as yours.
King of the Road Vacation
Exchange
117 Poland Road
Danville, IL 61832

International Directory of Access Guides

Guides for 15 countries in North America and Europe, covering air and rail travel wheelchair accessibility to hotels, restaurants, and leisure facilities. To order write to

Rehabilitation International USA
20 W 40th Street
New York, NY 10018

National Easter Seal Society for Crippled Children and Adults supplies handicapped travelers with listings of current access guides to hotels, theaters, shopping, and tourist attractions. Write to

National Easter Seal Society
Information Library
2023 W. Ogden Avenue
Chicago, IL 60612

New Horizons for the Air Traveler with a Disability

This 33-page booklet by the U.S. Department of Transportation has tips on planning a trip and explanations of accommodations, facilities, and services required of U.S. airports and aircraft. To order send 50 cents to

Consumer Information Center
Department 100
Pueblo, CO 81002

Tour Agencies
For a list of agencies that specialize in arranging tours for the disabled, write to

SATH (Society for Advancement of Travel for the Handicapped)
26 Court Street
Brooklyn, NY 11242

SATH also serves as a clearinghouse for information about accessible domestic and international transportation and lodging facilities.

Health Care While Abroad

The following companies provide coverage to travelers up to age eighty four.

Access America: 800-284-8300
Health Care Abroad: 800-237-6616
Mutual of Omaha Travel Assure: 800-228-9792
Travelers' Travel Insurance Pak: 800-243-3174
US Assist: 800-756-5900

Helping Out in the Outdoors

This directory of volunteer work and internships on America's public lands is published as a public service by the American Hiking Society and published semiannually in February and August. Write for information to

The American Hiking Society
1015 31st Street NW
Washington, DC 20007

Healthy Eating on the Road

Heart Smart Restaurants International (HSRI) gives seals

of approval to restaurants offering foods lower in fat, sodium, and cholesterol and for accommodating special dietary requests made in advance. For a list of 800 restaurants in 44 states or for more information, call 800-762-7819.

Home Exchange

Intervac US: 800-756-HOME

International Home Exchange Service
P.O. Box 3975
San Francisco, CA 94119

Vacation Exchange Club, Inc.
12006 111th Avenue
Unit 12
Youngstown, AZ 85363
800-638-3841

Hostelling International— American Youth Hostels

HI-AYH has a brochure listing its 149 hostels in the United States and locating them on a map. Each listing has address, telephone number, and open dates. (Some are seasonal.) Request a copy from

HI-AYH Map Brochure
733 15th Street NW,
Suite 840
Washington, DC 20005
203-783-6161
202-783-6172 fax

Hostelling International Hostel Reservations

To reserve a bed in one of more than 200 hostels linked through

International Booking Network (IBN), operated by Hostelling International, call 800-444-6111

Hostels

The Rucksackers North America offers a map that covers the locations of 55 independent hostels in the United States, four in Hawaii and one in Mexico. Some of the hostels also offer camping sites. For a free copy send a self-addressed, stamped envelope to

Rucksackers North America
250 West 77th Street
New York, NY 10027

Hotel Room-rate Bargains

Room Exchange is a wholesale agency that specializes in brokering leftover space at more than 22,000 hotels in the United States, Canada, and the Caribbean and can offer 20 to 50 percent savings. Call 800-846-7000.

Hotel consolidators offer discount services that can cut the cost of a room by 35 to 65 percent off quoted prices. Quickbook has bookings in U.S. cities and Hotel Reservations Network has bookings in 24 U.S. cities plus London, Paris, and Disney World. There is no fee or service charge.

Hotel Reservations Network: 800-964-6835
Quickbook: 800-789-9887

Information Sheets on More than 200 Countries

For information on a particular
 country (or countries), write to
  American Citizen Services
  2201 C Street NW
  Washington, DC 20520
  202-647-5225

Interhostel

An international study/travel program for adults age 50 and over.
 For a free catalog or more information, call or write
  Interhostel
  University of New Hampshire
  6 Garrison Avenue
  Durham, NH 03824
  800-733-9753

Lesser Known Areas of the National Park System

Listings by state of more than 170
 national parks, their accommodations, locations, and historical sig-
 nificance. Available for $1.50 from
  Consumer Information Center
  P.O. Box 100
  Pueblo, CO 81002

National Parks Information Kit

For information about the national
 parks, the Golden Age Passport
 for park patrons over 62, and the
 Golden Eagle Pass for people
 under 62, send for the free
 National Parks Information Kit
 from
  Department of the Interior
  National Park Service
  P.O. Box 37127, Room 1013
  Washington, DC 20013-7127

National Trails System Map and Guide

This full-color map describes eight
 national scenic trails and nine
 national historic trails. Available
 for $1.25 from
  Consumer Information
  Center
  P.O. Box 100
  Pueblo, CO 81002

National Wildlife Refuges: A Visitor's Guide

Full-color map shows the best
 viewing seasons and recreational
 and educational opportunities of
 nearly 400 wildlife refuges
 nationwide. Available for $1.25
 from
  Consumer Information
  Center
  P.O. Box 100
  Pueblo, CO 81002

Seniors Abroad

A home-stay program for those over
 age fifty includes visits with fami-
 lies. Participants reside with hosts
 in homes where they also have all
 meals family-style. For details and
 itinerary call or write to
  Seniors Abroad
  12533 Pacato Circle North
  San Diego, CA 92128
  619-485-1696

Solo Travelers

Travel Companions locates people
 of similar tastes for anyone traveling alone. The group then
 books tours and cruises with savings of up to 40 percent.

Membership is $40 annually. For more information call 800-383-7211.

The Safe Travel Book

This 14-page booklet put out by SmithKline Beecham Pharmaceuticals has tips on how a traveler can prepare for medical emergencies and includes information on vaccinations, infectious diseases, and what supplies to pack. To order call 800-HEP-A-VAX

Travel Companion Exchange offers same-sex and opposite-sex listings. A six-month introduction rate of same-sex listings is $36.00. For a free sample copy write to

> Travel Companion Exchange
> P.O. Box 833
> Amityville, NY 11701
> 516-454-0880

Travel Safely

Ask your travel agent for a copy or send a self-addressed stamped business-size envelope to

> Fulfillment Department
> American Society of Travel Agents
> 1101 King Street
> Alexandria, VA 22314

Traveler Safety Tips

Send a self-addressed, stamped business-size envelope to

> American Hotel and Motel Association "Tipsm"
> 1201 New York Avenue NW
> Washington, DC 20005-3931

Using Credit and Charge Cards Overseas

Explains how your credit is protected and how to get cash, tips on shopping, renting a car, and making lodging and travel reservations. Available for 50 cents from

> Consumer Information Center
> P.O. Box 100
> Pueblo, CO 81002

Volunteering

Global Volunteers is a nonprofit, nonsectarian organization that offers travel alternatives within the United States and in 13 countries worldwide. Volunteers pay a tax-deductible fee to work in one- to three-week service programs. For information on the program and a catalog of volunteer opportunities contact

> Global Volunteers
> 373 E. Little Canada Road
> St. Paul, MN 55117-1628
> 800-487-1074

1996 Back Door Guidebook

This guidebook by Michael Landes (*Back Door Experience*) lists more than 1,000 organizations that offer opportunities ranging from internships and seasonal work to volunteer programs and adventure careers. The majority are in the United States, but the book includes a chapter on overseas opportunities covering volunteering and internships. Look for it at your local library or order a copy from the author at 800-552-7284. It's expensive—$30.

When Things Go Wrong: Where to Lodge Travel Complaints

American Society of Travel Agents (ASTA)
1101 King Street, Suite 200
Alexandria, VA 22314

Consumer Affairs Department handles problems with travel packages bought through travel agencies.

National Fraud Information Center
P.O. Box 65868
Washington, DC 20035
800-876-7060

Check the local phone book for your State Attorney General's office. The State Attorney General enforces a wide range of laws that affect consumers and reviews consumer complaints.

U.S. Department of Transportation
800-322-7873

Handles problems with bumping, charter flights, baggage loss and damage.

U.S. Tour Operators Association (USTOA)
211 East 51st Street, Suite 128
New York, NY 10022
212-750-7371

Has a code of standards and funds to reimburse consumers if a member of the association goes out of business without making refunds.

World Climate Charts

A set of 24 charts detailing climate, clothing suggestions, sanitary conditions, water and food purity worldwide, and specifics for 1,440 cities. Donation requested. Write to
IAMAT
417 Center Street
Lewiston, NY 14092

World Immunization Chart

Lists required and recommended immunizations and routine immunizations that may need boosters. Free from
IAMAT
417 Center Street
Lewiston, NY 14092

YMCA Booking

The YMCA of Greater New York publishes a 23-page guidebook of Y's and budget hotels in the United States and worldwide that participate in its central booking service. Rate information and package programs are also described. To obtain a copy, send a self-addressed business size envelope, stamped with 65 cents postage, to
The Y's Way International
224 East 47th Street
New York, NY 10017

Youth Hostel Reservations

To reserve a bed in one of more than 200 hostels linked through the International Booking Network (IBN), operated by Hostelling International, call 800-444-6111

Youth Hostels

To obtain a membership card or for information on hostelling, call or write

> Hostelling International-
> American Youth Hostels
> P.O. Box 37613
> Washington, DC 20013-7613
> 202-783-6161

Check if your city has a youth hostel. Many have stores where you can purchase a wide array of travel items, such as money belts, lightweight luggage, water purification kits, books, maps, etc. Some youth hostels also offer informative workshops on traveling abroad.

U.S. GOVERNMENT SALES

Are There Any Public Lands for Sale?

Describes the federal program to sell excess undeveloped public land and why there is no more available for homesteading. Available from

> U.S. Department of the
> Interior
> Bureau of Land Management
> Washington, DC 20240

Guide to Federal Government Sales

How to buy land, houses, cars, and other items from 18 federal sales programs, including seized and unclaimed property. Available for $1.75 from

> Consumer Information
> Center
> P.O. Box 100
> Pueblo, CO 81002

How You Can Buy Used Federal Personal Property

Describes how the U.S. General Services Administration advertises and sells used government equipment and industrial items. Lists where to call for more information. Available for 50 cents from

> Consumer Information
> Center
> P.O. Box 100
> Pueblo, CO 81002

The nearest regional General Services Administration office can also supply details. If you can't find it in your phone book, call the Federal Information Center at 301-722-9000.

Small Business Administration Sales

The Small Business Administration sells off property used as security for business loans that the borrower has defaulted on. The agent's nearest district office can tell you when the next sale will be held in your area. If you can't find the Small Business

Administration in your phone book, call
800-827-5722.

U.S. General Services Administration Guide to Federal Government Sales

To obtain this free publication on U.S. Government surplus merchandise, write for the Consumer Information Catalog to
Consumer Information
Center
Department 100
Pueblo, CO 81002

U.S. Real Property Sales List

Lists government properties for sale that are sold by auction or sealed bid. Tells how to get more information on specific properties.
Free from
Consumer Information
Catalog
Consumer Information Center
P.O. Box 100
Pueblo, CO 81002

U.S. Department of Defense Surplus Items

To receive a catalog, write to
DRMR Headquarters
74 North Washington
Battle Creek, MI 49017

How to Buy Surplus Personal Property from the Department of Defense

Lists types of items for sale and includes bidder's application. Order this 51-page booklet for $1.00 from

Consumer Information Center
P.O. Box 100
Pueblo, CO 81002

U.S. Marshals Service

For information on auctions, or more details, get in touch with the district U.S. Marshal in your phone book or write to
Office of Congressional and
Public Affairs
U.S. Marshal Service
600 Army Navy Drive
Arlington, VA 22202
202-307-9221

TOLL-FREE NUMBERS FOR THE CONSUMER
Appliance Hotlines

The following manufacturers offer free repair instructions over the phone. Before calling, write down the appliance's model number, serial number, and date of purchase and have the appliance in front of you while you talk.

Admiral: 800-477-1305
Amana: 800-843-0304
General Electric: 800-626-2024, 24 hours a day, 7 days a week
Frigidaire: 800-777-8349 M–F 8 A.M. to 8 P.M. EST
Hotpoint: 800-626-2000
KitchenAid: 800-253-1301
Maytag: 800-688-9900 M–F 8 A.M. to 5 P.M. EST
RCA consumer electronics: 800-336-1900
RCA major appliances: 800-626-2000

Roper: 800-253-1301
Westinghouse: 800-245-0600
Whirlpool: 800-253-1301
  seven days a week from
  7 A.M. to 11 P.M. EST
Sears Technical Assistance
  Line charges $9.95. You
  can make unlimited calls
  back about the same repair
  for 30 days at no extra
  charge. Call 800-473-7247
  24 hours a day, 7 days a
  week.

Car Rental Agencies

Alamo: 800-327-9633
American International:
  800-527-0202
Avis: 800-331-1212
Budget: 800-527-0700
Dollar: 800-421-6878
Enterprise: 800-325-8007
General: 800-327-7607
Hertz: 800-654-3131
National: 800-227-7368
Thrifty: 800-367-2277
Value: 800-327-2501

Federal Information Center

If you need help finding a Federal
  agency or office, call
  800-688-9889.

Hotels, All Suite, Central Reservation Numbers

Embassy Suite Hotels:
  800-EMBASSY (located in 28
  states, some kitchen appliances, full breakfast included
  in price)
Guest Quarters Suite Hotels:
  800-424-2900 (located in

15 states, outfitted with some
  kitchen appliances)
Quality Suites: 800-221-2222
  (located in 18 states, some
  kitchen appliances supplied,
  breakfast included)
Radisson Hotels International:
  800-333-3333 (located in
  17 states, cooking appliances
  vary with the properties, breakfast usually supplied)
Residence Inn by Marriott:
  800-331-3131 (located in 41
  states, full kitchens available,
  continental breakfast included)

Hotlines for This and That

American Dietetic
  Association Hotline
  800-366-1655
Registered dietitians answer your
  questions on food.

Auto Complaints, call
  Council Better Business Auto
  Line Program
  800-252-0410

Auto Safety Hotline
  800-424-9393
Operated by the National Highway
  Traffic Safety Administration, it
  provides information on cars,
  tires, the results of government
  crash tests, and other useful
  safety information.

Consumer Infoline
  800-344-9940

Consumer Loan Advocate
  Hotline
  800-767-2768

Advises consumers regarding loans and mortgages. Also provides a booklet to help consumers audit their adjustable rate mortgages.

Emergency Planning and Community Right-to-Know Information
Hotline operated by the U.S. Environmental Protection Agency: 800-535-0202

Garlic Information Hotline
800-330-5922

Internal Revenue Service Information line
800-829-1040
To order the free publication *The Guide to Free Tax Services*, which also lists IRS publications, call 800-829-3676

International Olive Oil Council's Hotline
800-232-6548

Meat and Poultry Hotline—
U.S. Department of Agriculture
800-535-4555
Home economists and registered dietitians answer questions about freezing, canning, and food safety.

Medical Information and Referral
800-446-9876

Medicare Hotline operated by Social Security
800-772-1213
Provides information on Medicare coverage and costs.

Medicare Hotline operated by U.S. Department of Health and Human Services
800-724-2233
Provides information on Medicare and Medigap coverage.

National Fraud Information Center
800-876-7060

National Pesticides Telecommunications Network
800-858-PEST
Provides information about pesticides.

Product Safety Hotline
800-638-2772
Recorded information is available 24 hours a day on safety tips, product recalls. Operators are on duty Monday to Friday from 10:30 A.M. to 4:00 P.M EST to take complaints about unsafe consumer products.

Safe Drinking Water Hotline
800-426-4791
Provides information on regulations under the Safe Drinking Water Act, filter information, and a list of state drinking water offices.

Seafood Hotline
800-332-4010
202-205-4314 in the Washington, D.C., area.

Social Security
Administration
800-772-1213
Call to order the following free
publications:
*Understanding Social Security,
How Work Affects Social
Security Benefits, Medicare,
How Your Retirement
Benefit Is Figured.*

Motels, Budget Chain, Central Reservation Numbers

Comfort Inn: 800-221-2222
(located in 48 states,
Canada, Mexico, Europe)
Days Inn of America:
800-325-2525 (located in
50 states, Canada, Mexico,
France, Netherlands)
Econo Lodge of America:
800-446-6900 (located in
47 states and Canada)
Hampton Inn: 800-426-7866
(located in 39 states)
Hospitality International:
800-251-1962 (includes
Red Carpet, Master
Hosts, and Scottish Inns,
and locations in 33 states)
La Quinta Motor Inn:
800-531-5900 (located in
29 states)
Motel 6: 505-891-6161
(located in 42 states)
Red Roof Inn: 800-843-7663
(located in 30 states)
Rodeway Inn International:
800-228-2000

Super 8 Motel: 800-848-8888
(located in 47 states and
Canada)
Travelodge International:
800-255-3050 (located in
47 states, Mexico, Canada,
and Great Britain)

Tourist Offices of the States

Alabama: 800-Alabama
Alaska: 907-465-2010
Arizona: 802-542-8687
Arkansas: 800-Natural
California: 800-to-Calif
Colorado: 800-433-2656
Connecticut: 800-CT-Bound
Delaware: 800-441-8846
800-282-8667 in state
District of Columbia:
202-789-7000
Florida: 904-487-1462
Georgia: 800-Visit-GA
Hawaii: 808-923-1811
Idaho: 800-635-7820
Illinois: 800-223-0121
Indiana: 800-289-6646
Iowa: 800-345-IOWA
Kansas: 800-2Kansas
Kentucky: 800-225-Trip
Louisiana: 800-33-GUMBO
504-342-8119 in state
Maine: 207-289-6070
Maryland: 800-543-1036
Massachusetts: 617-727-3201
Michigan: 800-543-2937
Minnesota: 800-657-3700
Mississippi: 800-647-2290
Missouri: 800-877-1234
Montana: 800-541-1447

Nebraska: 800-228-4307
Nevada: 800-NEVADA-8
New Hampshire:
    603-271-2343
New Jersey: 800-Jersey-7
New Mexico: 800-545-2040
    505-827-0291 in state
New York: 800-CALL-NYS
North Carolina:
    800-VISIT-NC
North Dakota: 800-437-2077
    800-472-2100 in state
Ohio: 800-Buckeye
Oklahoma: 800-652-6552
Oregon: 800-547-7842
Pennsylvania: 800 Visit-PA
Rhode Island: 800-556-2484
South Carolina:
    803-734-0235
South Dakota: 800-843-1930
Tennessee: 615-741-2158
Texas: 800-8888-TEX
Utah: 801-538-1030
Vermont: 802-265-4763
Virginia: 800-Visit-VA
Washington: 800-544-1800

West Virginia: 800-225 5982
Wisconsin: 800-432-Trip
Wyoming: 800-Call-Wyo;
    307-777-7777 in state

Tourist Offices of Canada

Alberta: 800-661-8888
British Columbia:
    800-663-6000*
Manitoba: 800-665-0040
New Brunswick:
    800-561-0123
Newfoundland:
    800-563-6353
Northwest Territory:
    800-661-0788
Nova Scotia: 800-565-0000
Ontario: 800-668-2746*
Prince Edward Island:
    800-565-0267
Quebec: 800-363-7777
Saskatchewan: 800-667-7191
Yukon: 800-789-8566

*Will make hotel reservations

Weights and Measures

Measures and Equivalents

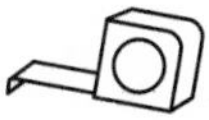

Tablespoon

1 tablespoon = 3 teaspoons
⅞ tablespoon = 2½ teaspoons
¾ tablespoon = 2¼ teaspoons
⅔ tablespoon = 2 teaspoons
⅝ tablespoon = 1⅞ teaspoons
½ tablespoon = 1½ teaspoons
⅜ tablespoon = 1⅛ teaspoons
⅓ tablespoon = 1 teaspoon
¼ tablespoon = ¾ teaspoon

Cup

1 cup = 16 tablespoons
⅞ cup = 14 tablespoons
¾ cup = 12 tablespoons
⅔ cup = 10⅔ tablespoons
⅝ cup = 10 tablespoons
½ cup = 8 tablespoons
⅜ cup = 6 tablespoons
⅓ cup = 5⅓ tablespoons
¼ cup = 4 tablespoons
⅛ cup = 2 tablespoons
¹⁄₁₆ cup = 1 tablespoon

Pint

1 pint = 2 cups
⅞ pint = 1¾ cups
¾ pint = 1½ cups
⅔ pint = 1⅓ cups
⅝ pint = 1¼ cups
½ pint = 1 cup
⅜ pint = ¾ cup
⅓ pint = ⅔ cup
¼ pint = ½ cup
⅛ pint = ¼ cup
¹⁄₁₆ pint = 2 tablespoons

Quart

1 quart = 2 pints
⅞ quart = 3½ cups
¾ quart = 3 cups
⅔ quart = 2⅔ cups
⅝ quart = 2½ cups
½ quart = 1 pint
⅜ quart = 1½ cups
⅓ quart = 1⅓ cups
¼ quart = 1 cup
⅛ quart = ½ cup
¹⁄₁₆ quart = ¼ cup

Gallon

1 gallon = 4 quarts
⅞ gallon = 3½ quarts
¾ gallon = 3 quarts
⅔ gallon = 10⅔ cups
⅝ gallons = 5 pints
½ gallon = 2 quarts
⅜ gallon = 3 pints
⅓ gallon = 5⅓ cups
¼ gallon = 1 quart
⅛ gallon = 1 pint
¹⁄₁₆ gallon = 1 cup

Pound

1 pound = 16 ounces
⅞ pound = 14 ounces
¾ pound = 12 ounces
⅔ pound = 10⅔ ounces
⅝ pound = 10 ounces
½ pound = 8 ounces
⅜ pound = 6 ounces
⅓ pound = 5⅓ ounces
¼ pound = 4 ounces
⅛ pound = 2 ounces
¹⁄₁₆ pound = 1 ounce

Oven Temperatures (Fahrenheit)

250°–275° = Very slow oven
300°–325° = Slow oven
350°–375° = Moderate oven
400°–425° = Hot oven
450°–475° = Very hot oven
500°–525° = Extremely hot oven

Linear Measure

1 hand = 4 inches
1 link= 7.92 inches
1 span = 9 inches
1 foot = 12 inches
1 yard = 3 feet
1 fathom = 2 yards; 6 feet
1 rod = 5½ yards
1 chain = 100 links; 22 yards; 66 feet
1 furlong = ⅛ mile; 40 rods; 220 yards; 660 feet
1 statute mile = 8 furlongs; 320 rods; 1,760 yards; 5,280 feet
1 international nautical mile = 1,852 kilometers; 6,076.115 feet
1 knot = 1 nautical mile per hour
1 league = 3 miles; 24 furlongs

Metric Conversions

Dry Measure

Metric	U.S.
1.00 gram	1,000 milligrams; 15.49 grains; 0.035 ounce; ¼ teaspoon
28.35 grams	1 ounce or 480 grains
43.00 grams	1½ ounces
57.00 grams	2 ounces
85.00 grams	3 ounces
99.00 grams	3½ ounces
113.00 grams	4 ounces
142.00 grams	5 ounces
170.00 grams	6 ounces
198.00 grams	7 ounces
227.00 grams	8 ounces

U.S.	Metric
9 ounces	*255.00 grams*
10 ounces	*283.00 grams*
11 ounces	*312.00 grams*
12 ounces	*340.00 grams*
13 ounces	*369.00 grams*
14 ounces	*397.00 grams*
15 ounces	*425.00 grams*
16 ounces (1 pound)	*454.00 grams*
1 pound (7,000 grains)	*0.454 kilogram*

Dry/Liquid Measure

U.S.	Metric	Imperial
A few drops	1.00 ml	
½ teaspoon	2.50 ml	
	3.00 ml	½ teaspoon
1 teaspoon	5.00 ml	
	6.00 ml	1 teaspoon
1 dessert spoon	8.00 ml	
	12.00 ml	1 dssp
1 tablespoon (½ ounce)	15.00 ml	
	18.00 ml	1 tbsp
1 ounce (2 tablespoons)	29.57 ml	
	36.00 ml	2 tbsp
2 ounces	59.00 ml	
3 ounces	89.00 ml	
4 ounces	118.00 ml	
	120.00 ml	4 ounces
	140.00 ml	5 ounces
5 ounces	148.00 ml	1 gill
6 ounces	177.00 ml	
7 ounces	207.00 ml	
8 ounces	237.00 ml	
8½ ounces	250.00 ml (¼ liter)	1 cup
9 ounces	266.00 ml	
	285.00 ml	½ pint
10 ounces	296.00 ml	
11 ounces	325.00 ml	
12 ounces	355.00 ml	
13 ounces	384.00 ml	

U.S.	Metric	Imperial
14 ounces	414.00 ml	
15 ounces	444.00 ml	
16 ounces (1 pint/4 gills)	473.00 ml (.4732 liter)	
	500.00 ml (½ liter)	
20 ounces (1¼ pints)	591.00 ml	1 pint
32 ounces (1 quart/2 pints)	0.95 liter	
1.057 quarts	1 liter (1,000 ml)	
128 ounces (1 gallon/4 quarts)	3.84 liters	

Metric Abbreviations

a	are
cbm	cubic meter
cc	cubic centimeter
cg	centigram
cl	centiliter
cm	centimeter
cm²	square centimeter
cm³	cubic centimeter
cu cm	cubic centimeter
dag	dekagram
dal	dekaliter
dam	decameter
dg	decigram
dl	deciliter
dm	decimeter
dm³	cubic decimeter
g	grams
ha	hectare
hg	hectogram
hi	hectoliter
hm	hectometer
kg	kilogram
kl	kiloliter
km	kilometer
km²	square kilometer
1	liter
m	meter
m³	cubic meter

mg	milligram
ml	milliliter
mm	millimeter
t	metric ton

Metric Measurements

Acre = 4,840 square yards; 43.560 square feet = 0.4047 hectare; 4,047 square meters

Are = 100 square meters = 119.60 square yards

Bushel = 4 pecks; 2,150.42 cubic inches = 35.239 liters

Centigram = 0.01 gram = 0.154 grain

Centiliter = 0.01 liter = 0.61 cubic inch; 0.338 fluid ounce

Centimeter = 0.01 meter =0.39 inch

Cubic centimeter = 0.0000001 cubic meter = 0.061 cubic inch

Cubic decimeter = 0.001 cubic meter = 61.023 cubic inches; 0.908 dry quart; 1.057 liquid quarts

Cubic inch = 0.00058 cubic foot = 16,387 cubic centimeters

Cubic foot = 1,728 cubic inches; 0.0370 cubic yard = 0.028 cubic meter

Cubic meter = 1.307 cubic yards

Cubic yard = 27 cubic feet; 46,656 cubic inches = 0.765 cubic meter

Decigram = 0.10 gram = 1,543 grains

Deciliter = 0.10 liter = 6.1 cubic inches; 0.18 dry pint; 0.21 liquid pint

Decimeter = 0.10 meter = 3.95 inches

Dekagram = 10 grams = 0.353 ounce

Dekaliter = 10 liters = 0.35 cubic feet; 2.64 gallons

Dekameter = 10 meters = 32.81 feet

Dram = 27.344 grains; 0.0625 ounce = 1.772 grams

Fluid ounce = 8 fluidrams = 29,573 milliliters

Fluidram = ⅛ fluid ounce; ¾ teaspoon = 3,697 milliliters

Foot = 12 inches; 0.333 yard = 30.48 centimeters

Gill = 5 fluid ounces; 8.669 cubic inches = 142.066 cubic centimeters

Grain = 0.037 dram; 0.002286 ounce = 0.0648 gram

Gram = 1,000 milligrams = 0.035 ounce

Hectare = 10,000 square meters = 2.47 acres

Hectogram = 100 grams = 3,527 ounces

Hectoliter = 100 liters = 3.53 cubic feet; 2.84 bushels

Hectometer = 100 meters = 109.36 yards

Hundredweight = 100 pounds; 112 British pounds = 45.36 kilograms

Inch = 0.12 foot; 0.36 yard = 2.54 centimeters

Kilogram = 1,000 grams = 2.2046 pounds

Kilometer = 1,000 meters = 0.62 mile

Liter = 1,000 milliliters = 61.02 cubic inches; 0.908 dry quart;
1.057 liquid quarts

Meter = 0.1000 kilometer = 39.37 inches

Metric ton = 1,000,000 grams = 1.102 short tons

Mile-See "Statute mile."

Milligram = 0.001 gram = 0.015 grain

Milliliter = 0.001 liter = 0.061 cubic inch; 0.27 fluidram

Millimeter = 0.001 meter = 0.039 inch

Ounce = 16 drams; 4,375 grains = 28.350 grams

Peck = 8 quarts; 537.605 cubic inches = 8.810 liters

Pint = 0.5 quart; 16 ounces; 33.600 cubic inches = 0.551 liter

Pound = 16 ounces; 7,000 grains = 453.59 grams

Rod = 5.5 yards, 16.5 feet = 5.029 meters

Square centimeter = 0.0001 square meter = 0.155 square inch

Square foot = 144 square inches; 0.111 square yard = 0.093 square meter;
929.03 cm^2

Square inch = 6.452 cm^2

Square kilometer = 1,000,000 square meters = 0.3861 square mile

Square meter = 1.20 square yards

Square mile = 640 acres = 2,590 km^2

Square rod = 30.25 square yards = 25.293 square meters

Square yard = 1,296 square inches; 9 square feet = 0.836 square meter

Statute mile = 1,760 yards = 1.6093 kilometers

Ton, short = 20 short hundredweight; 2,000 pounds = .0.907 metric tons,
907.18 kilograms

Ton, long = 20 long hundredweight, 2,240 pounds = 1.016 metric tons,
1.017 kilograms

Yard = 3 feet; 36 inches = 0.9144 meter

To Convert:

Celsius to Fahrenheit:	multiply by 9, divide by 5, add 32.
Centimeters to inches:	multiply by .394.
Cubic feet to inches:	L × W × H, then multiply by 1,728.
Cubic feet to cubic meters:	multiply by .0283.
Cubic meters to cubic feet:	divide by .0283.
Fahrenheit to Celsius:	deduct 32, multiply by 5, divide by 9.
Fluid ounces to liters:	multiply by .0296.
Gammas (micrograms) to milligrams:	divide by 1,000.
Grams to pounds:	multiply by .0022.

Inches to cubic feet:	L × W × H, then divide by 1,728.
Kilograms to pounds:	divide by 2.2046.
Liters to fluid ounces:	multiply by 33.81.
Liters to quarts:	multiply by 1.057.
Milligrams to gammas (micrograms):	multiply by 1,000.
Milligrams to grams:	divide by 1,000.
Ounces to grams:	multiply by 28.35.
Pounds to kilos:	multiply by 2.2046.

In a Nutshell . . .

Centimeter =	a little more than the width of a paper clip (about 0.4 inch)
Gram =	a little more than the weight of a paper clip
Hectare =	about 2.5 acres
Kilometer =	somewhat more than 0.5 mile (about 0.6 mile)
Liter =	a little larger than a quart (about 1.06 quarts)
Meter =	a little longer than a yard (about 1.1 yards)
Metric ton =	about one ton
Millimeter =	about the diameter of a paper clip wire

Oven Temperatures

Fahrenheit	Celsius	Fahrenheit	Celsius
200°	90°	*400°*	200°
250°	120°	*425°*	218°
275°	135°	*450°*	232°
300°	150°	*475°*	246°
325°	163°	*500°*	260°
350°	177°	*525°*	270°
375°	190°	*550°*	290°

Baking Pans

13 × 9 × 2 inches	33 × 23 × 55 centimeter oblong pan
8 × ½ inches (round)	20 × .4 centimeter round pan
9 × 1½ inches (round)	23 × .4 centimeter round pan
8 × 8 × 2 inches	20 × 20 × .5 centimeter square pan
9 × 9 × 2 inches	23 × 23 × .5 centimeter square pan
8-inch pie plate	20-centimeter pie plate
9-inch pie plate	23-centimeter pie plate
1-quart casserole	1-liter casserole
2-cup mold	500 milliliter mold

CLOTHING SIZES FOR USA, GREAT BRITAIN, AND EUROPE

Women's Garments — Sizes

United States	8	10	12	14	16	18
Great Britain	10	12	14	16	18	20
Europe	38	40	42	44	46/48	50
Inches	32/34	34/36	36/38	38/40	40/42	42/44
Centimeters	81/88	88/91	91/96	96/102	102/107	107/112

Women's Hosiery — Sizes

United States & Great Britain	8	8½	9	9½	10	10½	11
Europe	0	1	2	3	4	5	6

Men's Shirts — (Collar Sizes)

United States	14	14½	15	15½	15¾	16	16½	17
Great Britain	14	14½	15	15½	16	16½	17	17½
Europe	36	37	38	39	40	41	42	43

Women's and Men's Shoes — Sizes

United States	4½	5	5½	6	6½	7	7 ½	8	8½	9	9½	10	10½
Great Britain	3	3½	4	4½	5	5½	6	6½	7	7½	8	8½	9
Europe	36–		37–		38–		39–		40–		41–		42–